October 1956

THE LIFE AND TIMES OF JOHN SHARP, ARCHBISHOP OF YORK

JOHN SHARP, ARCHBISHOP OF YORK.

Frontispiece.

THE LIFE AND TIMES OF
JOHN SHARP
ARCHBISHOP OF YORK

By the Rev.
A. TINDAL HART, M.A., B.D.

Published for the Church Historical Society

LONDON
S·P·C·K
1949

To

MY WIFE,

WITHOUT WHOSE ENCOURAGEMENT

THIS BOOK

WOULD NEVER HAVE BEEN WRITTEN

MADE IN GREAT BRITAIN

CONTENTS

ACKNOWLEDGMENTS

Although solely responsible for this book, I should like to thank all those who helped me to produce it. First and foremost Archbishop Sharp's descendants, Lt.-Col. A. B. Lloyd-Baker and Miss Olive Lloyd-Baker, but for whose generosity in allowing me free access to their family papers my task would have proved impossible.

I am also much indebted to Professor Norman Sykes, who read this work in MS. and offered a great deal of valuable constructive criticism. Among others I must mention, especially, Canon S. L. Ollard; the Reverend J. S. Purvis, F.S.A.; Mr. E. Welbourne, M.A.; and Mr. F. S. E. Bardsley-Powell, the present owner of Horton Old Hall, Bradford, the ancestral home of the Sharp family.

NOTE

The spelling of all original letters has been modernised.

The Lloyd-Baker-Sharp MSS. appear in the notes under the abbreviation L-B-S. MSS. The box, bundle and letter numbers are given in each case.

FOREWORD

ICOUNT it an equal honour and pleasure to accept Mr. Hart's invitation to write a short introduction to his biography of Archbishop John Sharp. I remember well his consulting me some years ago about the choice of a subject for his researches; and I replied by suggesting that if he could discover the papers on which Thomas Sharp's life of his father had been based, a most useful and interesting study might result. The story of Mr. Hart's quest for and final discovery of these papers (almost when on the point of abandoning the chase) has the properties of a detective romance, and I could wish that in his own preface he had told it in full. Once the discovery was made and the correspondence opened to his researches, I anticipated confidently a rich harvest.

The measure to which this anticipation has been realised will be evident to all readers of this book; and it is not the province of an introduction to disclose all the riches of the author's work. I will content myself with saying that in my opinion Mr. Hart has presented a biography which is both full and definitive. It is true that in the delineation alike of Sharp's character and of his public policy Mr. Hart has reached the same conclusions as the archbishop's son. But the picture is now filled out with a great deal of valuable illustrative detail; and the reader can form a clear and conclusive estimate of Sharp's principles and of the part which he played in the religious and political events of the important and influential quarter of a century between 1689 and 1714, which constituted the testing of Revolution principles. It would be easy to point to particular and detailed ways in which this biography expands our knowledge both of its subject and his times. But that would be to steal Mr. Hart's thunder and to blunt perhaps the curiosity of his readers.

I would like to emphasise that the researches for and the

vii

writing of this book have been undertaken during Mr. Hart's discharge of the exacting office of a parish priest, for part of the time in a busy industrial suburb, and during the difficulties and distractions of a world war. When the full implications of these circumstances are realised, the reader will be at once more grateful and admiring in his recognition of Mr. Hart's success. "We live in a troublesome and tumultuous age", observed Thomas Fuller; "and he needs to have a very soft bed who can sleep soundly nowadays, amid so much loud noise, and many impetuous rumours. Wherefore it seemeth to me both a safe and cheap receipt, to procure quiet and repose to the mind which complains of want of rest, to prescribe unto it the reading of history." Both on the ground of its intrinsic merits and in echo of Fuller's recipe for quiet and repose of the mind, I commend Mr. Hart's biography to the perusal of all interested in English history. It is a source of great gratification to me to have been instrumental in helping Mr. Hart to begin his study and an occasion of high privilege to be associated with its publication.

NORMAN SYKES,
Emmanuel College, Cambridge.

August 17, 1947.

PREFACE

MY only excuse for inflicting another *Life* of John Sharp upon the reading public, when the admirable and authoritative two-volumed biography by his son, Thomas Sharp, archdeacon of Northumberland, edited by the Reverend T. Newcome, is already so widely known and appreciated among scholars of the Queen Anne period, lies in my recent discovery of the archbishop's entire correspondence and other private papers now in the possession of his direct descendant, Lt.-Col. A. B. Lloyd-Baker of Hardwicke Court, Gloucester.

Curiously enough, the Lloyd-Bakers are also sprung from another Queen Anne bishop, Sharp's very good friend and predecessor at the Almonry, William Lloyd of Worcester.

The Lloyd-Baker-Sharp MSS., as I have entitled them, contain several thousand documents, including letters, sermons, petitions, memoranda and accounts, the vast bulk of which have never before been published in any shape or form; and, so far as I am aware, their very existence is completely unknown to the argus-eyed Historical MSS. Commission.

Admittedly some of the most important letters have already appeared in the archdeacon's biography; but, as he himself assured us in "The Author's Preface", he could, had he so desired, have inserted a very great many more from the same source.[1] Thomas Newcome, who likewise had access to these MSS., respected the archdeacon's reticence, and gave his biography to the world without attempting to add anything further to a lengthy and undeniably authoritative study of the archbishop's career. This authority, of course, is based on the claim that the archbishop's own diary, five quarto volumes in shorthand, is the foundation of the whole

---

[1] "The compiler, indeed, of this work, was in justice to the Archbishop's correspondents, very scrupulous on that article, and very sparing in embellishing his work with original letters, when he might have done it, such was his opportunity, with a liberal hand, had it been consistent with the honour and respect due to them": *Life of Archbishop Sharp*, vol. i, Preface, xxi.

work.[1] Unfortunately that diary has since disappeared, although quite probably, like the archiepiscopal correspondence, it is still extant but in private possession.[2]

The Lloyd-Baker-Sharp MSS. remain, and their chief value lies in the fresh light that they throw on the activities, troubles and problems of the early eighteenth-century parochial clergy in York-shire and Nottinghamshire, and on their relations with their arch-bishop. Furthermore, the numerous letters from contemporary bishops, especially from Sharp's fellow-metropolitan, Tenison, give us some added information about the Queen Anne episcopate. There is much else, part of which has been made use of in the following pages, but no more than a fraction of the material pro-vided. This may perhaps be remedied at a later date by my pro-jected biography of William Lloyd.

Here space permits me only to hint at some of the more interest-ing but subsidiary topics. There is, for example, a packet of letters addressed to the archbishop from the Reverend Samuel Noyes, who was serving with the British Expeditionary Force in the Grand Alliance. "I am", he told Sharp, "Chaplain to my Lord Orkney's Regiment, the same person, who had the honour to be introduced to your Grace at London by the Dean of Lincoln."

Noyes' epistles, which are extremely lengthy and closely written, describe in detail his own personal experiences and observations during the campaigns of 1703 and 1704, and must be of the greatest interest to all students of the Marlborough wars.[3] Again, another bundle of papers displays the archbishop in a very different light, as the student not of war, but of the supernatural. He made, apparently, a considerable collection of reputed miracles, apparitions and strange disturbances, including the famous story of Mary Clarke, apprentice at Ashford (1698). His friends, learning of this obsession, used to send him any unusual stories on which they could lay their hands, as when Lord Notting-ham reported a wonderful cure in June 1706, and the Lord Mayor of York told him the tale of a woman who came to York

---

[1] Op. cit., vol. i, Preface, vii.
[2] Another loss is the correspondence between the archbishop and Dr. Jablonski over the proposed introduction of a form of the Anglican Liturgy into the Prussian Church.
[3] L-B-S. MSS., Box 4, Bundle A. 74-81.

from London on the pretence of delivering a message from a spirit.[1]

Inevitably, any biography of John Sharp must be based primarily on his son's account of him;[2] not only because of the archdeacon's claim to the diary, but also as a contemporary record by one who had personal knowledge of many of the actors involved, and, no doubt, personal experience of his father's private life. Nevertheless, so far as it has been possible to do so, I have neglected this obvious source in favour of the newer material available; while, at the same time, endeavouring to check and co-ordinate all the relevant documents, both published and unpublished, in order to try to produce something like a true portrait of one of the most remarkable of the archbishops of York.

A. TINDAL HART,
Sometime scholar of Emmanuel College, Cambridge.

St. Paul's Vicarage,
Bordesley Green,
Birmingham.
August 1945.

---

[1] L-B-S. MSS., Box 4, Bundle Y.
[2] Colonel Lloyd-Baker also possesses the original MS. of the published *Life*, edited by T. Newcome.

CHAPTER I

THE YORKSHIRE ECCLESIASTICAL BACKGROUND[1]

JOHN SHARP was a Yorkshireman. He was born of an ancient Bradford family, which had its roots deep down in the history and soil of Yorkshire.

At the very time that he was being reared, and educated in the local grammar school, members of that family were helping to defend the sturdy independence of her people against the autocracy of king and Church. Some forty years later he became archbishop of York, and ruled that gigantic archdiocese for longer than any of his predecessors since the Reformation.

It will not, then, be out of place to devote a few introductory pages to a brief glimpse of this vast ecclesiastical field, in which he was ultimately destined to make no inconsiderable mark, and to consider the shape and kind of obstacles he had to surmount there, and the different types of parson with whom he had to deal.

At the beginning of the eighteenth century the diocese was very much larger than it is now; for, besides the whole of Yorkshire, always excepting the archdeaconry of Richmond, it also included Nottinghamshire and that part of Northumberland which was known as Hexhamshire. This unwieldy territory was divided into four archdeaconries: York,[2] Cleveland, the East Riding and Nottingham; and further subdivided into seventeen deaneries: City of York, New Ainsty, Old Ainsty, Pontefract, Craven and Doncaster in the archdeaconry of York; Bulmer, Cleveland and Ryedale in the archdeaconry of Cleveland; Buckrose, Dickering, Harthill and Holderness in the archdeaconry of the East Riding; and, finally, Bingham, Newark, Nottingham and Retford in the archdeaconry of Nottingham.

Among the Lloyd - Baker - Sharp MSS. are some interesting "Rules and Orders to be observed by Rural Deans . . . declared and enjoined by his Grace John Lord Archbishop" of York, which were issued in 1705. Here, among other things, they are warned

[1] Based on the Lloyd-Baker-Sharp MSS. and the Bishopthorpe MSS.
[2] "This Archdeaconry", wrote Sharp in his Bishopthorpe MSS. volumes, "takes into it the city and the county of the city of York and much the greatest part of the West Riding of Yorkshire viz. all that lies south of the River Nid. That part of the West Riding which is North of that river belonging to the Archdeaconry of Richmond which is now in Chester Diocese."

"that they transgress not the limits of their Commission by invading the districts of other Deans, whereby happen great uncertainty and confusion by their returns of business into the Public Registry".[1] Their principal duties, apparently, consisted in granting matrimonial licences, giving "timely notice of the vacancy of any livings or curacies or vacant schools within their several districts", making returns of "all notorious dilapidations", notifying to the ecclesiastical courts at York "all notorious and scandalous offenders (especially those of the higher rank) who escape presenting", summoning incumbents together for the purpose of electing proctors to Convocation, and, most important of all, receiving "the Registers of every parish or chapelry brought to them after the 25th of March and before the 25th of April, and send the same into the Registers' Office before the 10th of May". They were helped in these tasks by sub-apparitors, whom they had themselves recommended, and for whose conduct and diligence they remained responsible.

Besides the deaneries proper there were the two districts of Ripon and Hexhamshire, which lay outside the archdeaconries; and groups of parishes in various parts of the diocese known as "peculiars". These "peculiars" were under special jurisdiction, and were mostly controlled by the chapters of York and Southwell.[2]

Of the Nottingham "peculiars" Sharp wrote in his famous *Notitia* of the diocese: "I meet with no Churches or Parishes in this County that are exempt from the Ordinary Jurisdiction, but only those that belong to the Dean and Chapter of York and the Chapter of Southwell. Both the Church of Lincoln and of Peterborough have Churches and Parishes here which they present to, and of which the Great Tithes, in some places all the Tithes, are appropriated to them, yet they are all in the Archdeaconry of Nottingham and under Ordinary Jurisdiction. The same is true of all those Churches or Parishes that are appropriated to Religious Houses. They are also as far as I can find under the Bishop's and Archdeacon's Jurisdiction.

"As to the places wherein some of the Religious Houses stood I am not so certain as to them. I am told that Welbeck and Rufford and Newsted are peculiars. That is as I take it they are in no

---

[1] L-B-S. MSS., Box 4, Bundle O. 15.

[2] The dean and chapter of York had "peculiars" in many different parts of the diocese, but Southwell's were confined to Nottinghamshire.

Other "peculiar" jurisdictions included some belonging to the bishop and dean and chapter of Durham.

For a full list see *Valor Ecclesiasticus*, vol. v, Appendix, pp. 333 and 334.

Parish. For I do not hear that they have any Churches in them. And particularly it is said that there are about 30 families in Rufford that are wholly destitute of ministerial offices. This deserves to be enquired into. . . . The Jurisdiction that the Dean and Chapter of York and the Chapter of Southwell have in their peculiars is the same viz. they have both Episcopal Jurisdiction viz. granting institutions to livings, licences to serve cures, probate of wills; right of visitation etc."[1]

The "peculiars" attached to the chapter of York in the archdeaconry of Nottingham consisted of five churches "with the chappells to them belonging"; but the jurisdiction of Southwell took in "24 parishes in which as Mr. Mompesson reckons are 26 churches".

This great diocese, which contained some 903 parishes and chapelries, could also boast of one superb cathedral, York Minster; and two smaller yet equally fine collegiate churches, SS. Peter and Wilfrid, Ripon, and St. Mary, Southwell. But, while York and Ripon were ruled by dean and sub-dean, Southwell had to rest content with a vicar-general.

The nomination to the York and Ripon deaneries lay in the hands of the crown, and frequently occasioned a trial of strength between the various clerical parties in order to gain the royal ear. Sharp, for example, representing the High Church party, failed to secure the appointment to York for his nominee in 1697, but succeeded five years later.[2] Christopher Wyvil, a native of the East Riding and grandson of the Earl of Holderness, became dean of Ripon in 1686, where he remained until his death in January 1710/11, wearying his metropolitan with long accounts of his perpetual squabbles with Alderman Sir Jonathan Jennings of the Ripon Corporation.[3] The queen, no doubt at the prompting of the archbishop, immediately presented this ecclesiastical plum to his chaplain and future son-in-law, Heneage Dering. Wyvil had also been Master of the hospitals of SS. John and Mary Magdalene, Ripon; and from his time onwards they became permanently attached to the deanery. At Southwell, on the other hand, where the archbishop controlled the appointments, the Mompessons, father and son, upheld his authority with admirable zeal and discretion.

Of the three chapters, that of York was the most imposing, con-

[1] *Archbishop Sharp's MSS.*, vol. iii (Bishopthorpe MSS.).
[2] On both occasions the archbishop's candidate was Henry Finch. William III turned him down in 1697, but Anne accepted him in 1702.
[3] L-B-S. MSS., Box 3, Bundle E. 26.

taining the dean, precentor, chancellor and treasurer, besides twenty-eight prebendaries and four vicars choral; Southwell came next with sixteen prebendaries and six vicars choral; while Ripon now possessed only six prebendal stalls (which since James I's restoration of the church were no longer to be identified with the old territorial prebends) and two vicars choral.

The gift of all these prebends was in the hands of the archbishop, except that his powers of patronage were somewhat qualified at Ripon, where "he was obliged to collate one of three persons presented and recommended to him by the chapter whenever a vacancy occurred. The sub-dean was elected from among the prebendaries."[1]

The vicars choral of all three foundations were often a source of trouble and anxiety to their archbishop,[2] a good example of which is to be seen in the following public confession and penance of Mr. Bland, one of the vicars of Ripon:

"Whereas I John Bland, Master of Arts and late Vicar Choral of this Collegiate Church of Ripon, not having the fear of God before my eyes, nor duly considering the Dignity and Holiness of my calling as a Minister of the Gospel, but suffering myself to be led by my own carnal lusts and evil affections, have been guilty of the great sin of fornication, to the high dishonour of God, the reproach of the Reformed Religion, the scandal of my profession, and the great offence of all good Christians, whereby I have incurred the displeasure of Almighty God, and the first censure of my superiors: Now I the said John Bland, being deeply sensible of the grievousness of my guilt, do here in the presence of God and in the face of this congregation declare my unfeigned sorrow and repentance for that grave sin; and I humbly beg forgiveness of God in the first place against whom I have sinned and then of all of you whom I have justly offended, and lest my ill example in this particular should give encouragement to others to commit the like sin, I do here declare my utter detestation of it and an abhorrence of myself for it, and do exhort you all to beware of and avoid it, as that which is highly dishonourable to Christianity and pernicious to your souls. I do also beseech you that you will not let the rest of my order suffer in your thoughts of them upon my account; and I do heartily desire your prayers for me, that God may be graciously pleased to have mercy on me, through the merit and mediation

[1] *Memorials of Ripon*, vol. ii (Edit. Surtees Society, vol. 78), p. 258.
[2] *Cf.* Chapter VII, p. 202.

of Jesus Christ our Lord and only Saviour; to whom with the Father and the Holy Ghost, three persons and one most glorious God, be all Honour and Glory now and forever-more. Amen."[1]

To turn to the parochial clergy: The 903-odd parishes and chapelries were served by about 710 clergy, probably by more when the majority of the prebendaries, who enjoyed livings as well as their stalls, are included. The great mass of cures were small and rural; but there were at least a dozen large market towns with populations running into some thousands of families, viz. Halifax, Leeds, Nottingham, York, Bradford, Sheffield, Birstall, Scarborough, Wakefield, Almondbury, Huddersfield and Hull. Most of these lay in the West Riding of Yorkshire. The value of the benefices varied enormously; the majority were quite incapable of providing any sort of decent livelihood. A return drawn up for the benefit of the Governors of Queen Anne's Bounty during 1704/5 showed that out of 10,000 parishes in the country as a whole, 5,082 were worth less than £80, and there were at least 471 under £10, 1,216 under £20, and 3,043 under £40.[2] Many out of these latter categories were found in the poor and sparsely populated Northern Province. Here are a few examples taken at random out of the diocese of York: Kildwick, value £38 8s. 8d.; Skipton, value £39 12s. 10d.; East Harlsey, value £12; Collingham, value £21; Swinton near Wath, value £24; Skipsey, value £16 4s. od.; Pannal, value £12 6s. od.; Horbury, value £7.[3] The figures given in each case are those prior to their augmentation by the Bounty.

On the other hand, the Reverend Samuel Dakeyne, vicar of Holme-on-Spalding-Moor, wrote to the archbishop during the autumn of 1701: "I confess my living is reputed worth £100 per annum, but I could never make so much of it."[4] The same gentleman, on falling into debt, endeavoured to retrieve his fortunes by turning farmer and "taking my glebe into my own hands". But the venture was scarcely successful, since his crops were "spoiled by cold and wet weather". He then adopted other and singularly unpopular methods of increasing his income, for, as he ruefully

[1] L-B-S. MSS., Box 4, Bundle N. 10.
[2] Le Fanu, *Queen Anne's Bounty*, p. 37.
[3] For a full list of livings and their values in the York diocese see John Ecton, *Liber Regis Vel Thesaurus Rerum Ecclesiasticarum*, pp. 1099-1188.
  Cf. also J. Ecton, *A State of the Bounty of Queen Anne*, pp. 137-148.
[4] L-B-S. MSS., Box 4, Bundle C. 6.
  N. Drake, vicar of Sheffield, informed the primate that the living of Mansfield was worth at least £200 per annum: L-B-S. MSS., Box 4, Bundle C. 7, Oct. 25, 1697.

remarked, "my parishioners were sworn together against me, saying, cursed be the man that raises the priest's rents".

Certainly, as regards his stipend the incumbent was often very
much at the mercy of the squire or churchwardens of his parish.
Mr. John Boulter, for instance, the patron and squire of the living
of Harwood, who, as he himself confessed, "voluntarily surrendered all my powers in choosing a Vicar to yourself" (*i.e.* the archbishop), became so incensed against the man whom Sharp had
chosen that he refused to fulfil his promise "to more than double
the Vicar's ancient pension out of my own pocket in order to make
the living worth £55 or £60 a year, which is an income considering the method of living and cheapness of provisions in these parts,
more really valuable to those who have a family than any £100 a
year in London".[1]

Again, Mr. Dade, the new vicar of Otley, found himself "opposed by Mr. Edmund Barker, who has bought a moiety of the
tithes there from Mr. Nevile";[2] while Mr. Baines, vicar of Kilburn, who had become involved in a protracted and expensive
lawsuit to secure his tithes, saw himself baulked of the fruits of his
labours because, as his legal adviser explained, "the new Lord
Holles and the Lord Chesterfield or one of them stand upon privilege and will not suffer you to recover your tithes of their tenants".[3]

Finally, out of many other examples of every type, we may
select the case of John Gee, rector of Plumptree, a sufferer from
"the business of enclosure" ruthlessly enforced by the local squire,
Sir Godfrey Copley, who—or so Gee declared—"instead of discoursing me upon the subject, sends for his tenants, tells them that
he had made Mr. Gee such proposals as should never be offered
again, orders them to enclose anything they thought convenient,
and promised to defend them; gives them peremptory charge,
upon the pains of ejectment, to lay half their land unploughed, to
the great diminution of my tithes". This action, Gee calculated,
"will depreciate the tithes to the value of about £30 per annum".
Worse was to follow: "But besides the laying it down, they enclose
it; and are now at work with all the force of the Lordship, and that
will deeply prejudice my glebe. Not only by being deprived of my
right of common, but in these other respects: It lies scattered
through the field, mostly by single lands, or but two together, and

[1] L-B-S. MSS., Box 4, Bundle Q. 11, Jan. 29, 1704/5.
[2] L-B-S. MSS., Box 4, Bundle Q. 19, May 20, 1701.
[3] L-B-S. MSS., Box 4, Bundle Q. 15, Jan. 4, 1693.

by ditching up close to the very furrows of my land, it must necessarily fall in on either side, and in the whole make considerable
waste. The hedges lying so near will give much shelter to the birds
that they will devour an incredible quantity of corn, far beyond
the apprehension of any but experienced husbandmen. There will
be no room for a carriage to turn, when we are to lead out manure
or fetch home the grain; nor breadth enough in many of them for
the cart to pass beside a cock or shock. It lies so encompassed on
every side, that should they enclose all theirs, they would cut off
all passage or access to mine, or, if they may leave what way they
please, may turn me many furlongs about to every land."[1]

The larger market towns were little better provided for than
the country villages. Nathaniel Drake of Sheffield and Francis
Pemberton of Bradford officially drew only £12 15s. 2d. and £20
per annum respectively from these livings.[2]

The harassed parson, seeking to escape from the cruel grasp of
poverty or debt, found various loopholes open to him. He might
become a pluralist—i.e., hold more than one living provided they
lay within thirty miles of each other—although owing to the
shortage of livings this practice was not encouraged. Again, he
could become a chaplain or lecturer in an institution, as when,
for example, the Duke of Norfolk appointed Drake, vicar of
Sheffield, to be the chaplain and governor of the hospital on the
outskirts of that town.[3] The favoured few, on the other hand, were
presented by their archbishop to prebendal stalls;[4] while, at the
other end of the scale, the poor curate sought to eke out his slender
stipend by turning schoolmaster.

The unbeneficed clergy, of course, suffered most of all. Thomas
Clark, rector of Kirk Heaton, promised to allow Jeremiah Kitching, as soon as he was ordained, "£10 per annum for reading
prayers at the Church, burying, christening, etc. in my absence as
I did Mr. Midgeley before him".[5] Kitching added another £5 to
his £10 by serving the school at Kirk Heaton. Drake also secured
an assistant to read prayers at the parish church in order to set

[1] L-B-S. MSS., Box 4, Bundle E. 2.
[2] These are the figures given by Ecton in the *Liber Regis*, pp. 1135 and 1154, which
he found "in the King's Books". No doubt their real value was much higher. Similarly
he gives: Almondbury, £20 7s. 11d.; Wakefield, £29 19s. 2d.; and Beverley, £31 6s. 8d.
[3] L-B-S. MSS., Box 4, Bundle C. 8, 9, 10, 11, 12.
[4] Lady Dixey of Selson, who had just appointed a new incumbent to a living worth
only a few pounds, besought Sharp: "If your Lordship would bestow a Prebend upon
him it would much oblige me, and fix him here which I cannot hope for unless you
please to remember him when one falls": L-B-S. MSS., Box 4, Bundle C. 20.
[5] L-B-S. MSS., Box 4, Bundle G. 16.

himself free to preach in the hospital, and informed Sharp: "He makes £40 a year of his school, and I shall allow him £10 a year more for reading prayers."[1] Such incomes were considered perfectly adequate for a curate. When the Earl of Thànet, a very good friend to the Church, promised to give £20 out of his estate to pay a curate to serve the new chapel of ease at Skipton, he seemed to think that this was an ample endowment.[2] Nevertheless, despite their miserable penury, the clergy were not deterred from matrimony, the founding of large families, and an attempt to equip their sons for following the same profession. Timothy Ellisonne of Coley, pleading for financial help from his archbishop, spoke of "my two youngest sons" who "are likely to be good scholars. I will do what I can to fit them for the University."[3]

Patronage was pretty evenly divided between the crown, the archbishop and the private patron. The last was usually a county magnate or a country squire, but occasionally the vicar of a neighbouring parish.[4] There were also, of course, the peculiars, College livings,[5] and the right of the Lincolnshire and Peterborough chapters to present to certain parishes in Nottinghamshire.[6] During his archiepiscopate Sharp displayed great skill in persuading the other patrons, especially the lay nobility, to accept his candidates or at least to consult him before nomination.[7] Naturally, however, there were exceptions to this unwritten rule, and on several occasions noblemen were charged, not unjustly, with prostituting their powers in the matter. Robert Banks, vicar of Hull, wrote on March 6, 1698: "About 8 years since the Duke of Norfolk made me a very solemn promise that he would give me the first living in his gift if I would accept. I never asked his Grace the question till about a month since that I heard Mr. Browne (who had two good ones) was dead, then I wrote to his Grace and desired a friend then at London to present it, which he did, and upon perusal of my letter his Grace owned his promise, but said he was sorry his circumstances were such that he could not fulfil it, for he had sold Treeton 3 months since to Mr. Jessop, and as

---

[1] L-B-S. MSS., Box 4, Bundle C. 10.
[2] L-B-S. MSS., Box 4, Bundle L. 107.
[3] L-B-S. MSS., Box 4, Bundle D. 11, Nov. 19, 1698.
[4] *E.g.*, the vicar of Almondbury claimed the right to present to Honley Chapel. See *Archbishop Sharp's MSS.*, vol. iii, Addenda: Honley Chapel.
[5] *E.g.*, Holme-on-Spalding-Moor, in the gift of St. John's College, Cambridge.
[6] This list is not exhaustive; *e.g.*, there were also the bishop of Durham and the dean and chapter of Christ Church, Oxford.
[7] *Cf.* Chapter VI, pp. 157-159.

for Handsworth, such were his necessities, that whoever had it he must have 200 guineas for it, and if any friend for me would give it I should be presented before another."[1] Banks promptly retorted: "I would not give 200 farthings for the best Rectory in England."

But if it could be proved that the parochial clergy were badly paid and often harshly used, what of their archbishop? In the second of his famous MS. volumes Sharp has set down a detailed account of "the estates belonging to the Archbishop of York with the several rents issuing from them". These consisted of the "exchange lands", three Yorkshire manors given in exchange for York House in the Strand;[2] some sixteen other manors, mostly in Yorkshire and Nottinghamshire, but including the "Mannor of Brighton" and "Mannor of Battersea"; thirty-five impropriate rectories; and a few lesser properties, e.g. "twelve farms called the Granges". The whole estate brought in an annual income of between £2,000 and £3,000. That was a great deal of money in Queen Anne's reign; but the archbishop's expenses were equally heavy. Considerable sums had necessarily to be expended on the upkeep of the estates themselves; while much more was needed to provide the lavish hospitality which was expected as a matter of course from the archbishop both in London and at Bishopthorpe. Charity, too, demanded its quota; and the expenses of the archiepiscopal office itself could not be dismissed as insignificant. When Sharp was enthroned "the Fees of Homage" alone came to £225 0s. 8d.[3]

During the winter months the archbishop was compelled to live in London, attending to his political duties; but his summers were normally passed amid the pleasant surroundings of Bishopthorpe Palace. He had, however, usually little leisure to enjoy them. The duties of visitation, confirmation and ordination, which Sharp so faithfully and regularly performed at this time of the year, will be dealt with in another place.[4] Here it is only necessary to recall them to our minds, together with their corollary of long, arduous and continuous journeys on horseback, or, when his physical powers were waning, in his coach, over bad roads, infested with highwaymen, and through one of the largest and wildest dioceses in the country. A pleasant glimpse of him at work is to be found

[1] L-B-S. MSS., Box 4, Bundle Q. 8, March 6, 1692.
[2] Beckhay, Acomb and Sancton.
[3] L-B-S. MSS., Box 4, Bundle O. 76
[4] Chapter VI, pp. 165-171.

in the memorandum book of Sir Walter Calverley, Bart., under the date June 7, 1698: "The Most Reverend Father, Dr. John Sharp, Lord Archbishop of York, came through the fold at Esholt, in his way to Bradford from the visitation at Otley, and made me a complement, and said he called only to see me to know how I did, but that it was so late he could not light off horse-back; and though I urged him to take a drink, yet he said he could not drink anything, but said he was to dine at Bradford on the day after, whither he invited me."[1]

At home he entertained the clergy and the county in princely style,[2] anyone, in fact, who cared to trespass upon his hospitality. Dr. William Grahme, writing to the archbishop on January 13, 1701/2, requested him to "be pleased to present my service to your excellent Lady with thanks for her respect and care of me, when I was indisposed. I confess I was never so ill of that distemper in my life."[3] The Reverend Peter Leigh of Settrington also informed the primate: "My Lord Warrington and Mr. Roberts dining with us yesterday took occasion to speak of your Grace's entertainment of them at Bishopthorpe in terms expressing a more than ordinary satisfaction."[4]

The hours of leisure stolen from his official duties, and not swallowed up by the composition of his great *Notitia* of the diocese,[5] were devoted to laying out the beautiful palace gardens. An interesting letter on this subject among the archbishop's muniments shows that Sharp had a taste for statuary and trees, especially the lime and poplar. "I have the honour", wrote J. Gibson of Welburne, "of your Grace's letter last night, intimating your intention of having a statue in the middle of your Parterre . . . I perceive your Grace is for lime trees for a hedge betwixt your upper and lower ground: I should not have advised to them, as not worthy to be planted within a walled enclosure, no more than hornbeam, and therefore I dare undertake to foretell that Your Grace will grow weary of them there, as you will also of your poplars so near your wall . . . I shall be glad to see the new plan Your Grace so much approves."[6]

[1] *Yorkshire Diaries* (Edit. Surtees Society, vol. 77), p. 74.
[2] *Cf.* Chapter XI, p. 293.
Thomas Norton, gamekeeper in the archbishop's "Liberty of Ripon", wrote on January 28, 1700/1: "I shall still endeavour that your Lordship's table may be frequently furnished with your own fowl; and I have sent your Lordship a day's work . . . and I hope I may live to send you many more": L-B-S. MSS., Box 4, Bundle A. 76.
[3] L-B-S. MSS., Box 4, Bundle E. 6.
[4] L-B-S. MSS., Box 4, Bundle J. 17, July 25, 1700.
[5] See Appendix A.   [6] L-B-S. MSS., Box 4, Bundle E. 8, Oct. 19, 1699.

But usually he sat in his study and wrote letters; letters replying to the thousands that poured in an unending stream into his letter bag. The great majority of these were from clergymen, ranging from the comparatively well-to-do and well-connected cathedral prebendary or market town vicar to the poorer country incumbent and the needy curate or clerical schoolmaster. The subject-matter of their long and often beautifully written and charmingly expressed epistles[1] provides the modern historian with a valuable cross-section on late seventeenth- and early eighteenth-century clerical life.

Manners, morals, intellectual activities, grouses, occupations, family problems and politics, all come under survey and must in their day have afforded many an archiepiscopal headache to their metropolitan.

Clergymen, who are professedly wedded to the ideal of Christian charity, frequently display little of this virtue in their dealings with one another. W. Savile, vicar of Mexborough near Sheffield, wrote of an offending colleague: "I was in hopes Your Grace would ere this have eased me of the burden I lie under by my scandalous curate, giving occasions to all persons to reflect upon my little regard I have to the peoples' souls, as well as to my own sense in placing and continuing so unfit a man in such a weighty concern . . . which I am sure must reflect upon your predecessor, that for a fee would ordain an ass."[2] Yet neither was the vicar wholly blameless, since he had detained his curate's salary without adequate cause.[3] Savile had complained of his assistant's ignorance, his misreading of the prayers and nonsensical preaching; while another incumbent, Mr. John Hepworth of Harwood, had an even greater cause for annoyance, for his curate, Mr. Cheldry, was not merely undermining the affections of the parishioners for their vicar, but had stolen those of his daughter, and had approached the patron on the question of ultimately succeeding him.[4]

The curates themselves did not fail to hit back at those who slandered them,[5] and even the downtrodden clerical school-

---

[1] Not a few, of course, are straightforward begging letters, but even these lose much of their crudity through the dignity and quaint simplicity of the parson's approach to his Spiritual Father.

[2] L-B-S. MSS., Box 4, Bundle K. 22, July 13, 1695.

[3] L-B-S. MSS., Box 4, Bundle K. 23.

[4] L-B-S. MSS., Box 4, Bundle F. 25, Sept. 2, 1699.

[5] E.g., Robert Lacock, curate of Rastrick-cum-Fixby, versus Mr. Petty of Elland: L-B-S. MSS., Box 4, Bundle Q.53, July 15, 1700.

masters were not afraid to stand up for their rights, with or without their archbishop's support. Edward Griffith of Nottingham had been informed by the mayor and corporation that, despite Sharp's intervention on his behalf, he must quit his school, because of his alleged "neglect and severity". Nevertheless, Griffith stoutheartedly determined "to keep my post (if I live so long) till Xmas, and so to fit my lads for an examination by any examiners that Your Grace or the Corporation shall appoint. And this I shall do (God willing) to vindicate my qualifications."[1]

Schools were not plentiful in Yorkshire. *Archbishop Herring's Visitation Returns* of 1743 record that "in some 266 places of the 645 Returns from Yorkshire there is no mention of a school or of any secular teaching whatever."[2]

This was particularly true of the East-Riding villages. Consequently there was a great demand for appointments, and a considerable amount of cut-throat competition; as, for example, at Guisborough, where Lisle and Jaques, clerical schoolmasters, fought each other so fiercely that they were at last both obliged to retire from the parish.[3]

Incumbents and their churchwardens were likewise frequently at loggerheads. Certain parishioners of Long Preston in the deanery of Craven deplored "a present debate springing up between our vicar and his churchwardens in respect to the most solemn act of our profession and provision for it, the sacramental bread and wine at Easter".[4] Mr. Spark, the vicar in question, had found various customs prevailing in his church which he rightly regarded as uncanonical, for example the performance of "the office of public baptism in private houses"; and, in face of bitter opposition from the leading members of his flock, courageously took his stand upon the rubrics, declaring "that without our conformity to the established rules of our profession, he cannot in conscience be a curate to our souls". "But", as another correspondent reported to the primate, "the people will not hear of anything save their own ways and Customs."[5]

Mr. Allen of Sneaton had similar trouble, although in his particular case it was more of a personal vendetta. Feeling in the parish, indeed, ran so high that he wisely arranged to exchange

[1] L-B-S. MSS., Box 4, Bundle E. 15, Feb. 11, 1698/9.
[2] *Archbishop Herring's Visitation Returns*, vol. i, Preface, xi.
[3] L-B-S. MSS., Box 4, Bundle H. 14, 15; and J. 8, 9, 10.
[4] L-B-S. MSS., Box 4, Bundle K. 64.
[5] L-B-S. MSS., Box 4, Bundle Q. 12, March 19, 1706/7.

pulpits with Mr. Bateman of Lith. But this attempt at compromise met with a rebuff, for "the Sneaton churchwardens would not let Mr. Bateman go into the church because sent by Mr. Allen. Nevertheless two or three Sundays passing without their having any minister they complained that Mr. Allen took no care to provide them with a minister, and therefore desired Mr. Wilson would go up next day which he did against afternoon service and for which they gave him ten shillings."[1]

On the other hand, it was sometimes the squire who fell out with the parson. Mr. Simpson was licensed by the archbishop in 1697 to officiate at Graisbrook, but he soon found himself opposed by the local squire, Major Gill, who denied him entrance to his own church. Whereupon the curate threatened "to break open the chapel door if they refused him entrance, which accordingly he did lately".[2] The major was helpless, but being a man of resource retorted by indicting "him at the sessions for practising physick without a licence" (October 1697).

At the end of the seventeenth century churches and vicarages must, generally speaking, have been in a deplorable state of decay, judging from the multitude of complaints from incumbents on the score of dilapidations, for which they were usually responsible. These were, undoubtedly, a perpetual source of preoccupation to many a harassed cleric, a drain alike on his energies and pocket.

The question of the dilapidated vicarage will be dealt with in another place;[3] but with regard to the actual church fabric it is interesting to note that when lay impropriators shared the burden they not infrequently strove to avoid their obligations, leaving the wretched clergyman to bear it all alone. Sir Willoughby Hickman was such a defaulter. As trustee of Mrs. Sandys' estate he was liable for £80 towards the rebuilding of Howden church chancel, but denied the charge and referred the matter to his lawyers.[4]

Even when repairs were begun, they did not always come up to the parson's expectations. Alexander Jameson, incumbent of Easington, wrote to the archbishop on June 12, 1700: "Mr. Tylor, who holds Easington lease of Your Grace, is come hither from Beverley and is now repairing the Chancel, but with so little decency that he has caused the workmen to build all the windows round half up (some more some less) with brick, which shamefully

[1] L-B-S. MSS., Box 4, Bundle V. 43, Aug. 7, 1705.
[2] L-B-S. MSS., Box 4, Bundle C. 7.
[3] See Chapter VI, pp. 147-148.
[4] L-B-S. MSS., Box 4, Bundle F. 1, 2, June 25, 1690.

defaces it. How soon I heard thereof I repaired to Church where I found himself and asked him whether he did so by Your Grace's order, who seemed not much to regard it, and told me for answer that I should have light enough for all my business, which may be all true; but since neither defacement nor alteration (as I conceive) ought to be in the Church (especially my part of it) without Your Grace's liberty, I hold myself obliged and do make bold to acquaint Your Grace therewith."[1]

Another potential source of trouble in the parishes was the Roman Catholic or the Dissenter.

In Yorkshire, especially the rural districts, the Roman Catholics were a small and largely aristocratic community. Theoretically they remained subject to the harsh and intolerant penal laws: "Roman Catholic priests were banished the kingdom, and if they returned they were to be hanged; a reward of twenty pounds was given for the discovery of a priest, and a papist refusing to tell where he last heard Mass, was to be imprisoned for a twelve month; no papist was allowed to keep a school, and severe penalties were announced against such as should go themselves or send others abroad to be educated in the Romish religion; no papist could be guardian to any child, and if the child of a papist became a Protestant the Court of Chancery might order any part of the father's estate to be applied to the use of the child;[2] no papist could be a barrister or solicitor; no papist was to serve on Grand juries or on any other jury if objected to; and other penalties and disabilities were inflicted, equally atrocious."[3] But in practice, provided they kept quiet, they were not seriously molested; except when, in times of crisis, the mob got out of control and indulged itself in the sacking of Catholic chapels. These chapels were generally situated in the houses or grounds of the landed Roman Catholic gentry, and remained well secluded from the public gaze. The officiating priests were their private chaplains. It is estimated that some fifty-nine parishes in the York diocese had regular Roman Catholic congregations, which were served by thirty-six chapels. Elsewhere there were only a few scattered families. As a rule they gave no trouble to the incumbent, who good-naturedly

---

[1] L-B-S. MSS., Box 4, Bundle H. 11.

[2] There is an interesting case of a young Roman Catholic named Hammond, who pretended conversion to Anglicanism in the not unjustified expectation that the archbishop would help him to secure part of his father's estate: L-B-S. MSS., Box 4, Bundle V. 50.

[3] Such were the laws as enforced by the whig Somers in the reign of William III. See J. Campbell, *Lives of the Lord Chancellors*, vol. iv, p. 227.

forbore to make any mention of them in the Recusant Returns of 1706.[1]

Nevertheless, on occasion, an Anglican parson would come into conflict with his papist parishioners. John Smith, curate of Egton, wrote to the primate on August 29, 1699: "May it please Your Grace—What encouragement the papists receive from a popish steward is so apparent, that we think it our bounden duty humbly to beseech Your Grace to use your influence over the Lord Egton that no popish man may be here."[2] Again, Richard Clegge of Kirkham bitterly complained of the papists in his parish, especially of Sir John Clifton: "I do not think any other papist, beside him, in this kingdom, doeth own or maintain 3 papist priests against our Church." As a result of Sir John's efforts two Roman Catholic congregations had been established in the neighbourhood, "in time of Divine service at Westbury Hall on Sundays and Holy Days, and at Salwicke Hall every other Sunday".[3]

The Dissenters were very much more dangerous and aggressive. The Toleration Act had allowed them to have their own properly licensed ministers and to hold their own services; although, on the other hand, Nonconformists were still expected to pay tithes and perform any parochial duty required of them.[4] The main sects consisted of the Presbyterians, Independents, Baptists and Quakers, of which the last, at any rate in Yorkshire, were by far the most numerous, and practically alone of the Dissenters penetrated into the country districts.[5] But it was in the larger market towns that they proved most troublesome. Robert Banks, vicar of Hull, mourned the loss of members of his congregation, "who are too often . . . seduced to a conventicle";[6] while Mr. Spark, the unfortunate incumbent of Long Preston, was personally attacked in argument by two leading Nonconformist divines of the vicinity, "Mr. Hill who married Mr. Frankland the great non-conformist's daughter and who keeps up the meeting house at Rawthmill, and Mr. Kirshaw who heads another party at Winterborn in the parish of Gargrave". They sought to draw the vicar into a public dis-

[1] Parish after parish records "no papist". See marginal notes in *Archbishop Sharp's MSS.*, vol. iii.
[2] L-B-S. MSS., Box 4, Bundle K. 15.
[3] L-B-S. MSS., Box 4, Bundle G. 37, June 7, 1695.
[4] H. Gee and W. J. Hardy, *Documents Illustrative of the History of the English Church*, p. 662.
[5] There were probably about 70 Presbyterian meeting-houses, 20 Independent, 20 Baptist and 100 Quaker in the diocese. See *Archbishop Herring's Visitation Returns*, Introduction, xi.
[6] L-B-S. MSS., Box 4, Bundle Q. 8, March 6, 1692.

putation; but he so completely turned the tables on them that "both these leading men did profess their willingness to conform upon a convenient occasion".[1]

At Sheffield, however, the Independents and Presbyterians stole a march on the Anglicans, as their parson was obliged to confess: "I have lately heard a piece of news, which does not please at all . . . The dissenters in this Town of Sheffield are going to build a new and large meeting house, the land is purchased, and the charge of all computed to £200. Most of which is raised by legacies, well wishers at London, etc. The reason of this undertaking is not the growth of either party (independents or presbyterians) who are here united, but rather the hopes of gaining by convenience of room great numbers who at present can neither find place in Church nor conventicle. I have therefore discoursed his Grace about the great want we have of another Church in this populous town. Sure I am that many go to the meeting-house purely for want of room in our Church, alleging that they must serve God somewhere. I know not how this can be remedied, for building of Churches in this age is a hard undertaking, and endowing 'em yet harder. Yet it grieves me to see ourselves out-done in this nature, and that Non-conformity is in such a way to enlarge its borders among us."[2] Drake went on to suggest two possible remedies: A large private house might be converted "into a place of divine worship", or the chapel in the hospital, of which he was chaplain, situated on the outskirts of the town, could be thrown open for public prayer. "It is capable", he urged, "of being enlarged both in length and breadth."

Not all the Yorkshire clergy found the Nonconformists hostile and intractable. At many places their ministers were welcomed into the newly formed Societies for the Reformation of Manners;[3] and the Reverend Clement Elis, rector of Kirby, became so friendly with one of them that he even had the temerity to approach his archbishop with the following request: This minister, Elis affirmed, had a meeting-house in his own private dwelling, which lay in a parish where the vicarage, worth about £7 per annum, had been vacant for some time. Two-thirds of the population attended his meeting-house. Under these circumstances would it not be possible for the primate to license him "to preach in the said church (i.e. the parish church), he using the Lordsday service, and preaching

[1] L-B-S. MSS., Box 4, Bundle K. 64, April 24, 1705.
[2] L-B-S. MSS., Box 4, Bundle C. 8, Sept. 14, 1699.
[3] Cf. Chapter VII, p. 180.

only truths and duties of our common Christianity, not meddling with any controversy between churchmen and dissenters"?[1] Or, if that was impossible, he might be admitted as vicar "with indulgence and favour in some points of conformity; having taken and being ready to take again the oaths to their present Majesties; having subscribed to the doctrinal articles of the Church of England and being ready to subscribe all in Mr. Chillingworth's sense, as it is with Preface to his book against Knox." The dissenting minister, however, refused point blank to be ordained deacon and priest, "accounting himself a Presbyter", but was perfectly willing for the archbishop, by imposition of hands, to commission him to serve that particular church. Elis was enthusiastically in favour of some such arrangement, and informed Sharp: "I must confess I am very desirous to gain him to us." Unfortunately Sharp's reply is not extant. It would make interesting reading.

Manners and morals were, on the whole, coarse and low at the beginning of the eighteenth century; and, judging from the archiepiscopal correspondence, which is full of references to the personal misdemeanours of his spiritual sons, the clergy were no exception to this general rule.[2] The Reverend Henry Greathead of Granby frankly admitted to tippling in the local ale-house, growing quarrelsome in his cups and knocking down those who differed from him.[3] Mr. Hill of Willoughby also confessed that he had neglected his cure and led the kind of life most unbecoming to a clergyman.[4] Yet perhaps the worst instance of all was that of Mr. Hewardine, vicar of Swine, who violently raped the daughter of a well-to-do neighbour, Mr. Rand, under the most shameful conditions; and then not merely admitted the charge, but put the entire blame on the girl, and brazenly proceeded to carry on his clerical duties beneath the very nose of the outraged father, as though nothing uncommon had occurred.[5]

Finally, here is the record of a casual observer, who happened to pay a visit to the village of Farlington, "where", as he observed, "I have a small concern": On arrival he was informed that a

[1] L-B-S. MSS., Box 4, Bundle D. 1, April 21, 1692.
[2] *Cf.* Chapter VI, pp. 150-152.
[3] L-B-S. MSS., Box 4, Bundle E. 5, May 25, 1698.
[4] L-B-S. MSS., Box 4, Bundle F. 15.
[5] L-B-S. MSS., Box 4, Bundle E. 21, 41, 42, Aug.-Oct. 1702; Bundle F. 20, Mr. Hewardine's defence.
Mr. Henry Gaches, another clergyman, was charged not only with seduction but also an attempt to procure an abortion: L-B-S. MSS., Box 4, Bundle E. 11, Aug. 17, 1695.

certain Mr. Clark was going to become the new incumbent, of whom many scandalous stories were being whispered. These our friend would have been reluctant to believe, "had I not", as he later informed the archbishop, "seen too much in a neighbouring village on Tuesday last . . . The man is a stranger to me. I never saw him, but the last Tuesday and never desire to hear or see him more as then."[1]

Neither were the clergy always as true and just in their dealings as their parishioners had every right to expect. A good example of this is to be seen in the petition of "Anthony Bickerton, Robert Harryman and Thomas Frank inhabitants of the Township of Knotingly in the parish of Pontefract being poor men and in an indigent condition, who stand indebted unto Mr. Drake Vicar of Pontefract the sum of eight shillings a man or less, for which debt the said Mr. Drake has served a citation on us the said poor inhabitants, we being willing to pay the said debt with lawful charges therewith, and have made a tender of the same, he the said Mr. Drake demanding the sum of forty shillings a man, which we are in no way capable of paying neither are we able to withstand or defend our cause in court".[2]

Mr. Kemp of Sand Hutton, on the other hand, attempted to deceive his congregation by posing as a priest, when he was still only in deacon's orders; "and I verily believe", reported an indignant fellow-cleric, "would not have stuck at administering the Sacrament at Easter if I had not made the discovery."[3]

Strangely enough, there are comparatively few letters dealing with such recognised evils as simony and non-residence,[4] which seems to show that in Yorkshire, at any rate, they were relatively scarce.

Certainly it would not be true to say that the Queen Anne parson was an idler; for, despite serious preoccupations with the recovery of his tithes, the farming of his glebe, and the dilapidations of his church and vicarage, he yet found ample time for the conduct of his services, the visitation of the sick and negligent, the

---

[1] L-B-S. MSS., Box 4, Bundle L. 37.
Even the prebendal clergy were not always above reproach. Mr. W. Mompesson, vicar-general of Southwell, was accused by Mr. Barton of Budley, with much circumstantial evidence, of seducing one of his maidservants: L-B-S. MSS., Box 4, Bundle Q. 1.

[2] L-B-S. MSS., Box 4, Bundle C. 24, undated, but Mr. Drake's letter defending himself to the archbishop was written on July 20, 1704. See Bundle C. 14.

[3] L-B-S. MSS., Box 4, Bundle F. 28, April 29, 1707.

[4] For a discussion of these problems see Chapter VI, pp. 161-163.

punishment of the impenitent, and the courageous protection of
the weak against the strong, as well as for reading, writing and
political controversy. One service a Sunday, either in the morning
or afternoon, was generally recognised as the indispensable
minimum. This consisted of morning or evening prayer, a sermon
and the Litany, followed on four occasions in the year by the Holy
Communion. But most parishes did better than that. The list of
his services which Richard Leake, vicar of Helmsley with Kirkdale, supplied to the archbishop is a fair sample of what the
majority of his brethren were conscientiously endeavouring to
provide, and is worth quoting verbatim:

"Helmsley Parish Church supplied with divine service, sermons
and Sacraments yearly as followeth (viz);

"Three Sundays in every month, divine service and sermon in
the forenoon, and in the afternoon of the same day prayers half an
hour after four till the days be somewhat short. The 4th Sunday
divine service and sermon in the afternoon except when a Sacrament at Kirkdale which is four times in the year.

"Divine service on all holy days (except when urgent occasion
abroad) as also on Wednesdays and Fridays all the year long,
which was not performed here till I came. Occasional prayers (and
sermon most commonly) on Fastdays and Thanksgiving days in
the forenoon.

"Catechising I must confess very much omitted, but shall endeavour to retrieve that by diligently employing what opportunities I can possibly meet with, especially once a month, while
I can assure myself of (God willing) Wednesdays and Fridays in
Lent, and to that purpose I have considered of the several methods
that many have made use of, and shall make the catechism as
plain as I can."[1]

Visiting, too, was not neglected. Mr. John Hewitt, vicar of
Harthill, wrote on June 8, 1698: "In my visitation of a sick illiterate neighbour, whom (though a good honest well meaning
man, yet) I could not make sensible by any Christian arguments
of the necessity of repentance, faith and prayer, even on his death
bed tho' I was often with him."[2]

Towards the impenitent, indeed, the clergy frequently resorted
to sterner measures, causing them to be "presented" in the ecclesiastical courts, and either fined or forced to do penance. Some
went even further and banded together in the Societies for the

[1] L-B-S. MSS., Box 4, Bundle J. 14.   [2] L-B-S. MSS., Box 4, Bundle F. 44.

Reformation of Manners, which sought to inform against the immoral, dissolute and irreligious for their punishment by the State. Yet, in their pursuit of the wrongdoer, they were not unmindful of the claims of the weak and oppressed, although their satisfaction might also entail the defiance of the strong. Edward Charingburn, incumbent of Conisborough, gave shelter to a daughter flying from the cruel usage of her father, Mr. Stanhope of Mansfield. For this action he was naturally enough vilified by her family, who put into circulation the wildest tales about him: That, for example (as he bitterly complained to the primate), "I had ordained Madame Catherine a deaconess making her to believe she had power *ex-officio* to pray with the sick, instruct the ignorant," or that "I would have persuaded her to auricular confession."[1] Mr. Stanhope was an important social figure in the neighbourhood, while Charingburn was only a poor parson with a family of five or six to maintain out of an income of £36 per annum. He certainly possessed courage as well as Christian charity.

The standard of culture prevailing among the clergy was, on the whole, unexpectedly high; and, although books were scarce and expensive, and their leisure for study strictly limited, they yet remained the best-educated section of the community, the *literati* and tutors of the nation.

It was suggested to the archbishop in February 1704/5 that Henry More's *Theological Works* should be "reprinted for the use of smaller livings, and 2000 of them to be printed and given gratis". Unfortunately the publishing costs were very heavy: "If the whole Theological volume is printed 'twill cost near £1000. If only the Mystery of Godliness and Mystery of Iniquity about £600."[2] Sharp himself gladly contributed 25 guineas towards so excellent an undertaking, which would have been warmly welcomed in the parishes; but, alas! there is no record of its ever having been accomplished. John Hewitt of Harthill, in particular, would have rejoiced over this addition to his library, since books meant more to him than any other worldly possession. In a letter to Mr. Drake of Sheffield he wrote: "As you tender the good and welfare of your people (which I know you do in a great measure) I beseech you not to slight my advice of getting Mr. Beverley's Prophetical Works"; and referring to a paraphrase on the Revelation by Edward Waple, rector of St. Sepulchre, in London, de-

---

[1] L-B-S. MSS., Box 4, Bundle V. 37, May 2, 1705.
[2] L-B-S. MSS., Box 4, Bundle C. 18.

clared: "I value the book above the purchase of all my temporal enjoyments."[1] Drake, who was not a whit behind him in his love of learning, commented with pride on the fact that at a neighbouring auction he had been able to buy "3 lumping volumes of St. Jerome, the paris edition of Marion Victor for one pound, which I think is not dear."[2]

The majority of the young men who came forward for ordination were of humble birth: "There were indeed many sons of squires in the priesthood. But most of the village clergy were themselves children of the parsonage or else of the farmhouse."[3] After attending the local charity school they proceeded to the University as "servitours", obtained their degree, and then often sought for employment as tutors or schoolmasters until they were old enough for holy orders.[4] Before presenting themselves to the bishop, however, they had first to secure the offer of a title to a curacy or chaplaincy, and testimonials as to character and learning.[5] Neither were the candidates themselves averse from pleading their own cause: "I have a great desire", wrote John Nowell from Botton-nigh-Bolland to his archbishop, "to commit my mite to the treasury and lay out myself for the salvation of some souls through the help of my Master and Redeemer, and if my prayers and entreaties can prevail with you I humbly beg and desire that you would suffer me to preach my first sermon before you and admit me into Holy Orders."[6]

Freshly ordained deacons were not as a rule encouraged to preach. Drake of Sheffield remarked concerning his newly fledged colleague: "I had much rather see him perform the office of deacon well in reading prayers for one year than have him leap so hastily into the pulpit."[7] Further testimonials had to be forth-

---

[1] L-B-S. MSS., Box 4, Bundle F. 44.

Thomas Beverley was the Nonconformist minister of a congregation at Cutler's Hall, London. He published a number of works on the biblical prophecies and other theological subjects between the years 1670 and 1701. "He fixed dates with great confidence and lived to find his calculations erroneous. He held the doctrine of the premillennial reign of Christ on earth": S. Allibone, *British and American Authors*, vol. i, p. 185. For a full list of his works see R. Watt, *Bibliotheca Britannica*, vol. i, p. 110.

Edward Waple, B.D., was archdeacon of Taunton and vicar of St. Sepulchre. His book on the Revelation first appeared in 1693. See also *British and American Authors*, vol. iii, p. 2568, and *Bibliotheca Britannica*, vol. ii, p. 947.

[2] L-B-S. MSS., Box 4, Bundle C. 8, Sept. 14, 1699.

[3] G. M. Trevelyan, *England of Queen Anne* (reprint of chapters i-iv of *Blenheim*), p. 76.

[4] L-B-S. MSS., Box 4, Bundle E. 24.

[5] *Cf.* Chapter VI, p. 165.

[6] L-B-S. MSS., Box 4, Bundle A. 79, July 16, 1703.

[7] L-B-S. MSS., Box 4, Bundle C. 10, Sept. 11, 1700.

coming for the priesthood. Lord Eglinton asked Sharp "to admit into the sacred order of Priesthood the bearer hereof Obadiah Porrit who is Bachelor of Arts of Lincoln College, Oxon, and late scholar of the same and does at present perform the office of Chaplain to me",[1] and then went on to give him full marks for learning and morals.

The favoured and well-connected few were usually ordained deacon and priest within the space of six months. Heneage Dering, for example, was made deacon in Bishopthorpe Chapel on February 9, 1701, and was ordained priest the following July.[2] On the other side, Maurice Lisle, the humble curate of Fishlake, wrote: "May it please Your Grace.—My Son, having continued in the office of deacon for the space of three years, being found faithful and diligent in the execution of it, intends, God willing, at the next time of Ordination to supplicate Your Grace for the order of Priesthood."[3]

Not all the clergy had degrees or were particularly well educated. The career of the curate at Mexborough was described in the following terms: "He was first admitted into the wood, his study to rive latts, his tutor a woodman, his degree a drummer to Oliver, then reader to old Jackson of Doncaster, another Oliverian, and then to Mexborough."[4]

But it was not only during the turbulent times of the Great Rebellion and Commonwealth that men strove to slip into the ministry through the back-door. Mr. Hewitt of Harthill endeavoured to persuade Sharp to ordain a young schoolmaster, who had no degree, as his curate, promising "I will join with him in a bond of an £100 that he shall never preach, nor attempt to expound the Scriptures, but only to read prayers."[5] But Sharp was not a bishop lightly to lower his standards.[6]

The Reverend Humphrey Bralesford of Southwell had, on the contrary, some interesting suggestions to make for the yet more intensive training of ordinands: "If such of the clergy", he urged, "who for learning and reverence are judged competent, were prevailed with by some recommendation that carries authority along with it, to entertain each some young scholar upon his

[1] L-B-S. MSS., Box 4, Bundle A. 30, May 3, 1695.
[2] See H. Dering, *Autobiographical Memoranda* (Edit. Surtees Society, vol. 65), pp. 340-341.
[3] L-B-S. MSS., Box 4, Bundle J. 9, May 28, 1707.
[4] L-B-S. MSS., Box 4, Bundle K. 23.
[5] L-B-S. MSS., Box 4, Bundle F. 44, June 8, 1698.
[6] *Cf.* Chapter VI, pp. 164-165.

leaving the University for a year or two, allowing him his board, the use of his library, direction in his studies, instructions in the Pastoral Care, and a good example." "'Tis certainly the case of many young scholars", he went on, "having commenced Bachelors of Arts, they are forced to quit the University; and either presently crowd into Orders, or else . . . wait for the Canonical Age. These on their own account may deserve our pity; and on the Church's account a remedy if . . . this might not be had in some measure by the project proposed." Bralesford then proceeded to outline his scheme, which provided that the candidate for orders, regardless of his worldly means, should live for some months or years with an approved incumbent, be supplied with all the books he needed for carrying on his studies, and initiated into the mysteries of pastoralia. "By this means", he concluded, "the giddiness and gaiety of youth would likely be fixed in a settled habit of regular living, by the sober conversation, good example and wise instructions they should meet withall, which would insensibly of its own force prevail upon them, without any form of discipline exercised upon them. The expenses of the venture must of necessity be borne by the Church itself, which should tax all the clergy for the purpose."[1]

In this brief survey of the Yorkshire parson and his problems, his more intimate family relationships cannot be omitted. Most clergymen had large families, including, perhaps, ten or more children. These youngsters had all to be fed, clothed and educated on something like £40 or £50 a year; while the Queen Anne parsonage that housed them was usually small and lacked the amenities of the better-equipped country house. "The house Mr. Davies should purchase seems to me", wrote a contemporary, "to be very convenient and advantageous to the vicarage. There may be a parlour an hall and kitchen with a chimney in every one, also a pantry and 3 chambers above all. There is in the yard a well which was much awanting to the vicarage house. The out-house is a stable. Those buildings will take very little repairs being free from storms."[2]

Within so narrowly confined an environment the family atmosphere was not always as harmonious as it might have been. It was, indeed, said of one vicar that he "was an honest industrious sober man for many years, till his wife's wickedness, and children's

[1] L-B-S. MSS., Box 4, Bundle Q. 17.
[2] L-B-S. MSS., Box 4, Bundle F. 35, June 2, 1703.

disobedience distracted him so much, that he endeavoured to drown his cares, till he was so besotted that the Cure and School was most miserably neglected".[1]

In these circumstances the value of the average parson in the matrimonial market could never be a high one; although, of course, the cathedral clergy were on quite a different footing. Mr. Ralph Lowther wrote to the archbishop in 1702 asking him to sound the new dean of York on the subject of a possible marriage with Miss Lowther, whose dowry would run to £3,000 or £4,000. He added, by way of postscript: "I hope her person (tho' fat) and humour would be agreeable to him."[2]

Such, in rough outline, is the background picture of the men and their times, drawn for us in faded ink by the pens of those long-dead Yorkshire and Nottinghamshire clerics, out of the depths of their very human hearts. And, as we fold their correspondence once again into the well-worn creases and return it to the muniment room, we must needs admit that Jonathan Swift was not so very far from the mark, at least in relation to the archdiocese of York, when he made his satirical comparison between the poor curate and the prosperous cathedral dignitary:

"Thy curate's place, thy fruitful wife,
Thy busy, drudging scene of life,
Thy insolent, illiterate vicar,
Thy want of all consoling liquor,
Thy threadbare gown, thy cassock rent,
Thy credit sunk, thy money spent,
Thy week made up of fasting-days,
Thy grate unconscious of a blaze,
And to complete thy other curses,
The quarterly demands of nurses,
Are ills you wisely wish to leave,
And fly for refuge to the grave.
And, O, what virtue you express,
In wishing such afflictions less!
But now, should Fortune shift the scene,
And make thy curateship a dean;
Or some rich benefice provide,
To pamper luxury and pride;
With labour small, and income great;
With chariot less for use than state;

[1] L-B-S. MSS., Box 4, Bundle Q. 63, Aug. 11, 1705.
[2] L-B-S. MSS., Box 4, Bundle J. 4, June 29, 1702.

With swelling scarf and glossy gown,
And licence to reside in Town,

. . . . .

With underlings thy flock to teach,
With no desire to pray or preach;
With haughty spouse in vesture fine,
With plenteous meals and generous wine;
Wouldst thou not wish, in so much ease,
Thy years as numerous as thy days?"[1]

[1] *Poetical Works of Dean Swift*, vol. ii, p. 52, edit. 1853.

CHAPTER II

EARLY DAYS

"I CANNOT leave this district", wrote Ralph Thoresby, "without notice of an ancient house . . . memorable for the birth of one, and the death of another learned and pious author, the late Reverend Mr. Thomas Sharp, whose family is of great antiquity in Bradfordale, particularly at Little Horton where there has been a succession of Thomas and John alternately for many generations; but the ancient writings being lost at the taking of Bradford in the Civil Wars, I cannot produce a pedigree, save what I have extracted from the several registers at Bradford and Leeds, which I the rather insert, though imperfect, because 'tis rare to meet with so many learned authors so nearly allied, though this branch be extinct in an ingenious and hopeful young gentleman, Dr. John Sharp, yet another is likely to continue in honour, being deservedly advanced to the Archiepiscopal see of York, not only to the comfort and honour of his native country and family but the universal satisfaction and joy of the whole nation."[1]

The Sharp family had certainly been seated for many generations at Little Horton. In the year 1365 the then lord of the manor, William de Leventhorpe, executed a deed conveying some land in Little Horton to Thomas Sharp, who was apparently a substantial yeoman farmer.[2] There is mention, too, of an Alice Sharp in the poll tax rolls of Richard II;[3] and in the Hopkinson MSS. James Sharp was stated to be living at a house in Little Horton, which had lately been the property of Kirkstall Abbey, during the thirty-sixth year of Henry VIII's reign. This house was probably on the site of the present Horton Old Hall.[4] James had a contemporary, Christopher Sharp, the elder, who owned a considerable property, since he was assessed to the subsidy roll, 34th Henry VIII, at £20, a big sum for Tudor days. Christopher's will, dated February 1, 1541, directed that his body should be buried in the church of St. Peter, Bradford, left 3s. 4d. to buy a "maniell", and 10s. to be expended on masses for his and all Christian souls. His son John

[1] Ralph Thoresby, *Ducatus Leodiensis*. Edit. T. D. Whitaker, p. 37, 1816.
[2] W. Cudworth, *Life and Correspondence of Abraham Sharp*, p. 1.
[3] A. Holroyd, *Collectanea Bradfordiana*, p. 105.
[4] Rev. J. Fawcett, *The Sharps of Horton Hall*: A lecture, 1873.

inherited not only the property but the Catholic piety of his father, commending his soul, when his turn came, to the Lady Mary and leaving 12d. for the high altar of Bradford parish church. But with the coming of the Reformation part of the family at any rate turned Puritan, for John's grandson, another John, was a strong supporter of the parliamentary interest in Bradford during the civil wars. The latter, according to the testimony of his faithful servant, Joseph Lister,[1] was a manufacturing clothier, a merchant, and a man of large estate at Little Horton. He married Mary Clarkson, whose brother David, after hair-raising adventures with Lister at Bradford when that town was taken by the royalists in 1643, later became fellow of Clare Hall, Cambridge, and the tutor of John Tillotson, the future archbishop of Canterbury.[2]

John Sharp, evidently an extremely well-educated man, was appointed Sir Thomas Fairfax's secretary and fought throughout the northern campaigns. He was present at the defeat of Atherton Moor, the siege of Bradford, and the subsequent victories at Nantwich and Marston Moor. For his great services he received from Parliament, during the Protectorate, a gold medal with the figure of Fairfax on the obverse.[3] It is a common fact, of course, that the Great Rebellion divided many ancient families, and so it is scarcely surprising to find that this was the case with the Sharps of Little Horton. John's uncle, yet another John, who had married the heiress of the Waterhouse estates at Shelf, proved himself to be a strong royalist, "having been in several battles on the king's side, in one of which he received a severe contusion on the head from a battle-axe, and though he lived to a good age, he was wont to say, that but for such a blow he might have lived to be an old man".[4] The same gentleman is also credited with never suffering "his beard to be shaven or his hair to be cut after the execution of Charles I".[5]

John, the parliamentarian, was the father of two famous sons, Thomas and Abraham.

The Reverend Thomas Sharp, M.A. (1633-1693), who was educated under the auspices of his uncle David Clarkson at Clare Hall, Cambridge, became vicar of Adel; but, after being ejected

---

[1] See *The Autobiography of Joseph Lister*. Edit. T. Wright. Also *cf.* J. Lister, *A Genuine Account of the Sore Calamities that Befel Bradford in the Time of the Civil War.*
[2] A. Holroyd, *Collectanea Bradfordiana*, p. 55.
[3] Now in the possession of Mr. F. S. E. Bardsley-Powell.
[4] A. Holroyd, *Collectanea Bradfordiana*. p. 55.
[5] W. Cudworth, *Life and Correspondence of Abraham Sharp*, p. 249.

from that living in 1662, set up as a Nonconformist minister of Call Lane Chapel, Leeds, where he created no small reputation. This was the Thomas Sharp to whom Thoresby referred, and whose son, a very promising medical student, died at Leyden, aged thirty.

Abraham Sharp (1651-1742), on the other hand, was the noted mathematician, the friend of Flamstead and Newton. For the greater part of his long life of ninety-one years he resided in Little Horton; but, as a young man, he had been appointed Flamstead's assistant at the Royal Observatory, Greenwich. Ill-health, however, eventually drove him back to Horton Old Hall, and here he became an habitual recluse.[1] "It is stated that when any particular friends came to see him, they were in the habit of rubbing a stone against a prescribed part of the outside wall of the house, and if he wished their company were admitted by him, otherwise they returned disappointed."[2] He carried on a regular correspondence with the greatest philosophers and mathematicians of his day, including, besides Flamstead and Newton, Halley, Wallis, Hodgson and Sherwin, all of whom held him in the highest esteem. Immersed in his mathematical calculations, he often forgot to take food for days on end; and there is a story to the effect that on one occasion, being unable to solve a mathematical problem, he travelled as far as Scotland in order to consult a scholar who had been recommended to him. This man told his visitor, who had evidently not revealed his identity, that there was only one person capable of unravelling the tangle, a certain Abraham Sharp of Little Horton.

Abraham was as strong a Presbyterian as his brother, and used regularly to attend the meeting-house in Chapel Lane, built by his father. On these occasions he filled his hands with copper coins, holding them behind his back in order that the money might be taken by people whose names he did not know; thus literally fulfilling the gospel command: "When thou doest thine alms, let not thy left hand know what thy right hand doeth." His portrait was taken and engraved by Vertue. After his death a monument was erected to his honour in St. Peter's, Bradford, which, in recognition, no doubt, of his great age, concluded its inscription with the

[1] The exact date of Abraham's introduction to Flamstead is uncertain, but from entries in his pocket memorandum books he was undoubtedly employed as an assistant at Greenwich from March 1684/5 to April 1690. He returned to Little Horton on March 29, 1694. See op. cit., pp. 12-22.
[2] Rev. J. Fawcett, The Sharps of Horton Hall: A lecture, 1873.

words: "Sated with human affairs he passed to Heaven on the 18th July 1742."[1]

Abraham and Thomas both attended Bradford Grammar School, where John Sharp, the future archbishop of York, was also a pupil. The exact relationship between them is, nevertheless, unknown. "There is no doubt," wrote Dr. T. D. Whitaker, "of the consanguinity with the Sharps of Little Horton; but Thoresby who, with a little more of that industry which he usually exerted on such occasions, might probably have discovered the connecting link, has in this instance neglected it."[2]

On Abraham Sharp's monument it is merely recorded that he was "united in the bond of relationship with the Archbishop of York of that name";[3] but Calamy went so far as to declare that Thomas, Abraham's brother, was the archbishop's cousin.

Be this as it may, it appears certain that the archbishop had descended from that James Sharp who was mentioned in the Hopkinson MSS. as living at Little Horton during Henry VIII's reign.[4] James was, apparently, a poor relation of Christopher Sharp, since he only paid a sum equal to one-fifth of the latter's taxation to Henry's subsidy; but again the exact connection has never been traced. However, the bond was sufficiently close for James to act as a witness both to the wills of Christopher and of his son John. He himself died about the year 1557. His son, another James, left Horton for Woodhouse in North Bierley, and henceforth this branch of the family became known as the Sharps of Woodhouse. They, too, were clothiers and farmers on a small scale. A third James, evidently the favourite name for the eldest son of the house, succeeded his father and begat four children: James, Elizabeth, Mary and Thomas. James, the fourth of that ilk, was the progenitor of the Sharps of Gildersome and Tong, from whom the late Canon John Sharp, vicar of Horbury, had descended; Elizabeth married Tempest Cordingley of Tong in 1625, and later undertook the duties of godmother to the archbishop;[5] and Thomas, the second son, ventured into trade and set up as a wet and dry salter and oil drawer in Bradford, residing at a house in Ivegate to the west of that now known as the Unicorn

[1] " Rerum Humanarum Satu in Cælum Demigravit XV Kalend August MDCCXLII."
[2] T. D. Whitaker, The Parish of Bradford, p. 25.
[3] " Et Archiepiscopo Eius Nominis Eboracensi Sanguinis Vinculo Coniuncti."
It may be of interest to state, in passing, that Cudworth asserts that Abraham was born on June 1, 1653, and was only just ninety when he died.
[4] See above, p. 38.   [5] Life of Archbishop Sharp, vol. i, p. 3.

Inn. Here he prospered and married "Dorothy, the eldest daughter of Mr. John Weddall of Widdington in the said county"[1] (*i.e.* York). John Weddell (or Weddall) was rector of Widdington,[2] where he also owned some property. His son John had settled in Bradford as an attorney. Thomas and Dorothy, in their turn, produced five children, four boys and a girl. The last married John Richardson of Birks Hall, Bradford, likewise an attorney-at-law,[3] in 1672. Little is known of the three younger sons, Thomas, James and Joshua, except that Joshua "received the honour of knighthood in London".[4] John, the eldest, was the future archbishop of York.

The dates of the archbishop's birth and baptism are uncertain. There is much evidence in favour of his birthday being February 16, 1644/5;[5] but the entry in the baptismal register of Bradford parish church, now the cathedral church of St. Peter, reads very differently:

"Oct. 2nd 1642. John, son of Thomas Sharp of Bradford."

Against the name, or rather above it, has been written in the same handwriting: "Afterwards Archbishop of York." There is no mention either of the clergyman who was responsible for the ceremony or of any of Sharp's sponsors. But if this entry is the original and correct one, then John Sharp was born nearly two years earlier than has generally been supposed, in the autumn instead of the spring of the year, and not so very long after that "very stormy and tempestuous day (22nd August 1642)"[6] when Charles I caused his standard to be raised at Nottingham, the sign that civil war had begun.[7]

---

[1] Op. cit., vol. i, p. 1.

[2] J. Venn and J. A. Venn, *Alumni Cantabrigienses*, Part I, vol. iv, p. 49.

[3] R. Thoresby, *Ducatus Leodiensis*, p. 23.

[4] W. Cudworth, *Life and Correspondence of Abraham Sharp*, p. 266.

[5] Ralph Thoresby (*Ducatus Leodiensis*, p. 36, edit. 1714) omits the dates of birth and baptism. But the second edition (edit. T. D. Whitaker, 1816) asserts that he was "born 16 Feb. 1664". The archbishop's monumental inscription in York Minster reads: "Natus Bradfordiæ in hoc Comitatu 16 Feb. 1644." *Alumni Cantabrigienses:* "B. at Ivegate, Bradford, Yorks, Feb. 16, 1644/5."

Life of Archbishop Sharp, vol. i, p. 3: "He was born at Bradford on Shrove Tuesday, February 16, 1664."

A MS. originally belonging to Granville Sharp: "Dr. John Sharp, Archbishop of York, was the son of Thomas Sharp, of Bradford, in the County of York, where he was born on the 16th February 1644/5."

On the other side, *cf.* the evidence of the *Lambeth Act Books*, vol. ii, p. 84, quoted on p. 5 of this book.

[6] J. R. Tanner, *English Constitutional Conflicts in the 17th Century*, p. 118.

[7] The entry appears genuine enough. It is made on vellum. There is no reason to believe that the registers were destroyed or tampered with in any way during the civil wars. However, it is possible that owing to the war the writing up of the register was

It has been claimed that Sharp was baptised by "Mr. Blazet, a person episcopally ordained".[1] The last statement was seemingly made on the authority of the archbishop himself, who prided himself on the fact of his regular baptism; since, sound churchman as he was, he thus escaped the ignominy, a very common one in those turbulent times, of an irregularly performed service. Such a misfortune, indeed, was continually and most unjustly fathered upon Archbishop Tillotson. The names of Sharp's godparents have also survived: Mr. Weddell, Mr. Drake and Mrs. Cordingley, the first and last of whom were, of course, a maternal uncle and paternal aunt.[2]

Mr. Blease (or Blazet) was the "under-minister" or curate of St. Peter's at this time. The vicar, Francis Corker, who had been appointed by the king in 1642/3, had so infuriated his puritanical parishioners by making use of the sign of the cross in baptism and other Catholic practices that he was compelled to leave the town and take refuge in the king's army of the north, where he resigned his clerical office for the profession of arms. The rectory and manor of Bradford, which had been sold by Charles immediately after the appointment of Corker, had come into the hands of Sir John Maynard, who appointed as his agent for collecting the rectorial tithes John Sharp, the parliamentarian and friend of Fairfax. Among the Sharp MSS. there is a letter from Sir John, dated August 13, 1649, that deals with the presentation to the living, which, evidently, Blazet had been demanding for himself. "I wish", wrote Sir John, "to be careful to consult the parish, so I advise you to agree in the choice of a minister. I have written to the town to satisfy Mr. Blease's importunity." Blazet was appointed in 1650; so in 1644/5 he was only the curate, and not the vicar, as has sometimes been supposed. It is interesting to note in this connection that after the Restoration and death of Corker, who had returned, Abraham Brooksbank, Archbishop Sharp's Cambridge tutor, was presented by Lady Maynard to Bradford in 1667, which living he held for some ten years.[3]

Thomas Sharp, the archbishop's father, was as strong a parlia-

---

delayed, and then the error occurred. The words "afterwards Archbishop of York" being in the same handwriting as the rest of the entry lend colour to such a theory.

[1] *Life of Archbishop Sharp*, vol. i, p. 3.

[2] John Weddell and Elizabeth Cordingley (née Sharp).

[3] *Christ's College, Cambridge, Biographical Register*, edit. J. Peile, p. 532: "He having been appointed by the Dowager Lady Maynard, and by Jonas Waterhouse . . . to the vicarage of Bradford on 19 April 1667." *Cf. Alumni Cantabrigienses*, Part I, vol. i, p. 229.

mentarian as his relation at Little Horton, and the occupation of
Bradford by the Roundheads during the civil wars certainly did
him no harm. Bradford, indeed, was violently puritanical and
resolutely supported Sir Thomas Fairfax, who, writing to his
father about his initial campaign in Yorkshire against the Duke of
Newcastle, remarked: "The first Action we had was at Bradford
where we had about 300 men. The enemy having about 700 or
800 and 2 pieces of ordnance came thither to assault us"[1] (October 1642). They were defeated and driven off. But on Sunday,
December 18, during Fairfax's absence, Newcastle decided to
make another attempt in the form of a surprise attack at night
from Leeds. He had considerable forces at his disposal, and, since
there were no regular parliamentary troops garrisoning the town
at the time, anticipated an easy victory. However, he had reckoned
without the Bradford men, who, turning out with clubs, scythes
and poles, fell upon the royalists and after a fierce hand-to-hand
mêlée in the narrow streets, routed them completely. A contemporary thus recorded the utter amazement of the cavaliers: "The
courage of our army astonished the enemy, who said that no fifty
men, unless they were mad or drunk, would have pursued a
thousand."[2]

Ferdinando, Lord Halifax, the father of Sir Thomas, in a letter
dated December 29, 1642, described this victory of the clubmen
in the following terms: "In which victory the hand and power of
God was most evident, the Town being open on all sides and not
defensible; assaulted on every side by a malicious and bloody
enemy; and defended by a few half armed men . . . so that the
slaughter was, for the most part, with clubs and scythes mounted
on poles, and came to hand to hand blows. With this defeat, the
enemy are so enraged that they threaten revenge to Bradford.
Whereupon Bradford men sent to me for succour of men and arms.
And I have sent my son (Sir Thomas Fairfax) and Sir Henry
Foulis to them, with 3 Troop of horse and 120 Dragoones; who
are safely arrived there, and have been received with great joy and
acclamation of the country; who flock to him and offer themselves
most willingly to serve against their Popish enemies, if arms could
be furnished them."[3]

[1] Thomas, third Lord Halifax, *A Short Memorial of the Northern Actions*. Edit. An
English Garner, vol. ii, p. 365.
[2] Pamphlet in the British Museum, *Bradford's Deliverance or The Rider of the White
Horse and His Army*, 1643.
See also *Fairfax Correspondence*, iii, p. 236.
[3] *A Short Memorial*, p. 370.

It is not known whether or no Thomas Sharp took part in this clubmen's victory; but, judging from his noted Presbyterian zeal and military leanings, it is highly probable that he did. At any rate Sir Thomas Fairfax, who now made Bradford his headquarters, singled him out for special attention by lodging at his house in Ivegate, and apparently offered him a commission in the Round-head army, which he would gladly have accepted but for the prayers and entreaties of his wife.[1]

After the heavy defeat of the Fairfaxes at Atherton Moor on June 30, 1643, Sir Thomas was surrounded in Bradford and had to cut his way out, leaving Lady Fairfax a prisoner in the hands of the royalists.[2] The town was then occupied by Newcastle and remained in his hands until the advance of the Scots and the victory of Marston Moor in the following year finally destroyed the king's power in the north. How the Sharps fared during the royalist occupation has not been recorded, but doubtless the wife's loyalty did much to compensate for the infidelity of the husband. For Dorothy was devoted to king and Church, and retained, despite repeated search, copies of the proscribed Book of Common Prayer. The fact that John Sharp later became the acknowledged head of the High Church party was largely due to his mother, who imbued her eldest son at an early age with a great love for the Anglican Liturgy, and a strong spirit of loyalty towards the exiled House of Stuart. Both these principles of the archbishop found their fullest expression when, during the reign of Queen Anne, he acted as her ecclesiastical adviser. The Prayer Book, he used indeed to declare in later life, was almost perfectly designed; and he strenuously resisted any attempt at its radical revision, although willing enough to introduce slight modifications in the hope of winning back the mass of the Dissenters to the Church. The Prayer Book also inspired him to undertake difficult and delicate negotiations with the ministers of Hanover and Prussia for the adoption by those countries of a form of the Anglican Liturgy.[3] Furthermore, throughout his entire life, he made the widest use of it for his own private and family devotions.

Nevertheless his father's puritanical beliefs left an impression equally deep, if not so direct, upon his mind. One of John's earliest recollections as a child was that of discovering, purely by chance,

[1] *Life of Archbishop Sharp*, vol. i, p. 5. [2] M. A. Gibb, *The Lord General*, p. 53.
[3] See Chapter X, pp. 264-274.

the manner in which Thomas conducted his prayers; and the earnest dignity and simplicity of those petitions attracted the boy's attention and presented him at a most impressionable age with an ideal of worship which was never forgotten.[1] It was not, however, to be his ideal; for the doctrines of Presbyterianism were irretrievably tainted with fanaticism and disloyalty, and consequently could take no permanent root in a heart already pledged to Church and king.

John's early education was mediocre. He attended Bradford Grammar School, which under its headmaster, Mr. Cotes, was a very flourishing institution. Several future celebrated savants, including Abraham Sharp and Dr. Richardson, F.R.S., of Bierley Hall, were pupils there about this period. Here he was taught an accomplishment that stood him in excellent stead for the rest of his life—namely, the art of shorthand.[2] In order to perfect himself he used regularly to take down the sermons preached on a Sunday and repeat them aloud from his shorthand copy to the family circle. This was no uncommon practice in the grammar schools of the time, where the scholars were usually required not only to reproduce the entire sermon, but the following morning to turn it into Latin. For such purposes some sort of shorthand was indispensable. John Sharp certainly found it of the greatest help to him throughout his whole career in every kind of literary work. His personal diary was written entirely in this form.

He went up to Christ's College, Cambridge, in April 1660, the year of the Restoration, and was placed under the tuition of his father's friend, Abraham Brooksbank.[3]

Thomas had four[4] other children to provide for out of a modest income. Nevertheless he was determined to maintain John at Cambridge for seven years, as liberally as possible, in order to give his quick-witted eldest son, who had shown great intellectual promise at Bradford, every opportunity of winning a fellowship. He confided him to the care of Brooksbank, then a fellow of Christ's, trusting implicitly in his friend's power to see these hopes realised. Brooksbank certainly paid particular attention to John's studies, and although he failed to provide the coveted fellowship,

[1] *Life of Archbishop Sharp*, vol. i, p. 6.
[2] For a note on seventeenth-century shorthand see the Appendix to Chapter II.
[3] *Biographical Register of Christ's College, Cambridge*. Edit. J. Peile, p. 590.
Cf. also *Alumni Cantabrigienses*, Part I, vol. iv, p. 49.
[4] *Life of Archbishop Sharp*, vol. i, p. 9, states that there were five, but only four can be traced—viz., Thomas, James, Joshua and Hannah. *Cf.* Thomas Sharp's will, dated Sept. 5, 1670.

yet so won his pupil's respect and admiration that when the latter
became archdeacon of Berkshire he procured for his old tutor,
through the interest of the Lord Chancellor, the living of St.
Mary's, Reading. That was in 1677; and later, after Sharp had
himself been raised to the archbishopric, he secured the same
friend a prebend in Salisbury Cathedral (1692).[1] Yet one of the
first services Brooksbank rendered John would probably not have
pleased Thomas, as he helped to disabuse the former's mind of
those rigid Presbyterian doctrines of predestination and reproba-
tion which he had imbibed from his father.

Sharp, like his "cousin" Abraham, had mathematical and
scientific leanings. Thus, besides attending the lectures of Brooksbank, he also studied natural philosophy under Thomas Burnet,
then a fellow of Christ's, but later, in 1685, to become Master of
the Charterhouse and chaplain and clerk of the closet to William
III.[2] Burnet taught the new Cartesian philosophy, which in the
eyes of all progressive scholars had already ousted the older
Copernican system. But an even brighter star, Newton, was now
in the ascendant, and Sharp with his clear mathematical brain,
which was unfortunately stinted of mathematics and forced into
classical and theological grooves, much admired his work, and in
after years defended it. He likewise took up botany and chemistry,
but had no time to do more than dabble in these subjects. However, he did actually go so far as to compile two volumes, written
in cypher, "containing transcripts of lectures, queries, and solu-
tions and large excerpts out of writers upon these subjects. The
larger book of botany, chemistry and physics was begun in the
year 1665; the lesser book was written before. And after both these
(but at what time is uncertain) he wrote out a fair copy in round
hand of certain chemical experiments and conclusions."[3]

He made use of his shorthand, in which he was now expert, in
another direction, when regularly week by week he took down the
University sermon or made copious theological notes for future
reference. He was known, too, to have been a great lover of poetry
and plays, particularly those of Shakespeare, and "whatsoever
was calculated to smite the fancy, and move the passions".[4] Such

[1] *Alumni Cantabrigienses*, Part I, vol. i, p. 229.
[2] Op. cit., Part I, vol. i, p. 261.
Cf. J. Peile, *Cambridge College Histories: Christ's*, vol. vii, p. 203:
"The earth, he said, was like an egg whose shell was crushed at the Deluge, when
the water inside the egg burst out and the fragments of the shell became mountain
ranges." (*Telluris Theoria Sacra.*)
[3] *Life of Archbishop Sharp*, vol. i, p. 11.   [4] Ibid., vol. i, p. 14.

facts are of interest as indicating his catholic tastes and wide intellectual sympathies, even at this early age.

The social life of the University, its political and theological heats, or the wild, gay, exuberant spirits riding the crest of Restoration reaction against the principles and practices of Puritanism, would make but little appeal to the serious young scholar drinking so deeply at the wells of knowledge. Not that Sharp was strictly puritanical in all his habits. He was as fond as any man of pleasant company, good plays and amusing conversation; neither was he by any means averse to "the soothing aid of a pipe of tobacco and the gentle stimulus of a glass of good wine".[1] His studies, however, were his first consideration, and so closely did he pursue them, rising early and retiring late, that his health became seriously affected. He fell a victim to "the quartan ague"[2] shortly after coming into residence, and took it very badly. So much so that he was compelled to return home in the hope that his native Yorkshire air would restore his vigour. Unfortunately the distemper, far from abating, developed into a form of nervous depression, which he found extremely difficult to combat. But he did not fall into the error, common enough at the time, of ascribing his melancholia to religious rather than physical causes. And by means of concentrating primarily on the improvement of his bodily health, together with a strong effort of will-power, he succeeded in curing himself so completely that he never again succumbed to hypochondria. Nevertheless the experience was to prove of considerable value to him in later years, when as a casuist he had to deal with similar cases. On one occasion, indeed, while rector of St. Giles-in-the-Fields, he preached a complete course of sermons on the subject, which aroused much interest, since he freely attributed the cause of this malady to physical disease and laughed to scorn the suggestion that it had any religious origin—i.e., in the work of an evil spirit.[3]

Sharp took his B.A. degree in 1663/4, and was shortly after-

[1] *Christ's College, Cambridge, Biographical Register*. Edit. J. Peile, p. 590.
[2] This malady, probably a form of malaria due to mosquito bites, was not uncommon in marshy seventeenth-century Cambridge.
[3] See Sharp's *Sermons*, vol. iii, edn. 1734.
Among the L-B-S. MSS. are many letters dealing with hypochondria, *e.g.* a letter to Lady Wild upon blasphemous thoughts: Box 3, Bundle H. 19; "Answering queries from an hypochondriack": Box 3, Bundle H. 20; "A letter from James Powell about a diseased mind": Box 3, Bundle O. 6; "An anonymous enquirer about hypochondria": Box 3, Bundle O. 7.

wards made a scholar of his college.[1] For the next three years he was to remain in or near Cambridge, perfecting his Greek and specialising in theology in preparation for the fellowship on which both he and his father had set their hearts .The famous Dr. Cudworth, the Cambridge Platonist, then Master of Christ's, was his friend, and so were most of the fellows, including the equally famous Henry More. More and Cudworth at this period represented the heart and brains of the Cambridge Platonist movement, of which Christ's College had long been a stronghold. This movement, which began with the revolt of John Hales and William Chillingworth in the early years of the seventeenth century against dogmatism in religion, condemned alike the Anglicanism of Laud with its ceremonies, and Puritanism with its insistence on the doctrines of election and predestination. It was composed of a group of deeply learned men with a philosophical outlook, who were convinced that human reason, illuminated by the Holy Spirit of God, could alone uncover the heart of truth and religion. Reason was to them the "candle of the Lord", the ultimate authority, the very voice of God Himself. That is not to say they set reason above either conscience or scripture, but merely claimed that it confirmed both. It was, however, the moral element in scripture, rather than the dogmatic or the mysterious, that appealed to them. Hence their interest in Neoplatonism and their attempt to combine its teaching with that of Christianity, not for the sake of its metaphysics, but on account of its religious spirit and ethical idealism. On the other hand, it would be definitely untrue to say that they were slavish imitators of the Neoplatonists, despite the fact that most of their writings were encrusted with quotations from classical moralists like Plotinus. They drew far more freely from the Bible and always acknowledged Christ as their Master.[2]

Cudworth, indeed, in his great work *Anima Mundi*,[3] strove to prove the existence of certain fixed divine moral laws, such as

[1] *Life of Archbishop Sharp*, vol. i, p. 12: "He had no college preferment till his fourth year, and then he was made scholar of the house."

[2] *Cf.* W. F. Mitchell, *English Pulpit Oratory*, chapter viii; E. T. Campagnac, *The Cambridge Platonists*, Introduction, pp. xi-xiv.

J. Peile, *Cambridge College Histories: Christ's*, chapter vii.

W. C. de Pauley, *The Candle of the Lord*, chapters iv and v.

F. J. Powicke, *The Cambridge Platonists*, chapter iv.

[3] *The True Intellectual System of the Universe*, 1678.

The Cambridge Platonists were reproached for being moral preachers only, and were even accused of Latitudinarianism. Political Latitudinarians they were certainly not, but it is possible to describe them as rationalistic Latitudinarians.

Christ expounded, which all men must observe, but declared that any narrow dogmatic forms, whether of Romanism, Anglicanism or Puritanism, were unnecessary and often definitely harmful. Nevertheless he then went on to oppose Hobbes' attempt in the *Leviathan* to reduce all morality to a matter of human expediency.

Sharp, himself a student of the classics, was not unnaturally interested in these views; although, it must be admitted, little if any such philosophical theism crept into his own teaching or preaching, which were always robustly dogmatic both in tone and content. Yet his youthful sympathies with the Platonists, as indeed with the scientific world as represented by such names as Descartes and Newton, gave a breadth and depth to his theology which it never entirely lost, and which so many of his more narrowly orthodox contemporaries lacked.[1] But the year 1665, which saw the passage of the Five Mile Act through the fanatically Anglican Cavalier Parliament, an Act forbidding dissenting ministers to come within five miles of any corporate town, or to qualify as schoolmasters, and so put the coping-stone on the repressive legislation of the Clarendon Code, that aimed at the total extirpation of dissent in England, was scarcely a favourable time for the realisation of academic ambitions by the son of a prominent Presbyterian, particularly in such a royal stronghold as the University of Cambridge. 1665 also witnessed the outbreak of the Great Plague in London; and it was not long before students, flying from its ravages, had carried the fatal germs into the University.[2]

Sharp refused to be discouraged by either event, but removed his lodgings first to Sawston and then to the little village of Dullingham near Newmarket, where he stayed with several college friends and quietly pursued his studies. One such friend was John Covell (or Covill), a fellow of Christ's and later to be its master from 1688 to 1722. Prior to this latter appointment, however, he became in 1672 chaplain to the Levant Company at Constantinople, where he made the acquaintance of Sir John Finch, English Ambassador to the Porte.[3] So in years to come the friendship of these two young men was to be cemented by their mutual regard for the family of Finch.

In 1667 Sharp took his M.A. degree, and promptly applied for

[1] Many of Sharp's sermons certainly go to prove that he was a disciple of the moral and practical school of preachers.
[2] *Life of Archbishop Sharp*, vol. i, p. 13.
[3] *Alumni Cantabrigienses*, Part I, vol. i, p. 406.

a fellowship at Christ's, at the same time petitioning the archbishop of Canterbury for both holy orders *extra tempora*. This petition is thus recorded in the *Lambeth Act Books*: "John Sharp, Master of Arts, being Candidate for Fellow of Christ's College in Cambridge and required by the statutes of the said College to be in Holy Orders. And being of the full age of 24 years, Petitions His Grace for a Faculty to enable him to receive both the Holy Orders together *extra tempora*; which upon good testimonials was granted him by Fiat upon his Petition directed to the Master of the Faculties, August 9th, 1667."[1]

Three days later, on August 12, together with James Leigh and Thomas Lovett,[2] who were both of the same college, he was ordained deacon and priest in the parish church of St. Margaret, Westminster, at the hands of Dr. William Fuller, then bishop of Limerick and later of Lincoln. The assisting priests were William Outram, vicar of St. Margaret's and formerly a fellow of Christ's; Thomas White, afterwards bishop of Peterborough; and Dr. Gardiner, the Duke of Monmouth's chaplain. These facts are of interest, since to receive both orders on the same day was a rare and uncanonical proceeding. It was, indeed, true that there had been many precedents in the past, especially during the Commonwealth period,[3] but these had been excused on the ground of necessity in a time of revolution.

No doubt Archbishop Sheldon felt perfectly justified in granting the dispensation in Sharp's case, yet it is perhaps significant that the latter's son and biographer, who was evidently unaware of the Lambeth Petition, felt bound to defend his father's ordination: "Dr. Fuller had something more for his justification, viz. a special dispensation from Dr. Sheldon, the Archbishop of the province: which, however extraordinary, was of sufficient authority, and a

---

[1] *The Lambeth Act Books*, vol. ii, p. 84. If it is true that Sharp was twenty-four on August 9, 1667, it seems possible that he was baptised on October 2, 1642, after all. In any case he could hardly have been admitted to Christ's at the age of fifteen, as Venn and Peile assert.

[2] James Leigh, the son of a schoolmaster at Bishop Stortford, was already a fellow of Christ's (1664-1676). Lovett was to become one at Sharp's expense.

[3] *E.g.*, Dr. George Bull, in 1655, at the uncanonical age of twenty-one. See R. Nelson, *Life of Bull*, pp. 21-24.

This irregularity is noted in a collection of queries, printed without date, and entitled *Some Queries recommended to the consideration of the more rigid and clamorous Rubicans.* The twenty-third and last of these reads as follows: "Whether bishop Taylor, bishop Bull and archbishop Sharp, who were all ordained priests before the age of twenty-four, and were allowed to have cure of souls in England, were yet not clergymen of the Church of England?" *Cf.* Rev. E. Burton, *Bull's Works and Life*, 1846. Sharp, of course, was twenty-four.

satisfactory reason why the three grave and worthy divines who assisted should, without scruple, concur in the act."[1]

But, despite the success of his Lambeth Petition and the favourable impression his industry and intelligence had created on the college authorities, Sharp failed to secure his fellowship. "Thomas Lovett was elected Fellow."[2] Probably his Calvinist antecedents, together with the lack of a Yorkshire "county" fellowship at Christ's, contributed to his defeat. Father and son were certainly bitterly disappointed; so much so that it is of lasting credit to them both that they rejected "certain proposals",[3] which were afterwards made through one of the fellows, for obtaining this preferment, but on conditions that they considered dishonest.

Failing, then, to secure any permanent position in the University, Sharp was compelled for financial reasons to retire home to Bradford. Thomas was only moderately well off, he had fulfilled his promise of maintaining John for seven years at the University, and had no great influence in the world. His Roundhead proclivities rendered him suspect in Restoration England, and were a hindrance rather than a help to his son's advancement. Besides, he had other children to consider, and John must learn to stand on his own feet. John might, under these conditions, have had to wait long before securing employment, and perhaps have been compelled to become a humble curate, passing his days in some remote country vicarage, struggling to keep up appearances and educate his children on a mere pittance. That is no wild speculation; for it was at this low ebb in his fortunes that he applied for the incumbency of Wibsey Chapel, "a mean thatched building",[4] not far from Bradford. This living was then in the gift of Richard Richardson of Bierley Hall, whose third son, also named John, was later to marry Sharp's sister, Hannah.[5] It was worth little more than £22 per annum. Yet even here he suffered defeat, "having been out-preached by some-one of superior lungs,

---

[1] *Life of Archbishop Sharp*, vol. i, pp. 16 and 17.
[2] J. Peile, *Biographical Register of Christ's College, Cambridge*, p. 590.
[3] *Life of Archbishop Sharp*, vol. i, p. 13. These "proposals" are not known. Perhaps bribes were demanded, or a declaration to pursue a line of College policy distasteful to the Sharps. The interference of the Crown in the election of fellows, at the request of one of the candidates' friends who had influence at court, was notorious.
In this particular case, "Jan. 16, 1666/7 Cudworth writes to recommend Tho. Lovett. . . . On the 19 January occurs the King's 'recommendation' of Lovett." See *History of Christ's*, p. 203.
[4] W. Cudworth, *Round about Bradford*, p. 38.
[5] John Richardson became a prebendary of York Minster in 1712.

but inferior talents".[1] It was said that when the future archbishop made a visitation in this part of his diocese, he always placed the incumbent of Wibsey[2] on his right hand at dinner, "saying with a degree of pleasantry, that he owed much to him for having stood in his way in former years, and thus prevented his settling down in a humble sphere and a retired district where he might never have been known".[3]

Fortune decreed otherwise. Cudworth and More had not forgotten him, and the latter, who had been much impressed by the manner in which, while still a B.A., he had read the lessons in the college chapel, recommended his name to Sir Heneage Finch, an old friend, as domestic chaplain and tutor for his sons.[4]

The Finches had always been strong royalists from the days when Thomas Finch, great-grandfather of the first Earl of Nottingham, was knighted by Bloody Mary for assisting in the suppression of Wyatt's rebellion. His grandson, Sir Heneage, became a barrister of the Inner Temple and a Member of Parliament, being made Recorder of London and Speaker of the House of Commons in 1626, where he defended the royal prerogative at law as zealously as his grandfather had once defended it on the field of battle. His son, the present Sir Heneage, also became a lawyer and joined the Inner Temple, specialising in the study of municipal law. He took no active part in the civil wars, but emerged in 1660 as M.P. for Canterbury and Solicitor-General, being generally regarded as the official representative of Church and Court in the House of Commons. As such he opposed all compromise on the question of Church government and urged the expulsion of the Nonconformist ministers from their livings. He was also averse from any form of toleration for dissent or Roman Catholicism. His zeal for the crown was equally pronounced, and for the many legal services he rendered the king, particularly in the realm of municipal law, he was created a baronet in 1660, and was soon to become Baron Finch of Daventry (1674), Lord Chancellor, and finally, in 1681, Earl of Nottingham.

It was remarkable that at a time when passions ran high and fiercely Finch never lost either the royal confidence or that of the

[1] Op. cit., p. 41. The curate in question was Samuel Crowther.
[2] Probably Henry Lund (1680-1699) or William Pollard (1706-1719).
[3] Op. cit., p. 41.
[4] More was in close touch with the Finches. He had been Sir John Finch's tutor (1649), and had corresponded with his sister, Lady Conway (1651-1664). See J. Peile, Christ's History, p. 203.

House of Commons, a fine tribute both to his honesty of purpose and powers of discretion. In the second part of *Absalom and Achitophel* Dryden paid him a splendid compliment, under the pseudonym of Amri:

> "Our list of nobles next let Amri grace
> Whose merits claimed the Abethdin's[1] high place
> Who, with a loyalty that did excel,
> Brought all the endowments of Achitophel.
> Sincere was Amri, and not only knew,
> But Israel's sanctions into practice drew;
> Our laws, that did a boundless ocean seem,
> Were coasted all, and fathom'd all by him.
> No rabbin speaks like him their mystic sense,
> So just, and with such charms of eloquence:
> To whom the double blessing does belong
> With Moses' inspiration, Aaron's tongue."

Such was the man who for the next decade largely determined John Sharp's career. For Sir Heneage took a personal interest in the young divine, treated him as a son rather than a servant, gave him ample leisure for study, nursed his preaching powers by not overstraining them, and ensured his rapid rise. It was a perfect example of the conscientious patron and the deserving protégé. Sharp fully repaid the debt, both in his devoted loyalty to the House of Finch and also by his ability and industry, which thoroughly justified Sir Heneage's attentions. In later life Edward and Henry Finch became prebendaries in York Minster under their old tutor, now their archbishop; while, although "Dismal", the second Earl of Nottingham, and the archbishop of York did not always see eye to eye, notably during the heated party struggles of Queen Anne's reign, they remained on the whole excellent friends and firm allies.

The Solicitor-General resided at Kensington House, and here it was that Sharp took up his abode and duties as tutor to John and Charles Finch, very promising youths, but doomed to death when still in their teens. Smallpox, a scourge little less dreaded than the Plague itself, carried them off in the flower of their age, the former before, the latter after, reaching All Souls, Oxford. Sir Heneage's younger sons, Edward and Harry, however, survived, and much to the gratification of their tutor, both eventually took holy orders.

---

[1] Lord Chancellor.

Sharp's tutorial duties were never heavy and he had ample leisure, of which he made good use, for private study. He had now definitely abandoned all thoughts of a fellowship,[1] and hence his classical, philosophical and scientific studies dropped into the background, and he devoted himself almost entirely to theology, for which purpose his patron abundantly supplied him with the necessary books.

It is interesting to note in passing that Sharp was present in 1669 at the opening of the Sheldonian Theatre, which had been built by Archbishop Sheldon, while Chancellor of the University, entirely at his own expense, employing Wren as his architect, and along with many other Cantabrigians became incorporated as an Oxford M.A.[2] The Finches themselves were all Oxford men.

He now engaged himself upon a commentary on the books of the Bible that took most of his spare time during the next few years, and when completed was certainly a lengthy and pains-taking work, although it would appear not a very inspired one. Nevertheless in its composition he went to endless trouble, not merely confining his researches to the Greek and Latin texts, but even venturing a little way into the Hebrew. So close, in fact, did he keep at his books that his health again broke down and he was compelled to return to Yorkshire once more, where he found his father fast declining towards the grave. The old man (he was now sixty-three) died in 1671, a month after John's return to London,[3] sincerely mourned by relations and friends and the people of Bradford alike, who had a warm regard for this honest Christian tradesman. In his will, dated September 5, 1670, "he bequeathed to his wife Dorothy £300 out of his personalty, besides a third part of all his lands for life, or if she pleases, she may have a third part of his personal estate in lieu of £300, and have the house they dwelt in, and all the garden for life. He gives to John Sharp, his eldest son, his dwelling-house and appurten-ances (garden, crofts, etc.) in Ivegate; also a close adjoining Brad-ford Mill Dam, called Bower Howme, which he purchased of Mr. Ellison, and another close in Little Horton, called Lowe Close, bought of Thomas Cooke. He gives to Thomas, his second son, six closes, viz. Upper Bower Royde, Nether Bower Royde (the one lying above Brick Lane, the other below), Hawkhead Close, or

---

[1] In 1669, when a vacancy at length occurred at Christ's, Cudworth offered to obtain it for him. Sharp, however, refused this offer. See *Life of Archbishop Sharp*, vol. i, p. 13.
[2] J. Venn, *Alumni Cantabrigienses*, Part I, vol. iv, p. 49.
[3] *Life of Archbishop Sharp*, vol. i, p. 19.

Sylbrigg Close, purchased of Thomas Cooke; two closes called Town End Closes or Millne Cliffs; another close called Sommer Butts and Long Lands, lying near to Sylbrigg's, which he purchased of Christr. Frickleton, the said Thomas to have £100 in money if he is a good son when he sets up trade for himself, if there be hopes of him. He gives to James Sharp, his third son, houses in Kirkgate which the testator lately built or purchased of Wm. Hemsworth; also a close called Morris Croft or Lower Millne Holme, bought of Ezekiea Taylor, gent.; also one close called Bricks or Brecks, in Manningham, bought of Susan Fearnley. He gives to Hannah Sharp, his only daughter, £350 and two closes called Cow Pastures or Bowling Closes in Bowling Yate. He gives to Joshua Sharp, his youngest son, the house next the one he (testator) lives in, in the occupation of James Snowdon and Aunt Alice Dighton; and a close called Mucky Close, in Millne Cliffe, bought of Susan Fearnley, besides £250 in money. Testator commits the tuition of his youngest children, James and Joshua, to his wife and appoints her sole executor. He desires, if she marry again, that she will be good to James and Joshua. He gives to poor of Bradford £3, which his wife is to distribute as she thinks fit; his brother-in-law John Weddell to assist in the distribution, and to have 20s. for a ring.

Witness—JOHN WEDDELL.

ABRAHAM BROOKSBANK."[1]

Unlike many young clergymen, even deacons, to-day, who are rushed into the pulpit Sunday after Sunday having little to say and no experience of how to say it, Sharp was able, during his long sojourn at Kensington House, to lay a good foundation of knowledge, particularly of the Scriptures, before he so much as set pen to paper in order to compose a sermon. Sir Heneage, although he often required his chaplain to read the sermons of others, especially those of Bishop Andrewes, Donne and Archbishop Laud, whose witty, metaphysical styles with their play on words and ideas were typical of the Anglo-Catholic preachers of the early seventeenth century, and which strongly appealed to him, long forbore to demand one of his own composition.[2] But when at length the ban was lifted the first he heard so pleased the Solicitor-General that he ordered his second son, also named Heneage, who in later

---

[1] W. Cudworth, *Life and Correspondence of Abraham Sharp*, pp. 267 and 268.
[2] Sharp detested this "witty" fashion. His own sermons were always plain, practica l and straightforward. See Chapter III.

life became the Earl of Aylesford, to go and thank him for it; a signal honour and of a kind which his chaplain would much appreciate. The six years spent in obscurity and comparative leisure within the precincts of Kensington House were of infinite value to the brilliant young cleric, so soon to emerge as one of the foremost Anglicans of his age. Here he learnt not only to write and preach a good sermon, to increase and expand his already considerable store of academic knowledge, but living as he was so intimately with one of the greatest lawyers and most impartial judges of his time, he acquired the art of rapidly summing up and assessing character, especially clerical character, at its true worth, and of judging a case, an opinion or a policy on its merits, and not in the light of party passion or prejudice.

He now began to reap the fruits of his chaplaincy in a long list of promotions, all of which were conferred upon him by the crown at the instigation of his patron, culminating in his appointment to the deanery of Norwich (1681). Yet Sir Heneage's first attempt in 1670 to obtain for his chaplain the rectory of St. Peter's, Cornhill, lately vacated through the death of Thomas Hodges, dean of Hereford, a friend whom Sharp had attended on his death-bed, failed completely. This living was in the gift of Bishop Henchman of London, who bestowed it upon his own chaplain, the learned William Beveridge, the future bishop of St. Asaph. The king, however, proved more accommodating than the bishop, and in 1673 the archdeaconry of Berkshire, vacant by the promotion of Peter Mews to the see of Bath and Wells, was conferred upon Sharp at the early age of twenty-eight.[1]

"When the Attorney-General (Sir Heneage Finch)", wrote Sharp's biographer, "told him (after he came from Court) that the King had given him the archdeaconry of Berkshire, he answered that he was too young for that office, and that he knew nothing of the nature of it: whereupon the Attorney-General bid him read Lyndwood; and for his further encouragement paid all the fees of the Seals for him, and shortly after, at his first visitation, he not only lent him horses and servants, but put money into his pocket to defray his expenses."[2] Despite these favours Sharp encountered considerable difficulties in taking up this appointment, largely, it must be admitted, because of his raw inexperience of such matters.

---

[1] *Life of Archbishop Sharp*, vol. i, p. 21. But if Sharp had been twenty-four at his ordination (August 12, 1667), he must now be thirty or over?

[2] Op. cit., vol. i, pp. 21 and 22.

For example, he was ignorant enough to hold his first visitation before his induction, with the unfortunate consequence that the dean of Salisbury refused to induct him at all, and sent him back to London on the ground that he had acted illegally and so invalidated his mandate. Whereupon Sharp wisely and promptly sought the advice of his patron. Pressure was quickly brought to bear on the refractory dean, and within ten days the young archdeacon-designate had returned to Salisbury and was inducted under the original mandate.

Sir Heneage, who was already Attorney-General (1670), had been made Lord Keeper towards the end of 1673, and eventually Lord Chancellor in December 1674, which office he held until his death. Consequently he became a rich patron of Church livings.

Robert Nelson, the future non-juror and biographer of Dr. George Bull, referred to the manner in which Finch carried out this latter duty in the following terms: "Among the very commendable qualities of this great man (Lord Chancellor Finch) his zeal for the welfare of the Church of England was not the least conspicuous; which particularly shows itself in the care he took in disposing of those ecclesiastical preferments, which were in the gift of the seals. He judged rightly in looking upon that privilege as a trust for the good of the Church of God, of which he was to give strict account; and therefore being sensible that the several duties of his great post, as First Minister of State, as Lord Chancellor, and as Speaker of the House of Lords, would not allow his Lordship time and leisure to make that inquiry which was necessary, to know the characters of such as were candidates for preferment, he devolved this particular province upon his chaplain, whose conscience he charged with an impartial scrutiny into this matter; adding withal, that he would prefer none but those who came recommended from him; and that, if he led him wrong, the blame should fall upon his own soul. It is true that this was a great testimony of my Lord's entire confidence in the uprightness as well as the capacity of his chaplain; but the world will quickly be satisfied with what caution and judgement his Lordship took his measures, when they shall know, that his then chaplain was Dr. Sharp, the present Lord Archbishop of York, who fills one of the archiepiscopal thrones of England, with that universal applause, which is due to his Grace's distinguished merits: whose elevation hath not deprived him of his humility, but he exerciseth the same affability and courtesy towards all men, which he practised in a lowly sphere; and that learning and piety, that integrity and zeal for the Glory of God, which influence his Grace in the government of his diocese, and of his province, were peculiarly serviceable to the Earl of Nottingham, in the charge his Lordship laid upon him with so much solemnity."[1]

Meanwhile Sharp's own career was not neglected. In the year 1675 he received no less than three preferments at the hands of his patron: a prebend at Norwich, the living of St. Bartholomew Exchange, and the rectory of St. Giles-in-the-Fields. "Each of these favours were accompanied with further marks of kindness, for his Lordship would not suffer him to pay seal fees for the two former; and when he gave him the last, he did it with this further promise, that if St. Martin-in-the-Fields would be more acceptable to him, if ever it became vacant in his time, he should have it."[2] This actually occurred shortly afterwards, but Sharp, thoroughly contented with St. Giles', refused the greater position, which was given to Tenison.[3]

As rector of St. Giles' Sharp had now developed overnight from being merely a promising young cleric, who pulled the Lord Chancellor's wires, into an important figure in the ecclesiastical field. For he had become one of that famous band of London clergy of whom Macaulay remarked that out of twelve, ten became bishops and four archbishops.[4] The influence of a powerful patron could effect a great deal, but if the protégé was lacking in real ability it had its limitations. Sharp's own merits came in for their first crucial test when he was instituted at St. Giles'. He stood or fell on his work as an important London parochial minister; for the London clergy were too much in the public eye to tolerate fools gladly, and where they led the greater part of the Church followed, even against the king himself. This fact was put to the proof during the reign of James II.

St. Giles-in-the-Fields, one of the foremost London churches of the day, had been built in 1623 on the site of the old lepers' hospital of St. Giles, founded by Queen Matilda about 1101. The new brick church was consecrated by Archbishop Laud, and abounded in ornaments, largely contributed by the Duchess

[1] R. Nelson, *Life of Bull*, pp. 278-279.
[2] *Life of Archbishop Sharp*, vol. i, p. 25.
[3] Tenison was appointed to St. Martin's in October 1680, where he was rector for eleven years.
[4] C. J. Abbey, *The English Church and its Bishops (1700-1800)*, vol. i, p. 95.

Dudley, who gave "six bells, communion plate and ornaments".[1] This was the church that Sharp knew, although somewhat stripped of its interior decorations by the Puritans. It exists no longer. The ground in the neighbourhood was gradually raised until it stood some eight feet higher than the floor of the nave, and consequently St. Giles' became very damp and unwholesome. Eventually it was found necessary to apply to Parliament to have the whole church rebuilt.

An Act of Parliament had been passed in 1710 providing for the erection of fifty new churches in London; and of these twelve were built before Queen Anne's death, while many of the existing churches were repaired. The funds for this purpose were secured by a duty on all coal brought into the Port of London, realising £350,000. Out of that sum £8,000 was granted to St. Giles', the old church was taken down, the site raised, and the first stone of the present building was laid in the year 1730. Only the vestries remain of the original structure.

Sharp was instituted into his new rectory on January 3, 1675/6, by Henry Compton, the new bishop of London, and a curious incident marked the occasion. While the new rector was treating his vestrymen after the institution, the vestry was broken into and the communion plate stolen to the value "of above £200".[2] An advertisement in the London Gazette, dated January 6/10, 1675/6, stated the facts as follows: "Jan. 4th out of the vestry of the Parish Church of St. Giles-in-the-fields four great silver flagons emboss'd double gilt. Two silver plain cups with covers, likewise gilt. If any person can make a discovery of the aforesaid plate, and give speedy notice thereof to Mr. Henry Rogers, or Mr. William Mathers, Churchwardens of the aforesaid Parish of St. Giles-in-the-fields, they shall have forty pounds for their reward." The plate, however, was never recovered, and the loss was made good by the generosity of the Lord Chancellor, who, hearing of the theft, "was pleased to order for the use of that Church, two large gilt flagons, and two chalices, for which he paid above an hundred pounds".[3] The present communion sets bear the date 1828, having been melted down and reformed in that year by the rector, James Endell Taylor, from original plate of 1681. The names of Sharp's churchwardens for that year are given as Edward Harris and Thomas Harris. In all probability this was the Lord Chancellor's gift set. It is of interest to note in passing that another attempt at stealing the plate in modern times was frustrated by the fact that the thief so liberally partook of the communion wine, which was stored with the silver, that he collapsed outside the building in a drunken stupor, where he was discovered with his spoils on the following morning.

CHAPTER III

THE NEW RECTOR

JOHN SHARP was already well known to the parishioners of St. Giles-in-the-Fields, not only as a friend of the late incumbent, Dr. Boreman,[1] but also as priest-in-charge during the vacancy, when his comparative youth, personal charm and considerable preaching ability ensured an early popularity. This favourable impression was confirmed by his marriage, which took place in the late spring (1675/6), to Elizabeth Palmer of the Palmers from Winthorpe in Lincolnshire.[2] She was to prove an invaluable helpmeet, whether within the boundaries of a parish or the precincts of a cathedral. Her mother, Mrs. Moseley,[3] who had married again, was puritanically minded and a great admirer of the saintly moderate Dissenter Richard Baxter, whose consent to the match she made conditional upon her own. Baxter, who now

[1] Robert Boreman, D.D., was a strong royalist divine who had suffered under the Commonwealth. A fellow of Trinity College, Cambridge, and prebendary of Westminster, he was, not unnaturally, a violent opponent of the Dissenters, and especially of their great leader, Richard Baxter. Baxter's subsequent attendance at St. Giles' during Sharp's incumbency is therefore a trifle ironical. At the time of the Great Plague, Boreman had had sufficient courage to live and work among his stricken parishioners, assisted by his sexton, John Geere, who dug the first plague pits in the churchyard. Yet he was never popular with the members of his vestry; and in 1670 he actually claimed the right of electing one of the churchwardens himself without the consent of the vestrymen. He lost his case, however, in the Court of Exchequer, where it was decided that the churchwardens should be elected by the parishioners, *i.e.* all who paid poor rates. See the Vestry Minutes (St. Giles-in-the-Fields), February 8, 1670.

[2] The Palmers were a yeoman family. They had long been resident in Winthorpe and were connected with important country people. There was also a Nottinghamshire branch, which, apparently, owned considerable possessions. The churches of Winthorpe, Ingoldmells and Burgh contain many Palmer brasses, and on the wall of the south porch at Winthorpe is the following, undated, inscription: "Robert Languay and Wylly Palm': they payd for this. God for hys mercy bryng them to his blys." One of Elizabeth's brothers, Colonel William Palmer, served under Marlborough in Major-General Wyndham's regiment. According to the Reverend Samuel Noyes, he was seriously wounded at the battle of Blenheim, and subsequently died. Among the archbishop's MSS. (L-B-S. MSS., Box 4, Bundle M. 4) is a letter from "Brother Palmer" describing the campaign of 1703 in Flanders. There are no Palmers of this family in or near Winthorpe to-day.

[3] In his correspondence with Archbishop Sharp, Clement Elis, rector of Kirkby and prebendary of Southwell, referred to Mrs. Moseley on several occasions while she was residing at Nottingham. For example, he remarked in one letter (L-B-S. MSS., Box 4, Bundle D. 3, Sept. 1, 1693) that Mrs. Moseley had sent a recipe for elder wine to Mrs. Sharp. Again (Bundle D. 6, Dec. 19, 1694): "I was in Nottingham . . . and I had but one day time to call on Madam Moseley, but at that time could not see her, she being gone to the Dissenters Lecture. But she is in very good health."

attended the services at St. Giles',[1] willingly agreed to this be-
trothal, declaring that if he had had a daughter of his own to give
away he would not have refused her hand to Sharp.

The marriage ceremony was performed at Clerkenwell by another friend, Dr. Tillotson. John Tillotson, a fellow-Yorkshireman,
was a member of a Puritan family settled at Sowerby, where his
father, a prosperous cloth worker, had been a pillar of the Con-
gregational church of Henry Root. More puritanically minded
than Sharp had ever been, he had accepted, under the Commonwealth Government, a fellowship at Clare Hall, Cambridge, from
which the Anglican Peter Gunning was ejected. At the Restoration Gunning, of course, got his fellowship back; and Tillotson,
who had now taken Anglican orders, became the curate of
Thomas Hacket, then vicar of Cheshunt in Hertfordshire, but soon
to be raised to the bishopric of Down and Connor. And when
towards the close of the year 1667 Sharp first became acquainted
with him, Tillotson was already rising rapidly to the top of the
clerical tree, having taken his D.D. degree, been appointed Tuesday lecturer at St. Lawrence Jewry and one of Charles II's chaplains. Shortly afterwards he was nominated to the deanery of
Canterbury (1672) and received a residentiary canonry at St.
Paul's (1675). The meeting of these two lifelong friends has been
described in the following terms: "Not long after he (Sharp) came
out of Yorkshire into the Solicitor's family, going to Mr. Joseph
Tillotson, the Dr.'s brother, a wet and dry salter in London, with
a bill from his father, he there happened to meet with the Dr.
Himself; who finding Mr. Sharp to be his countryman, setting out
in the world, did, out of his usual goodness and humanity, take
particular notice of him and entreat him courteously, and having
entered into some familiar conversation with him, was pleased, at
parting, to give him leave, whenever he would, freely to come to
his own house, and to have recourse to him as often as he thought
it might be serviceable to himself. Mr. Sharp judged this a lucky
interview, and thought himself blessed in so valuable an acquaintance and ever afterwards spake with pleasure upon the occasion:
for here commenced a friendship which lasted as long as Dr.
Tillotson lived, improved perpetually by an intimate conversation

---

[1] "My judgement was for the holding of communion with assemblies of both parties;
and ordinarily I went to some parish church, where I heard a learned minister that
had not obtruded himself upon the people, but was chosen by them and preached
well, and I joined also in the common prayers of the church": Sylvester, *Life of Mr.
Richard Baxter*, p. 437. The reference is to Sharp at St. Giles'.

for many years, and cemented by repeated returns of good offices to each other, and some of them, on either side, considerable, as will hereafter be shown."[1]

One such "good office" Tillotson performed for his friend was to secure him the Friday lectureship at St. Lawrence Jewry in March 1679, a very much coveted post. "The London churches . . . set forth the best divinity and oratory of the time, and even into their inferior pastoral offices clergy of talent and ability were recruited in the hope of commending themselves to the notice of influential patrons. The brightest young divines from the Universities accepted curacies or lectureships in the capital as a recognised vantage point for future preferment. The position of the lecturer was particularly coveted and the list of prelates who had adorned this office testified to its importance as a first stage on the ladder to promotion."[2]

This made a suitable return for Sharp's previous efforts on Tillotson's behalf, which through the influence of the Lord Chancellor resulted in the exchange of the less important Ealdland for the Oxgate prebend at St. Paul's.

The newly married couple, in order to be near St. Giles' parish, took up their abode in Chancery Lane at the house of their brother-in-law, Mr. (later Sir William) Rawlinson,[3] who practised as a barrister of Gray's Inn. Consequently Sharp, although he remained the Lord Chancellor's titular chaplain until the latter's death in 1682, found himself obliged to quit Kensington House, where he had now lived for nearly nine years. Such a break marked the opening of a fresh chapter in his career.

Of Sharp's next sixteen busy years as a parish priest at St. Giles' little enough has been recorded; yet there is sufficient evidence to give a clear insight into his parochial plan of campaign and the methods he adopted to carry it through. Preaching was, of course, the main weapon in his armoury, as indeed with most of his contemporaries, whether of High or Low Church persuasions. For the marked stress laid nowadays upon the celebration of the Eucharist as the core of the Church's life is an entirely modern feature of Anglo-Catholicism, and was noticeably absent from seventeenth-

[1] *Life of Archbishop Sharp*, vol. i, p. 29.
Mr. Joseph Tillotson's name appears in the London Directory of 1677 as Tillingson, an oilman. He died on September 16, 1678. See *D.N.B.*: "Tillotson."
[2] N. Sykes, *Church and State in the Eighteenth Century*, p. 254. Benjamin Whichcot, the Cambridge Platonist, who was vicar of St. Lawrence Jewry, also helped to secure Sharp's acceptance of the lectureship. See *Life of Archbishop Sharp*, vol. i, p. 31.
[3] William Rawlinson married Elizabeth's sister.

century clerical opinion and practice. So at this point in the narrative a short digression on the subject of the Restoration sermon in general and the preaching of John Sharp in particular will not be out of place, especially as it was during his sojourn at St. Giles' that the majority of the archbishop's published sermons were written.[1]

The chief interest of Restoration preaching centres in the change of taste from the elaborate, witty, metaphysical sermons of Andrewes, Donne or Cosin, full of classical tags and Hebrew quotations, to the simple prose style, which found its highest expression in the works of Tillotson. Naturally such a change only gradually made itself felt; being brought about by the combined influence of preachers from various schools of thought, among whom the best of the Puritan divines like Tuckney and Baxter, the rationalists Hales and Chillingworth, the Cambridge Platonists More and Cudworth, and members of the newly formed Royal Society, all played their part. On the other hand, much Restoration preaching was merely a resumption of the pre-Commonwealth effusions,[2] as can be seen, for example, in the gorgeous rhetorical orations of men of the stamp of Jeremy Taylor, Robert South or Isaac Barrow. The last, indeed, member of the Royal Society though he might be, had more in common with that arch-Anglo-Catholic Donne than with the majority of his contemporaries.

But preaching, which previously had been in vogue chiefly among the intelligentsia, had during the turbulent times of the Great Rebellion and Protectorate become popularised by the Puritans; and subsequently the demand for the simple, straightforward sermon was greatly increased. So much so that conservative churchfolk got seriously alarmed, declaring that "the sermon jostled out catechising" and "people began to learn at the wrong end and ran to the lecture before they had been at the catechism";[3] with the result that when Sharp himself began to attract attention in the sixteen-eighties he found that the tide had set strongly in the direction of plainness, simplicity and shortness. Classical quota-

[1] *Life of Archbishop Sharp*, vol. i, p. 33: "And now it was, and chiefly in those midnight hours, which he borrowed from his rest, that he composed most of those discourses, which afterwards, with a little revisal and finishing he made use of to his dying day."
[2] A good example of the kind of "witty" saying to be found in these sermons is Archbishop Laud's remark on the scaffold: "I am going apace, as you see, towards the Red Sea, and my feet are now upon the very brink of it; an argument, I hope, that God is bringing me into the Land of Promise." See *The Archbishop of Canterbury's Speech, the 10th of January, 1644*.
[3] J. H. Overton, *Life in the English Church (1660-1714)*, p. 231.

tion, on the contrary, although far too deeply entrenched to be entirely omitted, was no longer made use of either so lavishly or openly. Tillotson became the model preacher.[1] The smoothness and simplicity of his style strongly appealed to the Londoners who flocked to hear him, and the fact that the subject-matter was trifling and the theology hazy did not greatly concern them.

Nevertheless Tillotson's sermons are forgotten to-day, and so to a certain extent bear out the opinion of the villagers of Kedington, who "did not relish the sermons and complained that they did not hear the Gospel".[2]

The religious revival that began about this period helped to stimulate a form of preaching more concerned with practical "good works" than either the elaboration of ceremonial or the incitement to hysteria. The Queen Anne sermon, in particular, was usually a plain practical discourse on Christian ethics, couched in simple terms, and no longer permeated with a wealth of quotation in foreign languages or the witty rhetorical expressions of which the Andrewes-Laud school of preachers had been accused. Furthermore, the length of the sermon was gradually shortened until the hour-and-a-half or two-hour discourses of the older Caroline preachers gave place to the one- or even half-hour lectures of Tillotson and Sharp. It is worth recalling in this connection that Burnet in his *Pastoral Care* advised the clergy never to preach above half an hour, for "this would not be endured by any nation but ours".

The written sermon, too, seemed to be giving place to the extempore oration through the intermediate stage of learning all addresses by heart.[3] A bad memory would be considered a serious handicap, sometimes preventing an otherwise suitable candidate from being ordained, and was always a constant source of worry. Some of the most popular preachers were Gilbert Burnet, Dean Comber, or George Bull, who spoke extempore, relying simply upon a few notes. Bull, while incumbent of St. George's, Bristol,

---

[1] Burnet, *History of My Own Time*, vol. ii, p. 135: "He was not only the best preacher of the age, but seemed to have brought preaching to perfection."

[2] J. H. Overton, *Life in the English Church (1660-1714)*, p. 247.

[3] G. C. Richardson, *English Preachers and Preaching (1640-1670)*, p. 65: "Seventeenth century congregations, established or non-conformist, had a distinct preference for sermons that were delivered, not read. A good memory was almost a necessity for a preacher who hoped for popular approval. Fortunately memory training was a part of grammar school experience and sermons were used for practical work in oral repetition. The rules for Eton scholars (1646) require: 'that those who can write take notes of sermons and those under the Master render them to him and those under the usher render them to him'."

saw on one occasion his notes blow out of the pulpit, whereupon
several members of his sailor congregation laughed aloud, expecting the preacher to falter if not to dry up completely. But Bull
continued his address quite unperturbed, and when the notes were
returned ostentatiously tucked them away into his Bible and concluded without another glance at their contents.[1] However,
people's taste varied, and the read sermon still commanded much
popular support in certain quarters. Sharp invariably read his,
and Tillotson his longer ones, although learning the shorter by
heart. It is not, indeed, until comparatively modern times that the
spoken word superseded the written in the vast majority of Anglican pulpits.

John Sharp's own sermons supply convincing evidence not only
of his infinite capacity for taking pains, but of the power of his
casuistical reasoning. On the other hand it must be freely admitted that none could be termed either great oratory or first-class
literature.

"Casuistry" is a word which has acquired an unfortunate reputation; but in Sharp's mouth it might have been rechristened
"psychology", since he merely endeavoured in a simple and practical form to anticipate the methods of the present-day psycho-
analyst. By its aid he was certainly able, sometimes from the pulpit,
more often through private correspondence or interview, to dis-
solve many a man's or woman's religious doubts and fears, and
disentangle a variety of delicate and often intricate problems in
practical everyday life. He never feared to look such problems in
the face, and rarely failed to provide a solution, which, whatever
its merits, or however unpalatable it might appear, yet was delivered with such tact, kindliness and honest goodwill that the
enquirer invariably went away with the firm impression that his
adviser had nothing but his welfare at heart. The archbishop's
MSS. are full of such enquiries. One typical example, culled from
many, the following letter of a certain Martha Fiennes, the sister
of the vicar of Broughton, is of interest:

"To the Lord Archbishop of York at his Palace in York.
LONDON. *Nov:* 7, 1692/3.
I fully designed to have waited on your Grace, when you were
in Town, not only to pay a Duty and Respect, which is infinitely
due, but to beg your opinion in two cases of conscience, which a

[1] R. Nelson, *Life of Bull*, p. 26.

friend of mine desired me to ask some person I most esteemed about. I cannot therefore be just to my friend, nor satisfy myself, without giving your Lordship this trouble, whose eminency is known so well and has been experienced by myself, in a case not much different from one of these, for which I shall always acknowledge myself much obliged to you: I have waited till now, to see whether you would come to Town again, before the Parliament rises, which being out of hope of, and having had the opinion of two eminent Divines in London, fearing you might blame my too great curiosity, the nothing could satisfy me, but yourself: in a place where there are so many learned men, but finding them of different opinions: I must beg your Grace to decide the point, though I know you must have many concerns of greater rate, in that great position you are in, which makes me in some confusion ask, what I hope your charity and desire of doing good will make you condescend to do; the scruple of kneeling at the Sacrament I acknowledge has been answered by several great men, but perhaps this person may not have had the good fortune to meet with it; could you satisfy them in this point, their example might have a great influence on a great party of Dissenters which would not only be a great service to God, but a considerable advantage to a friend of mine: as speedy an answer to this, as your affairs will permit and a pardon for the trouble will be a very great demonstration of your abundant goodness."

The rest of this very long letter deals with other matters. The two "cases", however, are attached as a postscript: "The cases are these following: When a minister will not administer the Sacrament unless kneeling and a person cannot be satisfied after his utmost endeavours, but these texts will obstruct:—He that doubts is, etc., and the said minister affirms that should he do it it would give offence, and some books lie in the way, the said persons receiving among the Dissenters, what shall such an one do?

"Suppose I have purchased a tenement upon a valuable consideration to me and my heirs, and in truth the seller had right but for his life, and the right heir comes to me and says, it is true you bought of my father, who thought he had right to dispose, and you also apprehended your title good, but in truth 'tis my estate; I in conscience have let you enjoy it 20 years, and so you have in small parcels resaved your money again you paid, and this time the title was in me, I pray you now restore the tenement else never seek to die comfortable etc. May the purchaser insist upon the 20 years possession by the statute of King James, or ought he to keep the land when in truth the right is in the heir?"[1]

Sharp's usual method in the pulpit[2] was to lay a scriptural text before his congregation, whether composed of his humble parishioners at St. Giles', of one of the Houses of Parliament, or of royalty itself, as though it might have been a mathematical problem, proceeding to its solution with a lucidity of mind and clear-cut simplicity of expression which enabled the dullest in his audience to follow his argument and profit from its conclusions. He prided himself, indeed, upon the practical and homely nature of his sermons, which despite their relentless logic were rarely couched in abstract or metaphysical terms, but dealt in the simplest of language with the immediate, apparent needs of his listeners. Yet, since fundamental human needs and desires do not alter with the changing years, no one with a serious turn of mind, who reads those sermons to-day from the point of view of their practical utility and not merely of their antiquarian interest, need feel, as he closes the volume, that he has been studying material which is quite unrelated to modern life. For example, let us take, quite at random, from Sharp's collected works the address he delivered at Bow Street in the January of 1675/6 on the text 1 Timothy iv. 8, "Godliness is profitable unto all things, having a promise of the life that now is, and of that which is to come."[3] Men, he began, do not usually trouble to put themselves out over the exercise of godliness as they will about other things, such as acquiring an estate or attaining to a competent skill in the human arts and sciences. Why? Because, unlike these possessions, its advantages cannot easily be seen or felt, and, indeed, it is often thought to be a definite hindrance to the realisation of worldly hopes and ambitions. This, Sharp declared, was quite untrue. And taking the three great worldly values of wealth, honour and pleasure he proceeded to show that godliness, far from proving an obstacle, was the most promising means to their attainment. First, in regard to riches: It is evident, he said, that the diligent man is

[1] L-B-S. MSS., Box 4, Bundle Q. 75.
[2] "And here I may justly add the good Archbishop [Sharp] who went before him [William Dawes]; a person truly excellent in all the perfections of good writing, goodness, fervour, strength and a true spirit of piety, run through his various compositions in plain, unaffected majesty of style": Dr. Henry Felton (1679-1740), Principal of Edmund Hall and chaplain to the Duke of Rutland, A Dissertation upon Reading the Classics and Forming a Just Style, p. 189, 4th edn., 1730.
[3] Archbishop Sharp's Sermons, vol. i, Sermon 2, edn. 1734.

made rich, and "religion obligeth us to mind our business, not only for our own but for God's sake . . . charging it upon our consciences as our Creator will account for every idle word". Furthermore, religion, "by dispelling those adventitious clouds that arise in the discerning faculty from the noisome fumes of lust and passion", gives to the business man the cool, clear brain needed for his transactions. But what of the argument that the hours spent in prayer and religious meditation were a waste of valuable business time? Sharp replied with sound common sense that there was no call to be always upon your knees—"We do as truly serve God and perform acts of religion when we labour honestly in our vocation, as when we go to church and say our prayers"—and concluded this section of his sermon by pointing out that "it is only shame and repentance that men buy at such costly rates. Godliness is saving and full of good husbandry."

Secondly, man's honour: This, he argued, was usually founded upon "the inward worth and dignity of his person, and his usefulness and serviceableness to others", which religion alone could give him, since neither the possession of wealth nor noble blood would make the complete man, but only "the right use of his reason, the employing his liberty and choice to the best purposes, the exercising of his power and faculties about the fittest objects", as God should direct him.

Thirdly, he drove home the lesson that "the excellent ministries of religion, above all other things add to the pleasures of human life." For religion was conducive to health, which was the necessary foundation of all pleasure, just as disease lay at the root of life's miseries, "cutting us off in the midst of our days and transmitting weakness and rottenness to our posterity". The religious man believed in the moderate satisfaction of his physical appetites; and it is by such an abstention that "our senses, which are the instruments of our pleasures, are always preserved in that due purity and quickness, that is absolutely necessary for the right performing of their offices and the rendering the perceptions of anything grateful and agreeable."

Inevitably excess defeated its own ends, but the lightness and cheerfulness of mind that religion supplied removed all such curbs on mirth as an evil conscience or a clouded understanding. On the other hand, once the senses were given a free rein they quickly became dulled and stupefied. Besides, godliness was "a most effective antidote against all those iniquities and evil accidents that do

either wholely destroy or very much embitter the pleasures of
life". As an example of such a ruined life Sharp quoted the case
of a man who had become a slave to his appetites, which he could
not suppress, and which shattered alike his peace of body and
mind. But the good Christian, he declared, "sits above the reach
of fortune . . . he can turn the basest metal into gold . . . and the
worst accidents that can befall him . . . shall be accóunted . . . his
enjoyments". For, Sharp continued, "when we become acquainted
with God and the infinite abyss of good which is in Him, when our
hearts are made sensible of the great love and good will He bears
us; and in that sense are powerfully carried out in joy and love and
desire after Him", then indeed, "while we live thus, things are
with us as they should be; our souls are in their natural pasture,
in that state they were framed and designed to live in". In fact,
he concluded, once men had tried God's way they would never
want to relinquish it, but would count the practice of godliness a
delight instead of a burden. The material world, they must needs
admit, could give no pleasure like this, to be a friend of God's,
accepted and beloved by Him, cared for in this life and in joy for
all eternity.

Here in this early sermon are all the main features of Sharp's
method in the pulpit: the strength and clearness of his critical
faculties, the simplicity of style and language, and the intimate
relationship between the religion he taught and the facts of everyday life.

Like the great majority of the Anglican divines of his day Sharp
was imbued with an exaggerated fear of popery, largely due to a
succession of contemporary happenings such as the Popish Plot,
the ever-present menace of a French invasion, and later the sinister
attempt of James II to grant the Roman Catholics complete
toleration. Hence much of his earlier preaching was devoted to
combating this supposed danger, and a good example of his anti-
papistical style is to be found in an address delivered before the
House of Lords at Westminster Abbey on November 5, 1691, the
anniversary of the Gunpowder Plot,[1] when he compared the mis-
guided zeal of the Scribes and Pharisees with that of the papists.
Zeal according to knowledge, he declared, had much to recommend it, but the ignorant enthusiasm of the Roman Catholics was
the work of the Devil. For like the Scribes and Pharisees in the
past they, too, had set up their traditions in opposition to all

---

[1] *Archbishop Sharp's Sermons*, vol. ii, Sermon 10.

sound reforms; and, while laying great stress on little, outward, unimportant ceremonies, forgot or ignored the great fundamental truths of the Faith. Ends were made to justify the means, however infamous, as when they burnt heretics or attempted a wholesale murder along the lines of the Gunpowder or Popish Plots.

Yet Sharp was sufficiently charitable on this occasion—the Roman peril had receded by the year 1691—to conclude his address on a more tolerant note: "Tho' we are sure they are mistaken, nay and dangerously mistaken too; yet if they have a zeal for God, if they be serious and sincere in their way; if their errors in religion be the pure results of a misinformed conscience; let us as the Apostles here did [in their attitude towards the Pharisees] take occasion from hence to pity them, and put up hearty prayers to God for them; and to endeavour all we can, by gentle methods, to reduce them to the right way: but by no means to express contempt or hatred of them with violence or outrage."

Nevertheless in the heat of battle he had not been so considerate. For in 1679, speaking before the House of Commons on the growing immorality of the times, he had roundly declared that unless the people repented God would hand them over to the Roman Catholics, who kept men ignorant, since "ignorance is the mother of devotion"; allowed no prayers in public, save the following of the service in Latin; compelled men to give up their Bible, and robbed them of half the sacrament; demanded that they should wholly submit their reason and understanding to an infallible judge; and denied them the use of their senses, affirming that a piece of bread was the very Body of Christ, which had been crucified in Jerusalem. A religion, in fact, that brought back the old pagan idolatries where the priests ate their gods and the people worshipped images of wood and stone. Above all, it was a faith which ran clean contrary to English ideas of personal liberty and national independence, for "you cannot therein be any longer good subjects to your prince than His Holiness will give you leave."[1]

Strong language, but it must have appealed strongly to a House that believed in the Popish Plot and favoured the Exclusion Bill. King Charles and his brother, the papist Duke of York, would not have been so easily satisfied; and the latter eventually put a spoke in the over-bold preacher's wheel, causing him to be suspended from all preaching activities in the year 1686. The address which

[1] Op. cit., vol. ii, Sermon 16.

then incurred the royal displeasure and led directly to the dramatic trial and suspension of Henry Compton, bishop of London, was preached at St. Giles-in-the-Fields, the second of a series confuting the Roman claim of being the only true Church of Christ in the world.[1] Later, speaking before the "Convention" House of Commons on January 30, 1688/9—a sermon that gave offence, but not for its antagonism towards Rome[2]—Sharp said: "It was the Pope of Rome who first taught the doctrine, and first gave the precedent of deposing and murdering sovereign princes in Christendom, and how tragical and mischievous an influence those principles have had in all countries where the emissaries of that see have got into credit and power, it is too evident in the histories of the several nations to be denied."[3]

This attitude towards the Roman Catholics was typical of the age; but in his dealings with the Nonconformists, particularly before he became archbishop, Sharp's opinions differed from those of the majority of his High Church contemporaries, who were opposed alike to comprehension and toleration, for political rather than religious reasons.[4] He certainly desired comprehension[5] and strongly opposed all forms of persecution. Nevertheless his whole soul always revolted against schism of any kind, and in a sermon preached at the Guildhall chapel in August 1674 he declared outright that "to make a rent in the Body of Christ is directly contrary to preserving the unity of that Body", and "we can have no just cause of withdrawing our communion from the Church whereof we are members, but when we cannot communicate with it without the commission of a sin".[6] Such an excuse as "the enjoying of a more profitable ministry, or living under a more pure discipline in a separate congregation, is not a just cause for forsaking the communion of the Church of which we are members". Sharp, a high-churchman, had not the same sympathy with dissenting scruples as some of his Low-Church friends like Tillotson or Teni-

---

[1] See Chapter IV, p. 92.

[2] It was thought to reflect on the Commons' recent vote that James had abdicated the throne by accusing them of deposing him. Actually it was an old sermon composed in Charles II's reign: *Life of Archbishop Sharp*, vol. i, pp. 98-100.

[3] Op. cit., vol. ii, Appendix I, p. 106.

[4] Defoe's *Shortest Way with Dissenters* represented satirically, but not on the whole unjustly, the lengths to which they were prepared to go in the interests of toryism rather than religion: "I do not prescribe fire and faggot, but as Scipio said of Carthage, Delenda est Carthago, they are to be rooted out of this nation, if ever we will live in peace, serve God, or enjoy our own." See *Select Documents of Queen Anne's Reign*, p. 55.

[5] *Cf*. Chapter IV, p. 90.

[6] *Archbishop Sharp's Sermons*, vol. i, Sermon 1.

son; but as the contents of this selfsame sermon[1] and his own
subsequent conduct on William III's "Commission of Inquiry" in
1691 go to prove, he was fully prepared to make substantial concessions in order to achieve unity, always provided that the Dissenters returned to the Church, and the Church itself surrendered
none of its fundamental principles.

The theme of many a Restoration preacher lay in attacking the
licentiousness, profanity and irreligion of the times, which, apparently, had the tacit, if not the open, support of the court. Sharp
was no exception to this general rule, as the following extracts
from some of his earlier sermons amply illustrate: "O the riots and
drunkenness; the frauds and cousenage; the filthy and lewd
speeches; the whoredoms and adulteries; the blasphemous oaths
and imprecations that are daily without any regret, any sense of
shame practised among us."[2] But it was not only immorality that
was practised. "Was there ever", he asked, "more atheism and
irreligion in a Christian nation?" and went on to suggest that
though few had sufficient courage to declare "there is no God",
because it would not have been safe to do so, yet in circuitous
ways, by innuendo, the ridicule of sacred things, and an openly
expressed contempt for instituted, revealed religion, many more
affirmed their disbelief in an all-controlling Deity.[3] In another
address he exclaimed in disgust: "What a world of open gross sins
and impieties do reign among us, and what a lewd, profane, hypocritical, atheistical spirit seems to have gone out of this nation and
to prevail upon it." There is much more in a similar vein. However, with the arrival of the austere William III—austere, at any
rate, in his public life—and the straitlaced Anne, public morals
took a distinct turn for the better, and there are fewer references
to them in Sharp's later sermons.

Another noteworthy characteristic of his preaching was its
homely common sense. In a series of lectures delivered before his
parishioners at St. Giles', under such titles as "Trust in God",
"Religious Melancholy and Desertion", "Loss of Spiritual Com-
forts", "The Devil and his Temptations", and "Faith when True,
Saving and Justifying",[4] Sharp made it perfectly clear that a great
many religious doubts and fancies were due to a disordered body;
and in nine cases out of ten of religious melancholy, sense of deser-

[1] *Archbishop Sharp's Sermons*, vol. i, Sermon 1: "I do not think in many points our
differences are near so wide as they are sometimes represented."
[2] Op. cit., vol. ii, Sermon 16.　　　　[3] Ibid.
[4] See *Archbishop Sharp's Sermons*, vol. iii, Sermons 1, 2, 3, 4 and 7.

tion or belief in one's own damnation, a physician should be consulted before a clergyman. He described melancholy as "a dejec-
tion of mind occasioned from the temperament, or most commonly
from the distemperature of the body accompanied with unreasonable fears and frights about our spiritual condition";[1] and went on
to say, like the good psychologist he was, that "there is something
in the mind itself, of which this distemperature of the body doth
commonly take advantage". Later, in a sermon preached before
William and Mary at Whitehall, he dissociated himself entirely
from all forms of religious mania or hysteria, and declared instead
for humanity and reason: "The truth of it is so long as we consist
of bodies and souls we cannot always be thinking of serious things;
they, indeed, are the wisest that think of them most, but it is even
dangerous to attempt to think of them always."[2] Sharp's method of
cure for those attacked by religious melancholy was first "that the
persons afflicted with it do take care of their bodies", and then
"they endeavour to get their minds truly informed about those
matters of religion from which their disease doth . . . take a handle
to vex and disturb them".

In his theological teaching Sharp was always thoroughly orthodox, as also in his literal acceptance of the Bible text. Indeed, it
was then considered a far greater heresy to criticise the Bible than
to mutilate the creeds;[3] and when the greatest and most deservedly
popular ecclesiastic of the age, Dean Tillotson, soon to be raised
to the archbishopric of Canterbury, dared ever so mildly to miti-
gate the torments of hell in a sermon preached before Queen Mary
during March 1689/90, he occasioned a popular uproar. Mr.
William Lupton, commenting upon this sermon, declared that it
was a plain example "that even the greatest of men have their
intervals of misapprehension and mistake".[4] Sharp could never
have been accused of such an error, yet in common with many
fundamentalists he did not scruple to twist his passages to suit his
purposes.[5]

Nevertheless his conception of the Catholic Church was broad

[1] *Archbishop Sharp's Sermons*, vol. iii, Sermon 2.
[2] Ibid., vol. ii, Sermon 14: "The Government of the Thought" (1693). This sermon
was at a later date presented to the Electress Sophia by the deist Toland. See *Life of
Archbishop Sharp*, vol. i, p. 274.
[3] F. W. Wilson, *The Importance of the Reign of Queen Anne in English Church History*,
pp. 72 and 73.
[4] T. Birch, *Life of Tillotson*, p. 218.
[5] He told the House of Commons in 1679 that the text Revelation ii. 5, "I will
come unto thee quickly and will remove thy candlestick out of his place, except thou
repent," referred to the Church of England See *Sermons*, vol. ii, Sermon 16.

and sound and is worth quoting verbatim: "I have given you the true notion of the Church which the Scripture always intends when it mentions the Church in general; when it speaks of the Church as the Body of Christ; when it speaks of the Church which Christ purchased with His Blood; when it speaks of the Church into which we are baptised; when it speaks of the Church to which all those glorious promises are made of the forgiveness of sins, of the perpetual presence and assistance of the Holy Spirit; of the gates of hell never prevailing against it, and of everlasting salvation in the world to come. I say that Church is always meant of the whole company of Christians dispersed over all the world, that profess the common Faith (though perhaps none of them without mixture of errors), and enjoy the Administration of the Word and Sacraments under their lawful pastors and governors; all these people, wherever they live, or by what name so ever they call themselves, make up together that one Body of Christ which we call the Catholic Church."[1]

In his references to the Devil, particularly during a discourse on 2 Corinthians ii,[2] Sharp expressed a belief, which was very widely held at the time, that Satan not only possessed a distinct personality of his own, but was attended by many legions of fallen angels and other evil spirits. In fact that the world around us, if men had eyes to see, swarmed with spirits, both good and evil, who continually strove together for the possession of our bodies.

Concluding this brief account of Sharp's preaching abilities and technique, "it may be added to his being a good preacher, that he was likewise a constant one. For several years he preached twice every Sunday in his own parish, besides his lecture in the city, and other occasional courses that he supplied in the week days."[3]

The practice of celebrating Holy Communion at least once in the week had become by the sixteen-eighties the rule rather than the exception. This was true not only of cathedrals but also in the more important London churches. Beveridge at St. Peter's, Cornhill, Tenison at St. Martin's, and now Sharp at St. Giles'

---

[1] P. E. More and F. L. Cross, *Anglicanism*, p. 40.

[2] "As there are good Spirits and good Angels, so there are evil Spirits and evil Angels; and of this latter sort is the Devil." See *Sermons*, vol. iii, Sermon 4.

[3] *Life of Archbishop Sharp*, vol. i, p. 42. The popularity of his sermons is illustrated by the following tribute from Mr. Hill of the Admiralty: "I should have thanked your Grace before now for two excellent sermons which I found left at my house by I know not whom. I must not only thank your Grace for the honour, but for the good which you have done me by them; and the rather because I fear I am not so good when your Grace is on the other side of Trent, as when you are in town: and these sermons come in aid of your absence": L-B-S. MSS., Box 4, Bundle F. 16, May 22, 1703.

celebrated as frequently as possible, besides restoring the Daily Offices. Sharp certainly deeply valued the Eucharist. In a sermon preached before Queen Anne on Good Friday, 1703, he declared that Christians ought to regard the Holy Communion as "the great and solemn Means . . . for the obtaining the Pardon and Forgiveness of their sins committed since their Baptism", and "strength against all our infirmities, physick for all our diseases, support against all the evils that oppress us".[1] He always insisted upon communicants kneeling at the altar rails to receive the sacrament, and refused to recognise the Puritan custom whereby they continued to sit in their pews and waited for the minister to bring it to them, although this was a custom that died hard, and persisted in the case of Christ Church, Oxford, even into the twentieth century, when it was far from being regarded as evidence of low-churchmanship.

Furthermore, he "had a very solemn way of reading the church service[2] and did great justice to the admirable form of prayer in the established liturgy", and "this is to be said for Dr. Sharp that the church service in his hands was executed to everybody's taste; and the common petitions, where they were put up by him to the throne of Grace, were so far from being liable to the imputation of dull performance, that they always affected his audience, though they did not seem always new. How far his happiness in these exercises was a natural gift in him, and how far it was an acquired perfection, it is not easy to determine; but which of them so ever it was, he never displayed it more than in the celebration of the Holy Mysteries. So distinct, nervous, devout and indeed seraphic was his elocution on those occasions, that he not only disposed the congregation present to seriousness and reverence, but inspired them with some degrees of that devotion, life and comfort which he expressed himself. In a word, if he ever distinguished himself in a more extraordinary manner under the character of a Christian priest, if ever he did justice to his function, or the liturgic offices, it is then when he stood before the altar."[3]

Preaching, frequent celebrations of the Holy Communion, the restoration of the Daily Offices, and his own personal charm in speaking and praying, represented Sharp's main accomplishments as a parish priest. But there were other equally important, if sub-

[1] *Archbishop Sharp's Sermons*, vol. ii, Sermon 20.
[2] J. Evelyn, *Diary*, April 26, 1696: "Dr. Sharp preached at the Temple. His prayer before the sermon was one of the most excellent compositions I ever heard."
[3] *Life of Archbishop Sharp*, vol. i, p. 43.

sidiary, branches of his work. First, the catechising of youth: This practice was strongly encouraged by the bishops, and was usually held on a Sunday afternoon. In the winter it could normally be combined with 4 p.m. Evensong, when the clergyman gave his instruction after the second lesson. "I catechise in my church", wrote Robert Marsden, sometime domestic chaplain to Archbishop Sharp and rector of Rempston, Bingham, in his visitation return of 1743, "every Sunday from ye first Sunday in Lent to ye first Sunday in November, and always (to ye best of my power) expound upon ye Catechism: this is done after 2d lesson at Evening-prayer."[1]

Sharp, while at St. Giles', became a particularly zealous advocate of catechising; and in later years, when archbishop of York, he remarked in one of his charges to his clergy that there could be no true reformation of manners or morals unless ministers early imbued the minds of the young with "serious and good notions".[2] He himself possessed to a considerable degree the art of teaching the young, clearly, simply and effectively; and on these occasions, unlike his usual practice in the pulpit, he always spoke extempore.

Secondly, the visitation of the sick: It was the custom at that time for the vicar of a large and important parish, which required several curates, to impose upon them the more arduous tasks in this field, especially where the dreaded smallpox and Plague were to be found. The Reverend Clement Elis, rector of Kirkby and prebendary of Southwell, wrote to Sharp on September 1, 1693: "Could I get an Assistant to my mind, which I find hard to do, I would make catechising and visiting my neighbours at their houses my chief work, as the former is indeed already."[3] Obviously Elis expected the curate would undertake the visiting, leaving himself free to continue his catechising.

Sharp employed two or three curates, but he made a point of bearing his fair share of such visitations, calling upon the very poor even in their cellars, as indeed Dr. Boreman had done before him. However, this faithful and conscientious discharge of his duties sometimes led him into dangerous places. For the parish of St. Giles, which has been described as "never at any time anything better than a squalid slum",[4] was a particularly ill-omened neighbourhood in the seventeenth century. Great Russell Street and the

---

[1] *Archbishop Herring's Visitation Returns*, vol. iv, p. 119.
[2] *Life of Archbishop Sharp*, vol. i, p. 45.
[3] L-B-S. MSS., Box 4, Bundle D. 3.
[4] Arthur Dasent, *Nell Gwynne*, p. 101.

lower portions of Drury Lane might house aristocrats like Lord Craven and the Earl of Southampton, and professional men like Sir Christopher Wren, but the neighbourhood of Holborn and Bloomsbury, taken as a whole, was a notorious plague-spot on the map of London where "bullies, knights of the road, cut-purses and brothel-keepers preyed upon one another and their betters".[1] The fields, still farmed, that lay behind Great Russell Street were little better, judging from the following advertisement in the *London Gazette*, dated October 5, 1693: "Whereas on Monday the 25th past in the night in the fields behind Southampton House, four milch cows, the cattle of Christopher Capper, of St. Giles-in-the-fields, were killed by stabbing in their bodies; and on Tuesday, the 3rd instant, in the same fields in the same night, two other milch cows of the said Mr. Capper were killed in like manner. Whosoever shall discover the Person or Persons concerned in this fact so as he or they shall be convicted of such offence, shall receive as a reward for such discovery by the said Christopher Capper the sum of £20." This Christopher Capper had two unmarried daughters, who were notorious for their spitefulness towards children, delighting in cutting the strings of kites flown by small boys, and confiscating their clothes when they were found bathing in the Capper ponds. It is recorded in the vestry minutes of 1695 that a child was accidentally drowned in one of these ponds.[2]

Irish immigration into London had begun towards the close of the sixteenth century. The first-comers were desperate men and adventurers fleeing before the Elizabethan oppression, and a large colony took up its abode in St. Giles' parish. "They were", wrote Strype, "builders' labourers, chairmen, porters, coal-heavers, milk-sellers and street hawkers, and they were publicans and lodging-house keepers, apparently catering for their own country-men." Such an element, Roman Catholic and irreconcilable, did not lend itself to the maintenance of parochial law and order. No wonder there were plenty of houses of ill-fame like Madam Ross's in Lewkenor Street, while the courts and alleys off Weld Street have been described as being "not over well inhabited, except some of them noted for the reception of the kinder sort of females",[3] *i.e.* nests of prostitution.

Certainly in the parish of St. Giles that Sharp and Nell Gwynne

[1] Ibid., p. 117.
[2] N. G. Brett-James, *The Growth of Stuart London*, pp. 403 and 404.
[3] Arthur Dasent, *Nell Gwynne*, p. 112.

knew so well, with its narrow, unlighted, unpoliced streets, abounding in criminals and desperadoes of all shades of political opinion, it was no light matter for a prosperous clergyman to stray off the beaten track. Londoners at no time have had any great regard for parsons, and particularly in the period that immediately succeeded the Plague they were not enamoured of the Anglican species. Such a gentleman might easily disappear down some unsavoury back alley and never be heard of again. Sharp himself had at least one narrow escape. During the reign of James II, when, owing to his uncompromising opposition to the Roman Catholics, he was out of favour at court, and therefore, as his enemies thought, less likely to attract attention by a sudden disappearance, two men called on him late one night. Their request was that he would accompany them in order to administer the last rites to a dying friend. Sharp's suspicions, however, were aroused, and fearing a trap he instructed a trusted and well-armed servant to follow them. Arriving at the house in question he bade the servant stand outside, on no account to enter it or leave the vicinity, and should he, Sharp, fail to reappear within a reasonable time, to give the alarm. The would-be assassins, observing these precautions and fearing to make an open assault, lost heart, informed the vicar that the patient was asleep and must not be disturbed, and allowed him to return home unmolested. Needless to say, Sharp never heard again either of this patient or his friends.[1]

Sharp worked his curates hard, but he paid them well according to contemporary standards. They each received £120 per annum, a princely sum compared with the more usual £20 per curate per annum.[2] These high stipends came, of course, out of the rector's own pocket, and were conditional on their scrupulous refusal to accept gratuities from tradesmen, which was a common and highly deplorable practice among inadequately paid assistants, leading to all kinds of bribery and sharp dealing, and lowering the moral and social dignity of the clerical office. In return for such an abstention Sharp allowed his curates, whenever possible, to perform any duties which carried with them as a matter of course large fees or perquisites.

[1] *Life of Archbishop Sharp*, vol. i, p. 47.
[2] Timothy Ellisonne, vicar of Coley and Haworth, writing to Sharp on August 8, 1702, about Haworth, remarked: "I would beg of your Grace the favour to keep Haworth a year or two, keeping an Assistant there and allowing him twenty pound per annum": L-B-S. MSS., Box 4, Bundle D. 13.

Without neglecting any of his parish work, Sharp did not hesitate to take advantage of the social opportunities that his new position afforded him. The London clergy were an influential body of men, containing in their ranks some of the ablest ecclesiastics of the day, such as: Tenison, vicar of St. Martin-in-the-Fields; Stillingfleet, dean of St. Paul's; Patrick, prebendary of Westminster; Beveridge, rector of St. Peter-upon-Cornhill; Whichcot, vicar of St. Lawrence Jewry; Calamy, vicar of St. Mary Aldermanbury; Scott and Sherlock, both prebendaries in St. Paul's; Wake, preacher at Gray's Inn; Clagget, lecturer at St. Michael Bassishaw; Cave, rector of All Hallows the Great; and naturally Tillotson, prebendary in St. Paul's. These men cordially welcomed him into their powerful yet exclusive circle; and regular meetings, almost partaking of the nature of conferences, were held at each other's houses, ostensibly for the purpose of reading and discussing the Scriptures, and criticising sermons and sermon technique, but also to decide on a common policy to be adopted towards the various outstanding ecclesiastical questions of the hour, of which the most burning were the popish, Socinian and Nonconformist controversies. This careful co-ordination of opinion and action enabled them at a later date successfully to resist James II's attempt to restore the power of the Roman Catholics; although on the more vexed problems of dissent and the nonjurors they found themselves in profound disagreement.

Sharp was, of course, fully aware that in the friendship of these men lay a sure road to promotion, since public attention largely centred upon the more important London divines. Certainly his own stock rose rapidly. In 1679[1] he took his D.D. degree, and the next year moved from Chancery Lane into the more aristocratic Great Russell Street. "A very handsome large and well built street", wrote Strype, "graced with the best Buildings in all Bloomsbury, and the best inhabited by the Nobility and Gentry, especially the North Side, as having Gardens behind the houses; and the prospect of pleasant fields up to Hamsted and Highgate. In so much that this place by Physicians is esteemed the most healthful of any in London." Shortly afterwards Charles II nominated him to the deanery of Norwich (1681) in succession to Dr. Astley. It is curious and a trifle ironical that James, Duke of York, and Lord Arlington, both militant Romanists, were promi-

---

[1] *Alumni Cantabrigienses*, Part I, vol. iv, p. 49. He took the degree by proxy: "Domino Doctore Beveridgio stante in comitiis in ejus vice."

nent in pressing Sharp's claims to this post upon Charles; probably because they were as yet unconscious of his sturdy, uncompromising, anti-Roman opinions. Lord Chancellor Nottingham, however, was also an active, and doubtless the more persistent, advocate.

Already a prebendary of Norwich, Sharp knew that diocese well, and was the more willing to accept the office of dean. But in order to fit himself thoroughly for his new task he spent the greater part of the year 1682 investigating the revenues of the cathedral and ascertaining exactly his own duties, rights and privileges. From that moment, although keeping a firm grip on the helm at St. Giles', his work as a parish priest was left more and more to his curates, men whom he had carefully picked and trained, and who could be depended upon to carry on this ministry as required. He had made his mark and could now afford to leave town for long periods at a stretch, both in the interests of his health, which had never been really robust since his Cambridge illness, and of his studies, for which he found more leisure in the country. Above all it gave him the chance "of improving in his spiritual life through the advantages of retirement and disengagement from company and business, which Norwich afforded him".[1]

The appointment to the deanery of Norwich, together with the deaths of his two close friends and staunch patrons, Sir John Finch and the Earl of Nottingham, which occurred in 1682, marked a definite line of cleavage in his career.[2] Behind him lay an apprenticeship where his natural talents had been fortunate enough to secure the training and patronage of so able and kindly a master as the Lord Chancellor and of so good a friend as John Tillotson; and so ample a field for their exercise as Kensington House and the parish of St. Giles-in-the-Fields. His feet had been firmly planted on the ladder of fame; he was recognised as one of London's foremost clerics, an able preacher and a conscientious parochial minister; royalty had smiled upon him both in the person of the reigning monarch and of the heir presumptive; and the Norwich appointment had marked him out unmistakably for a future bishopric. His friends were numerous. They were drawn from all walks of life and shades of religious opinion, from the dissenting

---

[1] *Life of Archbishop Sharp*, vol. i, p. 51.

[2] Sir John Finch was a graduate of Christ's, Cambridge, and a fellow of the Royal Society. He had been a pupil of Sir Henry More, and founded two additional fellowships at Christ's, to which he, and later his nephew Daniel, the second Earl of Nottingham, had the right to nominate. Among those whom Daniel appointed was Sharp's old friend and rival, Thomas Lovett. See J. Peile, *History of Christ's College, Cambridge*, pp. 196-198.

Baxter and Low-Church Tillotson and Tenison to the high-flying Atterbury and later non-juring Nelson, while the eccentric Whiston and free-thinking Toland were also his admirers.

Along with Tillotson at St. Paul's, Tenison at St. Martin's and Beveridge at St. Peter's, Cornhill, he seemed fated for swift promotion; and that he had to wait another six years for his bishopric (or rather archbishopric) was due partly to the politico-religious situation, which, after the comparative calm of the last five years of Charles' reign, developed alarmingly and burst in the Revolution of 1688, and partly to his own honest, if at times somewhat tactless, championship of the *via media* of Anglicanism. But in the long run he did not fail to reap the reward of his constancy, emerging from the three great religious controversies of these years, the Nonconformist, the Roman and the non-juring, with an enhanced reputation as a scholar and the character of a safe yet moderate churchman.

CHAPTER IV

NONCONFORMIST, ROMAN CATHOLIC, NON-JUROR

PURITANISM, the left wing of the Reformation, drawing its inspiration first from Geneva and then from Scotland, had reached the zenith of its power in England during the period of the civil war and Commonwealth. But even at that time it had never commanded a majority in the country. It would, indeed, be true to say that the autocratic misgovernment of Charles I and Strafford was no less responsible than the Arminianism of Laud for the revolt of the Long Parliament against the Crown.[1] The success of Puritanism, in fact, lay very largely in its close alliance with the House of Commons and professed regard for constitutional liberty, just as the eclipse of the Church of England was due to its having linked its destinies for good or ill with the fortunes of the King. Constitutionalism and Nonconformity, however, parted company when Cromwell and his Ironsides began to act even more despotically than Charles himself. Puritanism, too, unlike Anglicanism, represented no one homogeneous organised Church, but was a wide term embracing a large number of different sects, which shaded off into violent extremes. Consequently the Presbyterians of the Long Parliament found themselves pitted against Cromwell's Independents, who, in their turn, had to suppress fanatics like Lilburne and his Levellers, Harrison and the Fifth Monarchy men, Winstanley and the Diggers.[2] The Restoration was, undoubtedly, due more to the rivalries among the Puritan sectaries themselves than to the efforts of the royalists, since Charles II was invited by the Presbyterian majority in Monck's Convention Parliament to return to the throne of his ancestors on the certain expectation that he would disband the Independents' army.

Once the Restoration was an accomplished fact, royalism and Anglicanism automatically reasserted themselves and Puritanism rapidly disintegrated. It had lost its place in the national affections as the champion of popular rights, and by its bigotry and

---

[1] J. R. Tanner, *English Constitutional Conflicts in the Seventeenth Century*, p. 79: "While the King's financial policy was uniting all classes against him, the ecclesiastical policy of Laud was making trouble in a different direction."

[2] R. H. Tawney, *Religion and the Rise of Capitalism*, p. 256.

cruelty had caused a revulsion of men's hearts so that they now revered Charles I as a martyr and a saint. Churchmen and kingsmen were also anxious, of course, to pay off old scores, and by their efforts successfully wrecked all the hopes of moderate men on both sides, including the king himself, to effect some sort of compromise and comprehension.[1] The collapse of the Savoy Conference, followed by the passing of the infamous "Clarendon Code", completed the downfall of the sects, who had now, in their turn, to face a period of persecution, inaugurated by Archbishop Sheldon, who was the bitter enemy of the Nonconformists.[2] Some 1,200 ministers were ejected from their livings, many of whom, including John Wesley, the grandfather of the famous Methodist, died as a result of their sufferings. During these lean years the various Nonconformist parties, which had previously been violently hostile to one another, drew closer together and presented a more united front to the world.[3] Gradually, too, the growing fear of Rome softened people's hearts towards men and women who were at least Protestant and opposed to the army of Louis XIV; and the larger that army loomed in the minds of Englishmen, the more rapidly Oliver Cromwell and his Ironsides faded into history.

Another attempt at comprehension, sponsored by Lord Keeper Bridgman and Sir Matthew Hale in 1668,[4] and Charles' famous Declaration of Indulgence four years later both failed to effect any outward change for the better, although practically they brought some relief. Eventually the growing dread of popery, which the passing of the Test Act did little to allay, reached its climax in the "discovery" of the Popish Plot; and this event, together with the new Dutch alliance, now cemented by the marriage of the Calvinist William of Orange to Mary, the eldest daughter of the Duke of York, and next after her father in the line

[1] H. Gee and W. J. Hardy, *Documents Illustrative of the History of the English Church*, p. 587.
"Because the passion and uncharitableness of the times have produced several opinions in Religion by which men are engaged in parties and animosities against each other, which when they shall hereafter unite in a freedom of conversation will be composed or better understood; we do declare a liberty to tender consciences, and that no man shall be disquieted or called in question, for differences of opinion in matters of religion which do not disturb the peace of the kingdom, and that we shall be ready to consent to such an Act of Parliament as shall be offered to us, for the full granting of that indulgence": Declaration of Breda, 1660.
[2] Calamy, *Abridgement*, vol. i, p. 328.
[3] *E.g.*, the Presbyterians and Independents. See *Calendar of State Papers Domestic* (1661-1662), p. 396.
[4] Sylvester, *Life of Baxter*, Part III, p. 25.

of succession, reacted in favour of the Nonconformists. The majority of the bishops were still their deadly enemies, but after 1670 moderate Anglican opinion definitely swung in their favour, and, indeed, even angled for their support, on conditions. Of this latter school of thought Sharp was by no means the least conspicuous member. He himself had sprung from a family of strong Puritan traditions, and in his extreme youth had favoured the doctrine of predestination; his best friend Tillotson had had yet closer affinities with Nonconformity; and Baxter, one of Dissent's most venerated champions, was actually worshipping in his church. All the omens, then, pointed to the young rector of St. Giles', who was closely allied to the Crown through the influence of the Lord Chancellor, a trusted friend and collaborator of the more important London divines, and *persona grata* with many of the bishops, especially Compton, the new bishop of London, as a natural mediator between the Protestant Churches.

As early as 1674 he clearly defined his own attitude towards the Nonconformists in a sermon preached before the Lord Mayor at the Guildhall during August, when he took as his text Romans xiv, 19: "Let us therefore follow after the things that make for peace." The main theme of his argument was the need for "peace, love and unity" among Christians, which could best be achieved by the "preservation of communion". But what communion? "We are bound to maintain communion with the Catholic Church . . . with that part of it within whose verge the Divine Providence has cast us"—*i.e.*, the Established Church—and "to make a rent in the Body of Christ is directly contrary to preserving the unity of that Body."[1] Then, having made plain the absolute necessity for Nonconformists to return to the Church of England, he proceeded to gild the pill for them. Mankind, he argued, must carefully distinguish between what is necessary and superfluous in religion, remembering that the articles of faith needful for salvation are few and simple, and clearly set down in the Scriptures. These must certainly be adhered to; but in matters of pure speculation men and women were perfectly free to think for themselves. It was silly to quarrel about words and phrases: "I verily believe that this is the case of several of those disputes in which we protestants do often engage at this day. I do not think in many points, our differences are near so wide as they are sometimes represented." Finally he pleaded for courtesy and tolerance in discussing each

[1] *Archbishop Sharp's Sermons*, vol. i, Sermon 1.

other's opinions, a vigorous pursuit of holiness by all, and a real endeavour to bring down religion from the head to the heart: "This is that which will restore to the world the Golden Age of Primitive Christianity, when the love and unity of the disciples of Jesus was so conspicuous and remarkable that it became a proverb, See how the Christians love one another."

This sermon attracted widespread attention, and by the desire of the Lord Mayor, Sir William Hooker, it was printed.[1] Thomas Wadsworth, a Nonconformist divine, who had lately been a fellow of Christ's and was the intruded rector of St. Mary's, Newington, replied to Sharp's arguments but in the same friendly and co-operative spirit that the latter had employed. Now, unasked by Sharp, the cudgels were taken up anew in a most violent fashion by the hot-tempered high-churchman Henry Dodwell, late fellow of Trinity College, Dublin, who, casting all idea of compromise and courtesy to the winds, loudly demanded the forcible destruction rather than the comprehension of Nonconformity, but at the same time defended Sharp's sermon, or rather his own interpretation of it, in his Book of Schism. This attack provoked Baxter into entering the arena,[2] and Sharp, who although he had been consulted by Dodwell about his work was not altogether satisfied with the manner in which he had conducted his case, decided to make his own position crystal clear, and, he hoped, conducive to that alliance between the Protestant Churches which the times so sorely required.

Shaftesbury and his Whigs had now been finally discredited and the Rye House Plot unmasked, leaving Toryism, royalism and Anglicanism more firmly entrenched than ever. But as Charles II's reign drew to its close, with a Roman Catholic heir-presumptive in full control of the reins of power, it behoved all loyal and far-sighted churchmen to be prepared for any eventuality; and as a step in the right direction it led them to make a great effort to

---

[1] Life of Archbishop Sharp, vol. i, p. 51: "He had in the year 1674, while he was yet domestic Chaplain to the Lord Keeper, and before he had any other preferment besides his Archdeaconry, preached before the Lord Mayor at the Guildhall, upon the subject of the Dissenters' separation from the Established Church, which his Lordship desired to be printed; and so it was; and it is now the first sermon in his collection. In this discourse, he showed a great deal of sound reasoning, and a great deal of temper too, more than men at their first setting out in the world, and especially at his age, are usually masters of."

[2] "The True and only way of Concord of all the Christian Churches: the desirableness of it and the detection of false dividing terms. Opened by Richard Baxter" (1680). See Annotated List of the Writings of Richard Baxter. Edit. A. B. Grosart, 1868. Dodwell promptly retorted with his Reply to Mr. Baxter (1681).

bring the Nonconformists back within the Anglican fold. They were too few in number to constitute a menace to the National Church, and minor alterations in the Prayer Book would be well worth so substantial an addition to the Church Militant in her struggle with the Beast of the Apocalypse. Hence the appearance, with the blessing of Henry Compton,[1] of Sharp's two celebrated treatises, *A Discourse Concerning Conscience* (1683) and *The Case of a Doubting Conscience* (1684). He was well aware that he had not done himself justice with the narrowly prescribed limits of a single sermon, and expressed as much to the Lord Mayor and aldermen in that sermon's dedication: "Right Honourable, The following discourse was never designed to go further than your own chapel, otherwise it had not been left so imperfect."[2] Now in these two later works, which are lengthy and very closely but clearly reasoned, he strove to bring home to his fellow-countrymen the following important points: The human conscience, he began by arguing, works only in respect of our actions, which are either commanded by God and so lawful, or forbidden and so sinful, or colourless and so unimportant. Our conscience bids us perform the first, abstain from the second, and please ourselves concerning the third. In each case the Will of God declares itself through the laws of Nature or those of Revelation, *i.e.* the Bible. From such general premises Sharp proceeded to urge that God, and so conscience, has commanded that every man should join in communion with the Church established by law in the place where he lives, so long as that Church is a true, sound part of the Catholic Church, and that it imposes nothing "repugnant to the laws of God or the appointments of Jesus Christ".[3] The Church of England, he declared, was innocent of any such offence; and hence the Dissenters had no valid plea for abstaining from her rites for conscience' sake. Their separation, in fact, was due either to ignorance or to a variety of personal motives: "a private grudge or spite . . . because their pastors and teachers are not permitted to exercise their functions in our church . . . mere dislike of several things in our church, officers etc. . . . . But none of these excuses can enable them justi-

---

[1] It is interesting to note that *A Collection of Cases and other Discourses lately written to Recover Dissenters to the Communion of the Church of England, by some Divines of the City of London,* was dedicated to Compton and published in 1698. This contained, besides Sharp's two treatises, works by Drs. Grove, Sherlock, Williams, Freeman, Calamy, Clagget, Fowler, Tillotson, Hascard, Patrick, Tenison and Cave.

[2] *Life of Archbishop Sharp,* vol. i, p. 53.

[3] *A Discourse Concerning Conscience* (from *A Collection of Cases and other Discourses,* etc.), Part I, p. 151.

fiably to plead conscience for their separation, particularly those who do communicate occasionally with us in our prayers and sacraments."[1]

Sharp, however, fully and frankly recognised the sincere, if mistaken, religious outlook of the vast majority of the Nonconformists; and suggested that they should study the whole question afresh, bearing in mind this direct divine command to communicate with the Established Church provided it was a sound part of the Catholic Church.

An additional reason for returning to the Anglican fold lay in the fact that by so doing they would promote and empower Christianity as a whole, since unity meant strength, but disunion weakness. They would also, of course, the more readily further their secular interests. "Besides the disturbances they have all along occasioned to the public peace and unity, they have also brought their estates and families into danger of ruin by the just persecutions they have drawn upon themselves, and all this for the sake of a course they themselves must confess they are altogether uncertain and unresolved about, since even their own divines could find nothing directly contrary to God's law in the Anglican Communion."[2]

In conclusion he issued an appeal and a warning: "By this unnatural separation, we do, for anything we know, put ourselves out of the communion of the Catholic Church; and consequently out of the ordinary means of salvation." At the same time it meant "giving occasion for a deluge of atheism and profaneness and impiety . . . and by putting affronts upon our lawful governors we give scandal to the brethren . . . lastly, as we offer a very fair handle and pretence to all discontented and factious men to practise against the best of Governments; so we take a most effective course to ruin the best constituted Church in the world, and with it the Reformed Religion in this kingdom".[3]

In these two treatises, the best known of all his works, Sharp clearly defined his own theological beliefs and churchmanship. He based his whole argument on the fact that the Bible, containing God's revealed commandments, and the laws of the state could and did work hand in glove to procure an unblemished Church, that embodied in the Anglican liturgy and constitution. He could

[1] Ibid., p. 158.
[2] *Case of a Doubting Conscience* (from *A Collection of Cases*, etc.), Part II, p. 201.
[3] Ibid., p. 203.

not for one moment understand the dissenting or the non-juring viewpoint, which he attributed either to interested motives or to a profound ignorance of the whole truth about religion.

Authority weighed very heavily with him; but in the last resort, should it offend against God's law as expressed either in nature or revelation, it must be resisted. Hence he never became a non-juror, putting the good of the Church as a whole before loyalty to any individual, however divinely appointed. These works were also an important contribution to the policy of comprehension, which, under pressure of the Roman menace, assumed more realistic proportions and bore fruit in the schemes of Archbishop Sancroft[1] and Dean Tillotson, and ultimately in the Toleration Act of 1689. Sharp played an important part in the two former; and, although becoming more hostile towards Dissenters as the years went by,[2] he never wholly abandoned the hope that one day in some way they would be won back to the Mother Church, from which they had originally sprung.

A puritanical upbringing had prejudiced Sharp against the Roman Catholics as he had never been prejudiced against the Nonconformists; and this sentiment was strengthened and deepened by contemporary events such as the Popish Plot and the Revocation of the Edict of Nantes. Nevertheless he welcomed the accession of James II to the throne, not only as that of the heir by law and divine right, but also as the champion of order and, he hoped, of the Church against a possible recurrence of the civil war and a restoration of a puritanical commonwealth, which might well have followed in the wake of the elevation of the Duke of Monmouth.

Consequently, on the Sunday after Charles' death and the pro-clamation of his successor he preached a sermon at St. Giles' in

---

[1] Bishop Wake, in his speech at the trial of Sacheverell, thus described Archbishop Sancroft's comprehension design of 1688: "The scheme was laid out to such divines of the church as were thought most proper to be entrusted with it. His Grace took one part to himself; another was committed to Dr. Patrick, afterwards Bishop of Ely. And the reviewing of the daily services and communion book was referred to a select number of divines, of whom Dr. Sharp, afterwards Archbishop of York, and Dr. Patrick were two. The design was to improve and enforce the Liturgy, by correcting some things, and adding to others; and, if it should be thought advisable by authority, when this matter should come to be legally considered, first in Convocation, then in Parliament, by leaving some few ceremonies, confessed to be indifferent in their natures, as indifferent in their usage, so as not necessarily to be observed by such, who should make a scruple of them." See T. Birch, *Life of Tillotson*, p. 154.

For Tillotson's own scheme see Chapter V, p. 128.

[2] See Chapter IX.

the course of which he ascribed the peaceful succession to God's providence; and later accepted an invitation to present "the address of the Grand Jury for the City of London, upon the King's happy accession",[1] where it was expressly stated that the undersigned would "serve your Majesty . . . to the utmost extremity".[2] He also cheerfully agreed to remain one of the royal chaplains, being "apppointed Chaplain in ordinary to his Majesty . . . the next year, April 20th, 1686".[3] Furthermore, he was fortunate in winning the friendship of the future Lord Chancellor, Jeffreys, and in later days he was thus the better able to help some of the wretches who had fallen into that vindictive man's clutches, notably the family of a certain notorious Presbyterian and Whig, Sheriff Cornish, who, as privy to the Rye House Plot, had been executed in 1683.

All this, however, and much besides, was only surface deep. In his heart Sharp thoroughly mistrusted the Romish king, and had made up his mind to do battle, if the need arose, in defence of his beloved Church. He was, of course, in an especially difficult position, since many of his parishioners were immigrant Irish Catholics, whose priests, encouraged by the turn of events and the tacit approval of the court, proceeded to stir up as much trouble for the rector of St. Giles' as they possibly could.[4] This was rendered all the easier after the complete defeat of Monmouth and his Protestant allies had emboldened James to come further into the open as a Roman Catholic dictator and a pale imitation of Louis XIV. But forewarned is forearmed. The Anglican clergy, foreseeing a renewal of the Marian persecution, looked first to the bishops and then to the more important London divines for a strong lead. Nor did they look in vain. The London clergy, headed by Bishop Compton, were a strong, able, and intensely anti-Roman set of men, who eagerly rushed into the fray, denouncing alike the power and evil purposes of Rome.[5] The king then proceeded to make matters worse by causing "The Directions for Preachers", which Charles II had originally issued in 1662, to be reprinted and authorised afresh "by letters mandatory to the two Archbishops".[6]

---

[1] *Life of Archbishop Sharp*, vol. i, p. 63.
[2] Ibid., vol. i, p. 64.   [3] Ibid., vol. i, p. 66.
[4] R. Dobie, *History of St. Giles-in-the-Fields*, pp. 95 and 96: "The receipts and expenditure on account of the poor, mention the Irish expressly and repeatedly by name, and from the number of entries of them, it may be inferred that they began to abound in the parish" (*i.e.* from 1640 onwards).
[5] Burnet, *History of My Own Time*, vol. ii, p. 296, edn. 1818.
[6] *Life of Archbishop Sharp*, vol. i, p. 69.

These injunctions forbade the clergy to touch on controversial matters, and thus constituted a deliberate attempt to muzzle the freedom of the pulpit. Not unnaturally they were completely ignored. Whereupon Burnet wrote: "The Popish priests enraged at this opposition made by the clergy, when they saw their religion so exposed and themselves so much despised, said, it was ill manners and want of duty to treat the King's religion with so much contempt. It was resolved to proceed severely against some of the preachers, to try if by that means they might intimidate the rest."[1]

Sharp,[2] who was especially prominent in this attack on popery, having suffered so much from its machinations within his own parish, determined to deliver at St. Giles' a series of addresses, fifteen in all, directed against its teaching. He preached the first of these sermons on May 2, 1686, but it was the second, given a week later (May 9), that led to his selection by the court party as their first victim. It was headed: "A discussion of the question which the Roman Catholics much insist upon with the Protestants, viz: In which of the different Communions in Christendom, the only true Church of Christ is to be found. With a refutation of a certain popish argument handed about in MS. in 1685."[3] At the conclusion of this address he quoted "a little manuscript paper that had come into his hands, whose argument is, that if we cannot show a visible church distinct from the Roman, that hath at all times, from the beginning, opposed the doctrines and practices of the present Church of Rome, then it will undeniably follow that the Present Church of Rome is the only Visible Church". The "little manuscript paper", which had been handed to Sharp as he came out of the pulpit on the previous Sunday, "purported", so Macaulay tells us, "to come from one of his parishioners, who had been staggered by the arguments of Roman Catholic theologians, and was anxious to be satisfied that the Church of England was a branch of the true Church of Christ".[4] But more probably it was a challenge, which Sharp could hardly fail to take up, concocted by a Roman priest with the deliberate design of catching him out in his words. If so he certainly fell into the trap; for information was quickly brought to the court that not only had the rector of St. Giles' transgressed the commandments of the "Directions to

---

[1] Burnet, *History of My Own Time*, vol. ii, p. 297.
[2] Other prominent names, according to Burnet, included: Tenison, Tillotson, Stillingfleet, Patrick, Williams, Clagget, Gee, Aldrich, Whitby, Hooper and Wake.
[3] *Archbishop Sharp's Works*, vol. vii, Sermon 6, edn. 1754.
[4] T. B. Macaulay, *History of England*, vol. ii, p. 745, edn. 1849.

Preachers", but had cast a reflection upon the king himself for changing his religion. Furthermore, it was said that he had spoken scathingly of the theological disquisitions which had been found in Charles' strongbox and published by James.

Without troubling to inquire whether all this information was true or false (actually it was certainly false, as Jeffreys, who saw Sharp and studied his sermon notes, well knew), Sunderland despatched a letter to the bishop of London by the hand of Atterbury the messenger, which was delivered in the afternoon of Thursday, June 17, 1686:

"JAMES. R.[1]

   Right Reverend Father in God.

   We greet you well. Whereas we have been informed and are fully satisfied that Dr. John Sharp, Rector of the parish church, St. Giles-in-the-fields, in the county of Middlesex, and in your diocese, notwithstanding our late letter to the most Reverend Fathers in God, the Archbishops of Canterbury and York, and our directions concerning preachers, given at our court at Whitehall the 15th day of March, 1685, in the second year of our reign. Yet he the said Dr. Sharp, in contempt of the said orders, hath in some of his sermons since preached, presumed to make unbecoming reflections, and to utter such expressions as were not fit or proper for him, endeavouring thereby to beget, in the minds of his hearers, an evil opinion of us and our government, by insinuating fears and jealousies to dispose them to discontent, and to lead them into disobedience and rebellion. These are therefore to require and command you immediately upon receipt thereof forthwith to suspend him from further preaching in any parish church or chapel in your diocese, until he has given us satisfaction, and our further pleasure be known herein. And for your so doing this shall be your warrant, and so we bid you heartily farewell. Given at our court of Windsor, the 14th day of June 1686, in the second year of our reign. By his Majesty's command.

SUNDERLAND."

On receipt of this autocratic missive Compton, after taking legal advice, promptly summoned Sharp to meet him the next day (June 18) at Doctors' Commons, when he "desired and advised him to forbear the pulpit till the king's further pleasure be known".[2]

---

[1] *Proceedings against the Bishop of London, 1686.* Additional MS. 15551, f. 43.
[2] *Life of Archbishop Sharp,* vol. i, p. 81.

To this Sharp readily agreed. Whereupon the bishop composed
what he imagined to be a suitable reply and sent it to Sunderland
by Sharp in person, together with the latter's own humble petition
for pardon and mercy, which declared that "if in any sermon of
his any words or expressions have unwarily slipt from him, liable
to such construction as to give your majesty cause for offence; as
he solemnly protests he had no ill intention in those words or expressions, so he is very sorry for them; and resolves for the future
to be so careful in the discharge of his duty, that your majesty shall
have reason to believe him to be your most faithful subject".[1]
For his part the bishop wrote:

"MY LORD
I always have and shall count it my duty to obey the King
in whatsoever commands he lays upon me, that I can perform
with a safe conscience. But in this I humbly conceive I am obliged
to proceed according to law, and therefore it is impossible for me
to comply, because though his majesty commands me only to
execute his pleasure, yet in the capacity I am to do it I must act
as a judge. And your Lordship knows no judge condemns any man
before he hath knowledge of the cause, and hath cited the party.
However I sent to Mr. Dean and acquainted him with your
majesty's displeasure, whom I find so ready to give all reasonable
satisfaction, that I have thought fit to make him the bearer of this
answer from him that will never be unfaithful to the king or otherwise than
My Lord
your Lordship's most humble servant
H. LONDON."[2]

Both Compton and Sharp thought that such submission would
end the matter, especially as Jeffreys, not to mention Nottingham,
Rochester, and even Sunderland, were the rector's very good
friends and could be relied upon to intervene on his behalf. Indeed, except in a purely legal sense, all the king's commands had
been promptly executed. But Sunderland, Jeffreys and James were
no longer interested in the minor misdemeanours of the dean of
Norwich; they had other and bigger fish to fry, none less than the
bishop of London himself, the arch-Protestant, who, so they

---

[1] Additional MS. 15551, f. 43.
[2] Additional MS. 15551, f. 43. *Cf. Life of Archbishop Sharp*, vol. i, p. 81.

thought, had been delivered into their hands by his refusal to suspend Sharp. Hence when the latter arrived at Hampton Court, letter and petition in hand, Sunderland, pouncing on the one and ignoring the other, put the single question: "Whether the Bishop had obeyed the order?" The answer "No" more than satisfied him, and Sharp was left to cool his heels in an ante-chamber until the court had removed to Windsor, where he could get no better attention. Lord Middleton, in whose hands he had placed his petition, informed him that "His Majesty would not suffer it to be read"[1] at the council meeting; and both Jeffreys and Rochester advised him to give up the attempt and "get out of the way" until such time as they had "done the Bishop of London's work". Consequently the dean, feeling convinced that he could do no good either for himself or the bishop by remaining, retired on July 1 to Norwich, "where he continued till the middle of December".

Meanwhile the full fury of James' wrath was directed against Compton, who not only possessed strong Protestant and therefore anti-Roman prejudices, but had recently in the House of Lords proved himself far from amenable to the royal will. The court party were also aware that something must be done to silence the criticism of their policy from the pulpit; and it was hoped that if the bishop could be effectively disposed of, then the fear of wholesale suspensions and deprivations of a similar nature might be calculated to intimidate the lesser clergy. For this purpose James decided to employ, and incidentally to test the strength of, his recently appointed Ecclesiastical Commission.[2]

Nevertheless the trial and suspension of the bishop, although carried through with all Jeffreys' accustomed ruthlessness and efficiency, were by no means a success from the king's standpoint. In the first place, the very men who were asked to serve on the Commission were only half-hearted. Archbishop Sancroft shuffled out of the responsibility altogether on the plea of business and ill-health; Lord Chief Justice Sir Edward Herbert was opposed to

---

[1] *Life of Archbishop Sharp*, vol. i, p. 85.

[2] This court, it was argued, was a revival of the Court of High Commission, which together with the criminal jurisdiction of all other ecclesiastical courts had been abolished by an Act of Parliament in 1641. The Act was, indeed, repealed in 1661 *except for the clauses that related to the High Commission*. The court, however, now set up by James differed from its Elizabethan predecessor in that it was not concerned with extirpating heresy and enforcing uniformity, but only in compelling the clergy to do the king's will under threat of suspension or deprivation. James based his right to set up such a Commission on the royal supremacy, which had been explicitly reaffirmed by the Act of 1661. But in view of the fact that the High Commission had also been expressly abolished by statute, the illegality of its revival could scarcely be questioned.

passing sentence; and the Earl of Rochester could only finally be brought to heel by a judicious combination of threats and flattery. The bishops of Durham and Rochester alone were subservient to Jeffreys' bullying. Furthermore, during the course of the trial, it quickly became apparent that the bishop's strong case could not be destroyed legally, only by means of hectoring or brow-beating him into submission. This last method Jeffreys attempted without much success.

"On Tuesday August 3rd the Commissioners opened their Commission and immediately sealed a citation to Atterbury the messenger, who upon Wednesday morning brought it to the Bishop of London at Fulham, for him to appear before the Commission on Monday the 9th of the same month . . . in the Council Chamber at Whitehall at ten of the clock of the morning to answer to such matters as on his Majesty's behalf shall then and there be objected against him."[1]

Compton began his defence by insinuating that the court was illegal and had no right to try him at all, demanding "a copy of your Commission and a copy of my charge".[2] This Jeffreys refused, cynically remarking that the court's Commission "was upon record in every coffee-house".[3] But later he had the grace to admit: "My Lord, when I told you the commission was to be seen in every coffee-house I did not speak it with any design to reflect upon your Lordship as if you were a haunter of coffee-houses. I abhor the thought of it and intend nothing by it than that it was common in town."

However, he quickly brushed the matter aside as unimportant, and asked why the bishop had not obeyed the king by suspending Sharp. Compton replied: "It was because . . . I could not . . . I could not legally do it, but by way of citation and hearing him."[4] He then pleaded for time to consider his defence, and was granted a week followed by a further fortnight. But when the hearing was resumed he returned to the attack on the constitution of the Commission, but was again repeatedly refused the right to question the legality of the court: "My Lord I must tell you, that we will not admit of any quarrelling with our commission, we are well assured of the legality of it, otherwise we would not be such fools as to sit here."[5] Compton retorted by demanding to be tried by his metropolitan and fellow-suffragans, since the present court, whatever

---

[1] Additional MS. 15551, f. 43.   [2] See Sloane MS. 3943, ff. 1-16.
[3] See Egerton MS. 2543, ff. 254-260.   [4] State Trials, vol. xii, p. 1157.
[5] Op. cit., p. 1159.

its validity, had no power to try past causes, *i.e.* those which had been committed before it was set up. Jeffreys, of course, denied this, affirming that the general clauses of their Commission covered such contingencies. Finding he was making no headway, the bishop did not press the point any further, but produced Sharp's petition instead, hoping that this would settle the case, only to be informed that it was now irrelevant, as he, not Sharp, was being tried for disobeying the king's orders. Thereupon Compton fell back upon his old argument that he had consulted counsel and they had told him it was against the law to suspend "before citing and hearing".[1] However, he had gone so far as to advise Sharp to "forbear preaching till his Majesty had received satisfaction concerning him", and he had agreed to do so.

Compton's counsel, Drs. Oldish, Price and Newton, also made it perfectly clear that legally there could be no absolute suspension without citation, but in this particular instance the bishop had effectively silenced Sharp. No judge, they argued, can condemn unheard, and since bishops are not ordinary court officials they cannot blindly carry out the king's orders. On the contrary, they were *custodes canonum* and could not deliberately break such laws themselves. It is interesting to note that Dr. Pinfold, the king's advocate, who listened to all this very attentively, had nothing to say in reply.

Sentence, however, was determined upon, and after a short adjournment was pronounced on September 6, 1686: "Whereas Henry Lord Bishop of London hath been convened before us for his disobedience and also his contempt mentioned in the proceedings of the case. And the said Henry Lord Bishop of London being fully heard thereupon. We have thought fit after mature consideration to proceed to our definite sentence: Declaring, decreeing and pronouncing that the said Henry Lord Bishop of London shall for his said disobedience and contempt be suspended during his Majesty's pleasure and accordingly we do by these presents suspend him the said Henry Lord Bishop of London peremptorily admonishing and requiring him hereby to abstain from the function and exercise of his episcopal office and other especial jurisdiction during the said suspension under pain of deposition and removal from his Bishopric. Given under our seal the 5th of September 1686."[2] The bishop, apparently, "desired to speak, which they would not permit of but adjourned the court".

[1] Ibid., p. 1161.   [2] Additional MS. 15551, f. 43.

7

So Compton was "effectively disposed of"; but not without first making him a popular hero and martyr and arousing the temper of the populace to an ugly level.[1] The charge of the London diocese was handed over to his two judges, Sprat, bishop of Rochester, and Crewe, bishop of Durham; but they were unable to evict him from Fulham Palace or to take over the episcopal revenues, since "it was known that, had any attempt been made to deprive him of his temporalities, he would have put himself under the protection of the Common Law; and Herbert himself declared that at Common Law judgement must be given against the Crown".[2] And as even James dared not always go so far as to pack the courts of Westminster, the bishop was left in possession. Burnet neatly summed up the whole affair: "According to the form of ecclesiastical courts, a person under such a suspension must make a submission within six months: otherwise he may be proceeded against as obstinate. So six months after the sentence, the bishop sent a petition to the king desiring to be restored to the exercise of his episcopal function. But he made no acknowledgement of any fault. So this had no other effect, but that it stopped all further proceedings: only the suspension lay still on him."[3]

But to return to Sharp, who was all the while quietly residing at Norwich, collecting rare coins in his leisure hours and corresponding with Ralph Thoresby and John Evelyn about them. Friends notified him that now the bishop of London had been dealt with he might safely emerge from the obscurity of Norfolk, return to Town and renew his petition to the crown to be restored to his function. In accordance with this advice Sharp first interviewed Jeffreys, and understanding that the omens were favourable, employed Henry Guy, the secretary of the Treasury, as his intermediary for handing Sunderland a shortened version of his old petition, which both expressed sorrow for his recent behaviour and a desire to be restored to his parish. Almost immediately he received a favourable reply:

[1] See Egerton: MS. 2543, ff. 254-260. "It was observed when the Lord Bishop spoke concerning the Commission, Sir Thomas Hedges with a loud voice, said, 'well put, well put, my Lord speaks nothing but reason.' There was another Gent. supposed to be Sir John Lowther, who as he was coming away in the crowd said 'there were some who presented me as a papist, but on the contrary I will not be ashamed or afraid to vindicate my Lord Bishop, also to vindicate my Lord Bishop's causes before the Commissioners themselves."

[2] T. B. Macaulay, *History of England*, vol. ii, p. 751.

[3] Burnet, *History of My Own Time*, vol. ii, p. 300.

"Sir—I have read your petition to the King, who is pleased to accept of your submission, and commands me upon it to acquaint you, that he allows you to return to the exercise of your function as formerly.

> I am, Sir,
> your friend and servant
> SUNDERLAND. P."[1]

Various people claimed to have been instrumental in getting Sharp restored to the royal favour, varying from his own brother-in-law, William Rawlinson, and the Earl of Rochester to Tenison[2] and Samuel Pepys. Of the last it was said: "Sharp at last representing his case to Mr. Pepys, as a good natured man with wife and children, Mr. Pepys went freely to the King and prevailed with his Majesty to restore him to the exercise of his office; till which time, he had a guard or sentinel to attend his lodgings."[3]

Actually such interventions were quite insignificant. The game had been played to a finish, and it mattered little to James what became of the pawn who had made the opening move.

Yet it needed courage of a very high order for the rector, as he did, to return to his pulpit and immediately renew his attacks upon the Roman Catholics. But he could hardly fail to do less, as the priests had taken full advantage of his temporary absence under a cloud both to undermine the confidence of his parishioners in his own personal integrity and to destroy their faith in the Anglican Church. Sharp's curates, good and able men as they were, had been quite helpless in stemming the Roman tide, backed as it was by the apparent authority, or at least benevolent neutrality, of James himself, Defender of the Faith.. Throughout the year 1687, with the pen as well as by the spoken word, Sharp skilfully and resolutely led his counter-attack. He had to face some very ticklish questions. "Reverend Sir", wrote Alice Kingesmill, one of his parishioners, on March 1, 1686/7, "if you can prove to me that Christ hath no infallible Church upon earth . . . I will promise you to be no Roman Catholic."[4] Another, an anonymous correspondent, questioned the royal supremacy: "How I may be assured that all the Christians in the first 400 years, believed no purgatory,

---

[1] *Life of Archbishop Sharp*, vol. i, p. 88.
[2] Le Neve, *History of the Archbishops*, Part I, p. 239: "It was chiefly by his [Tenison's] interest that Dr. John Sharp, Rector of St. Giles-in-the-fields, at that time under suspension, was restored to the exercise of his ministerial office."
[3] "John Sharp" in the *Biographia Britannica*, 1763.
[4] L-B-S. MSS., Box 3, Bundle H. 1b.

no real presence as the Roman Catholics do now, no praying to
saints, no veneration towards holy pictures, and whether they
swore their temporal princes to be the heads of their Churches, for
unless I can understand how they had heads like us, I am puzzled
to conceive how the Church of the faithful was of the same nature
with ours."[1]

Gradually he won back the loyalty of his people and rebuilt and
strengthened the parochial life of the parish. This was made all the
easier by the Roman Catholics themselves, since the more extreme
their onslaught became, the less acceptable their arguments appeared to the mass of the people. Yet neither directly nor indirectly, by word or deed, did Sharp seem to reflect upon the king
or the royal policy, always being careful to distinguish between the
Roman Catholic monarch to whom he owed obedience and the
mass of the papists, whom he regarded as aliens and enemies, and
the fair and lawful target of his eloquence. Once bitten, twice shy.

An interesting sidelight on this "Roman Controversy" is its supposed connection with the source of Jonathan Swift's *Tale of a Tub*.
It has been suggested[2] that the story of the *Tale* was borrowed by
Swift from one of Sharp's sermons, *i.e.* the notorious address
which brought about his suspension in 1686 and contained his
answer to "the little manuscript paper" concerning "the only
visible Church". That answer proceeded as follows:[3] "Why now
methinks, this is just such an argument as this:—A Father be-
queaths a large estate among his children, and their children after
them. They do for some generations quietly and peaceably enjoy
their several shares, without disturbance from each other. At last
one branch of the family (and not the eldest house neither) starts
up, and being of greater power than the rest, and having got some
of the same family to join with him, very imprudently challength
the whole estate to himself, and those that adhere to him; and
would dispossess all the rest of the descendants, accounting them
no better than bastards, though they be far more in number than his
own party, and have a far greater share in the inheritance. Upon
this they contest their own right against him, alledging their
father's will and testament, and their long possession, and that
they are lawfully descended from their common ancestor. But this
gentleman, who would lord it over his brethren, offers this irre-

---

[1] L-B-S. MSS., Box 3, Bundle H. 2b.
[2] *The Protestant Advocate*, May 1814 (afterwards reprinted in the *Gentleman's Magazine*),
pp. 356-360.
[3] *Archbishop Sharp's Works*, vol. vii, Sermon 6, edn. 1754.

NONCONFORMIST, ROMAN CATHOLIC, NON-JUROR 101

fragable argument for the justice of his claim. If, says he, you deny me and my adherents to be the sole proprietors of this estate, then it lies upon you to show, that ever since the death of our progenitor, who left us the estate, there hath appeared some of the family, who have always opposed my claim to this estate. But THAT you cannot show; and, therefore, I have an undoubted title to the whole estate: I am Lord of the whole inheritance.

"I do appeal to any man living, whether this plea would pass in any court of judicature; nay, whether any private man, tho' never so learned, can believe that this insolent Pretender doth offer any fair reason for the disseising the coheirs of their inheritance. And yet this is just the argument with which those learned gentlemen would persuade us to give up our birthright, to depart from that share of the inheritance we have in the Catholic Church.

"Well, but what will the coheirs that are concerned say to this argument? Why, there are three so obvious to be said to it, that if the persons concerned have not the wit to hit upon them, they are fit to come under the custody and guardianship of this pretended heir-general. May they not say to this gentleman that makes so universal a claim: Sir, your claim was not so early as the death of our fore-father, who left us this joint inheritance. Your ancestors and ours lived a great while peaceably together, without any clashing about this estate; and we were suffered for some ages to enjoy our own right, without any molestation from you or those you derive from: And the case being so, there was no need of opposing your pretences, because you made none. But then (which is the second thing) when you did set up for this principality, and wheedled some of our family and forced others to join with you, you know that you were presently opposed by others of our family, who would not so easily part from their rights. You know that as soon as ever you made your claim, there were some that stoutly declared against it, tho' they had no power, and strength and interest enough in the world to stem the torrent of your ambition.

"But then thirdly may they say; supposing it was not so; supposing you had met with no rub in your pretences (which yet you know you did); supposing our family were not so suddenly aware of the mischief that would come upon them from those your usurpations, as to make a present opposition; doth not it follow that because no opposition was just then made to your pretences, that therefore your pretentions to the whole estate are justifiable? No, we can prove that they are not so; for it is plain by the testament, by the settlement of our common father, that we have as much right to our parts in this estate as you have, or as your ancestors ever had. Tell not us, that you were not at first, or that you were not always opposed in your claim. But tell us by what right or justice you can pretend to be the sole lord of this inheritance. Let the will of our common ancestor be produced, and that will plainly show, that we have as much a share in this estate as you have.[1] The allegory is so pat to our business, and the application of it so easy to our present case, that I think I should injure the most vulgar understanding, if I should suspect his ability to make that use of it, which I intend."

The general resemblances between this allegory and Swift's story in the *Tale of a Tub* are perfectly obvious; but to say that "the sermon referred to is one of fourteen which are devoted to an elaborate exposure of the errors and corruptions of the Church of Rome, furnishing indeed, even to minute details, the whole text for Swift's satire, which follows Sharp's commentary step by step",[2] is an entirely different question. Indeed, there are very strong reasons for doubting whether Swift ever made use of the sermon at all. It is to be noted, for instance, that this series of sermons was not printed until thirty-one years after the *Tale of a Tub* had been published. Swift was in Ireland at the time when the first sermons were preached at St. Giles';[3] and there is good reason to believe that the *Tale* already existed in manuscript at this date. Furthermore, a careful comparison of the two allegories shows marked divergences. For instance, Swift's "heirs" were three sons, while Sharp's were "some generations"; and again, in Swift's satire the plot hinged on the coats which the father gave to his sons, but Sharp's allegory centred round "the insolent Pretender" who made such preposterous claims. In fact, when the matter is closely sifted, there is little in common except the ancestor, the will and the descendants. Swift may well have heard of Sharp's sermon—it caused enough stir at the time—but on the other hand he could quite easily have thought of the father, the will and the sons for himself. Stories of a similar nature were much older than Sharp's version, and Dryden had already made use of one in his *Religio Laici* (1682).

But the interesting part about all this is the legend which grew up in the eighteenth century that Sharp, angered by the *Tale*, was

---

[1] *Cf.* Dryden's reply in *The Hind and the Panther.*
[2] Churton Collins, *Jonathan Swift*, p. 47.   [3] May 1686.

mainly responsible for Swift's failure to secure a bishopric. Swift himself lent colour to this supposition by declaring in his *Apology for the Tale* that sensible clergymen ought to be pleased at having the errors and superstitions of religion so clearly exposed, but "he (the author) has now given over these thoughts since the *weightiest* men in the *weightiest* stations, are pleased to think it a more dangerous point to laugh at those corruptions in religion, which they themselves must disapprove, than to endeavour pulling up those very foundations, wherein all christians have agreed".[1] Here he was certainly alluding to Sharp; and in his famous poem "The Author upon Himself", published during 1714, we find the lines:

> "By an old —— pursued
> A crazy prelate and a royal prude."

Relying on this and other contemporary evidence,[2] Dr. Johnson wrote in 1781: "Archbishop Sharp and the Duchess of Somerset by shewing it [*Tale of a Tub*] to the Queen debarr'd him from a bishoprick."[3]

Thomas Sheridan, on the other hand, suggested some three years later that while the intervention of the "crazy prelate" failed, "the old ——" was more successful, since the queen became so incensed by Swift's attack on the duchess contained in the *Windsor Prophecy* that "as a mark of her displeasure, passed Swift by, and bestowed the Bishoprick on another".[4]

The true facts, however, are somewhat different. Sharp had nothing whatever to do with Swift's failure to secure the see of Waterford in 1708;[5] and in 1712, when the deanery of Wells fell vacant, his influence was only one of several exerted against Swift's promotion. It was then, probably in 1713, when the vacancy had still not been filled, that he showed Anne the *Tale of a Tub*, but apparently quickly repented of his action and promised Swift he would never speak against him more.[6] Possibly this was because he had just read the latter's *Project for the Advancement of Religion*

---

[1] *Prose Works of Jonathan Swift*, vol. i, p. 15. Edit. Temple Scott.

[2] See Abel Boyer, vol. vii, p. 163; and Macpherson, *Original Papers*, ii, 563. A letter from Schutz, Hanoverian envoy to Robethon in Hanover: "He [Sharp] hindered her Majesty from giving a Deanery in England to the Sieur Savist, the favourite and creature of the Prime-minister, who gave him since a Deanery in Dublin."

[3] Johnson, *Lives of the Poets*, vol. iii, p. 10. Edit. Hill.

[4] *Life of Doctor Swift*, p. 84, edn. 1787.

[5] C. H. Firth, "Dean Swift and Ecclesiastical Preferment" in *Review of English Studies*, Jan. 1926, p. 3 (reprinted pamphlet).

[6] *Journal to Stella*, pp. 460 and 461: "The Archbishop of York says he will never more speak against me."

and the Reformation of Manners. Moreover, Swift himself seems to
have regarded the archbishop as a tool rather than a principal.
"York is from Lambeth sent", he wrote, "to show the Queen a
dangerous treatise writ against the spleen"; and dismissed him as
"Poor York! the harmless tool of others' hate."[1] Tenison, Nottingham and the Duchess of Somerset all played an equally subordi-
nate part in his discomfiture. His chief and immovable enemy was
the "royal prude" herself, who refused to permit Oxford to badger
her into richly promoting one whose reputation was so un-
pleasantly notorious. Thus, just as Bolingbroke had to rest content
with a viscounty, Swift received no more than an Irish deanery
from a mistress of high moral sensibility.

If the rector of St. Giles' had proved himself a redoubtable
opponent of Nonconformity and Roman Catholicism, he was to
show an equal hostility to the non-jurors, although with considerably more reluctance.

The non-juring position was simple and logical, but narrow-
minded and impracticable;and while no one could fail to admire
the high principles of the seven bishops, four hundred clergy and
many laymen who went out into the wilderness rather than accept
the Revolution settlement, it is perfectly legitimate to question
both their statesmanship and loyalty to the Anglican Church.
The famous non-juror John Lake, bishop of Chichester, summed
up their attitude succinctly enough on his death-bed (August 27,
1689): "That religion of the Church of England taught me the
doctrine of Non-Resistance and Passive Obedience, which I have
accordingly inculcated upon others, and which I took to be the
distinguishing character of the Church of England, I adhere no
less firmly and steadfastly to that, and in consequence of it have
incurred a suspension from the exercise of my office and expected
a deprivation. I find in so doing much inward satisfaction, and if
the Oath had been tendered at the peril of my life, I could only
have obeyed by suffering."[2] Why such a saintly man and many
like him made this choice, while other equally good churchmen,
such as Sharp and Tillotson, took the opposite decision, is worth
considering in some detail.

Charles I had broken his pledged word to Strafford, to Cromwell and to the New Model Army; but neither by word nor deed

[1] "The Author upon Himself."
[2] P. E. More and F. L. Cross, *Anglicanism*, p. 695.

would he swerve a hand's breadth from his determination to defend and uphold the Anglican Church. It was that determination as much as anything else which brought him to the scaffold. On the other hand, the Puritans had done their best to destroy Anglicanism. Episcopacy was abolished, the use of the Prayer Book was forbidden, and the clergy were turned out of their livings. Consequently the Restoration meant more to the Church than to any other section of the community; and when restoration was crowned by the dominance given by the Clarendon Code the cup of its joy and thankfulness brimmed over. Charles II, the son of a martyred father, the healer of the Church's wounds, the donor, albeit a trifle unwillingly, of the Clarendon Code, came to be regarded not only as the saviour of his children, the Anglican clergy, but as their sole barrier against renewed spoliation and persecution.

James I's dictum "No Bishop, no King" had been proved in the realm of practical politics; and hence James' further teaching about the divine right of kings, summarised in his political treatise *True Law of Free Monarchies, or the Mutual Duty betwixt a Free King and his Subjects*, was now zealously embraced by all Anglicans, many of whom had formerly been but lukewarm, as the sole bulwark against republicanism and Puritanism. This doctrine maintained that monarchy is divine, that hereditary right was unassailable, that kings were accountable to none but God, and all resistance to one's lawful prince was unforgivable and indefensible.[1] That Charles himself proved to be no such good churchman as his father was certainly disappointing. Nevertheless the deliberate attempt by Shaftesbury and the whigs, by the exploitation of the Popish Plot, to undo the work of the Restoration, restore the power of the sects, and perhaps even, under cover of championing Monmouth against James, bring back the Republic, rallied tory statesmen and Anglican churchmen alike to the side of strict hereditary succession. They cast out the Exclusion Bill, drove Shaftesbury into exile, beheaded the republicans Russell and Sydney, muzzled the press, renewed the persecution of the Dissenters, and smashed the whig strongholds in the towns by compelling the corporations to surrender their charters and receive new ones at the king's hands. In fact, during the last four years of Charles' lifetime, churchmen, tories and royalists were everywhere triumphant and the pulpits rang with perfervid and extravagant declarations concerning the divine right of kings

[1] See G. P. Gooch, *Political Thought from Bacon to Halifax*, p. 12.

and the sin of any form of resistance, in any conceivable circumstances, to the royal will.

The lesson of the Great Rebellion had now been reinforced by the struggle over the Exclusion Bill, and James as the rightful heir, despite his Romanism, became more popular with the Church than Charles himself. The defeat of Monmouth, the acknowledged leader of the sects, merely confirmed that allegiance. "I die a Protestant of the Church of England," Monmouth affirmed on the scaffold, which immediately earned the rebuke, "My Lord, if you be of the Church of England, you must acknowledge the doctrine of Non-resistance to be true."[1] No wonder, then, it seemed an impossibility that churchmen, even moderate and far-seeing churchmen, would ever run so counter to their beliefs as actively to resist the king. But James, who believed in miracles, made that impossibility come to pass.

When the most loyal parliament that ever sat refused to sanction his schemes, it was prorogued and did not meet again before the Revolution. Instead, James sought to attain his ends through the direct prerogative powers of the crown, aided and abetted by a packed Judicial Bench. By means of his "dispensing" power he filled the army with Roman Catholics and introduced them into the ministry and civil service, while corporations, lord lieutenancies and justiceships of the peace were purged of their too independent tories. The Church herself, as has already been seen, was directly attacked by the setting up of the Ecclesiastical Commission, which suspended the bishop of London and put three great Oxford colleges (Christ Church, University and Magdalen) under Roman rule, expelling the fellows of Magdalen for refusing to elect a Roman Catholic as their president. Meantime Cambridge had lost its vice-chancellor, and in London "popish institutes were established, a chapel in the City, a Jesuit school at the Savoy, a girls' school in St. Martin's Lane, a Franciscan Friary in Lincoln's Inn Fields, one for the Dominicans near by, a Benedictine house in Clerkenwell. A papal nuncio was publicly received at court. Steps were taken to revive a Roman Catholic hierarchy by the consecration of bishops. Pressure was put on corporations of various kinds, such as the Inns of Court, to admit papists."[2] James even went so far as to appoint Roman Catholics to church livings. The very freehold of the clergy was in danger; for if he remained

[1] J. R. Tanner, *English Constitutional Conflicts in the Seventeenth Century*, p. 250.
[2] G. N. Clark, *The Later Stuarts*, p. 118.

unchecked, the king could turn them all out on one trumped-up excuse or another. Finally there came the first Declaration of Indulgence (April 1687), whereby James hoped to secure the active co-operation of the Dissenters in his plans, not only by ceasing his previous intense persecution of the sects, but by granting them religious toleration and introducing them into political and civil offices. He sought, however, to soften and disguise the blow to the Anglicans by promising to maintain the Established Church, and by confirming the tenure of "the holders of monastic and church lands secularised in Tudor times".[1] The Church was not deceived. Cromwell's men, along with the Romanists and placemen, were to be introduced haphazard into the corporations, lord-lieutenancies and justiceships of the peace, with the eventual purpose of returning a parliament to Westminster of their own kind which would repeal the Test and Habeas Corpus Acts and legalise the Ecclesiastical Commission and all the rest of James' despotic creations and actions.

Matters came to a head with the birth of the "Old Pretender" (June 10, 1688), who displaced his Protestant half-sisters, Mary and Anne, from the direct line of succession and foreshadowed a long list of Roman Catholic kings. James was but mortal, and loyal churchmen had, throughout all his illegalities, clung desperately to the hope that his works would perish with him. If, however, the present king could now live long enough to stabilise the edifice that he had raised, popular liberties and the Protestant Faith, judging by continental precedents, would quickly and permanently disappear. So, despite all the doctrines of divine right and non-resistance, the highest of high churchmen could no longer acquiesce in the royal policy or even passively submit to it. Their allegiance was, indeed, soon put to the test, for James commanded that the second Declaration of Indulgence (April 27, 1688), which approximated very closely to the first, should be read from every pulpit in the land on two successive Sundays. Any clergyman who refused to carry out this order was liable to be deprived by the Ecclesiastical Commission; while every clergyman who obeyed would condone the illegalities of the crown. The time had come for united action; and after anxious and protracted consultations Archbishop Sancroft, with the approval of the majority of the bishops and lay nobility, advised disobedience. It was a momentous decision, for it was equivalent to saying that the Declaration

[1] Op. cit., p. 120.

was illegal and that the king by himself had no right to suspend statutes. Sharp, who accepted the archbishop's guidance, excused his flouting of the royal order on the following grounds: "All the law that I know of, which relates to the publishing or declaring things in the Church, is the rubric in the Communion Service which follows after the Nicene Creed. 'Nothing shall be proclaimed or published in the Church during the time of divine service, but what is prescribed by the rules of this book, or enjoined by the king or by the Ordinary of the Place.' . . . We have taken an oath to obey our Ordinaries in all lawful and honest things; and a higher obligation cannot be laid upon us to obey the king. . . . Even our obedience to the king is to be extended no further than *licita et honesta*."[1]

Here, then, we are given, by a typical tory clergyman, who believed in divine right, passive obedience, and that the king could do no wrong, a precise statement that the law is above the king, which was formerly a purely whig conception of authority. There could be no more striking commentary on the follies of James II.

Acting upon the advice of the archbishop, the mass of the clergy refused to read the Declaration of Indulgence, and some even went so far as to preach against it, like Samuel Wesley, who is supposed to have taken as his text those famous words from the third chapter of Daniel: "Be it known unto thee, O king, that we will not serve thy gods, nor worship the golden image which thou hast set up." A few placemen and vicars of Bray obeyed the royal command, but when Bishop Sprat, who was officiating at Westminster Abbey, began to declaim its provisions, the entire congregation walked out in protest.[2]

The famous trial of the seven bishops, five of whom, including Lake and Sancroft, afterwards became non-jurors, was the final straw that broke the Church's allegiance. They had petitioned the king in the most moderate terms against the reading of the Declaration, and their brutal treatment left churchmen no choice but to resist. On June 30 the bishops were acquitted. Nevertheless James refused to own defeat. "Orders had been given July 12th, and were directed to all Chancellors, Archdeacons, Commissaries, and officials, to enquire strictly within their respective jurisdictions, in what churches or chapels his Majesty's Declaration had

[1] *Life of Archbishop Sharp*, vol. i, p. 94.
[2] J. R. Tanner, *English Constitutional Conflicts in the Seventeenth Century*, p. 259.

been read or omitted, etc. And to transmit an account thereof."[1]
These orders were ignored. Whereupon the Commissioners summoned the archdeacons to appear before them on August 16,
1688, and explain the reason why. Instead they met two days
previously at Doctors' Commons and, after a protracted discussion,
decided to stay away. Sharp, as archdeacon of Berkshire, attended
the meeting and voted with the majority.[2]

Fearing a repetition of the Seven Bishops fiasco, the Commissioners wisely forbore from proceeding to extremities, contenting
themselves with demanding that the archdeacons should "make
this a matter of their enquiry at their visitation",[3] and render an
account to them before December 6. By that date William III was
in England and the Revolution had begun.

Taking all these facts into consideration, it is scarcely remarkable that erstwhile loyal tory churchmen so far forgot their principles as to desert and resist the king *de jure*, and eventually swear
oaths of fealty to the king *de facto*. Sharp and his many tory friends
were, in fact, practical statesmanlike churchmen, who realised that
the spirit of non-resistance and passive obedience had already been
shattered beyond repair; and it would be well, alike in the interests of their country and of their religion, to make a fresh start
with leaders whom they could trust. Inevitably they were accused
of taking the new oaths simply in order to secure promotion or to
retain their present positions in the Church. This was quite untrue
and most unfair. Sharp, as will be seen, actually went so far as to
refuse point-blank to accept a bishopric from which a non-juror
had been evicted.[4]

The non-jurors, on the other hand, although the majority had
certainly resisted James over the Declaration of Indulgence, and
were perfectly willing in practice to submit to the rule of his successors, yet, when it came to the point, could not bring them-

[1] *Life of Archbishop Sharp*, vol. i, p. 93.
[2] "He was summoned with the other Archdeacons before the Ecclesiastical Commission, for disobeying the King's orders in respect to the 'Declaration for liberty of
conscience'. But they agreed not to appear before that court, and Dr. Sharp drew up
the reasons for their refusal." See the article "John Sharp" in the *General Biographical
Dictionary*, 1816.
[3] *Life of Archbishop Sharp*, vol. i, p. 96.
[4] "Beveridge was not the only clergyman who refused to succeed to a see vacated by
deprivation. Sharp, who had acted a conspicuous part previous to the Revolution and
who afterwards became Archbishop of York, entertained the same scruples. He was
mentioned by the King as a proper person to succeed to one of the vacancies. Norwich
was pressed upon him; but he refused to accept of any; not from scruples of conscience
respecting the oaths, but from affection to the Deprived Bishop." See T. Lathbury,
History of the Non-Jurors, p. 91.

selves to accept as valid the Revolution Settlement, which had not only decided that James by his flight had "abdicated" the throne, but that this throne was now "vacant" and could lawfully be bestowed as the Convention Parliament thought fit. James was not dead; neither had he voluntarily abdicated. Actually he was making vigorous efforts to recover his own. Hence, whatever might be their personal opinion concerning the birth of the Prince of Wales, the king was still king by reason of his divine right; they had sworn to obey him; and they could not in consequence take similar oaths to another, intruded, monarch. The political expediency of politicians of the type of Danby, who drew a distinction between a *de facto* and *de jure* recognition, appeared merely hypocritical and time-serving; and the purely whig contention that there was a "contract between King and People, involving the forfeiture of the Crown in case of breach of that contract"[1] seemed sheer blasphemy. Consequently, they followed Bishop Lake into the wilderness for the selfsame principles: non-resistance, passive obedience, the divine right of kings.

They were, indeed, comparatively few in number, but powerful alike in intellectual ability and personal prestige. Archbishop Sancroft might be old and broken in spirit; yet nothing could dim the saintliness of Ken, bishop of Bath and Wells, the fighting strength of Hickes, dean of Worcester, and Jeremy Collier, and the high intellectual qualities of Charles Leslie. Neither were they prepared to take their eviction lying down. The peace-loving Frampton, bishop of Gloucester, and the saintly Ken were certainly ready to sacrifice everything without a struggle; and Ken was even willing to go on communicating with the Revolution Church, while others like the laymen Robert Nelson, Brokesby and Henry Dodwell eventually returned to the fold. But the majority, led by Lloyd, bishop of Norwich, White, bishop of Peterborough, Wagstaffe, Hickes and Jeremy Collier, turned fiercely on their pursuers. For they not only promptly organised their own *Ecclesia Anglicana* outside the official Establishment, but proceeded to argue in an acrimonious pamphlet offensive that theirs was the one true Catholic Church in England, that the bishops who had accepted the sees vacant by deprivation were schismatical, and those who communicated with them were committing sin. These claims were bolstered up by the theory, put forward by Leslie, that the Church was, in the last resort, entirely independent of the

---

[1] G. M. Trevelyan, *The English Revolution, 1688-89*, p. 140.

State. Church and State might normally be bound together by the bonds of self-interest, co-operating to promote the good government of the people in temporal and spiritual matters. In civil affairs the Church would be subject to the State, even to the administration of her own temporal possessions; but similarly the State must submit to the Church in regard to the things of the spirit. Miss Hawkins, speaking of this conception of Leslie's concerning the right relationship between Church and State, writes: "The one possible way out of the impasse caused by the Regale was, in Leslie's view, that the Church should make good her claim to complete spiritual independence. 'The right to meet, to consult, to make rules or canons for the regulation of the society is essential to every society as such and consequently to the Church as she is a society.' This right the Church must never renounce, for it is essential to her being. Nothing short of insistence upon her continued existence as a society separate and distinct from the State could preserve her from extinction. She must be as ready to renounce her claim to authority in civil affairs as she was valiant to deny the like claim to interference in spiritual matters by the State. 'Let in the State upon the circumstances of the Church, or the Church upon those of the State, they will soon draw the essentials with them. Therefore, in order to their good agreement, it is necessary they be kept wholly independent and unlimitable by one another in their several spheres. The medium betwixt these is plain, and it is to keep those powers, the sacred and the civil as they are in their own nature, distinct and independent of each other. They act in two spheres, and therefore, can never interfere. But if either encroach upon the other there is confusion without end or remedy.' "[1]

Thus the non-jurors strove to reinforce their purely political revolt against the Revolution Settlement by a more convincing and high-souled spiritual revolt against an encroachment by the State, in the person of William III, upon the independence of the Church. The State, they admitted, had every right to deprive them of their temporalities, but the spiritual powers and functions of bishops and clergy had been conferred by Christ Himself, and only He could recall them. For certain great offences the Church authorities, acting as His representatives, could unfrock, suspend, or otherwise punish a guilty cleric; but no one had

[1] L. M. Hawkins, *Allegiance in Church and State: The Problem of the Non-Jurors in the English Revolution*, p. 157.

attempted—it would have been ridiculous to have tried—to convict them of any spiritual or moral misconduct. They had been evicted simply and solely for the political offence of refusing to take the oaths to William and Mary or to recognise the work of the Revolution Government. Unfortunately for these non-juring professions of martyrdom for the sake of spiritual freedom, history, and indeed recent history, confuted them completely.

If William had no right to nominate Tillotson to Canterbury in place of the evicted Sancroft, then certainly James II had no power to suspend the bishop of London, nor Charles II or James for that matter to omit to issue a licence to Convocation, from 1664 to 1688, so that it could sit and act. Besides, to push their own arguments to their logical conclusion, the State had the *right* to deprive bishops of their temporalities, and of their work within the specific diocese to which they had been nominated by the crown. Meanwhile no attempt was ever made by William or any other sovereign to unfrock or degrade the non-jurors or challenge their authority to administer the sacraments.

In fact, everything in Leslie's eyes hinged on whether or not the king was *de jure*, when churchmen must all submit to his decrees; or *de facto*, when resistance and secession was the only possible course to adopt.

The non-jurors were bound to secede, since they could not take the oaths to or pray in public for William and Mary; but naturally enough, in order to avoid the taint of schism, they sought to justify their conduct to themselves, their contemporaries and posterity, and not, it would seem, entirely without success. They sincerely believed at the time that they and they alone out of the entire Anglican Church had preserved the spirit as well as the letter of their shibboleths.

Never before or since has the Established Church found itself in such a humiliating and difficult position. It had, indeed, been hoist with its own petard. But unfortunately the non-jurors made matters even worse by launching bitter attacks against the compromisers.

On June 28, 1691, Sharp preached a farewell sermon[1] at St. Giles' before leaving that parish for the archbishopric of York. This sermon was examined in an open letter published shortly

---

[1] *Archbishop Sharp's Sermons*, vol. ii, Sermon 9. Here he directly referred to and condemned the non-jurors: "What an unaccountable Humour it is to make a rent and Schism in the Church upon a mere Point of State."

afterwards and addressed to the archbishop. The author remained anonymous, although in all probability Hickes, if not the actual writer, instigated the composition of the epistle, which contained a bitter attack on Sharp's supposed apostasy: "I find you so altered like many of your brethren from yourself, though Dr. Sharp is still the same person, yet I do not find that the Dean of Norwich and the Archbishop are the same men . . . I hope to see such Bishops and Priests become base and contemptible, that expound St. Paul as you and Dr. Sherlock have done, and advance allegiance to the Government upon a principle that is destructive to it, and the true and lasting peace of the kingdom, in which our happiness does consist. . . . Two years ago you were not of opinion, at least you were not fully persuaded, that the text (Romans xiii. 1) allowed us to pray on behalf of the king *de facto* against the king *de jure* or on behalf of a king in possession against the legal king, as you and Dr. Sherlock still acknowledge King James to be, though he is out of possession: or else why did you, at his House in the Temple, express so much dislike and dissatisfaction at the prayers in the office for the first General Fast? But the World is since well mended with you and what was a matter of difficulty to you then is not so now: for since that time you have better studied the Great Apostle at *Canterbury* than you did at Norwich, and plainly discovered that he is and always was for the *uppermost*, and directs us to pay our allegiance and devotion without enquiring into titles, to the king on the Throne."[1]

However, the more moderate Dodwell wrote very differently in *The Case in View*: "Our truly Catholic doctrines of passive obedience and non-resistance are still maintained by many of our late Fathers and brethren, notwithstanding their new erected altars. But by none more openly and avowedly than the present excellent Metropolitan of York."[2]

It must certainly never be forgotten that despite their many personal faults and shortcomings the high-churchmanship of Sharp and his conforming tory friends did much by its wise compromise to preserve the continuity of Anglican thought and teaching. The doctrines advanced by whig low churchmen of the

---

[1] Hickes continued: "But, my Lord, besides that point which you call a State point, there is also a Church point, of which you take no notice . . . and that is the putting of new Bishops into the thrones of the old ones, whose deprivation they pretend to be null and unjust." See *An Apology for the New Separation: in a Letter to Dr. John Sharp, Archbishop of York, occasioned by his Farewell Sermon*, 4to, 1691, p. 1.

[2] T. Lathbury, *History of the Non-Jurors*, p. 117.

type of Tenison or Burnet led directly to Erastianism and to the Church becoming a mere department of State; while the non-jurors by their separation, although their consistency and courage under adversity may be respected, bear the charge of deserting their Church in its hour of need. It was Sharp and his friends who, by their fierce attachment to its creed, constitution and independence, and by their steadfast opposition to the deism, agnosticism and latitudinarianism of the day, not only kept Anglicanism alive, but triumphant over all its enemies.

Sharp's personal dealings with the more prominent non-jurors, although they carry us on to a later stage in his career, are worth considering in the present context. He was a good friend of Robert Nelson,[1] whose warm admiration for Tillotson made a strong link between them; and was at length instrumental in bringing this saintly man back into the Anglican fold.[2] For, after the death of Lloyd of Norwich in 1709, Nelson, Dodwell, Brokesby and others wrote to Ken, as the last surviving non-juring bishop, asking him, 'as the only survivor of the invalidly deprived bishops, and as thereby having it in his power now to free, not only his private diocese, but the whole National Church from the Schism introduced by filling the sees, whether he insisted on his rights as diocesan".[3] Ken replied that far from doing so he was himself considering the possibility of communicating with his successor at Bath and Wells. Consequently, "on the first Sunday in Lent (February 26th) Cherry and Dodwell went to their Parish Church with their families for the first time since the secession. Archbishop Sharp, who had taken a leading part in bringing about the healing of the Schism, administered the Communion to Nelson on Easter Day (1709). The bells rang out their peal of joy for the termination of the Schism, which had vexed the Parish as it had vexed the Nation."[4] Their example was followed by others.

Sharp interested himself in the Scottish non-jurors and kept up a regular correspondence with Bishop Rose;[5] and also apparently with Archibald Campbell, who wrote to the College of Bishops on

[1] Cf. J. H. Overton and C. J. Abbey, *The English Church in the Eighteenth Century*, p. 44 *et seq.*

[2] *Life of Archbishop Sharp*, vol. ii, p. 32.

[3] E. H. Plumptre, *Life of Thomas Ken*, vol. ii, p. 195.

[4] Ibid., p. 195. Sharp records that on February 15 he received "the good news of Mr. Nelson's intention to return to our Communion", and on "April 9th being Easter Day I preached at St. Mildred's Poultry, and administered the Sacrament; where was present Mr. Nelson, which was the first time he had communicated in the Sacrament since the Revolution." See *Life of Archbishop Sharp*, vol. ii, p. 33.

[5] J. H. Overton, *The Non-Jurors: Their Lives, Principles and Writings*, p. 435.

April 13, 1722: "If I could have complied with the times the late Archbishop of York offered me from his then Mistress the first Bishopric that should fall unless it were one of the biggest of all."[1] It was the archbishop, too, who counselled the queen to make renewed advances to Ken, and, even when this offer had been rejected, remained on the most cordial terms with him until the end of his life. Another correspondent was Thomas Brett, vicar of Betteshanger, who indeed only became a convert to the non-jurors in July 1715.[2]

The whole non-juring controversy was certainly utterly repugnant to Sharp, who, while sympathising deeply with their theories and admitting their courage and consistency, was yet a sufficiently practical churchman to realise the folly of their action. When every hand was needed on deck to keep the ship afloat amid the storms of the Revolution Settlement, the captain and some of the ablest of the crew did their best to scuttle her. That was how Sharp saw it. However, unlike Burnet and other whig bishops, he opposed the idea of trying them by court-martial on the grounds that their skill, courage and craftsmanship were still sorely required to bring the whole ship's company safely to shore.

[1] The Brett MSS. See H. Broxap, *The Later Non-Jurors*, p. 13.
[2] H. Broxap, *The Later Non-Jurors*, pp. 20 and 21. Sharp also reviewed Hickes' book *Answer to the Rights of the Church*, which Nelson sent him, very favourably. See L-B-S. MSS., Box 4, Bundle R. 29.

CHAPTER V

RECTOR, DEAN, ARCHBISHOP

JOHN SHARP took no active part in the Revolution. His reactions, such as they were, were purely negative.

When, after the birth of the "Old Pretender", the clergy were commanded to keep Sunday, June 17, 1688, as a day of national thanksgiving "for her Majesty's happy delivery",[1] Sharp, who was preaching at Gray's Inn, completely ignored the order. Again, as has already been noted, he voted with the majority of the archdeacons at Doctors' Commons against appearing before the Commissioners.[2] Otherwise he divided his time as usual between his parish of St. Giles and the deanery at Norwich. The only indication he gave of the gravity of the situation was to be seen in the longer periods spent, especially at Norwich, in religious meditation, as though he had convinced himself that a period of trial and possibly persecution lay ahead, and by hard spiritual training he must fit himself to meet and endure it. This rigorous striving after perfection, of which more will be heard at a later date, brought on a recurrence of his old Cambridge fever, and from October 1688 until the following Christmas he was confined to his bed. That he had relinquished all hope of further preferment can be seen from an interview with White, the engraver, which had taken place two years previously. It was at the time when Compton was being tried by the Ecclesiastical Commission, and White, no doubt regarding all this publicity as a good advertisement, was anxious to take and publish his portrait. It would certainly have sold well; but Sharp, who was always averse to publicity, declined to be drawn. However, on being pressed he smilingly consented to allow the engraver to take his picture "when he was a Bishop . . . supposing himself safe in such a promise".[3]

Now the tables had been turned with a vengeance, and a new and Protestant king and queen sat on the throne of England. Even so it appeared that he would be passed over. William, himself a Calvinist, distrusted the high churchmen who had been mainly responsible for the persecution of the Dissenters, and no one could

---

[1] *Life of Archbishop Sharp*, vol. i, p. 92.   [2] August 14 and 15, 1688.
[3] *Life of Archbishop Sharp*, vol. i, p. 89.

deny that Sharp, unlike Tillotson, was a strong Anglican and sympathised with the non-jurors. Then, he had taken no very active part in the Revolution and its Settlement was not entirely to his taste, although eventually he accepted both with a good grace. But perhaps his principal offence was that he refused point-blank to quit his allegiance to James until Parliament had declared that the exiled monarch's desertion of the government and king-dom constituted an abdication.

Preaching before William on January 27, and again before the House of Commons on the 30th, 1689/90, while the abdication and vacancy of the throne were still under discussion, he boldly prayed for King James. This was a particularly courageous action the second occasion, since on the 28th the House of Commons had voted for both abdication and vacancy, and certain members con-strued Sharp's prayer as a condemnation of their action. But as the Bill had not yet passed the Lords he was perfectly within his rights in doing so. Nevertheless there was much resentment among the Commons, and some heated talk of showing their displeasure by not granting him the customary vote of thanks. More moderate opinions finally prevailed, and they "Resolved, *Nemine Contra-dicente*. That the Thanks of this House be given to Dr. Sharp, Dean of Norwich, for his sermon preached before this House on Wednesday last, and that he be desired to print the same. And that Sir John Knight and Mr. Auditor Dane, do acquaint him with such, the thanks and desire of this House."[1]

The indignation of the Commons was the more understandable since the sermon itself, as well as the prayer, appeared to be deliberately offensive. It contained an attack on the Jesuitical doctrine affirming the legality of deposing and even murdering heretical princes,[2] and was taken to imply that James II had been wrongfully expelled from his kingdom. Actually Sharp, who was preaching on the anniversary of Charles I's execution,[3] made use of an address which had been composed as early as 1679 and had been delivered more than once before without causing any com-ment. As soon as these facts were made clear all feelings of resent-ment quickly died away. None the less John Evelyn's comment in

---

[1] Ibid., vol. i, p. 99.   [2] L-B-S. MSS., Box 4, Bundle P. 1.
[3] The Prayer Book of 1662 contained three additional Red-Letter Days, namely: January 30, May 29 and November 5. Services suitable to these occasions and ap-proved by Convocation were also added, but only by means of a Royal Mandate issued afresh at the accession of each new sovereign. Of the three, that on January 30 commemorating the martyrdom of Charles I was the most popular. In 1859 these services were withdrawn from the Book of Common Prayer by Royal Warrant.

his diary, under the date of January 30, 1689, is quite under-standable: "Dr. Sharp preached before the Commons, but was disliked and not thanked for his sermon"; and Sharp himself wisely recorded in his own memoranda: "I did not print my sermon."[1]

Sharp seemed to have the happy knack of winning the favour of royal princesses. Queen Mary, who admired his preaching, now became his strong supporter, just as in later life he was to win the affections of Anne, and finally of the Electress Sophia. William profoundly distrusted the tory high churchmen and was con-temptuous of the ceremonies of Anglican worship;[2] but policy demanded that such men should be placated. Sharp, as the friend of Tillotson[3] and the Queen, and a moderate, if firm, Anglican, was consequently among those marked out for early promotion. "Burnet as usual was ready with his own advice. Either at Windsor or Sion he had drawn up, for the Prince's perusal, a curious paper of ecclesiastical counsel. Ten clergymen are recommended to the Prince's particular notice: Tillotson, Tenison, Sharp, Wake, Stillingfleet, Patrick, Fowler, Horneck, Sherlock and Ayrshott. . . . Great was Burnet's relief when the appointments were gazetted; for they were such as he would himself have desired. Tillotson, with unfeigned reluctance, for his health was failing and his temper pacific to a fault, was raised to the invidious eminence whence Sancroft perforce descended. Political differences at a subsequent date affected Burnet's estimate of Sharp, who had been raised to the metropolitan chair of York, but on the whole he concludes 'in two years' time the King has made fifteen bishops; and excepting what is to be said as to myself, it is visible that they are the worthiest and learnedest men, the best preachers, and the men of the gentlest and prudentest tempers that could be found'. . . . It was also observed that these were men not past fifty, whereas generally men had not been promoted formerly till their strength and parts began to sink with age."[4] But Sharp did not immediately become a bishop. His first preferment under William was to the deanery of Canterbury;[5] and he knew well enough to whom he

[1] *Life of Archbishop Sharp*, vol. i, p. 100.
[2] G. J. Renier, *William of Orange*, p. 147.
[3] *Cf.* A. H. Hore, *The Church in England from William III to Victoria*, p. 128 *et seq.* William had a tremendous admiration for Tillotson; and when he died the king said with tears: "I have lost the best friend I ever had, and the best man I ever knew."
[4] H. C. Foxcroft and Clarke, *Life of Gilbert Burnet*, pp. 257 and 304-305.
[5] *Calendar of State Papers Domestic: William and Mary*, p. 271: "Sept. 23rd, 1689. Warrant for a grant to John Sharp, D.D. of the Deanery of Canterbury, void by the Translation of Dr. John Tillotson to the Deanery of St. Paul's." *Cf. State Papers Domestic: William and Mary*, 2, No. 60.

was chiefly indebted for this fresh advancement, replying to the Earl of Nottingham's letter of congratulation in the following terms: "Be pleased to accept my most humble thanks for this new instance of your favour and kindness. . . . It is to your Father, my Lord and yourself that under God I owe all that I have in this world."[1]

The Finches had certainly been excellent patrons, and "Dismal" was now a power at court as one of the heads of the conforming tory party which had done so much to bring the Revolution to a successful conclusion. Towards the close of William's reign, however, he not only fell from power and out of favour, but was even suspected of conspiring against the crown.

The acceptance of Canterbury meant, of course, the vacation of Norwich. Of Sharp's work there during the eight odd years that he held the office of dean little of interest has survived. But in two particulars, at any rate, he impressed his personality upon the cathedral. Soon after his arrival in 1681 he was instrumental in commencing the building of the present library. The chapter minute book records that the dean gave £20 and each of the six prebendaries £10 for this purpose. At the same time there was a dispute as to whether or not the bishop's excommunications could be published in the cathedral. Sharp and the rest of the chapter withstood the bishop on this question and maintained successfully that the dean was the only ordinary of the cathedral church.[2]

Among the Lloyd-Baker-Sharp MSS. is a letter[3] addressed to "My worthy friend, Dr. Sharp, Dean of Norwich", which came from a certain Mrs. Frances Pullin. It is undated, but is worth quoting verbatim as giving some idea of the high esteem in which the dean was held:

"WORTHY SIR

You may as well wonder as I blush at my own confidence in giving you the trouble of perusing these impertinent lines of mine, but you have shown such a particular favour to me by affording me both your prayers and also some advice in my great distress that I should have thought myself the ungratefulest person living had I in silence buried such favours as I have received from you, and lest any other messenger should have mistaken their errand I thought fit to employ my pen that by it you may know

[1] *Life of Archbishop Sharp*, vol. i, p. 104.
[2] See *The Norwich Cathedral Chapter Minute Book*, 1681-1689.
[3] L-B-S. MSS., Box 4, Bundle M. 22.

my heart that it is full of thankfulness and real acknowledgements for your kindness towards me. Sir, I am now about leaving this place since the blessing of success is at present denied to those who have undertaken me. I shall endeavour to follow your wise and holy counsel and with patience submit to God only for a release out of these great afflictions which lie heavy upon me. I only now beg that to the rest of your favours you will add yet one more, which is to continue me in your address to heaven, that my weaker faith may not fail, and that upon my true repentance I may receive such a pardon, that though my body may be afflicted even to death yet my soul may be made fit to enjoy heaven at last. Sir, there is no possibility for me to render sufficient thanks to you, but if . . . you will make . . . myself happy in enjoying your company no place nor person shall make you more really welcome than her who takes upon her to subscribe herself etc.

Frances Pullin."

Sharp's appointment to the deanery of Canterbury did not as such affect his incumbency of St. Giles-in-the-Fields; but his subsequent promotion two years later to the archbishopric of York inevitably entailed its resignation. It will not then, at this juncture, be out of place to summarise and complete the story of his activities in this particular sphere of operations.

Something has already been said of his spiritual labours in the parish; but as the rector of an important London district he was also a lay administrator compelled to deal, in the widest sense of that word, with men and affairs both in and out of church, where his success or failure would often have decisive results. The problems were many and varied, but they can be roughly grouped together under the following heads: church buildings and properties, poverty, the "selected vestry", and personal.

Church Buildings and Properties.—Despite the fact that St. Giles' had been entirely rebuilt in 1630, and through the extraordinary generosity of the Duchess Dudley had been beautifully furnished and decorated, Sharp, when he first arrived there in 1675/6, quickly discovered that his new church was still sadly in need of repair. In fact, the builders had done their work so badly that, notwithstanding repeated reparations, it slowly but surely fell to pieces, until by 1715 it had reached a state of total decay, and a completely new building, with the exception of the vestries, was erected. Sharp, who had to contend with the old rotting fabric, found himself involved in the endless task of raising the necessary sums of money to prevent the entire structure from collapsing on his head. This entailed a perpetual drain on his own purse, time and energy. The churchyard was also a source of trouble and expense. The sexton, for example, on his own authority had made "lights" into the yard from his house, and refused to remove them; but was eventually forced to agree to give "as an acknowledgement to the Rector and Churchwardens yearly on Tuesday se'nnight after Easter, two fat capons ready dressed".[1]

It was, moreover, far too small and overcrowded. Nearly a century later an observer exclaimed: "I have, in the Churchyard of St. Giles, seen with horror, a great square pit with many rows of coffins piled one upon the other, all exposed to sight and smell; some of the piles were incomplete, expecting the mortality of the night. I turned away disgusted at the view, and scandalised at the want of police which so little regards the health of the living, as to permit so many putrid corpses tacked between some slight boards dispersing their dangerous effluvia over the capital."[2] The overcrowding was, of course, far worse in the seventeenth century, and additional pieces of ground could only be obtained by conceding unwarrantable privileges to individuals or by agreeing to vexatious conditions. A certain Mr. Speckart had in Charles I's time given some land, and was allowed in return to make a private entrance from his back premises into the churchyard. Lady Dudley and two other benefactors had already been granted similar privileges. They were all, of course, abused, causing considerable inconvenience to the churchwardens. After the Restoration Sir Richard Stiddolph gave another quarter of an acre on condition that it was devoted solely for the benefit of the poor and not in any way for that of the rector.

The one substantial improvement made to the yard by Sharp was the erection of the celebrated Resurrection gate, whose design was copied from Michael Angelo's "Last Judgment". It has been described in the following terms: "Under a large compass pediment over the gate near the West end is a prodigious number of carved figures, being an emblem of the Resurrection, done in relievo very curiously, and erected in the year 1687."[3]

St. George's, Bloomsbury, the daughter church of St. Giles', was

[1] R. Dobie, *History of St. Giles-in-the-Fields*, p. 122.
[2] Pennant, *Account of London*, p. 157.
[3] *New View of London*, 1708. The whole structure cost more than £185.

not in commission until 1730, and during Sharp's incumbency there appears to have been only one chapel of ease, Joseph Read's Presbyterian chapel, which was situated in Dyott Street and built about 1672. Read, its minister, who was a great friend of Richard Baxter, was imprisoned in 1677 under the Conventicle Act; and, no doubt with Baxter's connivance and goodwill, it was made over to St. Giles' in 1684 at an annual rental of £30. Here in all probability worked that Good Samaritan Mr. Cothorne, reader in the church of St. Giles-in-the-Fields, who befriended the luckless mathematician John Pell.[1]

The year after the Restoration Mr. William Shelton founded a school in Parker's Lane, which ran between Drury Lane and Little Queen Street, for fifty poor children, all of whom had to be drawn from the parishes of St. Giles, St. Martin-in-the-Fields and Covent Garden. The cost was defrayed by the rents of certain properties which he owned in the neighbourhood. Shelton died in 1668 and his widow in 1681, when the trust "devolved on the rector and churchwardens of St. Giles, under the superintendence of the vestry";[2] and included, besides the school itself, the presentation every Michaelmas Day of green gowns to fifty poor old men and women from the same parishes. This was not made any easier by a proviso to the effect that the heir-at-law must also receive £10 per annum, since the whole of the expenses of the trust had to be met out of an annual income of barely £72, which rapidly dropped to £60 and less. The heir was eventually, by the year 1687, prevailed upon to accept £7 10s. as his portion of the estate; but even so St. Giles' found the Shelton trust a considerable liability, and by the middle of the eighteenth century it was estimated that "a considerable sum" was "due to the churchwardens".

Another trust was inaugurated by William Baynbrigge, Esq., who in 1672 gave £300 to build a south gallery in St. Giles' Church. The profits arising from the seating accommodation were to be distributed among the poor of the parish, and again the rector and churchwardens became responsible for carrying out these provisions.

Poverty.—The parish of St. Giles had long been familiar with the text "For the poor ye have always with you", and indeed found them a very serious problem. By 1680 there were probably some 2,000 houses and 10,000 permanent inhabitants in the dis-

---

[1] See *D.N.B.*: "John Pell."
[2] R. Dobie, *History of St. Giles-in-the-Fields*, p. 253.

trict; but the latter grew fast during the next ten years with a large influx of French refugees, Irish and other immigrants, all of the very poorest description. It was about this time that St. Giles' grew infamous for its numerous cellar-dwellings, and the expressions "a cellar in St. Giles' " and "a cellar-mate" became proverbial in London as being used to denote the most abject poverty.[1]

The interest of the vestry in these conditions was necessarily very real and active, as the following typical extracts from their minutes of this period amply illustrate:[2] "Ordered that special chardge be given to the constables, beadles etc to search diligently for women great with child, that they be either removed or good security got by the churchwardens in discovering and avoiding inmates, cellermates and new comers." Or, "1675. Whereas the charges of the poor do daily increase by the frequent resort of poore people from several countries and places, for want of due care to prevent the same; it is ordered, that Giles Hanson be elected an assistant beadle, with a salary of £40 a year, to find out and notice all new comers, inmates etc; and that a coat and badge be provided for him, that he be the better known in his office."

Overseers of the poor were appointed in increasing numbers from this date onwards, and by 1679 a special paymaster was employed to deal with casual relief. A building in Brown's Gardens[3] had already been established and fitted up by the churchwardens to serve as a workhouse; and when in 1680 this structure had to be pulled down, an order of the vestry directed "that certain houses neare Whetstone should be enquired for to accommodate the poor with habitations".[4]

The rector, as head of the vestry, had naturally to play an important part in these administrative acts;[5] and was especially brought into violent collision with the poor Irish, of whose doings, or rather misdoings, particularly their alarming tendency to increase and multiply, the vestry minutes are extremely full. They were, of course, Roman Catholics, and Sharp personally suffered

[1] Op. cit., p. 195.
[2] Parton, *Some Account of the Hospital and Parish of St. Giles-in-the-Fields, Middlesex,* p. 301.
[3] Part of the churchyard had, before the Restoration, been bounded by a garden plot, which was let to a man named Brown. Later, buildings were erected upon it.
[4] R. Dobie, *History of St. Giles-in-the-Fields,* p. 233.
[5] Among the archbishop's papers is the copy of a will of a certain Madam Goodman of the parish of St. Andrew, Holborn, containing the following provision: "I give three-hundred pounds to be given to Dr. Sharp of St. Giles for him to give as he shall think fit to the poor." See L-B-S. MSS., Box 4, Bundle N. 3.

heavily at the hands of their priests during the unfortunate "Roman Controversy".

The "Selected Vestry".—Something has already been said about the vestry. What exactly was this "selected vestry" that ruled at St. Giles' in Sharp's day, and for more than a hundred years after? An assembly of all the parishioners in the vestry room in order to discuss the business of the parish was, of course, a manifest impossibility, with the inevitable result that they were compelled to delegate their powers to certain "selected" vestrymen. But how were these vestrymen elected? Occasionally by direct annual elections, but more often they laid claim to their office on the ground of immemorial custom or through an Act of Parliament. One of these methods had to be adopted before the vestry could hope to be recognised by authority. The "selected vestry" at St. Giles' based its powers on "immemorial custom". Parton, who was parish clerk there from 1814 to 1822, declared that the vestry, which was select by prescription, consisted of the rector, church-wardens, and thirty-six other resident householders. Its powers, he went on to say, had been confirmed by episcopal mandate on April 27, 1628, which authorised its members "to do and exercise all things belonging to vestriemen, for the good and benefit of their church and parish". Vacancies due to death or removal from the parish were to be filled by co-option. However, the validity of Parton's pronouncement is open to grave doubt. To begin with, "immemorial custom" supposedly commenced from the reign of Richard I; but St. Giles' was not even a parish until after the dissolution of its hospital at the hands of Henry VIII. Furthermore, it was necessary for a "selected vestry" dependent upon immemorial custom to be regularly uniform in numbers. Yet whereas Parton mentioned thirty-six, the bishop of London's mandate referred only to twenty-five members, while the vestry minutes themselves record various numbers ranging from thirty to thirty-nine.

Whatever the rights or wrongs of the "selected vestry" at St. Giles', there were some parishioners, at any rate, who, during Sharp's incumbency, were not quite satisfied either with its numbers or constitution, as the following entry in the minutes proved: "Dec. 21st 1681. Whereas Mr. John Morris, and Mr. Nathaniel Chandler, in behalf of themselves, and divers other inhabitants, have requested of the Vestry, that some addition or alteration may be made to the present Vestry; the Vestry upon debate thereof, do order: That the said John Morris and Nathaniel Chandler, and the rest, do give in writing their desires touching the premises at the next Vestry to be considered of. And it is further ordered, that there be a summons for timely notice to Mr. Dean Sharp, and likewise to all Vestrymen, to desire them to meet at a time certain at the Vestry-house; and that intimation be given in the summons of the occasion of that meeting."[1] The outcome of what must have been an extremely interesting session has not been recorded, and the result can only be gauged from the fact that the "selected vestry" continued to function much as before. There are, nevertheless, two later comments upon this incident, which in their complete contradiction of one another are worth including verbatim:

"Whether these advocates for innovation afterwards discovered that the Vestry, which had, as shewn, been time out of mind by custom and established usage invested with extensive authorities for the government of the parish, could neither increase their number of THIRTY-SIX, nor with safety make any other alteration, does not appear. But some such reason did, in all probability, occur, for they did not afterwards make any further application to the vestry on the subject."[2]

"These two patriotic men were no doubt aware of the usurpation of their rights as parishioners, and the baneful effects resulting therefrom, and were aroused to make an effort to rid the parish of the odious tyranny; but probably they were appalled by the expense, the unfavourableness of the slavish times they lived in, and perhaps the little support they met with from their fellow-parishioners."[3]

Personal.—Sharp had a large circle of friends and acquaintances in London, for whose sake he would, if need be, put himself to considerable trouble and expense. One or two incidents are especially worth recalling. "On Wednesday, March 28th, 1688, his dear friend Dr. Clagget died."[4] Dr. William Clagget (or Claget), who was a particularly close friend of Sharp, held the appointments of preacher at Gray's Inn and lecturer of St. Michael Bassishaw, besides being one of the chaplains-in-ordinary to the king. They were in the habit of visiting each other at all hours and times, studying together and sharing confidences. Clagget, who was an

[1] Parton, *Some Account of the Hospital and Parish of St. Giles-in-the-Fields, Middlesex* p. 276.
[2] Ibid.
[3] R. Dobie, *History of St. Giles-in-the-Fields*, p. 288.
[4] *Life of Archbishop Sharp*, vol. i, p. 90.

able controversialist and a violent anti-Romanist, had, in support of his friend, taken a leading part in the Roman controversy of James II's reign. Suddenly he was struck down by smallpox while preaching one Sunday evening at St. Martin-in-the-Fields, and was dead within the fortnight. The Sharps did all in their power for the unfortunate family. The friends were together at the end; and the unhappy widow, although herself infected by the same dread disease, found a kindly refuge at the Sharps' house in Great Russell Street. Nevertheless, despite assiduous nursing, she survived her husband for less than three weeks. Sharp himself preached Clagget's funeral sermon, and his words express his own terrible sense of loss: "I am now to speak of a man whom I loved as my own soul! Something I ought to say concerning him, for he was not a common man: but God direct me how or what I should speak, for I am not yet myself, since I heard of this great loss."[1]

Two years earlier he had performed a similar act of charity and respect for the Reverend Dr. John Pell, who will be remembered as the inventor of the sign for division ($\div$), and was a man of considerable learning, especially in mathematics. He had been one of Cromwell's diplomatic agents in Switzerland under the Commonwealth, but after the Restoration he took orders and was successively domestic chaplain to Archbishop Sheldon, a fellow of the Royal Society and a D.D. of Lambeth. A bishopric was confidently expected for him, but he became hopelessly insolvent and, despite repeated attempts by John Collins and other wealthy patrons to befriend him, was twice thrown into prison and eventually found refuge, utterly destitute, in the College of Physicians under Dr. Daniel Whistler. One of his grandchildren at length took pity on him and procured him a lodging in Dyott Street, where dwelt the same Mr. Cothorne who served the church of St. Giles. Here, no doubt, Sharp, as rector, visited the poor old man; and on his death, which took place in December 1685, with the assistance of Dr. Busby of Westminster, secured his interment at their own expense in the rectors' vault at St. Giles'.

Four years later, this time in partnership with Tillotson, he undertook an act of far heavier responsibility. This was the Aske Trust. Robert Aske, an alderman of London and founder of a hospital in Hoxton for supporting twenty poor men of the Haberdashers Company, of which he was himself a member, and also for providing twenty boys with a decent education,

[1] *Life of Archbishop Sharp,* vol. ii, Appendix I, p. 103.

died in 1689, having made Sharp and Tillotson executors of his will. By its terms they were themselves left £200 apiece, together with a commission to allocate a further £400 to each of twenty poor clergymen nominated by them, while the residue of the Aske property passed to the Haberdashers Company. The executors, apparently, handled the matter with the greatest discretion, making over the custody of all the ready money and bonds to an agent of the Company, which obtained the largest interest under the will, until such time as the provisions of the will had been completely carried out. "Nor was there anything transacted relating to this trust from the time that the Will was opened, till that of the surrendering all their concerns into the hands of the Company, but in the presence, and with the advice and consent of the deputies of the Company, particularly Sir Thomas Vernon and Mr. Mould; which latter kept the account of all things done in this affair."[1] That was a very wise decision, since at a later date when both the executors had become archbishops they were accused of having "disposed of some of the Alderman's effects, before they delivered in the schedule to the Company".[2] Among the Lloyd-Baker-Sharp MSS. there is a copy of an undated letter from the archbishop to a certain Captain Richardson on this subject, evidently written as a reply to some such criticism. "I want no good will", wrote Sharp, "to give you a perfect satisfaction in the matter you write about. But I fear it is impossible for me to do it having kept no memorandums of or transactions as to that business. . . . But this I dare say with assurance that all due care was taken by us, both to have perfect inventories taken of all his estate both in ready money, debts, goods, household goods, etc. and likewise that all should be forthcoming to the Haberdashers Company (whom we knew he had made his heirs) over and above what he had disposed of otherwise in his Will. . . . And I am very sure from the time the Will was opened to the time we surrendered up all our concerns to the Company, we did not do any one act relating to this executorship (excepting the nomination of the 20 poor clergymen that were by the Will to be nominated by us) but what the deputies of the Company were privy and consenting to." The archbishops had been accused, among other things, of disposing of the alderman's library and part of his plate to his niece, Mrs. Denham, without the consent or knowledge of the Company. This, as Sharp goes on clearly to explain, was quite untrue, re-

[1] T. Birch, *Life of Tillotson*, p. 215.   [2] Ibid.

ferring Captain Richardson for the facts to Mr. Mould's papers: "I have told you sincerely how far the Archbishop [Tillotson] and I were concerned in this affair and must refer you entirely to Capt. Mould's papers, which I hope will settle all things."[1] Such a reference to the available evidence, of course, immediately exposed this gross calumny and cleared their characters entirely.

It is time, however, to return to the main story. Hot on the heels of Nottingham's letter informing Sharp of his appointment to the deanery of Canterbury came a second to acquaint him with the tidings that he had been appointed one of the Commissioners "to review the Liturgy, the Canons and the ecclesiastical Courts".[2] On receipt of such important news Sharp immediately returned to London and, after waiting upon the king and kissing his hand for the deanery, plunged into his new task. The Commission met for the first time on October 3, 1689, in the Jerusalem Chamber, where eighteen full sessions were held before November 18. These were principally devoted to a revision of the Prayer Book, similar to that contemplated by Archbishop Sancroft. William III, Tillotson, Burnet and Nottingham, the chief architects of this new Comprehension Scheme, set great store on its successful conclusion; but the Lower House of Convocation, which saw no need for further alliance with, and still less for incorporation of, dissent, and which thoroughly mistrusted William as a Calvinist and Occasional Conformist, skilfully engineered its downfall. The first step in this direction was achieved when on November 21 Sharp, acting in the royal interest, failed to secure the election of Tillotson as prolocutor.[3] Dr. Jane, a rabid high-churchman, was chosen instead, and the scheme, after being cold-shouldered, was finally scotched by the high-fliers. William in disgust adjourned Convocation on December 14, and it did not meet again for ten years. Actually Sharp himself played but a small part in this affair, being absent most of the session at Canterbury, where he was installed as dean, and returning to London only just in time for the adjournment. His earnestness in the matter was not, however, lost upon William, and in the next year (1690) he received the command to preach twice before the queen, at Whitehall in April and again at

[1] L-B-S. MSS., Box 4, Bundle T. 44.
[2] H. C. Foxcroft and Clarke, *Life of Gilbert Burnet*, p. 274.
[3] T. Birch, *Life of Tillotson*, p. 184. Birch quotes as his authority a letter written to him by Thomas Sharp, archdeacon of Northumberland, and dated November 7, 1751.

Kensington in May; while in the latter month he also delivered his third sermon before the House of Commons.

During that summer he paid a long visit to his native county of Yorkshire, staying with his mother, who still resided in Bradford, and renewing many old friendships both there and at York, "where he also paid his respects to Archbishop Lamplugh".[1] Lamplugh, who was now an old man of seventy-six, had shown himself to possess more than a touch of the vicar of Bray. As bishop of Exeter at the time of William's landing in the west, he had made himself conspicuous by his vigorous championship of James' cause; and in return for these services the king appointed him to the archbishopric of York, which had been kept vacant since Dolben's death in 1686 with a view to the ultimate succession, when the king's "Roman-autocratic" policy had beaten down all opposition, of that ardent Jesuit Father Edward Petre. But now, in a last-minute attempt to bring the nation over to his side against the Dutch invaders, the Protestant but time-serving Lamplugh was enthroned by proxy in York Minster on December 19, 1688, the very day that William entered London. Needless to say, the new archbishop was one of the first ecclesiastics to hail his triumph, and later helped to place the crown upon his head.

On his return to London in the autumn Sharp, through the agency of Tillotson, had pressure brought to bear upon him by the king to accept one of the vacated bishoprics. Norwich, it was hinted, might, from his past associations with that diocese, prove the most acceptable.[2] But as has already been noted, he steadfastly refused to step into another man's shoes.[3] Nevertheless Sharp made it perfectly clear that in doing so he was concerned only with his own individual conscience and did not expect others to follow his example. "He readily went down to Canterbury to elect Dr. Tillotson to the throne of that church where he himself was dean; and was himself afterwards consecrated (as archbishop of York) by Dr. Tillotson, in company with others who succeeded to these vacant bishoprics. Neither of which had been consistent with his principle, had he thought it absolutely unlawful or irregular to take those bishoprics in those circumstances."[4] Unfortunately his conscientious scruples angered William, who, remembering his former attacks on dissent and stout championship of a high type

[1] *Life of Archbishop Sharp*, vol. i, p. 108.
[2] T. Birch, *Life of Tillotson*, p. 253.
[3] T. Lathbury, *The History of the Non-Jurors*, p. 91.
[4] *Life of Archbishop Sharp*, vol. i, p. 108.

of Anglican churchmanship, feared that he had been harbouring a wolf in sheep's clothing, and determined that no further promotion should be offered to him. But powerful friends were pleading the dean's cause, and both Tillotson and Nottingham were equally determined that he should be made a bishop as soon as possible. York and Lincoln, owing to the advanced age of their present occupiers, were certain to become vacant in the very near future; and in the meantime they contented themselves with securing Sharp's collaboration on several important commissions. William was now reducing Ireland to order, and issued a warrant on November 6, 1690, for an ecclesiastical commission to consider the needs of the Church there. This included six of the bishops,[1] together with Tillotson and Sharp, the deans of St. Paul's and Canterbury, and Dr. Tenison, and ran as follows: "Almighty God having of his Great Goodness blest our arms with so much success in Ireland that it is now almost reduced to our obedience we esteem it our duty in the first place to provide for the settlement and government of the Church there by such rules and orders as may most effectually encourage piety and promote the worship of God. For this purpose we have made choice of you, as persons whose zeal, judgement, prudence and experience we are all well satisfied and do hereby require you to meet and consult of such means as may be most proper for attaining this great end. We recommend it particularly to you to consider the ecclesiastical preferments in our said Kingdom now void, and of the persons best qualified to fill them, in respect of their learning, exemplary life, and fidelity in the discharge of their duty, by a due residence upon the place. And upon this and all other matters which may most conduce to the good of the Church and the establishment of the Protestant religion in our said Kingdom, we expect a report of your opinion in writing, as soon as may be; wherein we doubt not your care and diligence."[2]

In January 1691 Queen Mary issued another warrant for a mixed commission of laymen and ecclesiastics, again including Sharp and Tillotson, to investigate alleged abuses and irregularities committed in hospitals and houses of charity. This contained important names like Marlborough, Nottingham, Fauconberg, and Godolphin.

[1] London, St. Asaph, Salisbury, Chichester, Worcester and Oxford.
[2] *Calendar of State Papers Domestic: William and Mary*, p. 158; *H.O. Church Book*, i, p. 65.

"The Queen is informed", it ran, "that divers great abuses and irregularities are committed in all or most of the hospitals or houses of Charity within this Kingdom whereby great wrong is done to the poor, and the charitable and pious intentions of the .Founders and Benefactors to the said hospitals are greatly perverted. The afore-named persons are therefore commissioned to visit the several hospitals here mentioned. . . . The Commissioners have power to call before them the masters, heads, governors, officers and ministers or any other person belonging to the said hospitals, to enquire, examine and inform themselves of the estate and rule of the said hospitals and of the masters, heads, poor people and others there abiding, and of the disposition and employment of the revenues given or purchased for the maintenance of the said hospitals, etc. and of all crimes, defects, excesses, abuses, corruptions, offences, and enormities in concealing, abridging, altering and diverting or misemploying the said hospitals or houses. The Commissioners have also power to enquire, hear, order, correct, amend and reform all defects, etc."[1]

Such work, which Sharp found congenial enough, had the effect of keeping his name alive and emphasising his many services to the crown, while Tillotson took occasion to inform William that the dean of Canterbury's refusal to accept one of the vacant bishoprics was due to his desire to wait for York.[2] William grudgingly agreed to accept this excuse on condition that it was confirmed by Sharp himself. Accordingly Tillotson visited his friend at Great Russell Street on Friday, April 24, 1691, explained the situation and secured his acquiescence in the scheme. Birch has admirably summed up this typical but subtle piece of ecclesiastical wire-pulling: "Dr. Tillotson came to his [Sharp's] house on Friday the 24th of April 1691, the day after his own nomination to the Archbishopric [Canterbury] and told him, that since he had so obstinately refused taking any of the vacant bishoprics he had thought of a method to bring him off with the King; which was, that he should promise to accept the Archbishopric of York, when it fell, as Dr. Tenison should take Lincoln . . . and directing him to go and acquaint the Earl of Nottingham with it; and, if his Lordship approved of it, he would himself propose it to the King on the Monday following. Accordingly on that day he acquainted

[1] *H.O. Warrant Book*, 6, p. 28.
[2] See J. le Neve, *History of the Archbishops*, Part II, p. 275: "To put his refusal upon his desire of staying till the death of Dr. Lamplugh, that he might be preferred in his own country."

his Majesty with what had passed between Dr. Sharp and himself and fixed the affair. In consequence of which on the next Council Day in the middle of the same week, the King declared there, who should fill the vacant sees and who should succeed to York and Lincoln when they should fall; and Archbishop Lamplugh dying on the 5th of May, Dr. Sharp was consecrated to the see of York on the 5th of July following."[1]

Eleven days later the new archbishop was enthroned at York by proxy. When the news of his nomination[2] got noised abroad there were, of course, many letters of congratulation, among them one from his old College of Christ's. Sharp's reply is still extant:

LONDON
June 13th 1691.

"MY HONOURED FRIENDS

I return you my most hearty thanks for the extremely obliging letter you were pleased to send me by my good friend Mr. Lovett. It is an honour as much beyond what I could expect as it is above what I could do or (I am afraid) ever can deserve. This I do assure you of, I shall always retain a grateful sense of it. And few things that have happened to me in my life will be remembered by me with greater delight than this testimony you have given me of your kindness and good wishes. I shall forever own the obligations I have to Christ's College; and as I do reckon it among the special blessings of God to me, that I had my education among you: So I shall always think myself concerned as much as in me lies, to serve your Society and every member of it.

I am with the Tender of my Hearty respects to everyone of you in particular—Gentlemen

Your obliged and Affectionate
Friend
J. EBOR. ELECT."[3]

Of Sharp's activities as dean of Canterbury as little has been recorded as of his time at Norwich. There is a bundle of papers

---

[1] T. Birch, *Life of Tillotson*, p. 254.

[2] "Whitehall, May 8th 1691: Warrant for a *congé d'élire* to the Dean and Chapter of York, empowering them to elect an Archbishop of that see now void by the death of Dr. Thomas Lamplugh, the late Archbishop thereof; and for a letter recommending to the said Dean and Chapter John Sharp D.D., Dean of Canterbury, to be by them elected Archbishop." See *H.O. Church Book*, i, p. 88.

"Whitehall, June 8th 1691: Warrant for the royal assent to the election of Dr. John Sharp, Dean of Canterbury, as Archbishop of York." See *H.O. Church Book*, i, p. 97.

[3] Additional MS. 22910, p. 398. *Cf.* L-B-S. MSS., Box 3, Bundle C. 6: The congratulatory letters from the College and University.

among the Lloyd-Baker-Sharp MSS. containing many of the acts of the dean and chapter during the vacancy occasioned by Sancroft's deprivation; but these are mainly concerned with testimonials to character, dispensations in order that livings might be held in plurality, or the deeds of presentation to the livings themselves. The two following are typical examples of the kind of requests made to them:

"Mr. Dean of Canterbury—I beg you will allow Mr. Geery the bearer a dispensation to hold All Hallows London with Islington—H. London."[1]

"To the Reverend the Deane and Chapter of Canterbury —I do hereby certify that the Rectory of Withycomb in the Diocese of Bath and Wells is not (as I am credibly informed) of greater yearly value than eighty pounds nor more than ten miles distant from the Vicarage of Stokegursy within the same Diocese. And that Stokegursy aforesaid is of about the same yearly value. And I think fit further to certify that Mr. Matthew Hale the present Vicar and Incumbent of Stokegursy aforesaid has promised that he will pay and allow the full moiety of the clear yearly value of the said Rectory of Withycomb to any curate that shall officiate for him there in case he can procure a dispensation to hold the same Rectory with the Vicarage—Gi. Sarum."[2]

There are also two interesting letters from the Reverend Jonas Proast, chaplain of All Souls College, Oxford. Proast had been dismissed by the Warden, Finch, and appealed to the College visitor against this decision, alleging that Finch was only "pretended Warden" and had never been properly elected, since "he was neither chosen nor constituted Warden as the Founder has ordained in his statutes". The interest of this letter, dated October 4, 1689, and of another, December 4, 1690, lies in the fact that owing to the vacancy in the see of Canterbury there existed no official visitor to the College at that time. Proast, nevertheless, declared that *sede vacante* he could be restored by "the Prior of Canterbury"; and then went on to enquire, "Who is now Prior of Canterbury; whether the Dean alone or the Dean and Chapter, in conjunction, it is not for me to determine."[3] Neither the dean nor

---

[1] L.-B.-S. MSS., Box 4, Bundle G. 12, April 16, 1691.
[2] L.-B.-S. MSS., Box 4, Bundle G. 10, March 13, 1690/1.
[3] L.-B.-S. MSS., Box 4, Bundle G. 21 and 62.

chapter appears, however, to have done anything to reinstate Mr. Proast.

There is another letter from a Mr. John Whitefoot of Norwich, written to Sharp while still dean of Canterbury, and congratulating him on his elevation to the archbishopric of York; and, with an eye to the main chance, recommending to him "the person of my son, who is not unknown to yourself, if it may be in your power to do anything for him". He suggested a prebend at Norwich, two of which "are like to fall void, in a short time"; and since their gift "will be the king's right . . . perhaps by that means will fall to the Archbishop of Canterbury".[1] Whitefoot, of course, was well aware of the close friendship existing between Tillotson and Sharp, and believed that the dean might influence his archbishop in this matter. It appears that he was mistaken, for Whitefoot junior received no preferment at Norwich.

[1] L-B-S. MSS., Box 3, Bundle C. 30.

CHAPTER VI

ARCHBISHOP OF YORK

"DURING his northern primacy Sharp was a just, liberal, and wise ruler of his diocese and province. He tried to exclude politics altogether from his work as an ecclesiastic, difficult though it must have been in those days of bitter controversy and party feeling. Even before coming to York he had shown great liberal-mindedness in his relations with such men as the non-conforming Baxter and Dean Tillotson with his sympathetic leanings towards non-conformity. And during his life and work in the north such large-heartedness was conspicuously displayed."[1]

Sharp, who had gone to York as the close friend and coadjutor of Tillotson, was looked upon by William as the advocate of a liberal, broad-minded type of churchmanship, desiring the comprehension of dissent and repudiating the narrow party bias of the non-juror and high-flier. But Sharp was also the friend of Nottingham, who expected, and not in vain, that he would prove himself a strong Anglican, resisting not only the papists and Nonconformists, but taking a bold stand against the latitudinarian doctrines of the day, infected as they undoubtedly were by rationalism and deism. Both these influences played their part in the archbishop's career. So long as Tillotson lived Sharp closely supported his liberal policy in Church matters, but with the accession to Canterbury of the yet more Protestant Tenison, York, although never actively going into opposition, became more and more to be regarded as the leader of the High-Church party—particularly so when on William's death he enjoyed the position of chief ecclesiastical adviser to the new queen. Gradually Tenison, who had been William's right-hand man in clerical matters, was forced into the background as Anne's High-Church sympathies became clearer; and from 1710 until Sharp's death in February 1713/14, York rather than Canterbury dominated the Anglican Church. But this change of front still lay far in the future. At first the new archbishop was only too glad to follow faithfully in the footsteps of his friend and fellow-metropolitan John Tillotson, with whose ecclesiastical

[1] Canon Solloway, *Archbishop Sharp* (York Minster Historical Tracts, No. 25), p. 4.

policy he was in complete agreement. Tillotson, writing to Burnet on April 12, 1692, about the impending publication of the latter's *Pastoral Care*, added the following postscript: "Yesterday morning I obtained a meeting here of eight bishops, York, London, Worcester, Ely, Gloucester, Chichester, Norwich, Lincoln. I proposed to them the heads of a circular letter; upon which we discussed very calmly and without the least clashing."[1] Indeed, at this stage Sharp was so far from criticising the actions of Canterbury that he hastened to bring his own problems to Lambeth. A good example of such a consultation is to be found in the case of the dissenting schoolmaster Richard Frankland. Frankland, who was also a graduate of Christ's College, Cambridge, had long been a thorn in the side of the Yorkshire clergy. He had set up an academy at Rathmell in 1670 for the training and recruitment of dissenting ministers, but later removed to Natland and other places, eventually returning to Rathmell in 1689. He had already once been excommunicated (1678) for instigating the first Nonconformist ordination in Yorkshire, and now, although the Toleration Act protected him as a preacher, a fresh attempt was made to suppress his academy. Accordingly, on September 17, 1690, he was cited by "several of the clergy in Craven . . . to appear at the Court[2] in York Minster the 25th of that month to answer certain articles especially his contempt of the law and jurisdiction of the Court in teaching youth at Rawthmell without licence from the ordinary".[3] Frankland never appeared; and finally, on October 24, 1690, the judge "decreed him to be excommunicate". The excommunication was pronounced on February 2, 1690/1, and "the 8th of that month it was published in Giggleswick Church." Frankland, however, had powerful friends at court, and at the instance of Lord Wharton, Sir Thomas Rokeby and others, William III ordered his absolution to be read at Giggleswick.[4]

But soon after Sharp's accession to the archbishopric of York the clergy were further excited and alarmed by a large and public assembly at Wakefield of twenty-four Nonconformist divines to consider the possibility of a union between the Presbyterians and Independents. Frankland, the senior Presbyterian minister present, strongly advocated such an amalgamation as a means of strengthening the Nonconformist position in the north; and thereby further increased the fear and dislike of the Anglicans for his formidable

[1] T. Birch, *Life of Tillotson*, p. 267.   [2] *I.e.*, the archbishop's (Lamplugh's) court.
[3] L-B-S. MSS., Box 3, Bundle B. 15.
[4] See *Dr. Calamy's Account*, pp. 284-288, 1713.

personality. The clergy of Craven therefore petitioned Sharp to suppress his academy, and compelled the archbishop, whose sympathies appear to have been with Frankland, to write the following cautious letter to the justiccs at Wakefield sessions:

"GENTLEMEN—Whereas a complaint hath been made unto us by several of the clergy of Craven in the West-riding of Yorkshire that one Mr. Richard Frankland a dissenting minister hath for some time taught and instructed youth as a tutor or schoolmaster within the Parish of Giggleswick in the said Deanery of Craven, and still continues so to do to the great disturbance and discouragement of them the said clergy (he pretending to train up youth for the Ministry and accordingly sending out his scholars to preach in their parishes and other places). We think ourselves bound in duty so far to take notice of this complaint, to signify to you that the said Richard Frankland hath no licence from the Archbishop or Ordinary of this Diocese to teach or instruct youth either within the Parish of Giggleswick or anywhere else."[1]

Once more Frankland's whig supporters rallied to his aid, and Lord Sydney addressed to Sharp a strong letter of remonstrance against the treatment meted out to him:

"MY LORD—Being informed that Mr. Richard Frankland of the parish of Giggleswick in the county of York, stands excommunicated before the Chancellor in Your Grace's Court on the second of February last, for non-appearance, tho' he had not any notice thereof till about ten days after the time he was cited to appear, the proceedings thereof being *ex mero officio* without any presentment or prosecutor, and the said Mr. Frankland being a person very well affected to the Government; and having taken the oaths appointed by law, I desire Your Grace will give order, that he may be permitted to appear in the said court, at a day to be appointed to make his defence to what shall be objected against him, and may in the meantime be absolved from his Excommunication; and if this will not stand with the course of the Court, that Your Grace will *ex officio* suspend the giving out of a significavit in this case."[2]

Sharp promptly consulted Tillotson, who replied: "I would send for him and tell him that I would never do anything to infringe the Act of Toleration; but I did not think his case came with-

---

[1] L-B-S. MSS., Box 4, Bundle P. 11.
[2] L-B-S. MSS., Box 4, Bundle L. 115, Whitehall, April 22, 1691/2.

in it: That there were two things in his case, which would hinder me from granting him a licence, though he were in all things conformable to the Church of England. First his setting up a school where a free school is already established: And then his instructing of young men in so public a manner in University learning which is contrary to his oath to do, if he has taken a degree in either of our Universities, and I doubt contrary to the bishop's oath to grant a licence for the doing of it; so that your Grace does not in this matter consider him at all as a dissenter."[1]

Soon afterwards Sharp saw Frankland at Skipton, where the archbishop was taking a confirmation, and invited him to Bishopthorpe. Here, in the library, cosily ensconced with a pipe of tobacco and a glass of good wine, they had a most friendly and confidential discussion. Sharp, however, having stated Tillotson's arguments and expressed his own personal sympathy with Frankland, refused courteously enough to be drawn into a religious controversy. Instead he seems to have questioned this prominent Dissenter, whose experience of Yorkshire must have been both wide and deep, about the state of his own diocese. Certainly they parted the best of friends, and the archbishop used his influence to quash an indictment brought against Frankland in 1695 and again in 1697. Nevertheless the latter continued to be persecuted by the Anglican clergy and was compelled to move about from place to place until his death at Kendal in October, 1698.

Frankland's case was a very fair sample of the kind of problem with which the new archbishop had to deal. Religion in England was passing through a critical period, with Church and State slowly but steadily drifting apart, and some of the old partitions dividing the former from the Nonconformists wearing a trifle thin. The non-juror shaded off into the high-flying Anglican, the Dissenter into the low churchman, the philosophical speculations of Locke and Berkeley into the free-thinking of Toland and Collins. The taking of oaths and the subscribing to set formulas might satisfy the State, but it could not and did not define Anglicanism or quieten the conscience of honest men. Sharp knew this, and in a spirit of revolt against political jobbery and party alliances threw himself into the work of setting his own province of York in order without reference to anything other than his own sense of justice, order, decency and godly fear. In the northern metropolitical see the lax administration of Archbishop Lamplugh had allowed

[1] T. Birch, *Life of Tillotson*, p. 272.

abuses and irregularities to creep into all walks of the Church's life, and it was left to the new archbishop to clean out these Augean stables. He began by laying down some hard-and-fast rules for his own observance, to be rigidly adhered to however tempting the offers made in exchange for their recantation. Lamplugh had brought the archiepiscopal office into contempt and dishonour by his warm championship of the tory party, and by making use of his ecclesiastical patronage for personal or political ends. Sharp openly renounced and condemned such practices; and so long as he remained archbishop his patronage, with certain marked exceptions, was used almost exclusively for the promotion of his own deserving provincial clergy. The exceptions were chiefly found among the members of his own family,[1] or great personal friends like the Finches. No man was ever a better friend and family man than Archbishop Sharp, and since in the eighteenth century the normal method of showing them a kindness lay in making use of an official position for their advancement, he felt it incumbent upon him to push his clerical relatives and friends, at least, as high up the ecclesiastical ladder as their natural abilities suffered them to go.

Nottingham's two brothers and the archbishop's ex-pupils, Edward and Henry Finch, both became prebendaries of Wetwang, the best prebend in the Minster. Henry was appointed in 1695, and on his promotion to the deanery in 1704 Edward succeeded to his brother's stall. Sharp had long striven hard to secure the deanery for Henry, but while William lived this was denied him, since the king distrusted the Finches and even suspected them of Jacobite activities. Henry, as he frankly acknowledges in his letters to the archbishop, had set his heart on becoming dean of York under his old tutor. For when Sharp secured him the offer from Lord Derby, in 1694, of the bishopric of Sodor and Man, he refused it on the ground that he preferred to wait for the deanery. "I thought it not proper for me," he wrote, and went on to suggest "that if your Grace thought fit you might renew your applications to their Majesties for the Deanery".[2] Subsequently Sharp suggested to Lord Derby the name of the latter's own chaplain, Thomas Wilson, who was to prove the ideal bishop for that island. "I did what service I could for Mr. Wilson with my Lord Derby," wrote the archbishop in a letter to Edward Finch,

---

[1] For a detailed account of the many benefits he conferred upon his relations see my article, "Archbishop Sharp and his 'Poor Relations' ", in *The Modern Churchman*, vol. xxxiv, Nos. 1, 2 and 3, April-June 1944, pp. 55-59.
[2] L-B-S. MSS., Box 3, Bundle B. 7.

"and recommended him for the Bishopric of Man as far as was decent, and all this before I had ever seen Mr. Wilson, and so I told my Lord, only I said I had had an extraordinary character of him. His Lordship seemed not to be ill pleased with the Freedom I took with him. . . . Upon that very little conversation with Mr. Wilson that I had I have a very great esteem of him, and think Harry and you have done him right in your representation of him."[1]

In 1697, on the death of Dr. Tobias Wickham, the battle for the York deanery really began. Sharp strove to enlist the help of Tenison, but not with any marked success, as the following letter from Henry Finch to the archbishop on this subject fully illustrates: "My Lord of Canterbury told the Bishop of Norwich on Monday last that he would speak with me at Whitehall on Thursday morning.and shew me that part of the letter which he had in answer to his which he wrote to the king: wherein he had in your name only recommended me to His Majesty. So I went accordingly. But he told me that he had wrote to Your Grace the Saturday before and had given you a full account of it. That . . . *The King would not approve of that recommendation by any means.* He then began to tell me some of the objections that were made against me; and particularly that mine and my brother's behaviour in the Lancashire Plot had been very ill presented to the King. . . . I took the freedom to tell him that since His Majesty did not approve the recommendation that he had already received, I thought His Grace [of Canterbury] could not only remove all objections, but give me one that would be effective. This he turned off at first by intimating that some such thing might be done hereafter upon some other occasion. But I told him that there was no preferment in England which I valued but this. Since there was nothing which could afford me an opportunity of being so near Your Grace, which was the chief, nay the only reason that I valued and desired this, and therefore I again told him that I was satisfied he could get this for me if he pleased (which he both times seemed to own he could) and therefore I should be extraordinarily obliged to him if he would do it."[2] Tenison, indeed, was more than half-hearted in the matter, being unwilling to offend the king by championing too readily an unpopular candidate. William certainly insisted on having his own way, since he distrusted the Finches and strongly favoured Dr. Thomas Gale, who was eventually appointed. In a

[1] L-B-S. MSS., Box 3, Bundle K. 3.
[2] L-B-S. MSS., Box 3, Bundle B. 5, May 22, 1697.

letter[1] to Sharp explaining Henry's failure and defending his own conduct, Tenison put the blame fairly and squarely upon the king's shoulders. This was undoubtedly true, but perhaps not the whole truth.

Members of the archbishop's own family who profited from his patronage included, among others, his son-in-law, nephew and niece's husband, all of whom received prebends in the Minster.[2]

Nevertheless nearly all the remaining forty-three stalls, which Sharp filled at the Minster and collegiate church of Southwell, were given to deserving Yorkshire and Nottinghamshire incumbents. Moreover, he was careful to distribute some of them among the vicars of large market towns like Hull, Beverley, Leeds, Wakefield, Sheffield, Doncaster, Nottingham and Newark, and so added not only to the dignity and effectiveness of their office, but also to their incomes, which, owing to the small endowments, had been out of all proportion to the size of the parishes.

Competition for such favours was, of course, exceedingly brisk. Francis Jessop, rector of Treeton, wrote to the archbishop on May 1, 1700: "These two things were formerly put to my choice: The living of Sheffield, or a prebend. I was to have the first, or am to have the latter. I most humbly appeal to Your Grace's words, in the manifest acceptation of them, and Mr. Drake's promise from Your Grace afterwards. I hope an honest man's just expectations are not to be suppressed."[3] To which Sharp indignantly replied:

"SIR—I received yours wherein you desire an answer to your last. . . . I wonder how you can say, that it was put to your choice, whether you would have the living of Sheffield or a prebend, if you mean that it was I that put it to your choice. For as for Sheffield you cannot but remember that I told you that if you thought of taking that, and keeping it with Treeton, I would oppose your dispensation as much as I could. And as for a prebend, tho' I did not say any words that might make you despair of one, yet I am sure I never entered into any engagement, or made any promise that I would give you one, or said any words that could be justly interpreted in that sense. What Mr. Drake might afterwards tell you, I

---

[1] L-B-S. MSS., Box 4, Bundle Q. 40.
[2] These were: Heneage Dering, John Richardson and John Clarkson. Another niece's husband, Edmund Wickins, received the wealthy living of Kirbythore in Westmoreland from the Earl of Thanet on Sharp's recommendation; and Cousin Dan Oughton was presented to the vicarage of Whitby. See "Archbishop Sharp and his 'Poor Relations' ", in *The Modern Churchman*, loc. cit., pp. 55-59.
[3] L.B.S. MSS., Box 4, Bundle H. 24.

know not, and therefore can say nothing to it. This is all I have to say in answer to your letter."[1]

Three years later Lord Burlington suggested to Sharp that a vacant prebend at York might be given to "Mr. Roe my chaplain", and in return he would appoint the archbishop's candidate, Dr. Fall, to the living of Londesborough, while also allowing the primate to choose his next chaplain for him "upon your own terms".[2] But this offer appears likewise to have been rejected. Sometimes, too, the application came through a friend. Clement Elis, incumbent of Kirkby, and later on himself prebendary of Beckingham in Southwell, a great favourite with the archbishop, wrote on behalf of a neighbouring clergyman: "I have heard there is now a Prebend in Southwell void. . . . If your Grace would be pleased to bestow it on Mr. Lalavel a Frenchman now minister at Eastwood in this county, whose living is not worth above £40 per annum . . . I most humbly offer this to Your Grace's thoughts without his knowledge whom I have neither seen nor heard from since last summer."[3]

The archbishop's manuscripts, indeed, contain large numbers of such applications, almost invariably unsuccessful, for Sharp was never the kind of bishop to be brow-beaten or cozened into bestowing his patronage upon the undeserving.[4]

Here, then, in conclusion, is one final and not unreasonable, even if ungranted, petition: The reverend Joseph Etherington, vicar of Dunham-nigh-Tuxford, wrote to the archbishop on April 10, 1700: "I am informed that Mr. Chadwick . . . (who is prebendary of Dunham) is desperately sick and in small hopes of recovery. If it should please God that he dies of his sickness, if it was not too much boldness in me to request such a thing, if I might find so much favour in Your Grace's eyes as to be accounted worthy of it, I should humbly petition Your Grace to annex the Prebend to the Vicarage of Dunham, which would be a good help and encouragement to this small living which requires so great labour and pains as to supply 3 churches in the same parish every Lord's day. And it would be a means to put the Vicar into a capacity to be able to hire a curate under him."[5]

---

[1] L-B-S. MSS., Box 4, Bundle T. 59, Aug. 24, 1700.
[2] L-B-S. MSS., Box 4, Bundle L. 116, Aug. 3, 1703.
[3] L-B-S. MSS., Box 4, Bundle D. 1, April 28, 1692.
[4] With the possible exception of his own relations, *e.g.* Dan Oughton. See "Archbishop Sharp and his 'Poor Relations' ", in *The Modern Churchman*, loc. cit., p. 59.
[5] L-B-S. MSS., Box 4, Bundle D. 20.

Willis, in his *Survey of the Cathedrals*, accurately summed up the archbishop's policy in this exceedingly ticklish problem of appointing the right kind of prebendary: "He [Sharp] made it his unalterable practice to elect them (viz. prebendaries) out of such as lived in his diocese and had recommended themselves by doing their duties in their respective parochial cures. By which means no Cathedral in England was better attended by clergy, and the service more regularly performed than at York; or the ministers of small livings in any diocese more encouraged to attend their charge; because this good bishop would reward their diligence by such compensations, more especially those in York city, on whose conduct the world had a more special eye, hoping his example would influence his successors to take the like course. Which certainly if other bishops had in like manner practised the dignity of Cathedrals would have been kept up as in primitive times and we should not have seen several of them so scandalously neglected."[1]

On the other hand, it is of interest to note that the offer of a prebend might occasionally be a source of embarrassment. Dr. Thomas Gale, the dean of York, wrote to Sharp on March 5, 1701, thanking him for the gift of the prebend of Botevant;[2] but five days later he hastily withdrew his acceptance on the ground that he had read that if the dean of York took either a prebend or a living, he immediately forfeited his deanery.[3]

As a general principle Sharp refused "to meddle or in any way concern himself in the election of members of parliament";[4] although apparently such an abstention did not apply to the borough of Ripon, where the archbishop possessed temporal as well as ecclesiastical jurisdiction. Here, indeed, he repeatedly intervened in order to secure the return to Parliament of his red-hot tory son, John Sharp junior, who never failed to hold that constituency during his father's lifetime. His refusal to meddle was confined, in fact, to the elections in the county and city of York, where his studied avoidance of any political entanglements was, on the whole, taken in good part by both whig and tory. Nevertheless on more than one occasion it required a great deal of high moral courage on the side of the archbishop to enable him to stick to his principles. During the general election of 1695 the Duke of Leeds, then Lord President of the Council, urgently pressed for the

[1] *Life of Archbishop Sharp*, vol. i, p. 120.　　[2] L-B-S. MSS., Box 3, Bundle N. 17.
[3] L-B-S. MSS., Box 3, Bundle N. 18.　　[4] *Life of Archbishop Sharp*, vol. i, p. 117.

primate's support of his candidates;[1] while in 1702 Lady Russell confidently expected him to promote the interests of Lord Hartington.[2] Sharp certainly found it a hard matter to refuse such powerful pleas for aid, but refuse them he did, and that in no undecided terms. Consequently he felt much aggrieved when in 1705 he was accused by Godolphin of being "one of those who made a noise and cry about the Church being in danger", and promptly retorted by demanding of the Lord Treasurer "whether his Lordship had ever heard that he had made any bustle about parliament men?" Whereupon "The Earl cleared him of that imputation, which was a better proof of his not having any such apprehensions of the Church's danger, as were suggested, and of his not being agitated by party zeal, as was rumoured of him, than any verbal remonstrances he could have made in his own vindication."[3] All this did not, however, prevent Sharp from taking a personal interest in election results, scarcely troubling to conceal his private preferences even if he declined out of principle to raise a finger on their behalf. In a letter to the Earl of Nottingham, written during the important general election in the summer of 1702, he described the contest in detail: "We are like to be very busy this week [the letter is dated July 10] both upon account of our Assizes and our Elections for the parliament. My Lord Hartington comes hither this night in order to his appearing for one of our knights of the shire. He joins with my Lord Fairfax, and Sir John Kay stands by himself. It is thought my Lord Hartington will be one that will be chosen, he having the interest of all the great lords that have estates here. The burgesses for York, Hull, Knaresborough, Burrowbridge, Pontefract, High Walton and Ripon it is thought to be the same that served in the last parliament. At Scarborough 'tis thought Mr. Hungerford will be chosen in the place of Sir Charles Hotham. And in Beverley it is talked that Sir Michael Norton will be thrown out and Sir Charles Hotham come in his place. At Alborough Mr. Jessop will come in the room of Mr. Arlington, the Duke of Newcastle having now the power to recommend both the burgesses."[4] These are certainly not the words of a man indifferent to election results.

It was one thing, however, to raise the archiepiscopal office and its patronage above political fears and favours, and quite another

[1] L-B-S. MSS., Box 4, Bundle K. 27.
[2] Life of Archbishop Sharp, vol. i, pp. 122-125.
[3] Ibid., vol. i, pp. 133 and 134.
[4] Additional MS. 29584, pp. 87-94.

to understand and efficiently administer the vast metropolitan see of York in the highest interests of the Church as a whole. Sharp took extraordinary pains to qualify himself for this task by obtaining a comprehensive grasp of its rights and duties. The knowledge he thus acquired he later set down in three volumes, which were based on the work of James Torre, antiquary and genealogist, who had practically devoted his entire life to research into the ecclesiastical antiquities of Yorkshire, and gladly lent its fruits to his archbishop. After Torre's death in 1699 Sharp purchased these MSS., five folio volumes in all, from his widow for the sum of twenty-five guineas,[1] and they were finally handed over to the dean and chapter library by the primate's own executors. Sharp's three MS. books, on the other hand, are still to be found in the archiepiscopal library at Bishopthorpe. The first two consisted of a number of separate treatises dealing in detail with the history, revenues, estates and patronage of the archbishopric and former archbishops, York Minster and its chapter, the collegiate church of St. Mary Southwell, and even a brief historical survey of the city of York itself. The general method appears to have been to set down the results of Torre's research verbatim, prefaced by a short introduction, and concluding, after the words "Thus far out of Mr. Tor", with various supplementary notes and comments of Sharp's own. The whole is a most careful and thorough piece of research, and reflects the greatest credit on the archbishop.[2]

"But the largest and most useful work of all, was that which related to the possessions and revenues of his clergy, with an account of all the parochial churches and chapels, whether under ordinary or peculiar jurisdiction, within his diocese; the value of the benefices, what rights were lost, and what preserved; in what hands the patronages were, and the impropriations and appropriations and whatsoever else could be learned of them useful to be known. This *notitia* of his diocese, as he called it, he distributed into four volumes folio, according to the division of the four archdeaconries. These were left at his death by his executors to the use of his successors."[3] This monumental work, the third and most important of Sharp's MS. books,[4] is of the greatest value to historians of the diocese, and can often prove of practical use to its modern possessors.

[1] See Appendix A, p. 325.
[2] See *Archbishop Sharp's MS. Books*, vols. i and ii (the Bishopthorpe MSS.).
[3] *Life of Archbishop Sharp*, vol. i, p. 136.
[4] It is known in the diocese as *Archbishop Sharp's Book*.

Characteristically enough, Sharp gave generous credit where credit was due, prefacing his learned survey with the following words: "For which account I am beholding in great measure to the accurate collections of the industrious Mr. Torre, who with incredible pains has transcribed out of the church monuments whatever he met with relating to the antiquities of every church or chappell in this diocese."

The archbishop knew only too well that the efficiency and reputation of the Church depended to a very large degree upon the lives of her parochial clergy; for they rather than the bishops or other ecclesiastical dignitaries were at close grips with the people of England. So first and foremost on his programme of reform he put the creation of a resident priesthood whose private lives, zeal, preaching ability and parochial efficiency should stand above reproach. It was an unfortunate age when want of discipline, poverty and party heats had already corrupted many of the clergy almost beyond reform;[1] yet more than any other bishop of his day Sharp saw his ideals realised. His methods were sound, for he was no inquisitor or busybody, and all forms of favouritism and toadying, either to persons or parties, were alike abhorrent to him. No clergyman was condemned unheard; no complaint or charge but was thoroughly and impartially investigated. No recourse was ever made to legal sanctions before there had been repeated appeals for reformation and fair warning had been given. All confidences were respected; and even when the law had to take its course the archbishop would often, out of the goodness of his heart and pocket, aid the unfortunate family whose head was alone to blame for their misfortunes. On the other hand, he seldom forgot a deserving cleric, however deficient he might be in worldly goods or influence, judging him in the light not of his political principles or family connections, but by his own moral character and the fruit of his pastoral labours. The recent discovery of Sharp's archiepiscopal correspondence throws a flood of fresh light on his dealings with the clergy, since the bulk of these letters, running into many hundreds, are from incumbents and curates within the York diocese. It will not, then, be out of place at this stage to quote passages from a few selected examples in order to illustrate Yorkshire clerical life as it was lived at the turn of the seventeenth century.[2]

[1] Abundant evidence for this is to be found in the Lloyd-Baker-Sharp MSS.
[2] *Cf.* Chapter I.

Some of the chief troubles that beset the Yorkshire parson during Sharp's day were: dilapidations; lawsuits arising out of tithe disputes; the malicious complaints of disgruntled parishioners or neighbouring clergymen, who seized on every trifling misdemeanour or omission of an incumbent in order to report him to the primate; the small endowments of livings, leading their possessors into plurality or debt; the difficulties of obtaining books or even newspapers; and, of course, the ever-increasing scramble for livings, of which there were never enough to go round. Faced by any or all of these worries, the Yorkshire and Nottinghamshire clergy in Queen Anne's reign knew that they had a staunch friend in their archbishop. And so, not unnaturally, the habit arose of writing to Sharp about it.

Dilapidations.—An interesting and typical case is that of Mrs. Tancred, the widow of the late rector of Barwick-in-Elmett: A certain Mr. Brook wrote to the archbishop on May 20, 1704, enclosing a document that he had received from Mrs. Tancred, with directions from her to transmit it to Sharp. "It contains the state of her case as she has drawn it up with reference to the contest about dilapidations between her and her husband's successor in the Rectory of Barwick, in Elmett, Mr. Plaxton."[1] The "enclosed paper"[2] made the following points: Mr. Tancred had himself found the vicarage in a deplorable state of disrepair, "an old ruinous decayed house"; but "for peace's sake" he had eventually accepted from his predecessor, Mr. Berrisford, the meagre sum of £50. Tancred, however, found the job an even bigger one than he had expected, for the foundations were rotten and the whole structure had to be created anew. The final contract arrived at with "one Richard Barrow" was for £260. Unfortunately the rector died before the work was finished, and £60 still remained to be paid. His widow allowed the contract to be completed, imagining that under the circumstances the new incumbent would settle the bill; yet Mr. Plaxton not only refused to do this but demanded £65 more for other dilapidations. The petition then went on to declare that Mr. Tancred had had little enjoyment of the living and none of the house, which was practically all paid for out of his own pocket. "He died above a year since and left a widow and a child. Query. Whether the present incumbent under these conditions is not obliged in all equity and good con-

[1] L-B-S. MSS., Box 4, Bundle Q. 2.
[2] L-B-S. MSS., Box 4, Bundle Q. 3.

science to acquit Mr. Tancred's widow and child from all dilapidations and further demands."

Mrs. Tancred put forward the viewpoint of the outgoing family, Thomas Heald that of the incoming vicar. Heald, the prospective vicar of Huddersfield, wrote to Sharp on July 15, 1696, about a conversation he had had recently with his predecessor, Mr. Clark, concerning the latter's payment for dilapidations: "He prevailed with me . . . to view the Vicarage-house. One part of it in which he himself lived, and has made some repairs, I confess is in a tolerable condition; but the other division which is the greatest (and was commonly let off to tenants) together with the barn is in a very miserable case, and all that Mr. Clark can say, is that he thinks that the new buildings may countervail the ruinousness of the others, and will spend a great deal more money *before* he makes anything at all of it good. I shall not insist much upon this, but refer myself wholly to your Lordship's will and pleasure."[1]

Tithe Troubles and Lawsuits.—Poor, uninfluential clerics often found themselves unjustly deprived of their rights, or compelled at ruinous expense to themselves to fight a losing battle in the law-courts. The archbishop was to prove a constant source of help to these unfortunate men. The Reverend W. Dealtry, curate of Egton, was such a one, who, finding his tithes sadly in arrears, wrote to Sharp as follows: "Upon the account of some arrears awanting to me as Curate of Egton . . . hearing that your Grace has been pleased long ago, to show the sympathy you bear to unrewarded labours in some instances of bounty to Mr. Baitman my fellow-sufferer; and being likewise told that, by a happy turn of affairs, you have been of late, put into the possession of the whole tithes of Lyth and Egton: I was encouraged to hope it would be no breach of modesty or forfeiture of your Grace's favour to offer a second request. I found myself now the main (and yet the most forgotten) loser in the case."[2]

Joseph Etherington of Dunham-nigh-Tuxford, on the other hand, found himself faced in the autumn of 1704, through no fault of his own, with a vexatious and expensive lawsuit, and also hastened to seek the archbishop's support and advice: "This is to signify to your Lordship that one Mrs. Flinton in my parish having without any consent brought a gravestone to be cut by the Communion Table in the chancel to the great hindrance of my doing

[1] L-B-S. MSS., Box 4, Bundle F. 32.
[2] L-B-S. MSS., Box 4, Bundle C. 5, undated.

the service of the Church and to the great offence of the communicants, by reason of the great interference that it has occasioned in
that sacred place. And still obstinately continuing it there, tho' I
never detained it or refused her to remove it out, but told her
withall that she could not appropriate a place to lay it in the
Churchyard (where there never was a precedent of any gravestone
before) without licence of the Bishop, order of the Court, and consent of the parson, paying the accustomed fees which are constantly paid to the neighbouring ministers, according to the
opinion of Sir Edward Coke. Notwithstanding that, my advice is
slighted, and obstinacy in her is encouraged by one who should be
a peacemaker betwixt minister and parishioners, yet threatens to
find £100 in her vindication (when he might better bestow it in
the Church's reparations) and no terms of peace can be accepted,
although I proposed to put the matter to reference to two clergymen, and would stand to their determination, and if it was not
my due I did not desire it, and if it was why should I not have it?
Nay rather than any trouble should come of it I propounded my
willingness to accept of half of the dues (which my neighbouring
ministers had) as an acknowledgement, for peace and quietness
sake. But I find the more I submit, the more refractory she is, and
nothing will please. She will not be friends with or reconciled to
me, but has visited her malice and hatred at me by arresting me
with a writ at the common law the last week . . . begging Your
Lordship's protection in the case and advice herein for peace
betwixt us."[1] Thomas Elcock of Rical was another who petitioned
Sharp in the most pitiable tones to "prevent the further consump-
tion of my poor income in a litigious law-suit";[2] while Henry
Elmsall of Thornhill, who found himself involved in a disputed
election of a schoolmaster at Stockton, wrote: "I hear Mr. Clarke
who is very foreign to his business (but to no litigeousness) concerns himself in applying to the Court of York to oppose our
methods herein."[3] Other complainants were John White of
Thorney[4] and James Earnshaw of Holme in Almondbury.[5]

[1] L-B-S. MSS., Box 4, Bundle D. 21, Sept. 16, 1704.
[2] L-B-S. MSS., Box 4, Bundle D. 24, Jan. 17, 1704.
[3] L-B-S. MSS., Box 4, Bundle D. 23, Dec. 29, 1700.
[4] L-B-S. MSS., Box 3, Bundle D. 4, Jan. 12, 1706/7.
[5] L-B-S. MSS., Box 4, Bundle D. 22A and 22B, May 24, 1703.
Unfortunately, in most of these and similar instances there are no indications as to
how the stories ended, since the archbishop's replies have not, apparently, been preserved. Sharp was, indeed, careful to make copies, either in long- or short-hand, of his
letters, of which only a limited number have survived. But wherever one is extant I
make a point of quoting from it.—A. T. H.

Complaints against the Clergy.—Jeremiah Bolton, incumbent of "Boutry", wrote to the archbishop on June 15, 1704, indignantly refuting the malicious accusations of his enemies. "I am not ignorant", he retorted, "that one of the clergymen who accused me to the Archdeacon had another thing in his view than my well-fare. I have been assured by a very virtuous person that his aim was at Boutry living. Your Lordship I doubt not is sensible that I living in a high road, all my relations and friends that travel this way will be calling upon me, which engages me in company much oftener than otherwise I should do. But I assure Your Lordship I ever took particular care to avoid scandalous drinking and unnecessary journeys to the ale-house and those I resorted to were no tippling houses, they were the best inns in the town.

"Besides, those that complain of me have no other information than of those who can love nobody long and have ever been fatal to the reputation of their ministers. I will not deny but my youth and the indiscretion that usually attends it, together with the little experience I had of some persons' tempers in our town, may sometimes have exposed me to the censure of the imperious and uncharitable, but never to those that are modest and humble and have a just sense of their own failings and miscarriages, and know how impossible it is to maintain an unblameable character in Boutry. We have some in our town will reproach persons for no other reason but because they are better than themselves and give a more constant attendance on the public worship of God. And God be thanked there are some of this sort, who would have scorned to have represented me so to Your Grace. I beg Your Lordship would consider under what difficulties I labour, there being so many divisions and parties in the town, that scarce one family loves their neighbour as is fitting. Tho' I have not been wanting to represent to them the ill consequences of rewarding tale bearers, which sets 'em on railing one against another. How contrary such things are to the nature and design of christianity, what abundance of ill blood those whispers create, and how fatal they were to the peace of the neighbourhood. For which I got thanks of some, and I suppose ill will of others. I could have added abundance more both in my defence and in representing the many bitter reflections I must bear with."[1]

Here is another from the Reverend George Holroid, vicar of Skipton: "The last time that I was at Bishopthorpe you were

[1] L-B-S. MSS., Box 4, Bundle Q. 39.

pleased to tell me I must answer the Court three things, viz. Neglect of the Church, boisterousness, and drunkenness. For the first the Church was never neglected but the service was performed either by myself or when I was not well by some neighbouring minister (on Sundays). The second: I live *in boriali plaga* and would not willingly so run I own. Third, let them name one particular place where, and tell the circumstances and prove them, and I'ill grant them their generals. And let them do it within the time of 7 years by past. Skipton is the poorest vicarage in Craven and they tell me by a monition that if I will retire I must have an allowance (never naming the fund) but I would where-ever it must arise, for I can scarce maintain myself although I live single. The reason why I make no defence to the Court is because (with submission to Your Grace) I think their proceedings are unjust; for 'tis unreasonable (I humbly conceive) that the Chancellor should both sue me and be likewise my judge, who is not my friend, but formost adversary. 'Tis not fair that two men who are mine accusers viz. Robert Kitchen and John Mitchill should be permitted to be witnesses against me. The first having perjured himself twice, once in the year 1696 he was instrumental in procuring the schoolmaster to make a clandestine marriage and did not present it being Churchwarden; and this last year being Churchwarden he never partakes the Sacrament. And he envies me because of the commission. Mitchill envies me because I'ill not go to his house for my Sunday dinner, but to Bankes'. And here's the ground of all their inventions lies and slanders."[1]

In this particular case, however, Sharp decided that the complaints were well founded, and replied: "I have . . . perused the depositions which were made against you, as also the defence that you made for yourself in writing. I am satisfied that the proceedings have been just and fair, and they certainly must and will end in a sentence of deprivation against you. . . . If you do not resign before the Michaelmas Term, you must expect to hear that you are deprived."[2] The conclusion of the story is to be found in a letter to the archbishop from the Earl of Thanet, the patron of Skipton living, who wrote on October 4, 1704: "I am very glad to find by Your Grace's letter to me Holroid has so much sense and respect to submit to your pleasure rather than be obstinate. And considering his unhappy circumstances 'tis very reasonable he

[1] L-B-S. MSS., Box 4, Bundle F. 39, Sept. 5, 1704.
[2] L-B-S. MSS., Box 4, Bundle T. 20.

should have £10 yearly secured towards his support, which I hope
you will see well secured to him."[1]

But once convinced of a clergyman's innocence Sharp stoutly
defended him against all comers. So when Timothy Ellisonne,
vicar of Coley, hastened "to inform Your Grace of the loose and
scandalous life which Mr. Cliff my neighbour lives, drinking whole
nights together and in his drink swearing and carrying on in a
most dreadful manner",[2] the archbishop coldly answered: "I received your letter this morning, and whatever the opinion I have
of the decency of it, I am willing to save you the trouble of a
journey to Bishopthorpe, Mr. Cliff is recommended to me, by a
great many of the inhabitants of Haworth to be their minister.
And I did not know that anybody's recommendation was wanting,
whose consent was necessary."[3] Neither did Francis Jessop, rector
of Treeton, receive any better satisfaction. He had written, quite
unsolicited, to Sharp about Dr. Halley, one of the prebendaries of
Ripon, in the following terms: "Often have I seen this man playing
the buffon in the coffee house without any regard for all sorts of
men there, some of which he knew, knew not and nobody knew,
yet he would take unwelcome liberties with me among such,
without occasion. Hereupon I was forced at last to foretell what
rough consequences would follow the next time. . . . I only beg
Your Grace will not suffer any longer, with Your Grace's pardon
again, a fool's cap longer on the Dr.'s head which suits not either
with the gown or hood or dignity of that most celebrated cathedral."[4] Certainly the manner in which many of the clergy abused
and accused one another was most unedifying.

Small Endowments, resulting either in Plurality or Debt.—"I must
acquaint Your Grace", wrote Timothy Ellisonne, "with my
straightened and mean circumstances. . . my maintenance not
being above 30 pounds a year, the greatness of my family,
six hopeful children . . . and having had much sickness in
my family I am become indebted £40. . . . I beg of Your
Grace to befriend me all you can."[5] The same gentleman later
received the offer "of two small places in Lancashire near to

[1] L-B-S. MSS., Box 4, Bundle L. 108.
[2] L-B-S. MSS., Box 4, Bundle D. 12.
[3] L-B-S. MSS., Box 4, Bundle T. 88.
[4] L-B-S. MSS., Box 4, Bundle H. 25. It is interesting to note that Jessop uses the
word "cathedral" in connection with Ripon, although the collegiate church of SS.
Peter and Wilfred did not become one before the nineteenth century. Twice, however,
in the same letter he also uses the term "Minster".
[5] L-B-S. MSS., Box 4, Bundle D. 11, Nov. 19, 1698.

Liverpool",[1] which he decided to accept, but at the same time pressed Sharp to allow him to retain Haworth: "I would beg of Your Grace the favour to keep Haworth a year or two, keeping an assistant there and allowing him twenty pounds per annum. And there will be only eleven pounds for myself which will discharge some small debts I have contracted in disposing of three of my children."[2]

Another impecunious clergyman was Richard Idle, rector of South Dalton, who wrote to the archbishop on May 19, 1707, after leaving the vicarage of Rothwell: "I was enabled by your Grace's bounty . . . to compound brother Jen. Thoresby's debts. Yet several of my own were left behind. And the removing of my family, repairs of house and chancel, with the payment of parish suits, took two years profits of this rectory entirely away from me. Besides the mismanagement of my wife, with her long sickness, run me sixty pounds into debts in these parts."[3]

In an undated petition John Tattershall, vicar of Sutton Panell, appealed to Sharp to help him to recover the small tithes from a farm, Stotfield, which were worth £150 per annum. Tattershall assured the primate that he had been "at great pains and charges in endeavouring to recover the said dues" both in the Court of Common Pleas and in the Ecclesiastical Court of York, but without avail, since he found himself opposed by the influential Lady Wentworth, the owner of the farm.[4] On approaching the latter, however, Sharp was informed: "I would not knowingly wrong the Church. I was very unwilling to enter into suit with Mr. Tattershall, and if I had not been satisfied it was our right I would not have continued it." She was very confident of a judgment in her favour.[5]

The Reverend Thomas Clark, vicar of Huddersfield, had been presented to the rectory of Kirk Heaton, and Sharp naturally expected him, after a reasonable time had elapsed to set his house in order, to resign the former living. This Clark obstinately evaded doing as long as possible,[6] and defended his conduct to the archbishop on the following grounds: "The whole benefit of Kirk Heaton is but £160 per annum. I have already laid out £50 in

[1] L-B-S. MSS., Box 4, Bundle D. 13, Aug. 8, 1702.
[2] L-B-S. MSS., Box 4, Bundle D. 13, Aug. 8, 1702.
[3] L-B-S. MSS., Box 4, Bundle H. 10.
[4] L-B-S. MSS., Box 3, Bundle F. 7.
[5] L-B-S. MSS., Box 3, Bundle E. 17, Dec. 11, 1701.
[6] Cf. Sharp's letters to Clark urging him to resign: L-B-S. MSS., Box 4, Bundle T. 17 and 18, July 6, 1696; Feb. 23, 1694/5.

making the house habitable, and £50 more will not set it in good repair (there is such a great pile of building belongs to it). I allow above £40 per annum to my curate and reader. I have paid at least £40 per annum past for taxes, assessments, pensions etc., besides first fruits, tenths. The Archbishop of Canterbury's dispensation together with the King's cost me in bare fees £24, besides 20 guineas more is charged upon me for soliciting, which I have not yet been able to pay. For clearing of my patron's title and . . . what was necessary for managing and improving the Glebe has caused me to contract above £300 debt, so that as I formerly acquainted Your Grace, tho' I live never so sparingly I shall not be reimbursed in 3 years. And therefore it was that I petitioned Your Grace at first . . . that I might enjoy but 3 years and then I would voluntarily resign it. . . . I think there are not many clergymen more adverse to pluralities than myself . . . should I die before I have paid the debt I have contracted my wife and children would be ruined."[1]

The Difficulty of Obtaining Books.[2]—Benjamin Brown, rector of Sundridge, near Sevenoaks, Kent, an old friend of Sharp during his Canterbury days, wrote to the archbishop on June 19 ,1695: "These are not sins, I confess, to be over-covetous of books, and I can tell by proportion, what great charges, great plans, required by the income and out-going of my little parsonage, which is just enough to keep me and my dear wife and children and pay taxes, and no more. But, my good Lord, books are such tempting things, that I for my part would be content to fare very hardly rather than be without some. Notwithstanding I have a greater library already, than is commonly seen in a country parson's house."[3]

Trouble with Parishioners.—John Wright, rector of Kirton near Tuxford, complained to Sharp on October 19, 1699, about the action of a certain Mr. Clarkson, whose sister resided in Kirton: "I beg leave to acquaint Your Grace that Mr. Clarkson (whom Your Grace (I presume) knows to be no great friend to the Church) has had his sister sick in our Parish but 3 houses from me, received

---

[1] L-B-S. MSS., Box 3, Bundle G. 17.   [2] *Cf.* Chapter I, pp. 32-33.
[3] L-B-S. MSS., Box 4, Bundle Q. 31. Brown continued: "I do not often receive the favour of a letter from an Archbishop: but once before I did from Archbishop Sancroft. Tho' seldomly I have such favours, the more I value 'ems. My Lord if you were not in that eminent station you are, I should count you as a dear friend and highly honour you, as all those do, and shall, that I have any interest in: for leaving aside your great character and considering you only as an excellent person and of a sweet temper and a courtious and most charitable gentleman. I think I and everybody else that values goodness and good manners, ought to show you all possible reverence and respect."

the Sacrament, dead and buried and a funeral sermon preached at my Parish Church and I never heard anything of this till all was past; they taking advantage of my being yesterday at the Synod of Southwell, for the funeral. My Lord all this was performed by Mr. Carter, Vicar of Little Markham, (who I thought could never have been guilty of so great an irregularity, but was) encouraged by Mr. Clarkson promising (as he says) to bear him out. I need not tell Your Grace that this is an affront to the ecclesiastical constitution of the Church as well as a slight upon myself."[1]

John Twitty, rector of Adwick, was troubled by "the malice of some evil men", who accused him of sanctioning "an incestuous marriage". He demanded that the archbishop should suppress such people: "I the Pastor of the Church of Adwick must find myself much more grieved if such enmities be not suppressed as disturb me in my ministry, while I cannot hope for any comfort of my travel and labour, nor have the blessed fruit of successful preaching, unless there be a public reformation of the offences mentioned."[2]

Many of the clergy were worried by the large numbers of moral offences committed within the boundaries of their parishes. John White, vicar of Thorney, informed Sharp on April 13, 1705, that one of his parishioners, George Neville, who had begotten an illegitimate child upon a servant girl of his, and had been duly "presented" for his crime, now desired to partake of the sacrament on Easter Day; and continued: "These are to certify to Your Grace within fourteen days according to the rubrick of the Church that I John White Vicar there durst not attempt to administer the Sacrament of the Lord's Supper to him upon Easter Day lest I might offend against the Church."[3] The inevitable Timothy Ellisonne of Coley complained of "one Timothy Stocks . . . in my chappelry, a filthy person having had three base begotten children fathered upon him. I have admonished and reproved him with all the earnestness I could. He glories in his shame. . . . I beg of Your Grace that he may be brought to open shame and punishment."[4]

Joseph Etherington of Dunham also "made bold to acquaint your Lordship with the incest that was committed in my Parish (for which reason I did repel them from the Holy Communion)".[5]

Others became involved with the sectaries. William Eratt, vicar

[1] L-B-S. MSS., Box 3, Bundle D. 26.   [2] L-B-S. MSS., Box 3, Bundle F. 30.
[3] L-B-S. MSS., Box 3, Bundle D. 37.
[4] L-B-S. MSS., Box 4, Bundle D. 12, Oct. 24, 1699.
[5] L-B-S. MSS., Box 4, Bundle D. 19, Sept. 16, 1700.

of Thorne, had on June 17, 1697, loudly praised his flock to the archbishop: "The peaceable and good genius of my parishioners . . . who as they are lovers of the Church, so also of decency and order."[1] But, alas! three years later a cloud appeared on the horizon. "There broke in upon me", he wailed, "that dangerous sect of the anabaptists." Dangerous and energetic they certainly proved; for they quickly got a meeting-house licensed, where they assembled two or three times a week, and, led by an ex-church-warden, "Jo: Woodward", startled and confused the Anglicans by calling their baptism into question. Eratt urgently desired the archbishop's advice on how to deal effectively with their argu-ments.[2]

On the other hand, several incumbents found themselves op-pressed or attacked by the local gentry. "The great kindness Your Grace has expressed", wrote Walter Hickson, rector of Cotting-ham, "in your repeated promises and endeavours, that my Lord of Chester may join with you in order to oblige Sir Michael Warton to pay to the Church of Cottingham what he is obliged to pay by lease."[3]

The dean of Ripon, Dr. Christopher Wyvil, was in a perpetual state of warfare with one of the aldermen, Sir Jonathan Jennings, and wrote long and exceedingly dull letters to the archbishop about his alleged iniquities; in particular that he caused disturb-ances in the Minster and abused the dean himself both publicly and privately. "My Lord", one of these letters complained, "I have been above eleven years Dean of Ripon, and have not been accustomed to be thus used."[4] Sharp, who did not care for Wyvil, refused to become embroiled in his quarrels. He therefore replied courteously but firmly that the archbishop had no power to inter-vene in this matter. Should, however, Sir Jonathan really make himself a nuisance in the Minster, the mayor and J.P.s could appoint their own officer to help the verger to turn him out, "provided it be done with all the quietness and gentleness that can be".[5]

The Scramble after Livings.—Much of the archiepiscopal corre-spondence is taken up with this subject, which was a very difficult

[1] L-B-S. MSS., Box 4, Bundle D. 17.
[2] L-B-S. MSS., Box 4, Bundle D. 18, May 16, 1700.
[3] L-B-S. MSS., Box 4, Bundle F. 30, Nov. 8, 1699.
[4] L-B-S. MSS., Box 3, Bundle E. 26, June 7, 1698. *Cf.* L-B-S. MSS., Box 3, Bundle D. 38, Sept. 7, 1698.
[5] L-B-S. MSS., Box 4, Bundle T. 66, Sept. 15, 1698.

and delicate one, involving all sorts of questions and interests. For example, there were frequent disputes as to patronage, which the following incident, culled from Sharp's own memoranda, amply illustrates: "A.D. 1704. Mr. Walker the late curate having quitted this chappell [Honley] a dispute arose between Mr. Philipson, the Vicar of Almondbury, and the inhabitants of this chappell, who should nominate the succeeding curate. Both parties pleaded a right. On August 2nd I had them before me at the Chancellor's chamber. The thing was doubtful. Mr. Philipson brought proof that he had named the two preceding curates. And they proved that he had taken money of both of them for their coming in. They pleaded that their consent was had as well as his. Nay further that they had an absolute right, for it did not appear the chappell was consecrated and so not under the ordinary jurisdiction. Tho' I believe this is false. And the lands out of which the curate was maintained being given to them they would not pay the rents to any but such as they choose. The Chancellor was of opinion that the right was in the Vicar, the chappell being within his parish and it not appearing that by any agreement or composition he had parted from his right or that the Ordinary had by an Act settled it upon the chappelry. They produced a letter under the Vicar's hand from Mr. Haigh wherein he declared that for this time the inhabitants might choose whom they would. And yet after this he names Mr. Porrit, and gets him licensed contrary to the consent of the inhabitants, who had choosen another and whom they would have had me to have licensed. After a great deal of squabble, both parties were content to submit the matter entirely to my determination. But yet as my award should only conclude them for this time, but should not affect the right of either party in time to come. My award was that both the present nominees should be laid aside . . . And that the inhabitants should pitch upon some third person, a sober unexceptionable man . . . and when they had chosen such a one they should present him to their Vicar and upon his approbation of him and signing their paper of election I would grant him a licence to serve the cure of that chappell."[1]

So the matter was amicably settled.

The majority of the livings in the York diocese were at the disposal of the archbishop himself, the crown or some great landowner. Sharp was as a rule on the best of terms with both the latter patrons, and they almost invariably consulted him before making

[1] *Archbishop Sharp's MSS.*, vol. iii, Addenda: Honley Chapel (Bishopthorpe MSS.).

an appointment. The many letters extant between Sharp and three of the Lord Chancellors of his day, Somers, Wright[1] and Cowper, were uniformly pleasant, consultative and informative;[2] and he was usually equally fortunate with the landed nobility and gentry.

In a letter to Lady Bridgewater dated April 1, 1703, Sharp admits that the "title to the Advowson of Agnes Burton" had finally been decided by law in her favour. To this decision the archbishop willingly submitted, but he goes on to beg her ladyship to confirm Mr. Richardson's appointment, "the man that I put in upon the death of the last incumbent."[3] In a charming reply Lady Bridgewater declared: "You may be sure that what you desire for the gentleman that you have collated there that will most readily be observed by me."[4] She was equally accommodating on another occasion: "I must now give Your Grace thanks for putting in Mr. Rose into the living of Normanby."[5] Lord Burlington also appreciated the archbishop's help and advice in this delicate question of clerical preferment. "Nothing", he wrote gratefully to Sharp on August 10, 1703, "can be more reasonable than to dispose of it as you intend."[6]

Frequently, indeed, the primate was consulted without having to ask. The Earl of Thanet hastened "to acquaint you that I have a living that hath been vacant above a month, would be above two hundred pounds a year, there are two chappells of ease which are fit to have £50 a year out of it, which I must take care to see secured, by reason the minister that is now dead was so remiss as to make so little allowances that the service of these chappells were seldom supplied. The parish is very large and requires a steady good man of 30 or 40 years old that would resolve to fix there and would have no higher thought of preferment, if Your Grace can recommend to me such a man, that has no exception to so cold a remote country, he may live as plentifully there . . . as one worth 400 pounds a year here. I have had application from

---

[1] Wright, in point of fact, was never more than Lord Keeper; while Harcourt, who became Lord Keeper in 1710 and Lord Chancellor three years later, only appeared at the end of the archbishop's life, and there is no record of any such correspondence with or from him.

[2] Cf. L-B-S. MSS., Box 4, Bundle B. 19, May 2, 1706; B. 20, April 20, 1706; T. 39, June 2, 1703; T. 40, July 9, 1700; T. 41, undated; A. 59, May 29, 1703.

[3] L-B-S. MSS., Box 4, Bundle T. 51, April 1, 1703.

[4] L-B-S. MSS., Box 4, Bundle B. 23, May 12, 1703. Her delay in replying was due to the death of her husband, which had naturally occupied her attention to the exclusion of everything else.

[5] L-B-S. MSS., Box 4, Bundle B. 29.   [6] L-B-S. MSS., Box 4, Bundle B. 26.

several of that country for it and have the most reason to be inclined to give it to a young man of that country now at Oxford;
but apprehending him to be young for me to be assured he would
acquit himself well of so great a trust . . . so that if Your Grace
know any Yorkshire or any other countryman so qualified that
will resolve to fix there, I know I shall be well provided when recommended by Your Grace. . . . The living's name is Kerbythure
(in Westmoreland) and the deceased parson's name was Hachill,
it being so remote cannot delay presenting so long as I might if it
was in Kent."[1] The archbishop was able to supply a suitable
candidate in the person of his own chaplain, Edmund Wickins,
who secured the benefice.[2]

Sharp could not always rely on such ready co-operation. Lord
Stamford, for instance, wrote on June 28, 1698, "I'm sorry to find
any reason to complain of Your Grace, as I must in refusing the
instituting of my Chaplain to Crofton,"[3] and went on to threaten
legal proceedings unless his request should be granted. A more
serious case was that of the Earl of Exeter, who had offered a
living as a bribe to a certain cleric on condition that he became
"Mr. P——'s son-in-law". Horrified, the primate begged him "to
consider the honour of God and religion, all of which cannot but
suffer by your permission of ecclesiastical benefices to be thus
prostituted".[4] Quite unrepentant, the Earl indignantly replied: "I
wonder why in good breeding your Lordship would pretend to
assume the liberty of becoming my censor? And endeavour to insinuate with your rhetorick that I prostitute (which by the way is
a very rough word) your ecclesiastical benefices, when God knows
that I give presentations but to those very men, that you Bishops
beforehand ordained and qualified to enjoy them. So that if they
are block-heads, scandalous to our church and gross ill-livers, the
fault lies at your own doors, and there I presume to leave it."[5]

But, on the whole, the lay patrons were very accommodating;
and as a result of their friendly consultations Sharp's powers of
and influence on patronage were vastly increased.

It is interesting to note in passing that yet another source of
patronage lay in the archbishop's right to options. "An option was

[1] L-B-S. MSS., Box 4, Bundle A. 52, Dec. 13, 1698.
[2] H. Dering, *Autobiographical Memoranda* (Surtees Society, vol. 65), p. 340. *Cf. Life
of Archbishop Sharp*, vol. i, p. 197; also "Archbishop Sharp and his 'Poor Relations'"
in *The Modern Churchman*, vol. xxxiv, pp. 55 and 56.
[3] L-B-S. MSS., Box 4, Bundle A. 55.
[4] L-B-S. MSS., Box 4, Bundle R. 3, July 27, 1695.
[5] L-B-S. MSS., Box 4, Bundle L. 113.

the right claimed by the Archbishops to 'chuse out of all the Pre-ferments belonging to the See of a new Bishop, what particular Benefice they would have, for the first Avoidance as a Fee due to them of Antient Right'.[1] During his two and twenty years at York Sharp secured several such options, notably when Nicolson became bishop of Carlisle and Wilson succeeded to Sodor and Man.

"I have here my Lord", wrote Nicolson on May 26, 1702, "enclos'd a list of whatsoever can be worth Your Grace's option on this occasion. The best living in the Diocese of Carlisle (and in the Bishop's gift) is the Vicarage of Torpenhow, worth about £140 per an. Its now enjoyed by (my brother-in-law) Mr. Nevinson; who is about 40 years old. The Rectory of Calbeck is the next in value . . . the rest are not worth naming to Your Grace. I have given the values, to the best of my knowledge."[2]

"I find", declared Wilson on February 6, 1697, "there is one Vicarage in my gift now vacant, which is at Your Grace's disposal . . . 'tis not worth above £8 a year."[3]

The greater his powers and opportunities the more careful was the archbishop to choose the right man for the right post, quite irrespective of any material considerations, although this scrupu-lousness sometimes led him into difficulties, and on one occasion compelled him to reject a candidate recommended by the powerful Duke of Leeds.

"In this particular", wrote Sharp to the Duke, "of recommend-ing Mr. Ferrand to the Vicarage of Wakefield in case Mr. Lee should die, I do most earnestly beg Your Grace, not to lay your commands upon me. For if you will give me leave to speak my sense freely, I do much doubt whether he have all the qualifica-tions necessary for the discharge of so great and so difficult a post."[4] The Duke accepted this rebuff in good part; not so the disappointed clerk.[5]

The clergy themselves were not diffident about approaching their metropolitan on the subject of preferment, and the arch-

[1] Edward Carpenter, *Thomas Sherlock*, p. 163.
[2] L-B-S. MSS., Box 4, Bundle L. 90.
[3] L-B-S. MSS., Box 4, Bundle L. 77.
[4] L-B-S. MSS., Box 4, Bundle R. 8, June 19, 1700.
[5] *Cf. Life of Archbishop Sharp*, vol. i, pp. 192-196. Another example of such a refusal is to be found in a letter to Lord Faulconbridge, concerning "Mr. Brown". The arch-bishop wrote: "I think he is no fit man for either Cuckwold or Kilburn . . . but what shall be done with Mr. Brown, since cures there are none in this country?": L-B-S. MSS., Box 4, Bundle T. 45.

bishop found that he had often to be firm as well as fair.[1] His methods can be illustrated from the two following examples: Dr. Nicholls, a notorious place hunter, was politely but firmly refused a prebend;[2] while Mr. Calvert, an obscure but industrious cleric, was warmly recommended for the living of Howden. "A grave, well tempered man", wrote Sharp, "and a very good preacher. He has been long a minister in this country."[3]

There is an interesting letter from the Reverend Harrington Yarborough, chaplain to the English ambassador at Constantinople. Yarborough desired the archbishop to secure him the living of Eperston, which was in the gift of Lord Howe, and hold it open for him until his return. "But, my Lord", he complained, "to repair to England so soon as may be requisite, is a great difficulty, by reason we have no free passage at sea; nor any ships in Turkey that are bound homeward. And overland, the distance is so great, and the countries so many and so various throughout which to pass, that it would be a journey of great expense and difficulty."[4]

There were three things against which the archbishop steadfastly set his face: simony, plurality and non-residence. Anything in the nature of a simoniacal contract immediately aroused his opposition. "Madam", he replied to a lady, who had asked him to recommend a suitable clergyman for a living in her gift, "I must beg leave to present to you, that if it be expected that the person . . . that is to be presented by your Ladyship, should enter into any promise or engagement of any kind relating to the rights and profits of the parsonage, I must humbly desire to be excused from recommending anyone."[5] It was, indeed, a matter of concern to all the bishops, who kept each other informed of any such illegality. The bishop of Chester, for instance, notified his metropolitan of the case of the living of Crofton in Lancashire, where it was alleged that the incumbent, in collusion with some of the trustees, had signed a bond resigning in favour of another clergyman, and accepted £500 as compensation.[6] And on August 27, 1698, Sharp received the following communication from Tenison: "My Lord's Grace of Canterbury is informed that Mr. John

---

[1] It is impossible to quote from all the correspondence available, but here are a few of the references: L-B-S. MSS., Box 4, Bundle T. 36, 43, 45; Box 3, Bundle B. 11: Box 3, Bundle E. 9.
[2] L-B-S. MSS., Box 4, Bundle T. 16, July 18, 1705.
[3] Letter to a Lord: L-B-S. MSS., Box 4, Bundle T. 27, 1707.
[4] L-B-S. MSS., Box 4, Bundle A. 69, April 24, 1702.
[5] Life of Archbishop Sharp, vol. i, p. 199.   [6] L-B-S. MSS., Box 4, Bundle L. 53.

Pighells, Rector of Patrington near Hull, came in by a simoniacal contract with my Lord Dunbar's steward to whom he paid £350, which Mr. Sissison, Rector of Headon, and his friends, are able to prove. The King's presentation will be granted to none till Your Grace have examined it, and please to let my Lord know your opinion, whether there is reason for it."[1]

There was a similar agreement in condemning pluralities. "I think", wrote Tenison, "Pluralities, as now the case stands, are a mischief to the Church, and . . . I should be glad if Your Grace and the rest of my brethren would join with me against them next Parliament."[2]

Sharp certainly did his best to stamp them out whenever practicable, as when he refused to allow Mr. Ellisonne to hold Haworth together with his two Lancashire livings, and compelled Thomas Clark to resign Huddersfield after his presentation to Kirk Heaton. Furthermore, he declined to appoint titular chaplains for the purpose of enabling his friends and protégés to hold more than one benefice, although this was a common enough practice among the bishops and lay nobility of the day.[3] In some instances, however, where the livings were small and close together and the clergyman poor with a large family, he did support a dispensation by the Archbishop of Canterbury.[4]

The archbishop likewise insisted, whenever possible, upon residence; yet here, again, each individual case had to be judged by its circumstances and on its merits. "I hope the prudent conduct of my curate", wrote Mr. H. Crisp, petitioning for leave of absence, "and the particular satisfaction my parishioners I understand take in him, render my presence among them less necessary. Not but that I intend sometimes to visit them."[5] This Mr. Crisp, who was vicar of Catton, was a highly unsatisfactory clergyman, and it is extremely unlikely that Sharp granted his petition. Tenison, who had had dealings with him, remarked: "He takes a good share of the profits of it [i.e. his living] with the consent of his parishioners as glad of his absence upon such terms";[6] and

---

[1] L-B-S. MSS., Box 3, Bundle B. 18.
[2] L-B-S. MSS., Box 4, Bundle A. 13, July 22, 1707.
[3] "The nomination to a chaplaincy became often a formality granted merely to furnish the legal qualification for plurality and without spiritual duties. This creation of titular chaplains in no wise added to the efficiency or credit of the Church": N. Sykes, *Church and State in the Eighteenth Century*, p. 170.
[4] *Life of Archbishop Sharp*, vol. i, p. 201.
[5] L-B-S. MSS., Box 3, Bundle G. 13, Sept. 12, 1699.
[6] L-B-S. MSS., Box 4, Bundle L. 67.

Sharp himself felt obliged to address the vicar with stern words: "Sir. It is complained to me that you have for some considerable time used your parishioners very ill in your performance of divine offices among them. As for sermons, you rarely give them any, and as for the divine service of the Church, you begin it so uncertainly as to the hour, and you perform it so indecently as to the manner, as if you really had in mind to show your hearers that you are so far out of charity with them, that you do not desire that they should receive any benefit, even by the saying of their prayers."[1]

Other would-be non-residents had more to justify their requests. Henry Finch, whose house in March 1695/6 had been searched by dragoons "as being a disaffected person to the government", felt obliged to quit his parish of Winwick for a time, "unless I can have some open satisfaction made me". But as this proved impossible, he was forced to "commit all the care of this place to my curates", and obtained the archbishop's permission to retire from it.[2] Mr. S. Terrick, one of Sharp's chaplains, pleaded the case of the vicar of "Brathwell, near Doncaster", who "says that Your Grace when at Hatfield in May last gave him a dispensation by word of mouth for not residing on his Vicarage House", because of "the great distance of it from the Church, its unhealthy situation, to which he desires may be added its great unfitness for his family, having many children (ten when all at home), and his being at present afflicted with an asthmatical distemper". Terrick went on to suggest that Sharp should confirm this dispensation in writing and so enable the vicar to move into a house nearer the church, while keeping the old vicarage in a proper state of repair.[3]

In order to get to know and improve the preaching abilities of the parochial clergy, apart from the cathedral staff, the archbishop instituted a Friday evening lecture, which was held every week in the city of York at the church of All Saints-in-the-Pavement, the preachers being drawn not only from York itself and the surrounding neighbourhood, but from all four corners of the diocese. Sharp, who constantly attended these lectures when in residence at Bishopthorpe, constituted himself a sort of father-adviser-cum-critic of the various preachers, who were afterwards invited to dinner at Bishopthorpe, where their addresses were analysed and discussed. Such proceedings, unless they had been extremely tact-

[1] L-B-S. MSS., Box 4, Bundle R. 16. *Cf. Life of Archbishop Sharp*, vol. i, p. 156.
[2] L-B-S. MSS., Box 3, Bundle B. 8, March 18, 1695/6.
[3] L-B-S. MSS., Box 3, Bundle F. 22, Nov. 27, 1699.

fully handled, might have aroused a good deal of opposition and ill-feeling; but on the whole this innovation, which ran from 1693 until 1707 without a break, was well received by the clergy, and certainly proved of considerable benefit mentally, spiritually and socially to all those who took part in it. Two of the earliest preachers were Clement Elis, rector of Kirkby, and T. Caryl, vicar of St. Mary's, Nottingham.

The archbishop, apparently, made a practice of entering each preacher's name together with notes on his discourse and character in his shorthand diary, which data often proved of value for future reference. Only twice were the comments of a harsh nature, and in each case the sermon under review had been a philippic against the Dissenters: "Mr. —— preached so furious a sermon against the dissenters as I never heard the like. I went out of the church before I came into the vestry because I knew not how to behave myself towards him." On the second occasion he wrote: "Mr. —— instead of preaching *railed* against the *dissenters*."[1]

Sharp was himself a constant preacher both at the Minster and elsewhere, having a great opinion of and belief in the value of the effect of simple, straightforward doctrinal sermons, free from controversial matter, but impregnated with practical Christian teaching. Certainly his own sermons of this type were much appreciated by his contemporaries and subsequent generations. "It has been one chief happiness", Mrs. Anne Wynne wrote to him on February 24, 1698, "that I have heard some of Your Lordship's sermons, wherein Your Lordship hath made religion very easy and pleasant."[2] Some eighty years later the Reverend Charles Simeon, while a young man on vacation in 1779, admitted that "having read a great deal of Hervey's Works, I was much perplexed in my mind respecting the nature of saving faith," and on asking his father's advice was told to consult Dr. Loveday of Caversham. "To him I did apply; and he lent me Archbishop Sharp's third volume; containing his casuistical sermons; these I read with great profit; they showed me that Hervey's view of saving faith was erroneous; and from that day to this I have never had a doubt upon the subject."[3]

Nevertheless it was the character rather than the learning or eloquence of a man that the archbishop bore constantly in mind

---

[1] *Life of Archbishop Sharp*, vol. i, pp. 143-144.
[2] L-B-S. MSS., Box 3, Bundle E. 189.
[3] *Memoirs of the Life of the Reverend Charles Simeon, M.A.*, p. 20. Edit. W. Carus.

when admitting candidates to ordination. For ordination was the gateway to the priesthood, and Sharp wisely took great care that it should only be opened to the deserving.

It was the custom for incumbents to send the men whom they desired as curates to the archbishop armed with a long and usually very flowery testimonial.

"The Bearer hereof, Mr. Jeremiah Kitching, Bachelor of Arts of Trinity College in Cambridge", wrote Thomas Clark, vicar of Kirk Heaton, of one such candidate, "comes to present himself to Your Grace to be made a Deacon, which I hope Your Grace will find him worthy of. He is well attested from the College from which he came but lately, and therefore I did not find the Canon required any other testimonial. He is chosen schoolmaster of our small school at Kirk Heaton, which is but endowed with £5 per annum; but for his better encouragement as soon as he is ordained Deacon I promise to allow him £10 per annum for reading prayers at the church, burying, christening, etc. in my absence as I did Mr. Midgeley before him. . . . He has demeaned himself very soberly since he came hither and seemingly pious and studious. I doubt not but he will give Your Grace satisfaction upon his examination, as to his learning."[1]

"Cousin Oughton", vicar of Whitby, also sent a candidate, a certain Mr. Kemp, and received the following cautious reply from the archbishop: "I am not against putting him into Deacon's Orders the next Ordination, provided he brings me a good testimonial of his morals, and a note that you appoint him your curate; with a certificate of an allowance to be made him either by you or the town."[2] It was not, however, always possible to accept a recommended candidate, and then the reply was not so easy to write: "Sir—It grieves me to tell you that I am forced to send back your son again without Orders . . . I had such an account of him that till these objections be cleared I cannot possibly with a good conscience admit him into Holy Orders . . . I should think it much more adviseable to put him upon some other calling than that of a clergyman. . . . I am engaged in no private interest, nor have any ends to serve but those of God and the Church in this affair."[3]

Sharp held ordinations "regularly at all the stated times, when

---

[1] L-B-S. MSS., Box 3, Bundle G. 16, May 15, 1700.
[2] L-B-S. MSS., Box 4, Bundle T. 70, July 30, 1702.
[3] L-B-S. MSS., Box 4, Bundle T. 78, Sept. 20, 1692.

he was in his diocese", and insisted upon his ordinands acquiring "a right notion of the main doctrines of religion, to understand thoroughly the terms of the new covenant, both on God's part and on man's: and to know the reasons and apprehend the force of those distinctions upon which the Church of England explained and stated those terms differently from the Church of Rome and other Communions separating from her."[1] Candidates who lacked such qualifications were sent back to their studies, taking with them not only the archbishop's wise counsels, but many of his books besides. Some, who were especially badly off, he actually "entertained . . . in his own family till they were so instructed, that he could satisfy himself they might be put into holy orders"; and when they were finally accepted he solemnly charged them all to do their duty, remembering that they were God's servants and He would one day demand a reckoning; to read the scriptures and other good books to help them in their profession; and always to preach "good sense and strong plain arguments" on Sunday, and "every day by their good life and conversation".[2]

There is certainly no doubt that Sharp took his ordinations very seriously and held them regularly: "Within the limits of the prevalent tradition which withdrew the episcopate from diocesan business for the greater part of the year, individual bishops strove often with diligence and perseverance to administer the rite of ordination with the solemnity and dignity appertaining to so high a transaction. Archbishop Sharp of York set a signal example of personal care and devotion to public duty in this, as in other branches of the episcopal character."[3] And yet curiously enough his Register and Act Books appear to contain no record at all either of his ordinations or confirmations, although, admittedly, it is unusual for the latter to be entered in the York Registers.[4]

Nevertheless it can be seen from the archbishop's letters that he was frequently in the habit of ordaining men from other dioceses in order to help some of his less conscientious brother bishops. "My Lord", he wrote to Lord Crewe of Durham on August 25, 1694, "There is one Mr. Swintoun a Scotchman in your Diocese whom the last Ordination I put into Priest's Orders, as I had done

---

[1] *Life of Archbishop Sharp*, vol. i, pp. 145 and 146.
[2] Ibid., vol. i, p. 149.
[3] N. Sykes, *Church and State in the Eighteenth Century*, p. 105.
[4] I am indebted for the above information to the Reverend J. S. Purvis, F.S.A., the learned archivist of the York diocese, who also tells me that for the duration of the war the York Registers have been widely scattered over the country, and it is quite possible, therefore, that some of Archbishop Sharp's records have been overlooked.

the year before into Deacon's. But I did not do it without your
Lordship's letters Dimissory signed by your Chancellor, nor without a good title to a Curacy then vacant at Barnard's Castle to
which he was nominated by the Minister of the Parish. I understand he is now a humble suitor to your Lordship for your licence
to serve that cure. I do my Lord join with him in his Petition, and
beg you would not refuse it him. I have by me as ample a testimonial of his virtue and good conversation as can be desired. And
for his learning he did so well acquit himself upon both his
examinations that if you dare take my word, I dare pronounce he
is very well qualified to serve a greater cure than that. I am told
likewise that he is very acceptable to much the greatest part of the
Chappelry. I should not, my Lord, have meddled in this affair had
it not been my fortune in your Lordship's absence to have admitted him into Holy Orders which puts some concernment upon
me to see that he be not turned to the wide world to seek his
bread."[1]

Stratford of Chester was another bishop whose candidates were
sometimes ordained at York. "I received by the last post", he
wrote to the archbishop on May 29, 1699, "a letter from Mr.
Stable (Rector of Goldsborough) with another enclosed from one
of the members of Parliament for Knaresborough, both requesting
me to give my consent, that your Grace might ordain one Richard
Petty, lately come from Cambridge. I freely give my consent. But
how the young man, when he shall be ordained, can serve as a
Curate at Tinghall without my licence, I do not understand."[2]

On occasion an incumbent, ignoring his own diocesan, would
send a candidate to Sharp. Dr. Todd,[3] the turbulent vicar of
Penrith in the diocese of Carlisle, sent a Scotchman named Murray
in December 1701. "His learning", wrote Todd in his testimonial, "I think is competent for he knows Latin and Greek indifferently well; and is well enough furnished with systematical
divinity,"[4] and went on to suggest that Sharp should ask for
Letters Dimissory. But in this particular case proceedings had to
be abruptly terminated as the would-be ordinand's past life
proved far from satisfactory.[5]

Sometimes a candidate who had been refused by his own
bishop would hopefully present himself at Bishopthorpe, trusting

[1] L-B-S. MSS., Box 4, Bundle H. 15.   [2] L-B-S. MSS., Box 4, Bundle L. 80.
[3] See *D.N.B.*, also Chapter VII, pp. 190 ff.
[4] L-B-S. MSS., Box 3, Bundle F. 9, Dec. 13, 1701.
[5] L-B-S. MSS., Box 3, Bundle F. 10.

that the primate's well-known warm heart would triumph over an equally cool head. "One George Burches", Stratford warned him, "formerly of Brasenose College in Oxford and now curate of Moghull in Lancashire applied to me last Ember-Week, for the Holy Order of Priesthood. I rejected him for insufficiency; for upon examination I found him grossly ignorant, that I cannot but wonder, how I came to admit him to the Order of Deacon. But which is worse, I have been lately informed, that the same Burches lives in the constant practice of the foulest immoralities, and I have now cited him to appear in my court to answer articles exhibited against him for very scandalous crimes. He therefore despairing of obtaining that Sacred Order from me, gives out (as I am told) that he will get it elsewhere. Lest therefore he should procure a false title from any clergyman of his acquaintance in Your Grace's Diocese, and thereby endeavour to impose upon Your Grace, I thought myself obliged to give Your Grace this short account of him."[1]

There is no record of Sharp having ordained anywhere but at York. Bishop Lloyd of Coventry and Lichfield, indeed, wrote in October 1698 concerning his son that he "took the boldness last winter at London to move it to Your Grace that you would be pleased to ordain him deacon"; but the rest of the letter clearly indicates that this young man was not immediately ordained.[2]

Before leaving the subject of ordination it may be of interest to note a curious case of supposedly forged orders, which James Gardiner, bishop of Lincoln, brought to the notice of the archbishop during the spring of 1700. Mr. Hide, a brother-in-law of the scandalous Watson, bishop of St. David's, and an unsatisfactory incumbent in the Lincoln diocese, was suspected by his bishop of this crime. Gardiner sent a copy of his orders to Sharp "desiring Your Grace to order your Books of Ordinations to be examined, whether there be such a name in the year mentioned." There were strong grounds for suspicion that the surname Hide had been written upon an erasure, and that the figure 8 in the year 1678 was likewise a later addition. Furthermore, the Cambridge College of Sidney-Sussex appeared in the orders, whereas the bishop had been given to understand that Hide was a graduate of St. John's. "I desire", Gardiner therefore continued, "the favour of Your Grace's answer to this, for if I have good ground to proceed against

[1] L-B-S. MSS., Box 4, Bundle L. 86, May 1, 1703.
[2] L-B-S. MSS., Box 4, Bundle L. 98, Oct. 3, 1698.

him for Forgery, it will be the most expeditious and effectual way."[1]

Sharp's archiepiscopal charges, delivered during his visitations, were directed towards impressing upon the clergy the paramount importance of a blameless life, both public and private, since the common people were sure to judge of their preaching and other ministrations in the light of their own personal practice and example. Nevertheless an ignorant priesthood was almost as bad as an immoral or lazy one; and so the archbishop earnestly besought them all "to study good authors and to use the best conversation they could meet with, and to improve themselves in all kinds of knowledge". An elaborate, witty or involved style of preaching should be avoided at all costs, as being just as objectionable in its way as either controversy or invective. But on the other hand they should be sure to "impress upon their flocks the substantial doctrines and indispensable duties of Christianity and the mighty arguments they had both for believing the one and practising the other: and that they should do this very plainly and affectionately."[2]

Constant personal residence within their cures was the indispensable obligation of a conscientious priesthood, while their time there should be occupied in catechising the youth of the place, administering the sacraments as frequently as possible, visiting the sick, and obeying all other rules and regulations "according to the rubrics and canons".[3] The archbishop also laid stress on the desirability of daily prayers in church, or, if that was entirely out of the question, at least on Wednesdays and Fridays and all recognised holy days. This latter injunction appeared to carry little weight with the majority of the incumbents, although there were many fine exceptions. Robert Marsden, rector of Rempston, formerly a domestic chaplain of Sharp and instituted in 1702, reported in *Archbishop Herring's Visitation Returns* some forty years later: "I reside personally upon my Cure, and in my Parsonage-house; as now I have done, for near forty years. . . . Public Service is duly performed twice every Lord's Day. We are, all, about a mile off the Church: else, I would be glad to have prayers daily. I catechise in my Church every Sunday . . . and always (to the best of my power) expound upon the catechism."[4]

---

[1] L.-B.-S. MSS., Box 4, Bundle L. 94.
[2] *Life of Archbishop Sharp*, vol. i, pp. 152 and 153.
[3] Ibid.. vol. i, p. 154.
[4] *Archbishop Herrings' Visitation Returns*, vol. iv, p. 119.

The following letter from the Reverend John Rawson warned Sharp of the manner in which idle clergy window-dressed on the occasion of his visitation, and then sank back into their old supineness as soon as his back was turned: "It is reported (although with some uncertainty) that Your Grace intends to visit your diocese this next summer. And I am of the number of those that believe it. And if I may be allowed the liberty of conjecture: I suppose Your Grace made your first visitation in order to be acquainted with the Estate of your diocese. And as it may be supposed that Your Grace might find several things out of order and give instructions for bringing them into order again; so your second visitation may be intended to inform yourself whether your instructions have been well observed: And, in my poor judgement, your first visitation will be lame, and imperfect without a second. It is usual for people to put their houses in order when they expect and are to entertain any extraordinary person. And afterwards they return to their old custom, and there are some people in the world that serve Your Grace so with respect to the Church: who at the same time endeavour to be thought to have the greatest respect for you, and although there is nothing more certain than that they do it wholly for their own ends. And if Your Grace would certainly know what zeal every man hath for your Church, and respect for yourself, you need but enquire into the particular orders that were given by you for the several churches of your diocese whether they have been observed, and how long they have been so."[1]

Nicolson, immediately after his installation as bishop of Carlisle, knowing the archbishop's interest in the subject, wrote on July 18, 1702: "The greatest want of this Diocese, in the late Bishop's time, was in the matter of confirmation; which his great age and infirmities had brought into a total neglect, for fourteen (or sixteen) years past. Your Grace's papers will give me great help in the recovery of my people out of this neglected state. And I shall (God willing) go round the whole Diocese before Michaelmas next, confirming in ten or twelve several churches."[2]

Sharp, when in residence in Yorkshire, held confirmations regularly, and if at all practicable made a point of laying his hands

---

[1] L-B-S. MSS., Box 4, Bundle E. 40.
[2] L-B-S. MSS., Box 4, Bundle L. 91. *N.B.*—Burnet was another "Revolution" bishop who was much concerned over confirmation. See Clarke and Foxcroft, *Life of Gilbert Burnet*, p. 290.

upon one or at most two candidates at a time in order to impress upon their minds the solemn nature of this sacrament. But at a period when the episcopate was bound to spend a large part of the year in London, and nearly all baptised persons came forward as a matter of course to be confirmed, which sometimes meant thousands of candidates at a service, such individual attention was not always possible. But Sharp's own deep sense of responsibility in the matter is well illustrated by the following account of one of his confirmations: "Upon one time, while he confirmed with the gout upon him that he could not stand, but sat in his chair at the communion rails, and the catechumens were brought to him, one after another, he first recovering so much strength as by resting one knee upon a chair, which was gently moved along, he could proceed as usual along the rails, and soon after he quitted that support and confirmed some thousands of persons, and after profuse sweating lost his distemper entirely."[1]

As the archiepiscopal correspondence fully bears out, Sharp was only too pleased to answer any question, to resolve any doubt, or to tender any advice, which it lay in his part to give to his clergy. Miles Gale, the rector of Keighley, found himself involved in a dispute with Daniel Craven, the Duke of Devonshire's tenant, who claimed two pews in the north aisle of the church as the duke's property. This happened to be false, as the pews in question had been built and were still being used by Mr. Starkey of Ridlesden Hall. Craven had apparently acted from two motives, "one to gratify his pride, in hopes he may be appointed to sit there, and the other his malice by doing Mr. Starkey an injury".[2] What is the rector to do? He has no desire to offend the Duke of Devonshire or Mr. Starkey; and Craven refuses to accept any alternative accommodation.

Again, Charles Wright, vicar of Normanton, discovered upon taking over the living that Mr. Charlesworth, a neighbouring clergyman who had officiated there for more than half a year during the vacancy, was now claiming what Wright considered excessive remuneration, i.e. £12 10s. Wright paid ten pounds, believing that to be sufficient, which was actually more than he could well afford. But Charlesworth refused to compromise and threatened legal proceedings, whereupon the vicar appealed to his archbishop: "I cannot tell whom to apply myself

---

[1] *Life of Archbishop Sharp*, vol. ii, p. 82.
[2] L-B-S. MSS., Box 3, Bundle D. 6, Oct. 28, 1705.

better, than to Your Grace, for some small redress in this matter."[1]

John Wilson, curate of Hollym, on the other hand, confided in Sharp that he was having trouble with his wife, whom he described as a shrew and a spendthrift. "I could heartily wish", he complained, "that she would be content to stay at home, and really to afford me her comfortable society, to mind her house, and to do the duties."[2] Mrs. Wilson made counter-accusations. "Her husband", she said, "promised to give her every year five pound to dispose of as she pleased . . . which he is unwilling to pay her: So her request to his Grace is, that he would write to Mr. Wilson to engage him to make good his promise to her, she obliging herself not to desire any more but the continuance of this annuitie, and that he would maintain her in such decent sort as befits his wife."[3] Sharp invited them both to Bishopthorpe and succeeded in effecting a compromise and a reconciliation.

Occasionally the archbishop had to write sternly and forcibly to an incumbent in order to correct proved cases of slackness and irreverence in the discharge of his duties,[4] or his unsatisfactory private life: "Sir, I should take notice . . . of the new difference or the old ones revived betwixt you and your wife; the blame of which is laid at your door . . . particularly the very severe, cruel and unmanly usage with which in your passion, you do sometimes treat her, and the just occasions you have given both to her and others to believe that you are not true to your conjugal vow."[5]

Yet he was never hard on anyone and gladly remitted punishment as soon as submission and reformation were forthcoming. A clergyman named Allen, incumbent of Sneaton, had been suspended owing to his many troubles with his parishioners and for the crime of having officiated at a clandestine marriage; but the archbishop was only too ready to reinstate him as soon as he displayed a genuine spirit of repentance and a real determination to do better in the future.[6]

Another task of the primate was to settle, without fear or favour, many questions arising out of the perpetual disputes and back-

[1] L-B-S. MSS., Box 3, Bundle E. 23, Sept. 22, 1701.
[2] L-B-S. MSS., Box 3, Bundle D. 19, Aug. 24, 1705.
[3] L-B-S. MSS., Box 3, Bundle D. 20.
[4] L-B-S. MSS., Box 4, Bundle R. 17 and 18.
[5] Life of Archbishop Sharp, vol. i, p. 157.
[6] L-B-S. MSS., Box 4, Bundle T. 10 and 11, June 25, 1705.

biting of the clergymen among themselves. Mr. Leech, curate of
Attercliffe, had refused to render an account of his burials,
christenings and marriages, which caused his vicar, Drake of
Sheffield, to complain to the archbishop. Sharp wrote kindly but
firmly to the curate: "I must confess to you I think there is no
colour of reason why you should deny the Vicar what he asks of
you. For if he have a right as Vicar to the profits of the christenings,[1] burials and marriages within your chappelry, he has also a
right to demand an account from time to time of these christenings, etc. . . . But there is another thing that shows the absolute
necessity of your doing this, for otherwise how can the marriages,
christenings and burials be entered into the Register book? . . .
You have my sense of your case. If I be out in the matter of fact
I shall be ready to receive better information as likewise to contribute what I can to a good understanding between the Vicar
and you."[2]

The vicar of Leeds and his curate, Mr. Banister, had quarrelled
over the question of erecting an organ in the new daughter church,
where the curate was in charge, and again the matter had to be
referred to Bishopthorpe. "I find," wrote Sharp to Mr. Banister,
"that the whole design is for an Organ in the chapel, or new
Church, and not at all for one in the Parish Church, and that as
it was begun without consulting the Vicar or Churchwardens, so
it is carried on against the Vicar's consent. . . . For these reasons
I can give you no encouragement to go on, in gathering subscriptions. On the contrary I desire you to lay the design aside, and to
think of it no more, for I shall never allow an Organ to be set up
in the new Church, till there be first one in the old. And I should
be sorry to see one there, if it cannot be had but at the expense of
peace and charity and goodwill among the inhabitants. I hear
there is a project now on foot at Leeds, which I could like abundantly better than that of the Organ. And that is the setting up a
Charity School for poor boys in the nature of that at York and
other places. If it be so I could heartily wish you would employ
your zeal in the promoting of that, rather than the other. I am
sure your pains would turn to much better account. For that is a
noble piece of service to the Publick and tends truly to the honour
of God, and the service of Religion. In getting subscriptions to
such a work as that, I should not only be willing to have my name

[1] See Appendix, p. 320.
[2] L-B-S. MSS., Box 4, Bundle T. 4, June 20, 1696.

used (if it would signify anything) but also be a subscriber myself if there be occasion."[1] This keen interest of the archbishop in his schools, and willingness to put his hand into his own pocket to help a deserving case or a worthy cause, will both be further illustrated in the next chapter.

[1] L-B-S. MSS., Box 4, Bundle T. 15, Sept. 17, 1705.

CHAPTER VII

ARCHBISHOP OF YORK (*Continued*)

THE Yorkshire and Nottinghamshire clergy quickly discovered that their new archbishop was as generous with his purse as with practical advice or pious exhortations: "His kind assistances to his poor clergy out of his own pocket were very great and many. To some he contributed towards the necessary repairs of their parsonage or vicarage houses. To others he voluntarily remitted their procurations, synodals, and pensions. To others he advanced money upon their taking their benefices, to be refunded again if they were afterwards able; if not, to remain with them as a gift. To others, who had large families, he contributed towards the education of their children at schools and the university. And many a poor clergyman, upon making a complaint of the narrowness of his circumstances, has gone from him with £5 in his pocket. Nor was he unmindful of their widows, after their deaths, but contributed to the support of such as were left in a deplorable condition."[1] Thomas Woodcock, curate of Rothwell, for instance, rejoiced to learn that "the £5 I borrowed . . . My Lord Archbishop would give it me"; and promised in return "greater circumspection in my behaviour and also more diligence in my duty."[2]

John Witty, another impecunious clergyman, acknowledged "Your Grace's goodness as to money, I can only return with my most humble thanks, I shall endeavour to live if possible upon my own bottom, and shall be very glad so to do till it shall please God by Your Grace's means to give me something."[3]

Sometimes his gift was in kind rather than cash. The Reverend J. White of Thorney found himself presented with a clerical gown, for which he returned a profuse letter of thanks.[4] Frequently Sharp preferred a less embarrassing and more indirect approach. "Sir", he wrote to Mr. Milner of Pudsey, "understanding that some of your ancestors left ten shillings per annum, or some such sum, for the preaching of a sermon every Trinity Sunday in Pudsey Chapel,

---

[1] *Life of Archbishop Sharp*, vol. ii, p. 58.
[2] L-B-S. MSS., Box 3, Bundle E. 8, March 31, 1707.
[3] L-B-S. MSS., Box 3, Bundle D. 7, Aug. 31, 1708.
[4] L-B-S. MSS., Box 3, Bundle E. 21, June 9, 1699.

and that usually you employ the Vicar of Calverly for the preaching of that sermon; I make it my request to you, that for this next time your own minister of Pudsey, Mr. Brown, may preach this sermon and receive the benefit of it. . . . I write this to you without any solicitation of Mr. Brown and indeed without his knowledge."[1] On another occasion he renewed the lease of Marton farm to Trinity College, Cambridge, remitting the entire fine of £120, on condition that the College "will oblige their tenant to pay five pounds per annum from henceforward to the minister that serves the cure of Marton", since the present endowment of that parish realised "no more than £5 per annum settled maintenance".[2]

The archbishop did not, of course, confine his generosity simply to the parochial clergy and their dependants. He subscribed handsomely to many schools. It has already been seen how he volunteered to contribute towards the founding of a charity school at Leeds; and this is what Thomas Mason, rector of Pateley Bridge, Ripon, reported to Archbishop Herring some forty years later: "We have one Publick School in Low-Bishop-Side, which was formerly endowed by his Grace my Lord Archbishop Sharp with five pounds yearly, which was deducted out of the Lord's Rent when paid to the stewards, but since his time never has been paid."[3] Church buildings, too, were the objects of his charity, of which an example is to be found at Hatfield, where he helped to repair its chancel.[4] Many indeed are the letters from distressed persons in all walks of life recording the ever-flowing stream of the archbishop's alms. "Your Grace", wrote Mrs. Katherine Taylor of London, "may see what great charity you did when you gave me them five guineas and sent me away with a glad heart giving God thanks."[5] Again, "Cousin Kitchin" of Edwinstow acknowledged an annuity of £10 for his daughter in the following grateful terms: "My humble and hearty thanks for your Grace's bounty so nobly and freely bestowed upon me, to my great comfort and the relief of my poor daughter and her four children."[6]

Two instances of his bounty are especially worth remembering. The first is the close attention he always gave to "the support of

[1] L-B-S. MSS., Box 4, Bundle T. 54.
[2] L-B-S. MSS., Box 4, Bundle R. 37. *Cf. Life of Archbishop Sharp*, vol. ii, pp. 57 and 58
[3] *Archbishop Herring's Visitation Returns*, vol. iii, p. 239.
[4] L-B-S. MSS., Box 4, Bundle D. 17, June 17, 1697.
[5] L-B-S. MSS., Box 3, Bundle F. 27, Oct. 16, 1705.
[6] L-B-S. MSS., Box 3, Bundle H. 6, Jan. 13, 1699.

the village and indigent neighbourhood where he lived";[1] and among the archbishop's funeral expenses is an interesting item: "To the poor at Bishopthorpe . . . £2. 0. 0."[2] The second concerned his old College of Christ's. "I understand last week from Mr. Cook at London", wrote Dr. John Covell, its Master, to Sharp on May 26, 1702, "that he had received £20 by your order for the use of our College. Give me leave now in the name of our whole Society to return our thanks and humble acknowledgements."[3]

A fine classical scholar himself, the archbishop naturally took a great interest in those schools which were subject to his visitation. He made a point of carefully studying and, if he thought it advisable, seeking to amend their statues. One practical suggestion of his in a letter to Sir John Kay, one of the governors of Almondbury school, was that poorly endowed schools ought to insist upon their scholars, when able to do so, paying something towards their education, if only the minimum fee of 3d. a week or 3s. 6d. a quarter.[4] On the other hand Greek, which formerly had been treated as an extra subject and paid for at a separate rate, should now be included in the ordinary curriculum. Other proposed reforms of Sharp were that no scholar should be received into a free grammar school unless he had already mastered the English language and could read it perfectly; that eight hours' work a day amply sufficed for both teacher and pupil; and finally that prayers should be said in the school provided they did not occupy too long a period and were of a suitable nature. "I have read over the prayers which you have composed for the use of the school," wrote the archbishop to Mr. Philipson, vicar of Almondbury, "and which you are all pleased to submit to my correction. . . . I like your contrivance both of the morning and evening prayers as far as to the end of the four collects. But every one of the prayers which you have added afterwards, is methinks too long for the occasion and . . . they are not so well adapted to the state and condition of children."[5]

Sharp was particularly strict and conscientious in perusing the testimonials and enquiring into the character of his schoolmasters prior to their appointment. "He thought that the capacity of a useful schoolmaster lay more in his temper, than in his parts, more in his taste than in his learning, and most of all in his virtue and

[1] *Life of Archbishop Sharp*, vol. ii, p. 61.   [2] L-B-S. MSS., Box 3, Bundle K. 17.
[3] L-B-S. MSS., Box 3, Bundle G. 6.
[4] L-B-S. MSS., Box 4, Bundle R. 35, June 15, 1700.
[5] L-B-S. MSS., Box 4, Bundle R. 36, Oct. 7, 1700.

sobriety."[1] Writing to one such applicant he quite frankly admitted: "It is not out of any mean opinion of your abilities, that I am adverse to doing that which you desire of me. So far from that, I really take you to be a person of extraordinary wit and parts, and I believe of very good learning, and I know you to be a singular good preacher, but I cannot satisfy myself that you will make a good schoolmaster."[2]

The archbishop was equally warm in their defence when he thought that they were being slandered. Mr. Lisle, a teacher at Guisborough, had been so misrepresented by a rival pedagogue, Mr. Jaques, and Sharp immediately took up the cudgels on his behalf with the vicar of Guisborough. "I humbly therefore beg of you", he exhorted the latter, "to give yourself a little trouble in inquiring into these complaints and if you find reason for them, that you would use your endeavours to bring Mr. Jaques to a better temper . . . or if that cannot be done, at least that Mr. Lisle may have your countenance and encouragement."[3] At the same time he wrote reprovingly to Jaques himself on the same subject: "I have heard of your ill usage of Mr. Lisle, and your endeavours to prejudice people against him by disparaging him and his performances. I would hope you were not guilty of this, because really it is so bad a thing. . . . I will stand by him and vindicate him."[4]

Incumbents and their schoolmasters, who were frequently also their curates, often found themselves at loggerheads and called in the archbishop to arbitrate or mediate between them. The Reverend John White, vicar of Thorney, who had quarrelled with and desired to get rid of his present schoolmaster, Mr. Charlesworth, dispatched another candidate for the post to Bishopthorpe, armed with a letter explaining the circumstances and appealing to Sharp to settle the case. "I am pretty apt to think", White wrote, "you will conclude Mr. Charlesworth can be no longer schoolmaster there, and if so, then, if you please to favour Mr. Taylor with a line or two to Mr. Charlesworth not to contest this matter, but quietly to resign."[5]

[1] *Life of Archbishop Sharp*, vol. i, p. 221.   [2] Ibid.
[3] L-B-S. MSS., Box 4, Bundle R. 20.
[4] L-B-S. MSS., Box 4, Bundle R. 21. Another example of this kind of thing occurred at Whitby, where one schoolmaster named Kemp tried, unsuccessfully, to oust another, Conyers. Sharp supported Conyers, who, he said, had been treated "very unfairly". See L-B-S. MSS., Box 4, Bundle T. 70, July 30, 1702.
[5] L-B-S. MSS., Box 3, Bundle E. 3, Oct. 20, 1699. *Cf.* L-B-S. MSS., Box 3, Bundle E. 18, April 14, 1702: the removal of the schoolmaster of Malton, Mr. Mills, and his replacement by Mr. John Stockdale.

Any consideration of Sharp in his purely administrative capacity
as archbishop of York would be incomplete without some account
of his relations with the Societies for the Reformation of
Manners, the diocese of Carlisle, and the collegiate church of St.
Mary Southwell.

"He always disliked and discouraged . . . the Societies for the
Reformation of Manners; which were begun to be set up within
his diocese (as they were in many others) about the year 1697."[1]
The archbishop was certainly not afraid to censure vicious clerics
and laymen, even those high up in the social scale,[2] or backward
in making use of his legal powers when necessary; but in the main
he was opposed to the methods applied by the Societies for the
Reformation of Manners, which were springing up all over the
country and had the approval of many of his brother bishops.[3]
"These societies", wrote Fowler, bishop of Gloucester, enthusiastically, "have already done such service . . . that lewd houses are
everywhere suppressed: taverns and ale-houses kept shut on the
Lord's days: And oaths and curses very rarely heard in comparison
of what they have been . . . many persons of these societies have
been miserably abused, and their very lives endangered, before
they had got this mastery over wicked people. . . . I profess our
whole Bench have never done the 40th part of that service and
honour to our Church, that these Church of England laymen have
done. And it hath grieved me to see, how much gladness they have
expressed, and how grateful they are, whenever they find any of
us giving them encouragement."[4] But these Societies, which aimed
at a complete reformation of public morals, strove to secure their
ends by encouraging informers and insisting on heavy legal
punishments. Sharp steadfastly set his face against them; for their
methods convinced him that they would never achieve any lasting
good. Reformation of character could come about only through
voluntary repentance and the real practice, as well as the profession, of Christianity.

The Church, indeed, as a whole was finding it more and more
difficult to enforce discipline, since in an age when toleration and
rationalism were acquiring a firmer grip on society, ecclesiastical
strictures were becoming more and more to be both resented and

---

[1] *Life of Archbishop Sharp*, vol. i, p. 170.
[2] See the case of Sir James Bradshaw of Hull, one of gross immorality: L-B-S. MSS.,
Box 4, Bundle R. 19; Bundle O. 47, 49, 62, 63, 64; Bundle T. 48, 49.
[3] *E.g.*, Gloucester, Chester and Worcester.
[4] L-B-S. MSS., Box 4, Bundle L. 87, April 6, 1699.

ignored. The temporal courts, for example, deliberately set themselves to whittle down the powers of the ecclesiastical, and complaints were easily set on foot against the inefficiency and tyran-
nical behaviour of the latter. Much, then, as Sharp personally
deplored the decay of discipline and the rapid growth of immorality and atheism, yet he had the sense to realise that the time
for its wholesale enforcement was past and gone by for ever; and
should it be attempted in the spirit that the Societies for the
Reformation of Manners desired, the people would only be exasperated into a further defection from religion. He himself took
good care to set his own courts in order so that no possible exception could be taken either against their procedure or personnel,[1]
and endeavoured to clear up all misunderstandings with the temporal courts. In a letter to the archbishop of Canterbury dated
March 11, 1698/9, he referred to "complaints of the frequent dis-
charging (of late) of excommunicate persons[2] out of the jail by
writs of supersedeas from the Chancery. . . . They encourage all
sorts of people to stand out in defiance of the Church censures, nor
have the Court powers to signify the excommunication and obtain
the Writ of Capias, because they are sure, that as soon as the
person is laid in the jail, he will be fetched out by a supersedeas,
grounded upon errors in the significavit, which yet they do not
know how to amend."[3] Sharp went on to press Tenison to persuade Chancery to draw in its horns. He himself took good care
never to press a case in the courts unless driven to do so by a deliberate breach of the Church's laws which no persuasions or
warnings could remedy.

As regards the Societies for the Reformation of Manners, Sharp
was more than doubtful concerning their legality, "whether they
come under those 'conventicles' which are forbid in the 12th and
73rd canons".[4] Moreover, he realised that it meant an association
of Anglicans with the Dissenters, who were even keener on these

---

[1] Cf. L-B-S. MSS., Box 4, Bundle O. 1-26.
[2] Archbishop Sharp, so his biographer noted, always displayed "great tenderness
. . . to particular persons under sentence of excommunication": Life of Archbishop
Sharp, vol. i, p. 217.
   Cf. L-B-S. MSS., Box 4, Bundle M. 25, April 8, 1704. Here a Mr. Pudsey, writing to
the archbishop about his brother-in-law, Robert Marsdon, who lay at death's door
and was under sentence of excommunication from the vicar of Gisburn, said: "Your
absolution . . . the only means to bring him comfort in this time of affliction and make
him with more cheerfulness resign his spirit into the hands of his Creator and Redeemer."
[3] L-B-S. MSS., Box 4, Bundle R. 2.
[4] Life of Archbishop Sharp, vol. i, p. 182.

Societies than the churchmen themselves. The archbishop was no persecutor of Dissenters and admired and befriended many of their leaders, but he foresaw in such a coalition the danger that the Nonconformists would deliberately make use of it to weaken the Church of England; as indeed proved to be the case. The Reverend T. Caryl, vicar of St. Mary's, Nottingham, wrote to Sharp in February 1697 about the Nottingham Society: "Altho' I believe this Society means honestly and well, yet I very much fear that it will not easily do so much good in this town, as those of the like nature may do in London; especially when I consider in what danger those churchmen (whom I believe to be the minority) among 'em will be in, of being first work'd into an indifferency and afterwards quite drawn off from the Establishment." [1]

The earliest Society to be established in the York diocese was set up at Nottingham. Several prominent Nottinghamshire clergymen, including T. Caryl himself, John Ellis of Gonalston, C. Elis of Kirkby and D. Chadwick of Southwell, were approached from London[2] and asked to join with the Dissenters, who as usual were the most enthusiastic,[3] in forming such a Society. The Londoners also sent down plenty of literature to be distributed amongst their brethren, a list of their own rules and a suggestion that it would be advisable to hold a quarterly lecture, delivered alternately by an Anglican and a Nonconformist.

Sharp was asked to give his sanction to these proceedings; but after some correspondence with Mr. Caryl on the subject, and a comparison of the Nottingham rules with those of London, he refused their request for the following reasons: "I am not against", he declared, "the coalition of churchmen with dissenters, in any matter where they can go together in promoting the common cause of religion or good manners. So far from that, I heartily wish them well. And it would be the most pleasing thing in the world to me, if we could all be united in one body. And, in the meantime, while we continue separate, I would have all possible tenderness and kindness shewed to all good men among them. But while

---

[1] L-B-S. MSS., Box 3, Bundle entitled "Letters relating to the Societies for the Reformation of Manners," No. 22.

[2] See L-B-S. MSS., Box 3, Bundle entitled "Letters relating to the Societies for the Reformation of Manners," Nos. 3, 19, 20. Mr. Clark of Nottingham, who had also been approached, refused to have anything to do with it, informing Sharp that in his opinion it was unfitting that such proposals should come from outside the diocese, and anyway the whole design seemed "a little presuming and uncanonical": No. 23.

[3] The Reverend C. Elis told Sharp: "The Non-conformist ministers seem very forward; and some applications have been made to some of the conforming clergy": Ibid., No. 20.

the laws stand as they do, I do not know how I can, without breach of that trust that is committed to me, come into the project and scheme that the gentlemen of your Society have laid down for themselves. You desire me to license a quarterly lecture to be preached to the Society. Is it not natural, that those of the Society who are dissenters, should also desire a lecture to be sometimes preached *to the Society in their meetings?* And can you deny this request of theirs? Is it not reasonable (since you are all on the same level as members of the Society) that you should comply with them as they with you? If now the case be thus, I must profess to you, I can by no means allow any clergyman of my diocese to preach as a lecturer to this Society, because it would be giving an encouragement to the breaking of those laws which I hold myself bound in conscience to see observed as far as I can."[1] Later, writing to Archdeacon Nicolson of Carlisle about another Society at Brampton in the Carlisle diocese, he said: "As for what you mention at Brampton, where the vicars have obliged themselves to take their turns with the minister of a dissenting congregation at a weekly lecture; if the meaning of that be that they are to take their turns in preaching at his meeting, or he is to take his turn in preaching at their churches, or lastly that they are to go and hear him preach in his turn at the conventicle, I say, if any of these things be meant in that article (and what other meaning it can have I cannot find out) I think the thing ought not to be suffered, but they should be admonished to forbear such practices; being directly contrary to our constitution, and to the engagement they are under to preserve it."[2]

And as a result of his intervention Nicolson was able to inform the archbishop that "the clergy about Brampton, who had associated, had now renounced the society they had joined with."[3] Sharp certainly found a zealous ally in the archdeacon, who strongly urged his own bishop, the old and infirm Thomas Smith, who was inclined to compromise, to withstand these Societies, especially one recently founded by the chancellor of Carlisle, Thomas Tullie, the archdeacon's *bête noire.*[4] In a letter to the archbishop dated February 5, 1700, Nicolson gives an interesting

[1] *Life of Archbishop Sharp*, vol. i, p. 177.
[2] Ibid., vol. i, p. 187. *Cf.* letter from Nicolson to Sharp, L-B-S. MSS., Box 4, Bundle K. 11.
[3] L-B-S. MSS., Bundle entitled "Letters relating to the Societies for the Reformation of Manners," No. 16.
[4] Ibid., No. 7. *Cf.* also L-B-S. MSS., Box 4, Bundle K. 10, March 7, 1699/1700: Letters from Tullie and Nicolson mutually accusing and excusing themselves before the archbishop.

account of a stormy meeting at Rose Castle where the bishop finally sided with his archdeacon against the chancellor, and declared that the Society proposed by the latter was contrary both to the 12th and 73rd canons. "I could not but concurr with my Lord", Nicolson blandly concluded, "in the plain meaning and interpretations of the canons; and, I added, that I thought these societies were conventicles, and unlawful assemblies in the voice of the statute law, till their meeting-houses were licensed: and that (even then) though they might be within the privileges of the Act of Toleration, they were without the pale of the Established Church."[1] Nicolson, however, proved rather too zealous an ally, becoming engaged in a lengthy and acrimonious correspondence with a number of his clerical brethren,[2] including Nicholas Stratford, bishop of Chester, on this subject. Nicolson accused Stratford of supporting the Carlisle Society; who retorted by expressing regret for the former's intolerant attitude towards the Reformers.[3] Stratford also wrote to Sharp commending a "book" drawn up by Fowler, bishop of Gloucester, capitulating the virtues and achievements of the Societies, which he was endeavouring to get all the bishops to sign. "It is therefore humbly hoped, that in order to the promoting of so great and glorious a work", begged Stratford, "Your Grace will be pleased to give leave, that your approbation (I mean not of every passage in the book, but) of the design and method of it, may be published."[4]

The bishops of Gloucester and Worcester joined with Chester in pressing for the archbishop's signature,[5] but in vain. Tenison, too, did not sign or approve this "book", which he regarded as exaggerated and provocative, but he himself issued a circular letter to the bishops[6] cautiously commending the Societies. Fowler, of course, was most indignant. "I could not but wonder", he wrote to Sharp, "how he should take the whole honour thus to himself. . . . And in short, I would not for twice his revenue that my name should run so low as his, for a lukewarm heavy man . . . I never saw two more like than him and his predecessor Sancroft; and particularly in their most obstinate wilfulness."[7]

---

[1] *Bishop Nicolson's Correspondence*, vol. i, pp. 147 and 148.
[2] Ibid., vol. i, p. 150 *et seq.*
[3] Ibid., vol. i, pp. 170-172.
[4] L-B-S. MSS., Box 4, Bundle entitled "Letters relating to the Societies for the Reformation of Manners," No. 9, March 25, 1699.
[5] Ibid., No. 11, March 25, 1699.
[6] L-B-S. MSS., Box 4, Bundle L. 58.
[7] L-B-S. MSS., Box 4, Bundle L. 88, April 18, 1699.

Nevertheless, the majority of clerical and lay opinion, numbering William III in their ranks, was on the whole so strongly in favour of the Societies that both York and Carlisle were compelled to modify their attitude. Sharp, indeed, stoutly maintained his decision to allow no Societies which contained Dissenters in the York diocese; neither would he license a special quarterly lecture. But, as he told Nicolson, he would not forbid them altogether, provided they contained only churchmen and did nothing contrary to the law: "Being sensible that a great many wise and good men do approve of these Societies, I will not think the worse of any man for engaging in them. Nor shall these Societies meet with any discouragement from me, so long as they keep within the bounds which the laws of the land and of the Church have prescribed. Letters to this effect I have written to some of my clergy who consulted me; but I must confess I came not to this degree of compliance till after a great deal of discourse with several of the bishops."[1]

Consequently Societies quickly sprang up at Nottingham, Hull,[2] York and elsewhere in the diocese[3] with the tacit consent, if not the very active approval, of the archbishop, who also permitted their members to "have a sermon once in a quarter, provided it was preached by a clergyman of known character and discretion and also on that day of the week on which the weekly lecture was preached".[4] In this way he strove to check any unseemly extravagance or illegality, while not openly hindering the work of the Societies. Yet in his own private opinion Sharp always considered that "the scheme of reformation which seemed . . . to bid the fairest for success was, that all they, whether of the clergy or laity, who undertook to promote it in others, should lay out their labours first of all in amending themselves; and that till they became exemplary men in their persons, they were not *duly and sufficiently qualified* to attempt the reformation of a degenerate age".[5] Subsequent events appeared to bear out this judgment, for with

[1] *Life of Archbishop Sharp*, vol. i, p. 185.
[2] The newly formed Society at Hull wrote to Sharp: "And for as much as we understand that it was of very great advantage to the like Society in Nottingham, that Your Grace was pleased to favour their enterprise; and excite their magistrates to do the like; we beg leave with the greatest humility to acquaint Your Grace, we promise ourselves the like, from your presence and countenance here." See L-B-S. MSS., "Letters relating", etc., No. 2.
[3] The vicar of Sheffield, for example, wrote to the archbishop: "A Society for the Reformation of Manners beginning to gather in this town": Ibid., No. 18.
[4] *Life of Archbishop Sharp*, vol. i, p. 179.
[5] Ibid., vol. i, p. 189.

the accession of the Hanoverians "Reformation of Manners" went rapidly out of fashion.[1]

In 1702 Nicolson became bishop of Carlisle and immediately took the usual steps to obtain a D.D. from Oxford, his old University; but to his amazement it was refused on the grounds that his previous attacks on the writings of Francis Atterbury, writings advocating the powers and privileges of the Lower House of Convocation, were a deliberate affront to that citadel of the high-fliers, Oxford. Nicolson promptly retorted by procuring the degree from Cambridge; but nevertheless the insult rankled, and when in 1704 Atterbury was nominated by Queen Anne to the deanery of Carlisle the bishop "determined to pay off old scores, by refusing to institute him unless he first revoked certain propositions relating to the royal supremacy, which might seem to be deducible from his Convocation book".[2] "The Queen", Godolphin wrote to Sharp with a certain dry humour on July 4, 1704, "designs to make Dr. Atterbury Dean of Carlisle for the present, and as an earnest only of her intention to give him a better preferment when an occasion shall happen for it . . . which will likewise give her an opportunity of pleasing the Bishop of Carlisle."[3] Anne did not like Nicolson, but she can scarcely have foreseen what the consequences of her action would be; for the matter quickly became a trial of party strength. Nicolson received the backing of the whig Tenison, archbishop of Canterbury, and of his chaplain Edmund Gibson; Atterbury, on the other hand, as the champion of the Lower and tory House of Convocation against the whig bishops, was a favourite with the high-fliers and indeed had the support of all the tories, including even the moderates like Archbishop Sharp and Robert Harley, one of the Secretaries of State.

On July 8, 1704, Atterbury wrote from his residence in Chelsea to inform Sharp of his appointment—"Her Majesty having thought fit to name me as the Dean of Carlisle's successor"—and went on to express the hope that the differences between himself and the bishop of Carlisle would be "buried in oblivion".[4] Later he wrote again to say that the bishop had not responded to his overtures: "I thought, as your Grace did, that the respect I paid to the bishop of Carlisle would have procured me a suitable return: but it hath not."[5]

[1] G. V. Portus, *Caritas Anglicana*, p. 182.   [2] N. Sykes, *Edmund Gibson*, p. 58.
[3] L-B-S. MSS., Box 4, Bundle L. 121.   [4] L-B-S. MSS., Box 3, Bundle N. 1.
[5] L-B-S. MSS., Box 3, Bundle N. 2, July 27, 1704.

Nicolson, however, professed to know nothing of these friendly advances; and announced that he had every intention of standing upon his rights. "The man", he told the archbishop, "has publicly traduced me as a *little, assuming Fellow*; and one that has *given up the rights of the Church*. . . . I have no occasion to capitulate with him for his respects in his new station. The statutes of the Church give me an ample power over the Dean; who is to receive institution from me, in the same manner with the meanest Vicar in my diocese."[1] At the same time Nicolson must have been well aware that Sharp was at any rate partially responsible for the offer of the deanery to Atterbury;[2] although this fact did not deter him from doing his level best to prevent its taking effect.

The bishop began with a letter to his friend and cousin, Archdeacon Pearson of Nottingham, condemning Atterbury's proposition concerning the royal supremacy—*i.e.*, that the queen in Parliament, and not the sovereign alone, was the supreme head of the Church. "I like Dr. A's position not one jot the better", declared Nicolson, "for his having a great many followers (or companions) in his new brooched opinions. . . . It makes it necessary for . . . us . . . to make a stand and bring the matter in controversy to a legal and authoritative decision."[3] Nicolson, in fact, intended to demand a recantation[4] from Atterbury before his institution as dean, and made it clear that it must be Pearson's task to try to get Archbishop Sharp, whom Atterbury was visiting on his way to Carlisle, to persuade the doctor to sign it. The bishop knew, of course, quite well that Atterbury never would recant; but he was extremely anxious to placate his metropolitan by a display of apparent magnanimity and injured innocence, and for this purpose actually went so far as to suggest that if his own conscience refused to allow him to institute the dean he would give Sharp permission to do so in his place, should that ever become necessary. The archbishop, although throughout the entire controversy he felt strongly that

---

[1] L-B-S. MSS., Box 4, Bundle V. 1, Aug. 17, 1704.

[2] Atterbury actually thanked Sharp for his help: "Your Grace's kind recommendations of me have a large share in procuring it." See L-B-S. MSS., Box 3, Bundle N. 1. This was also the opinion of Dr. John Smith of Durham: "We all expected that the Deanery of Carlisle would have fallen to Mr. Archdeacon Booth, which made me take it for granted that he had been the first person nominated by Your Grace. But it is no small surprise that Dr. Atterbury should accept it, especially considering what had passed betwixt the Bishop of Carlisle and him": L-B-S. MSS., Box 4, Bundle K. 12, July 26, 1704.

[3] L-B-S. MSS., Box 4, Bundle V. 2, August 24, 1704. *Cf.* also *Bishop Nicolson's Correspondence*, vol. i, p. 267.

[4] L-B-S. MSS., Box 4, Bundle V. 19.

Atterbury was both legally and morally in the right, strove hard
to pour oil on troubled waters. He pointed out courteously but
firmly, and at considerable length, that Nicolson's arguments concerning the royal supremacy were fallacious,[1] and jumped at the
latter's suggestion that he should perform the institution himself
and send "my mandate to the Chapter for his installment".[2] However, Nicolson's bare consent to such an institution, as the bishop
very well knew, was not enough. "They tell me here", continued
the archbishop, "that there must be an instrument under your
episcopal seal, to give me this authority; an instrument of remission, I think they call it, by which you refer this whole matter to
me. If your Lordship will please send me such an instrument, I
hope there will be an end to this dispute. There is likewise another
way, I am told, whereby this may be done; viz. by your granting
a commission under your episcopal seal, to such persons here as
you shall think fit, to give the Doctor institution . . . your Lordship
may choose which of these ways you will. But I beg that you would
come to a resolution as soon as may be, for so long Dr. Atterbury
will stay here. Indeed my opinion is, that you should put him to
no more expense, trouble and delay, than you needs must; for
that will serve to no other end than to inflame the differences
between you; and it is certain he will carry his point after all."
This was not at all to the bishop's liking, who had no desire to be
taken so literally, and hastily replied: "I shall never grant a Commission to others to do any act for me (and by my authority) which
I cannot in conscience do personally: For this I take to be such a
shuffling as no man of integrity can submit to."[3] He also summoned Atterbury, who had been cooling his heels at Bishopthorpe
for some seven days, to come to Carlisle and discuss the matter
directly in order to reach a solution. "The Dean set out accordingly as soon as possible."[4] At the same time Sharp wrote again to
Nicolson pleading for a rapid institution, or if that appeared quite
impossible in the bishop's opinion, "then I have this to beg of
you, that you would at the first give him your positive denial, and
not insist upon the 28 days which the Canon gives you to deliberate about the matter, that so he may, without more loss of
time, make his appeal."[5]

[1] *Life of Archbishop Sharp*, vol. i, p. 236.
[2] L-B-S. MSS., Box 4, Bundle R. 22, Sept. 4, 1704. *Cf.* also *Bishop Nicolson's Correspondence*, vol. i, p. 269.
[3] L-B-S. MSS., Box 4, Bundle K. 9, Sept. 7, 1704.
[4] *Bishop Atterbury's Epistolary Correspondence*, vol. i, p. 351.
[5] L-B-S. MSS., Box 4, Bundle R. 23, Sept. 11, 1704.

Nicolson took no notice of this advice; but the archbishop's strong condemnation of the proposed form of recantation seemed to have some effect, for he no longer insisted upon Atterbury retracting his three famous propositions concerning the royal supremacy. Instead, having called the canons of the cathedral together, the bishop produced another and equally obnoxious declaration of submission, which the dean was expected to sign. Atterbury, of course, refused and appealed to his supporters, including Sharp, to do battle on his behalf. "Since the Bishop", he wrote, "was resolved upon rough measures, I must take care of myself as well as I can, and am not answerable for the consequences of it. I thank Your Grace for the dispatch you were pleased to use in your's to Secretary Harley. I know Your Grace must needs be very tender in a point, where a Bishop, and one of your Province is concerned."[1] He added by way of postscript: "Your Grace cannot but take particular notice of the Bishop's taking the whole 28 days allowed by the Canon, when he himself had by his request to Your Grace detained me 7 days before that at Bishopthorpe, and hindered me by that means from producing my patent to him."[2] Nicolson also approached the primate seeking to justify his refusal to institute the dean and telling of his counter-appeal to Sir Charles Hedges, the other Secretary of State.[3] Both the protagonists hoped for the archbishop's approval and support; but this was given to Atterbury in a letter to Robert Harley, wherein Sharp urged him to use his influence with the queen to enforce institution. Harley had already heard from Atterbury about the affair, but was unwilling to trouble Anne in the matter unless the archbishop considered such action unavoidable. "I hope", he said, "this affair is already at an end by Your Grace's prudent conduct, and therefore I will forbear to take any notice of it to her Majesty. These are frailties which ought to be covered as much as possible and particularly now when the Queen hath so great hopes to heal that breach which hath been so long amongst the clergy, so much to their reproach and the weakening their interest."[4] But on receipt of the archbishop's own appeal he wrote again in a very different style: "My Lord, I received yesterday the honour of your Grace's letter. I have acquainted her Majesty how

---

[1] L-B-S. MSS., Box 4, Bundle V. 9.
[2] L-B-S. MSS., Box 4, Bundle V. 11, Sept. 16, 1704.
[3] L-B-S. MSS., Box 4, Bundle V. 3.
  For a note on the "Secretaries of State" see the Appendix, p. 320.
[4] L-B-S. MSS., Box 4, Bundle V. 17, Sept. 14, 1704.

much pains your Grace hath taken to cure this unhappy affair at Carlisle, with which her Majesty is as much pleased, as she is dissatisfied with the Bishop of Carlyle's indiscretion. And she thinks it very hard treatment from him, what he would not have ventured to have acted towards one of the meanest patrons in his own country: Your Lordship's goodness is such there is no need to desire the continuance of your good offices. On this occasion I suppose Secretary Hedges will write plainly her Majesty's mind to the Bishop by this post. . . . I hope the Bishop will not oblige the Queen to come to extremity upon this occasion, which I find . . . hath rendered him liable to very great penalites."[1]

Tenison, who had taken the opposite line and refused "absolutely to allow Atterbury to wait upon him",[2] was thereby indirectly administered a severe rebuke by the queen; while Nicolson, besides being compelled to institute Atterbury without delay, found himself in deep disgrace at court.[3] The fact that he relied upon the archbishop of York to make his peace with Anne is a striking testimony to the fairness and goodwill with which Sharp had treated both parties to the dispute. "Whether Her Majesty", Nicolson ruefully remarked, "will admit me into Her presence, without your Grace's intercession, I know not. But, I presume, it will not be reckon'd any new crime to live retired from Court, till your Grace come there."[4]

Atterbury was naturally jubilant at the turn events had taken and informed his patron that Hedges' letter had "dispelled all the doubts and difficulties both in law and conscience, which his Lordship was under".[5] Furthermore, he followed up this victory, again very largely with Sharp's help, by defeating an attempt by the bishop to dispute the validity of his patent. Ever since his nomination Atterbury had been uneasy about its legality,[6] as his predecessor, Dr. Grahme, who was translated to Wells, had never formally resigned Carlisle; and the Lord Keeper had once

---

[1] L-B-S. MSS., Box 4. Bundle V. 18, Sept. 21, 1704.
[2] N. Sykes, *Edmund Gibson*, p. 59.
[3] "I think myself obliged in duty", wrote the bishop to his metropolitan, "to give your Grace an account of my having on Friday last, given institution to Dr. Atterbury; in pure obedience to her Majesty's commands, signified to me by Mr. Secretary Hedges. . . . What sits most heavily on me is, my being wholly ignorant wherein I have so far offended the Queen as to deserve so severe a correction. I hope she will compassionately let me know my crime; that I may avoid the incurring her displeasure for the future": L-B-S. MSS., Box 4, Bundle V. 4, Oct. 2, 1704.
[4] L-B-S. MSS., Box 4, Bundle V. 5, Oct. 9, 1704.
[5] L-B-S. MSS., Box 4, Bundle V. 10, Sept. 28, 1704.
[6] L-B-S. MSS., Box 3, Bundle N. 2.

"observed that a second deanery did not make the first void, without a resignation, being no more incompatible than two archdeaconries".[1] There was, however, a recent precedent for such an action in Sharp's own career, when he became dean of Canterbury, and when Dr. Fairfax succeeded him at Norwich, both of which deaneries were only vacant by translation. Atterbury decided to be on the safe side and, as he informed the archbishop, "to have a resignation from Dean Grahme".[2] He also "had his patent passed the great seal a second time by warrant from the Queen, after the date was so adjusted that the resignation might precede the grant, and the grant precede the institution".[3] In this he was probably wise, for Nicolson showed himself inclined to dispute the validity of his possession and only desisted when the archbishop coldly reminded him that it was not the patent but the institution which legally constituted Atterbury dean of Carlisle, and he could now be ejected by the crown alone.[4]

The war between bishop and dean continued, nevertheless, to rage at full blast, and the next year (1705) the latter obtained a royal dispensation from residence. "I have", he told Sharp, "procured from the Queen a licence of perpetual absence under her seal, so that whatever the Bishop's power is, I am no ways obnoxious to it."[5] But he proceeded to grant proxies to his friend, and Nicolson's enemy, Dr. Todd, the vice-dean. The bishop promptly hauled him before his metropolitan: "Dec. 7th, 1705. Mr. Dean and I adjourned to my Lord of York's; where we debated ye controversy in Chapter before His Grace. The Dean produced several precedents (out of ye Chapter-Books) of such proxies as he had granted to Dr. Todd; but, in conclusion, offered to draw ye case fairly and refer it to my counsel."[6]

Atterbury also made himself a nuisance by refusing to accept the decisions of the chapter and insisting upon every tittle of his rights.[7] Consequently the chapter, urged on by Nicolson and his friend Edmund Gibson, appealed to the bishop to visit and decide. The dean promptly retorted by declaring that since Carlisle was

[1] *Life of Archbishop Sharp*, vol. i, p. 248.
[2] L.-B.-S. MSS., Box 4, Bundle K. 67, Aug. 8, 1704.
[3] *Life of Archbishop Sharp*, vol. i, p. 249. *Cf.* L.-B.-S. MSS., Box 4, Bundle V. 15, May 25, 1705.
[4] H. C. Beeching, *Atterbury*, p. 142.
[5] L.-B.-S. MSS., Box 4, Bundle V. 15.
[6] H. C. Beeching, *Atterbury*, p. 150, quoted from Nicolson's diary.
[7] *E.g.*, there are many letters to Sharp among the L.-B.-S. MSS. concerning his "right" as dean to appoint to "the Cook's place", which "right" was strongly disputed by the other members of the chapter.

a royal foundation the bishop possessed no right of visitation. This raised a question of national importance, and Archbishop Tenison took the matter up. He sent a circular letter to his suffragans wherein he warmly applauded Nicolson's action as being "a common cause and of great importance to the Church, which would never be quiet as long as that evil generation of men, who made it their business to search into little flaws in ancient charters and statutes and to unfix what laudable custom had well fixed, met with any success". The archbishop further expressed his readiness to concur with his brethren "in any proper and legal means, whether by bill or otherwise to make this excellent Church safe in this point, both now and to late posterity".[1] Accordingly a bill declaring all Henry VIII's statutes, which had been acted upon since the Restoration, good and valid in law was introduced into the House of Lords by the whig Lord Somers during January 1707/8; and Nicolson and Gibson immediately set to work to canvass as many votes for it as possible. Sharp's was not one, since he "more frankly than kindly" told his suffragan that "he'd oppose his Bill"—an episode that caused Tenison to be "much concerned at the odd behaviour of his Brother of York".[2]

The bill passed the Lords and, despite the opposition of Harley and "spitfire" John Sharp, the House of Commons also. Nicolson was not entirely surprised at the attitude of the Sharps, since he had become convinced that his metropolitan stood behind every move of Atterbury, Todd and their friends. Writing to William Wake, bishop of Lincoln, on November 29, 1707, concerning his excommunication of Dr. Todd, Nicolson said: "To be serious with you, my good Lord, I am very much concerned at the unavoidable course (*i.e.* the excommunication of Todd) I have taken in punishing the vilest contempts, affronts, and indignities, that ever were put upon any man of our orders, in the exercise of his Episcopal Jurisdiction. I know not what hand it is that moves behind the curtain. But certainly no presbyter would bid that defiance to his Ordinary, which Dr T. (countenanced by Dr A.) has done to me without a supporter of Power and Authority equal to his own insolence."[3]

The reference here is obviously to the archbishop of York. But with the passing of this Cathedral and Collegiate Churches Act, which contained the saving clause "Provided always and be it

---

[1] N. Sykes, *Edmund Gibson*, p. 59.   [2] Ibid., p. 60.
[3] H. C. Beeching, *Atterbury*, p. 153.

enacted that it shall and may be lawful for her Majesty during her life (which God long preserve) to alter, amend, correct, or enlarge the said statutes or any of them",[1] there was a general reconciliation. Nicolson had already lifted Todd's excommunication; and now, much to Gibson's wrath, even extended the hand of friendship to Atterbury. "The keeping of our ecclesiastical discipline within its ancient and known bounds", the bishop apologetically wrote to Sharp, "was all that I aimed at in my late extraordinary contest; wherein nothing . . . went so near my heart, as the trouble of finding your Grace's sentiments in this matter to be so different from my own."[2] For his part the archbishop cordially expressed the wish "that their warmth in ye House of Lords might be mutually forgotten".[3]

An interesting sidelight on this "Carlisle Affair" is the three-cornered correspondence between Sharp, Nicolson and Todd during 1705 and 1706 on the subject of the latter's curates.

Todd, vicar of Penrith and prebendary of Carlisle, was an old enemy of Nicolson (an enmity dating back to a dispute over the chapter library in 1696)[4] and a firm friend of Atterbury, whom he supported in his repeated conflicts with the bishop. The vicar, too, like the dean, was fond of appealing to Sharp over Nicolson's head.

On September 8, 1705, Todd wrote a long letter to the archbishop complaining about his curate, Paton. The facts were these: Two troops of dragoons had been stationed in Penrith, who seemed to have got slightly out of hand, drinking ale and causing a disturbance in the church. Todd preached a sermon on the subject, which Paton, hoping for promotion through the army and desiring to curry favour with the soldiers, had reported to the commanding officer in a grossly distorted form. For instance, he declared that Todd had referred to the dragoons as the very "virmin of sinners".[5] Todd, who had said nothing of the sort, was justly incensed; but as he informed Sharp, "I am obliged to do the officers right in this matter. They were somewhat fierce against me; till I shewed them my sermon, and Paton made his recantation: but now they have such an opinion of the falseness and baseness of his behaviour, as every impartial man ought to have."[6]

---

[1] H.M.C. *House of Lords MSS.* (1706-1708).
[2] L-B-S. MSS., Box 4, Bundle V. 23.   [3] N. Sykes, *Edmund Gibson*, p. 62.
[4] *Cf. Bishop Nicolson's Correspondence*, vol. i, pp. 43-51.
[5] L-B-S. MSS., Box 4, Bundle V. 26.
[6] L-B-S. MSS., Box 4, Bundle V. 28, Sept. 13, 1705.

Paton, who happened to be only on probation, was promptly paid and dismissed; but instead of taking his punishment lying down appealed to the bishop, who was his friend and, according to Todd, had foisted him upon Penrith in the first instance. Nicolson immediately flew to Paton's rescue, granted him a licence to continue at Penrith and demanded that the vicar should take him back. In the meantime, however, Todd had secured another curate named Langhorne, but on his explaining the position to Nicolson the bishop flatly refused to grant the latter a licence. Hence the vicar's appeal to Sharp to intervene in the dispute. At the same time Atterbury also wrote to the archbishop suggesting that he might license Langhorne in the bishop's place. "I reckon it to be in your Grace's power", insinuated the dean, "to grant a provincial licence to any proper person Dr. Todd shall pitch upon for his curate, if the Bishop of that Diocese shall persist in denying him this licence."[1]

Nicolson likewise hastened to state his point of view, insisting that he had not originally sent Paton as a curate to Penrith at all. "The Dr.", he declared, "took this man out of another curacy, to which he was ordained and wherein he was fix'd, without ever advising with me: And, after he had kept him near two years in his service, he's now for leaving him to shift for himself."[2] The bishop could not possibly allow this to happen, but when he intervened mildly on Paton's behalf, Todd vouchsafed him the insolent reply "that he's resolved that this person shall have no more to do with his affairs; and that he has as much power over his own curate as I have over my domestic chaplain." A reply, in fact, that had obliged Nicolson to retort by "injoining the Churchwardens to take care that none officiated in their parish-church, but either the Vicar himself or such assistant as they were sure had my licence. I also directed the present curate to attend, and offer his service as formerly; which was not accepted." The bishop, too, strongly resented Todd's action in appealing to Sharp over his head; for even if he had refused to accept the episcopal good offices, he should first have "articled against his curate in the consistory".

The archbishop was able successfully to solve the problem by bringing the principals together and persuading them to thrash the whole matter out in a friendly atmosphere. Todd, on Sharp's

[1] L-B-S. MSS., Box 4, Bundle V. 25.
[2] L-B-S. MSS., Box 4, Bundle V. 20, Sept. 24, 1705.

advice, met Nicolson and Archdeacon Pearson at Rose Castle, where, as he afterwards informed the archbishop by letter, the following compromise was arrived at: "That Paton may attend in my absence, by direction of the Churchwardens by the Bishop's order, till the end of October, which will be the end of the quarter, and then go off quietly. My Lord will then, or before, licence Mr. Langhorne to serve the cure, when I am willing to give a nomination as the Canon requires. Thus by Your Grace's good mediation there is an end to this dispute, and I am at ease in the discharge of my duty; and most highly obliged . . . upon all accounts."[1]

But as soon as one quarrel was patched up another broke out. Todd appointed his new curate, Langhorne, to be his churchwarden; and directly Nicolson heard about it he decided that his enemy had been delivered into his hand. "My Lord", he hastened to inform his metropolitan, "I humbly beg Your Grace's direction in a new difficulty which Dr. Todd has put upon me. As Vicar of Penrith he has nominated his curate to be a churchwarden; and by virtue of a surrogation from the Chancellor, has sworn him into office. I had promised the young man, who is sober and well-deserving, to ordain him priest on Sunday last; but this voluntary engaging himself in secular business (as I take it to be) stopped my hand; and I know not whether (in strictness instead of being capable of new orders) he has not rashly incurred the censure of the 76th Canon. . . . How to absolve him from his oath, or how to let him officiate as a curate, where he is also a churchwarden, I cannot tell. In this extra-ordinary case I am forced (very unwillingly) to trouble Your Grace with requesting your instructions, or your Chancellor's; which will be punctually and thankfully observed by . . . W. CARLISLE."[2]

Langhorne himself expressed to the bishop his willingness to drop the office of churchwarden, and in order "to make both your Lordship and myself easy I have declared myself to be out of the office of churchwarden and refused to act as one last Wednesday". But he then went on to insinuate that Nicolson had in the first instance deliberately encouraged him to undertake that office, saying "it was not inconsistent with my character as deacon". Nicolson accepted Langhorne's submission and ordered Todd to choose another churchwarden.[3]

[1] L-B-S. MSS., Box 4, Bundle V. 29.
[2] Bishop Nicolson's Correspondence, vol. i, p. 308, May 23, 1706.
[3] Ibid., vol. i, p. 313.

Todd, however, fiercely maintained his position, claiming precedents for his action and accusing the bishop, or so the latter complained, of "discouraging piety and conformity" in his parish, of having "threatened Mr. Langhorne with excommunication", and of being "under suffusions of prejudice". Furthermore, he pointed out that Nicolson himself held the lay office of J.P.[1]

Sharp now intervened and, while deploring Todd's action, urged the bishop to show moderation in dealing with the case, being well enough aware of Nicolson's violent temper and narrow legalistic mind, and of the open enmity existing between the two men. Nicolson had a strong ally in his cousin, Archdeacon Pearson, who strove to counteract Atterbury's influence with the archbishop. "I should be very glad", he told the bishop, "that I might have an opportunity of satisfying his Grace of the Doctor's . . . way of proceeding. . . . For I know the smooth Dean's talent at putting fair glosses upon the foulest actions, and how industrious he will be to do it in favour of his friend."[2]

Todd at first remained obdurate and, supported by Atterbury and the chancellor of the diocese, refused to make any concessions whatsoever, returning contemptuous answers both to Nicolson and Pearson. But on September 14 Sharp wrote sternly to him, quoted the bishop's own suggestion that "what had passed in passion might be forgotten", and pointed out that he ought first to apply to his own bishop and chapter for redress of grievances, rather than appeal over their heads to the archbishop. "I have considered of this matter as well as I can," the archbishop continued, "and taking altogether what you have owned to have writ to the Bishop, and what the Bishop says in his own defence and what the prebendaries say in confirmation of it in their letter: I must confess I am of opinion that you will get nothing by contesting this matter further. . . . I could therefore heartily wish, that instead of prosecuting this quarrel any farther, you would think of some method for the having both it, and all other differences between you amicably made up."[3] Whereupon Todd and the bishop begged each other's pardon, and the affair was settled by the appointment of a fresh churchwarden. But again the peace was no more than a truce to be violated as soon as concluded.[4]

[1] L-B-S. MSS., Bundle V. 21, July 31, 1706. *Cf. Bishop Nicolson's Correspondence,* vol. i, p. 315.
[2] *Bishop Nicolson's Correspondence,* vol. i, p. 319.
[3] L-B-S. MSS., Box 4, Bundle T. 81.
[4] The rest of the story, however, concerns the Carlisle diocese alone.

Since the close of the sixteenth century the affairs of the collegiate church of St. Mary, Southwell, had been governed in accordance with the statutes of Queen Elizabeth, which were administered by the chapter. The new establishment consisted of sixteen prebendaries headed by an elected vicar-general, six vicars choral, an organist, six singing-men, five choristers and one verger. But from the time of the Great Rebellion the chapter had, apparently, largely ceased to maintain discipline, and much scandal was caused by absenteeism and non-residence both on the part of the prebendaries and vicars choral alike; while the collegiate buildings were allowed to fall into disrepair, the register was badly kept, services had lapsed, and revenue had been lost. Sharp determined on Southwell's reformation. For, according to its constitution, the archbishop of York was not only the patron of the church, disposing of the prebendal stalls, but was also visitor, inspecting the chapter and peculiar every three years, and instituting an enquiry into their behaviour.

On the strength of this right Sharp came to Southwell for three nights, arriving on May 8, 1693, and commencing his visitation in the famous octagonal chapter-house on the 10th. The following questions were asked and answered:

> "1. What statutes, etc. have you and do you all own and submit to them?
> 2. Do any members hold offices in your Church inconsistent one with another or any other places or preferments that render their due attendance at your services impracticable, and are none of their dues, stipends, etc., unjustly detained?
> 3. Are there sermons preached on Sundays, etc. by the Prebendaries if present, and if absent are their courses supplied by able preachers?
> 4. Are the keys of the Treasury and chest disposed of as the statutes require?
> 5. Are all the Vicars Choral provided with houses?
> 6. Are all the prebendal houses in good repair?"

Answers:

> "1. We have the statutes of Elizabeth which we all own and submit to.
> 2. We know of none.
> 3. The sermons are preached by the Prebendaries in their course or supplied by the allowance of the Residentiary.

4. The keys are disposed of by the order of the Archbishop.
5. The Vicars Choral houses are to be determined by his Grace according to the statutes.
6. Some of the prebendal houses are in good repair, others in bad, and others are not to be found at all in being."[1]

These answers were evasive and unsatisfactory. Questions 5 and 6 had already been asked by Sharp's predecessor, Lamplugh, in his visitation of 1690, when he was answered that the vicarage-house, the proper dwelling-place of the vicars choral, was occupied by three of the prebendaries, "under whose orders we know not." This vicarage consisted of a courtyard with a communal hall on the east and the chambers of the vicars on the other sides. The prebendaries, who had their own houses, had no right to live there at all; but apparently several of the prebendal establishments were in a state of chronic decay, and since the vicarage originally contained chambers for sixteen vicars (the proper number before Elizabeth's statutes reduced them to six) the three offending prebendaries had squeezed themselves in. The chapter now tried to get round this difficulty by causing the hall to be pulled down and a house for the residentiary prebendary built in its place, for which purpose Lamplugh gave a present of wood from Norwood Park. But little seems to have been done until Sharp appeared on the scene, persuaded the Earl of Clare to give "one hundred pounds towards completing the residence-house, and furnishing the library",[2] and gave £20 himself. A certain John Chappell of Mansfield Woodhouse also contributed £150 to the same object.

Shortly after this visitation, while the archbishop was considering issuing his famous injunctions, he received a spate of anonymous letters from Southwell describing the bad conditions prevailing there. One of these, an extremely long and virulent epistle, was written in defence of "poor Ben: Adams", a vicar choral who had been compelled by Sharp to resign his place "upon account of its inconsistency with his other benefice". But Adams, or so the writer declared, was the least among a multitude of sinners, of whose crimes the archbishop was evidently unaware. A few of these are recounted in detail: A certain member of the chapter, for example, was "Vicar of two vicarages yet resides on neither, but lives in a gentleman's house, and at the same time

---

[1] *Southwell MSS.* These questions and answers are taken from a MS. note-book belonging to one of the prebendaries. Unfortunately the chapter registers from 1672 until 1727 are missing.
[2] W. D. Rastall, *History of Southwell*, p. 216.

takes a corporal oath to his personal residence for five quires together at Southwell and performs not that neither scarce one day in seven". But as "kin to a great man . . . may reasonably be connived at; especially having wrought such reformations in the Court as the smoking away pipes of tobacco from the residence and sinking the great cup to three spoonfuls". Each instance cited by the anonymous correspondent is worse than the last (one gentleman having a fresh office "for every day of the week"), and he ends up with "a certain layman, one of the singing men, who when he comes to Church acts that part tolerably well, only he cannot read a chapter in the Bible. But then he has places besides beyond my reach to muster up, which reward him so much foreign business that he employs two horses to carry him about the same, and is seldom a day off the back of one of them. So it may easily be guessed what sort of attendance on the Church and daily service his is."[1] Here is another letter in full:

"MY LORD—I make bold to inform your Grace that the eyes of many are upon you (as well of the laity as clergy) in expectation of the Injunctions you are about to send to this place. That you never wanted trouble ever since you have been concerned here, is almost everybody's observation, and possibly the wished for Injunctions may bring with them a writ of ease to your Grace. There is a noise in all parts of the country how miserably neglected the school is; possibly had not the Master neglected the Clubhouse, the noise had not gone so far. Nor the point of inconsistancy so much insisted on . . . inconsistances there are, by which means either the Collegiate or some parochial churches are scandalously neglected as much to the derision of some, as they are to the detriment of others. And the country round cry shames of these things. And now that all these matters are brought to your cognisance and laid before your Grace, at your Grace's door will the future blame lie, if they be not amended. We live in a partial age, where each person will be concerned as his friend or interest lies at stake. So you will be troubled with restless importunities, in case you do but seem to hearken to them. And as justice is pictured blind, so I'm sure both blind and deaf too must you be, if you do justice in this place.

It is an egregious shame that some who have taken cures upon them, where they are under so many obligations to be resident,

---

[1] L-B-S. MSS., Box 4, Bundle Q. 49, Feb. 13, 1693/4.

and at a time of liberty when common prudence bespeaks their presence to prevent the sowing of tares by others, yet they must be busied elsewhere, and to so little purpose to themselves and families as if £15 per annum with a resident dinner, should out-balance all other considerations of either duty or prudence. I can hear many say, that it is a great pity your Grace should not be rightly informed of these matters, which I hope will excuse the trouble now given."[1]

It was about this time that the archbishop himself wrote to the chapter at Southwell in the following terms:

"My Reverend Brethren

    I take this opportunity of your meeting in Chapter to recommend one or two things relating to your church to be considered of by you. And I earnestly desire that some care may be taken about them as soon as may be.

    First that whereas for about two years last past the duty of residence hath been wholly cast upon one person you would so order the matter among yourselves that it may be divided among four of your body, as I am told, hath been heretofore accustomed; each of which to keep residence a quarter of a year. Mr. Porter I am informed will not decline this piece of service to the church, neither as I believe will Mr. Mompesson nor Mr. Chadwick refuse to take their turns.

    Secondly I do heartily wish, and I do as far as I have power enjoin the restoring the afternoon sermon on Sunday which hath for some years been disused, as also the practise of catechising which latter thing your statutes do expressly require. If you elect a catechist out of your body as your statutes do order, I do not see why his performance to which he is bound, may not easily serve or at least be easily turned into a sermon. If you cannot among yourselves agree upon the method of having these things done: I will upon the application of any of you to me appoint a Divinity Reader out of your body (whom you may likewise make your catechist) and consign him a salary; as I conceive your statutes empower me to do. And this person so appointed may both catechise and preach in the afternoons on Sundays. I insist upon these two things now because the neglect of them proves matter of complaint in the country.

[1] L.-B.-S. MSS., Box 4, Bundle Q. 50, Jan. 17, 1693/4.

Thirdly I do earnestly recommend it to the Residentiary from time to time diligently to look after the Quire that the worship of God in the Church be solemnly, decently and regularly performed; that the office on the Fast days and the occasional Prayers enjoined by Authority be duly read; and that if any of the Quire men be failing in their duty as to these matters or do otherwise give any scandal to the Church or Government in their conversations; that they may be seriously admonished of their faults. And if upon that they do not reform thoroughly they may be punished as the 21 chapter of the statutes (*de excessibus corrigendis*) doth direct.

I do not doubt but you are all as ready to contribute what is in your power to the good government of your church and to the removing of all exceptions, as I can be to put you upon it. But I thought it would quicken your acting in these matters for me to put you in mind of them. Especially when I do assure you (as I do now) that nothing shall be wanting on my part for the supporting and encouraging all your endeavours for the good and happiness of your Church which is heartily wished and prayed for by

Reverend Brethren,
Your Affectionate Brother
Jo. Ebor.''[1]

The subject-matter of this letter foreshadowed the archbishop's injunctions which were issued on March 24, 1693/4.[2] These dealt, as in the letter, with the questions of residence: "That all the Prebendaries of the church (except Mr. Smith)[3] do, according to their respective seniorities, keep a quarterly residence by their turns for the future"; of the divinity lecture: "The Residentiary for the time being shall be the divinity lecturer, and as such shall preach, or procure to be preached, a sermon every Sunday in the afternoon, at the collegiate church of St. Mary in Southwell, for the encouragement of which Sunday lecture or sermon their present Majesties have been graciously pleased to order, that the sum of £500 shall be paid out of their treasury to the Chapter of Southwell as a fund for a perpetual salary to the preachers of it"; and of the choir: "Whereas we have been informed that some of

---

[1] Bishopthorpe MSS., Bundle 17, No. 125.
[2] "Injunctions and Orders of John Sharp, Archbishop of York": W. D. Rastall, *History of Southwell*, pp. 173 *et seq.*
[3] See L-B-S. MSS., Box 4, Bundle K. 13, Jan. 27, 1692/3. Mr. Smith successfully pleads for exemption because of his age.

the Vicars and Quiremen have been too negligent in giving that
due and constant attendance upon the service of the Quire which
their local statutes oblige them to . . . we do earnestly exhort them
to amend that fault . . . and we do enjoin and require that the
statute concerning this matter (cap. 2) be strictly observed, viz.
that none of the Vicars or Singingmen or Choristers, be at any
time absent from the service of the Quire, but for some just and
reasonable cause to be approved of by the residentiary." The
remaining injunctions were concerned with the proper division of
the vicarage among the vicars choral, the creation of a registry,
the tightening up of discipline, the vicar of the parish, the schoolmaster of Southwell Grammar School, and the dilapidations of the
prebendal houses. It had now been firmly established that, apart
from the new residence house, only the vicars choral were to
inhabit the vicarage, which was to be divided into five sections for
their convenience. One of the sections, however, would have to
supply two rooms for the registry: "We do enjoin, that at the same
time that the Chapter makes such a division of the vicarage into
five dwelling-houses, as is before specified, they do so order that
division, that in one of those houses two convenient rooms, viz. a
ground room and the chamber over it, with the staircase leading
thereto, may be reserved and set apart for their Register's office,
and what rooms they pitch upon for this purpose a memorandum
thereof shall be entered into their Chapter book; nevertheless we
do enjoin, that these two rooms shall not actually be applied to
that use till after the death or removal of that Vicar Choral, who
happens to be in the possession of that house in which these two
rooms are when the division is made, the present possessor shall
enjoy them as long as he stays there, but whoever succeeds him is
to take that house upon terms of being without them." This provision left out of account the sixth vicar choral, for the simple
reason that at the particular moment the injunctions were issued
he did not exist. But Sharp sternly reminded the chapter of the
statute requiring six vicars, and demanded that they should immediately fill up the vacancy. Where should he live? The archbishop replied: "We do consider that in all probability one of the
Vicars Choral will always be Vicar of the parish, and therefore . . .
we do enjoin, that he that is Vicar of the parish shall dwell at the
Parish Vicarage-house." Another of the vicars choral was usually
the schoolmaster, and he, later, also helped to relieve the conges-
tion at the vicarage by residing at the school-house in a different

part of the town. The schoolmaster became the subject of yet another injunction, which reproved him for putting his church work before his teaching and declared "that from henceforwards the Master of the Grammar School strictly and constantly attend his school on all school days, and at all school hours, as much as any former Master of the school that was no Vicar Choral was accustomed to do, or as much as he himself, if he was no Vicar Choral was accustomed to do". And on occasions when these two duties conflicted the chapter were to secure a fit substitute for him at the church, "provided, that he himself do in person perform the duties of his Vicar Choral's place on Sundays and Holydays".

The vicarage, it seemed, possessed some convenient back stairs and side entrances, which enabled the more adventurous vicars to indulge their taste for late nights. Vicars choral, apparently, had rather a reputation for this sort of thing; as, according to Torre, those of York Minster at one period "were in the habit of living so high, and heating their blood so much that it was dangerous for a female to come within reach of them". Sharp therefore ordered "that all the private back doors or outlets of the Vicars' houses be stopped up; and that there be no entrance into, or passage out of the Vicarage but through the gates, which gates we do order to be locked up at ten of the clock every night, and the key to be carried to the Residentiary".

Finally, as regards the dilapidations of the prebendal houses, which Sharp suspected were not being made good, despite the chapter's promises, he said: "We do enjoin that the longest time we give for the finishing of them is till our next Visitation; and if by that time all the houses be not in full and good repair, we shall think ourselves obliged to prosecute those that are faulty, in such methods as the law allows and directs."

Naturally enough these injunctions were not very popular with the more easy-going members of the chapter, and were especially resented by the vicars choral, "who complained that he had exceeded the limits of his power".[1] Nevertheless they were obeyed; and the government of the church was carried on under them, with, of course, necessary modifications as the years went by, until the Cathedral Act of 1840 put an end to the old collegiate system altogether. For example, the archbishop himself altered the second injunction by persuading the chapter in 1705 to permit the parochial vicar of Southwell, who was not a prebendary, to preach

[1] *Life of Archbishop Sharp*, vol. i, p. 229.

the divinity lecture on a Sunday afternoon. Some attempt was made by the vicars choral to obtain from Sharp's successors, Archbishops Dawes and Blackburn, a relaxation of the regulations concerning them; but in both cases they were met with a steady refusal. Nor did they achieve any better success in the secular courts, being referred back to their visitor, the archbishop.

In all his actions Sharp had the constant support of the vicar-general, the Reverend W. Mompesson, and repaid the debt by shielding the latter when he was attacked by the chapter in 1694 for overstepping the bounds of his jurisdiction. He died on March 7 1708/9. "On the 7 instant at night old Mr. Mompesson died," wrote William Popely of Southwell, and immediately went on to request the archbishop "to bestow the prebend on one Mr. Ellis", Popely's friend, and not on Mr. Bralesford, who "is so conceited and imperious that the Choir will be made very uneasy. We have now a good Choir and agree very well together."[1] This last piece of news must have pleased Sharp.

The great fire at Southwell occurred on the night of November 5, 1711. A contemporary thus describes it: "On the evening of the 5th of November in the year above mentioned, a very violent storm, attended with thunder and lightening, passed over the town. Between eleven and twelve o'clock, a small flame, not larger than a candle would emit was perceived by those who lived near the church, to rise from the very summit of the south spire. There was a very high wind the whole night, which blew the timber and woodwork of the spire, as it burned, on the roof of the church; so that, before midnight, the spire and the roof of the whole west end of the building were in flames. Before morning the fire was communicated to the roof of the middle tower, and had melted the bells, and destroyed the organ. The damage was estimated at four thousand pounds."[2] Three thousand pounds were needed for repairs, and the greater part of this amount was raised by means of a brief, which was issued at York, begging for donations. Among the Southwell MSS. are lists of parishes in Nottinghamshire, and the names of people in Southwell and its neighbourhood, who subscribed to the repair fund. The archbishop's name does not appear here; but his son and biographer has put it on record that "He [Sharp] gave himself two hundred pounds. He procured a grant of licence to cut down a wood in the Queen's forest of Sherwood, from the Duke of Leeds, to the value of £200; and

[1] L-B-S. MSS., Box 4, Bundle M. 16. [2] W. D. Rastall, *History of Southwell*, p. 461.

from the Duchess of Newcastle, £500."[1] The last noble lady was certainly mentioned, for the vicar of the parish, the Reverend Beckwith Spencer, celebrated her munificence in a fulsome poem entitled "The Benefactress". The archbishop was thus responsible for raising a third of the sum required; an event, one might have thought, worthy of better commemoration.

But this was not the only time that their patron had exerted himself on Southwell's behalf. A decree of the chapter in 1693 declared "that they held themselves wholly obliged to the extra-ordinary diligence of the Archbishop of York (John Sharp) for the recovery of five hundred pounds of arrears due to the Church of Southwell from the Crown". These arrears dated back to 1641, when a pension of £10 per annum, settled upon the chapter *in perpetuum* by Edward VI to pay the salary of a divinity lecturer,[2] had dropped. Sharp suggested that King William might care to make good this amount by a grant of wood from Sherwood forest; but on Nottingham's advice the money was paid in cash over a period of years, and, as has already been seen, it was devoted to the provision of a Sunday afternoon sermon (second injunction).

[1] *Life of Archbishop Sharp*, vol. i, p. 232. *Cf.* L-B-S. MSS., Box 4, Bundle R. 24. A copy of Sharp's appeal to the Duchess. He adds this footnote: "The effect of this letter was that her Grace gave five-hundred pound."
[2] See L-B-S. MSS., Box 4, Bundle K. 56: A letter to Sharp concerning these arrears from Dr. W. Stainforth, one of the prebendaries.

CHAPTER VIII

POLITICS

IF politics are a sorry business, then certainly of all politicians
bishops are the sorriest. When John Sharp entered the House
of Lords[1] in his capacity of archbishop of York, various persons
and parties competed for his support: William III naturally expected his nominee to vote consistently for the crown; Nottingham
and the high-fliers took for granted that he would side with the
tories; Tillotson and the low churchmen hoped much from one
whose sympathies had always been broad and very deep; even out
and out whigs like Burnet and members of the Junto were not
unfriendly and waited to see which way the cat jumped. Sharp
didn't jump at all. He preferred to sit on the fence. Furthermore,
he made it his rule never to speak for or against a measure unless
it happened to concern him directly as an ecclesiastic, or to be of
paramount national importance.

His first intervention came during a debate on "the Quakers'
bill"[2] (February 12, 1691). For some time the Quakers had been
petitioning Parliament to be allowed to substitute an affirmation
in cases where the law required an oath, because of their inability
to swear "for conscience sake".[3] That plea was finally granted, in
a modified form, by the Act of 1696. Sharp's speech on this occasion has not been recorded; but in a letter to Nottingham at a
later date he expressed his desire to get a clause preventing
Quakers from disinheriting their children who had come over to
the Church of England included in a bill aimed primarily at controlling the estates of papists.[4] "I writ", he said, "to some of my
friends in that House [of Commons] to assist in getting this clause
into that Bill, which they promised. But thro' the earnest opposition of Sir Richard Cox, who brought in that bill, the clause was
rejected in the Committee, and afterwards in the House, thro' the
absence of some of those gentlemen who had promised to espouse
t. . . . Now that this Bill is brought into your House I would

---

[1] October 1691. "The 5th instant the parliament met, but did no business: the two
new archbishops of Canterbury and York were sworn, and took their places in the
House of Lords": N. Luttrell, *A Brief Relation*, vol. ii, p. 289.
[2] *Life of Archbishop Sharp*, vol. i, p. 285.   [3] *Parl. Hist.*, vol. v, p. 754.
[4] "A Remarkable Act against Papists" (1700).

humbly beg your Lordship to give yourself the trouble to look over
the clause that is offered below. . . . And if your Lordship approve
it, and think it may do service, that then you would be pleased
to favour it with your assistance."[1] No such clause, however, was
accepted.

The archbishop also spoke four days later (February 16, 1691)
"about the lawfulness of divorce in the case of adultery"[2] during
the debate on the bill for the dissolution of the Duke of Norfolk's
marriage.

In 1694 he good-naturedly "took upon himself the conduct of a
bill about small tithes".[3] This bill had been framed by Stillingfleet,
the bishop of Worcester, who was apparently unable himself to
undertake its introduction in the House of Lords. The primate
afterwards noted in his diary under the date of April 7, 1694:
"On Monday night I went to the Bishop of Worcester, about the
bill of small tithes. On Tuesday I spoke largely to that bill; and it
was ordered, that we should bring in some amendments, and such
provisos as we had to offer. That afternoon five or six of us met
at the Bishop of Worcester's, and agreed upon alterations and a
proviso. On Wednesday I offered them to the House and spoke to
them. That day the bill passed. One alteration was allowed, but
the proviso thrown out. In the afternoon I went to the Bishop of
Worcester, to give him an account of that matter."[4]

On these occasions he spoke and voted strictly according to the
dictates of his conscience, but often to the alarm and discomfiture
of his friends. During the trial of Sir John Fenwick, "for being
concerned in the assassination and invasion plot"[5] (1696), William
pressed upon the bishops the necessity for passing an act of attainder against him; confident, no doubt, that the men whom he
had recently promoted could not fail to support his policy. None
the less Sharp informed the king that he had always been opposed
to bills of attainder,[6] and led seven other bishops into the opposition lobby: "The Bill having passed the Commons, was sent up
to the Lords, where it occasion'd long and vehement debates, the
House appearing to be equally divided in their opinions; and even
some of the best friends of the present government remained stiff
against this extra-ordinary proceeding; but a court-prelate (now

[1] L-B-S. MSS., Box 4, Bundle T. 62.
[2] *Life of Archbishop Sharp*, vol. i, p. 285.   [3] Ibid.   [4] Ibid.
[5] *Proceedings of the House of Lords*, edit. E. Timberland, vol. i, p. 463.
[6] Again in March 1697/8 he voted for the discharge of Mr. Duncomb: N. Luttrell
A Brief Relation, vol. iv, p. 356.

without occasioning a severe reflection on his character) having
made a long speech to show the necessity of passing this bill, he
drew the casting votes on his side; and so the bill was carried by
a majority of seven voices only, there being sixty-eight for it, and
sixty-one against it."[1] The "court-prelate", Burnet, referring con-
temptuously to the new episcopal creations, exclaimed: "How
could they who eat of the king's bread oppose measures necessary
to his service." To which Kidder of Bath and Wells retorted: "If
he might be said in any sense to eat another man's bread, it was
Bishop Ken's."[2]

A protest against the passing of this bill was signed by forty-one
peers, including six of the bishops. But Sharp did not carry his
opposition so far as to join them, since apart from his general
objection to acts of attainder he had little sympathy for Sir John
Fenwick, and had the previous year readily added his own name
to the association for William's defence against assassination. His
hypersensitive conscience, however, had also compelled him to insist upon a definition of the word "revenging"—i.e., "It should be
meant in a legal sense, either in the prosecution of justice at home,
or of war abroad"[3]—being entered upon the journals of the House
of Lords (February 27, 1695).[4] Nevertheless Burnet had high
words with the archbishop in the lobby of the House after the vote
had been taken, evidently and rightly regarding him as the leader
of the dissentient bishops. Later he wrote Sharp a letter full of
spiteful invective. William proved more generous and "received
him without any sign of anger".[5] (January 1, 1696/7.)

The king knew his friends.[6] He recalled the archbishop's speech
in defence of the prerogative during 1693, when in opposition to
the Triennial bill he had declared: "I am afraid this bill is a little
too hard upon the King; and doth in some measure tend to the
making a change in our constitution."[7] The Declaration of Rights
had laid down that parliaments should be held frequently; but
there were decided differences of opinion between the king and
his ministers as to the exact meaning of such a statement. Legis-

[1] *Proceedings of the House of Lords*, edit. E. Timberland, vol. i, p. 463.
[2] *Life of Archbishop Sharp*, vol. i, p. 295.
[3] Ibid., vol. i, p. 298. See also *Parl. Hist.*, vol. v, p. 992.
[4] *Somers Tracts*, vol. xi, pp. 139 and 140. *Cf. Dalrymple Memoirs*, vol. iii, pp. 99 and 101.
[5] *Life of Archbishop Sharp*, vol. i, p. 297.
[6] Tenison wrote to Sharp on February 2, 1694/5, expressing William's goodwill towards the latter, and remarked that he "spake with very much kindness concerning you": L-B-S. MSS., Box 4, Bundle L. 52.
[7] *Life of Archbishop Sharp*, vol. i, p. 287.

lation on the subject was introduced in the Lords as early as 1689, but the prorogation and dissolution of Parliament in January 1689/90 rendered the attempt abortive.

Nothing more was done for nearly three years; but in January 1693 the Duke of Shrewsbury sponsored a bill which advocated annual parliaments and authorised the chancellor to issue the necessary writs with or without the king's consent. Eventually this was watered down to triennial elections and annual sessions; and, having passed both Houses, was vetoed by William. Sharp had been absent from the Lords during the spring session when these events were taking place, but returned in November to speak against the bill, which had been reintroduced in the Upper House. He argued that "our monarchy is now equally balanced by the prerogative of the King on one side, and the privileges and liberties of the subject on the other." The proposed bill would upset this balance, for "if once the King be obliged to hold parliaments every year . . . methinks it makes the way easier, from an annual session, to come to a constant session," which might in time render the royal office a mere cypher. Besides, annual sessions of Parliament "would prove so intolerably vexatious and chargeable to the members of both Houses, who live at any great distance from the town, that it would be much more heavy than any taxes that have ever been laid upon them". Finally, frequent elections led to drunkenness and idleness among the common people, while encouraging "factions, and piques and quarrels".[1] The primate's speech failed to prevent the passage of the bill through the Lords, but did elicit from them a definition of the phrase "holden annually", in the sense of an annual assembly rather than a full session of Parliament. This proviso, however, was largely responsible for its rejection by the Commons.

In the following year a compromise agreement was arrived at between king and Parliament, and the Triennial Act became law, without attempting to define the controversial word "holden".

William was also grateful to Sharp for his stout championship of the Revolution Settlement. Replying to a query "whether from anything acted by King James there can arise a real nullity of the allegiance we once owed him?" the archbishop made the uncompromising point: "I think there needs no Apollo to unriddle the matter to you, for the answer to the question is easily deduced

[1] *Life of Archbishop Sharp*, vol. i, pp. 287-293.

from what you own and allow in the very putting of it. Viz. that King William and Queen Mary are in the eye of the law of England our real sovereigns."[1]

Again, in a charge to his clergy (1693) he remarked "How unaccountable a thing it was, that any person who had already taken an oath of allegiance to their present Majesties, should refuse to pray for them."[2]

There is an interesting anonymous letter written to Sharp on October 27, 1695, suggesting the course of action he ought to adopt during William's coming visit to York. The clergy of the diocese should be especially summoned to meet the king in the Minster, when the archbishop himself must publicly adjure his majesty never to "give way to the intended novelties of uneasy and ill-designing men" in the Church, and "be pleased to encourage the return of peaceable moral and modest men and well-wishers to kingly Government to be members of the ensuing Parliament". The writer concluded by expressing the opinion that if William agreed to these things it would be "a better security of our Ecclesiastical State and Interest . . . than his Majesty ever yet gave us: notwithstanding what passed at the Coronation".[3] There is no record that this suggestion was ever put into operation.

In the summer of 1696 Sharp, in conjunction with the archbishop of Canterbury and twelve other bishops, condemned the conduct of three non-juring clergymen, Collier, Cook and Snatt, at the execution of Sir John Friend and Sir William Parkyns. These two gentlemen, albeit the former only indirectly, had taken part in the assassination plot, and were condemned to death for high treason. The famous non-juring divine Jeremy Collier attended them at Newgate Prison, where Parkyns at least confessed his complicity in the plot and desired the absolution of the Church. This Collier promised to give him; but on the day before the execution he was refused admission to the prison. Nothing daunted, together with Cook and Snatt, he followed the prisoners to Tyburn, mounted the scaffold, and after prayers had been read placed his hands on the heads of the condemned men and pronounced the form of absolution contained in the service for the visitation of the sick. Such an action caused great indignation both among the whigs and tories. First, because the prisoners had made no public confession of their guilt in attempting the assassination

[1] L-B-S. MSS., Box 3, Bundle H. 28.   [2] *Life of Archbishop Sharp*, vol. i, p. 265.
[3] L-B-S. MSS., Box 4, Bundle N. 8.

14

of William, and thus the public absolution on the scaffold looked as though the priests concerned did not consider such an act sinful; and secondly, because the absolution, with imposition of hands, was not practised by the Church of England. Cook and Snatt were arrested, tried and found guilty of absolving traitors (July 2, 1696), but were shortly afterwards released. Collier went into hiding and was outlawed. Yet, far from repentant, he secretly published a detailed defence of the absolution. It was this "defence" that provoked Sharp and the other bishops into signing a declaration which stigmatised the whole episode as "an open affront to the laws both of church and state" and as "insolent and unprecedented in the manner, and altogether irregular in the thing".[1] The archbishop's frank repudiation of the Jacobite and non-juring position was confirmed two years later in a letter to the Earl of Portland, wherein he confessed "He had never, he believed, done anything that might give his Majesty occasion of displeasure; and as I do every day . . . pray to God for his Majesty's health and success in all his affairs; and so I desire to live no longer than I do uprightly and conscientiously endeavour to the utmost of my poor power, faithfully to serve his Majesty in that station wherein his mere goodness, without any desire of mine, hath placed me."[2]

Just as the archbishop had surprised William III by his conscientious scruples regarding acts of attainder, so despite his tory leanings, personal friendship with high-fliers like Nottingham and Rochester, and abhorrence of the principle of occasional conformity, he violently opposed the attempt of the tories to thrust their Occasional Conformity bill upon Parliament tacked to a money bill in 1704. He threw the whole weight of his personal influence against it in the Lords, and through his son John canvassed votes in the House of Commons. Here the "tack" was finally defeated by more than a hundred votes, many of them due to the energetic efforts of the Sharps. "That design", wrote Burnet,

---

[1] See *Somers Tracts*, vol. ix, p. 541.

[2] *Life of Archbishop Sharp*, vol. i, p. 298. There is an interesting letter from John Moore, bishop of Norwich, to Sharp on March 7, 1701/2, describing William's last illness: "On Tuesday his Majesty walked in the Gallerie by his closet, the sun shining and the weather being pleasant and no fire in the Room; at length sitting down there he fell asleep and did awake in a shivering fit; of these he has had 2 or 3 since; one this afternoon, which is now pretty well off; his spirits are very low, and his physicians fearful of his want of strength to go thro'; otherwise there be no malignant symptoms attending the disease. They have begun tonight with the bark, God grant it may succeed, for his own benefit, and the good of the nation": L-B-S. MSS., Box 3, Bundle O. 26.

"was lost by those who had built all their hopes upon it, and were now highly offended with some of their own party, who had by their opposition wrought themselves into good places, and forsook that interest to which they owed their advancement."[1] And yet at the same time Sharp assured Anne "how good a House of Commons she had this Parliament",[2] and advised her to oblige them by herself adopting the Occasional Conformity bill,[3] freed from the "tack", and to get it passed on the shoulders of the "Queen's Friends". It was the "tack" of which the archbishop disapproved; it appeared to him to be an attempt to pass a good measure by dishonest means. Again, in spite of his loyalty to the Act of Settlement and friendship for the Electress of Hanover, he opposed the motion of the tory Lord Haversham in November 1705, adopted for purely party reasons, to invite her over to England. "He could never endure it, as being in his apprehension calculated only to vex the Queen and distract her councils."[4] For the same reason he voted in favour of the Regency bill, which was moved by Wharton and supported by the whig Lords, but opposed by Nottingham and the tories.

If Wharton, Burnet and their friends, however, cherished the illusion that they had won a new and powerful friend, they were quickly disappointed when Sharp spoke in the debate on the Church being in danger during December 1705. "Then the Archbishop of York stood up and said, He apprehended danger from the increase of dissenters, and particularly from the many academies set up by them, and moved, that the judges might be consulted what laws were in force against such seminaries, and by what means they might be suppressed."[5] Yet, when finally the Church was voted to be in a flourishing condition, the archbishop forbore to sign the official protest against this decision. Nevertheless the journals of the House recorded that "The Archbishop of York, and the Bishop of Rochester (Thomas Sprat) protested afterwards."[6]

In connection with the Treaty of Union now pending between Scotland and England, Tenison, archbishop of Canterbury, introduced a bill into the House of Lords "for securing the Church of

[1] Burnet, *History of My Own Time*, vol. iv, p. 73, edit. 1818.
[2] *Life of Archbishop Sharp*, vol. i, p. 307.
[3] Usually he was a strong supporter of this bill. See N. Luttrell, *A Brief Relation*, vol. v, p. 369.
[4] *Life of Archbishop Sharp*, vol. i, p. 307.
[5] *Proceedings of the House of Lords*, edit. E. Timberland, vol. ii, p. 158.
[6] Ibid., vol. ii, p. 161.

England"[1] (1706). This was to be the Church's reply to an Act
recently passed by the Scottish Estates for the security of the Kirk
in Scotland. Sharp, who considered himself the champion of the
hard-pressed Scottish episcopalians, had been horrified by the
Scottish action, which had openly declared that Presbyterianism
was the only true Protestant religion, and enforced its government in Scotland. Accordingly, during the debates in the Lords
on the articles of the Act of Union, he violently opposed the
ratification of this measure;[2] but without success, although strongly
supported by Haversham, North and Grey, Nottingham, Rochester and other high tory Lords.[3] For the same reason he opposed
Tenison's bill, not because it protected the Church against dissent,
but as not going far enough in that direction, since it omitted all
mention of the Test Act. Consequently both Sharp and the tories
immediately clamoured for the following amendment: "That it be
an instruction to the Committee of the whole House, to whom the
Bill for the Security of the Church was committed, that there
should be inserted in the said bill, as a fundamental condition of
the intended Union with Scotland, particular and express words,
declaring, perpetual and unalterable, An Act of Parliament, made
the 35 Car. II. entitled An Act for the preventing dangers, which
may happen from Popish Recusants."[4] The archbishop had, indeed, always been a strong supporter of the Test Act.[5] During the
debate on the Regency bill he was, on his own confession, "one of
those who voted for their [i.e. the Regents] being restrained from
altering the Test Acts, in which vote I was against the Court".[6]
Queen Anne, who feared for the safety of the Union, knowing
that Nottingham and his friends were bitterly hostile to it, used
all her influence to persuade Sharp to break with the tories and
support Tenison, but in vain. "I told her", he wrote in his diary,
"I had seen the bill, and that some of the Lords made a wonder
that the test act was not mentioned in that bill to be continued
as well as the act of uniformity, and that I believed several of the
Lords would insist upon it that it should be, and I was of the same
mind."[7]

[1] *Proceedings of the House of Lords*, edit. E. Timberland, vol. ii, p. 167.
[2] A. S. Turberville, *The House of Lords in the Eighteenth Century*, pp. 83-99.
[3] The majority of the bishops were against him. The exceptions were London, Bath
and Wells and St. Asaph.
[4] *Proceedings of the House of Lords*, edit. E. Timberland, vol. ii, p. 168.
[5] At first mainly as a bulwark against the Roman Catholics, but in later life for
restraining dissent as much as popery.
[6] *Life of Archbishop Sharp*, vol. i, p. 310.   [7] Ibid., vol. i, p. 391.

The amendment was defeated by sixty votes to thirty-three. Five of the bishops voted with Sharp, twelve were against him. Together with twenty other Lords the archbishop signed a strong protest against its rejection.[1]

Yet, in spite of this uncompromising attitude, he was the recipient some two years later of an impassioned anonymous plea for the abolition of the Test. "The popular argument of its being the barrier against popery and fanaticism", wrote this correspondent, "has little weight; when its considered that the oath of supremacy and renouncing of the doctrine of Transubstantiation are the effectual tests against popery; and as to the dissenters it is notorious that few or none of them have declined any employment either of profit or power upon this account. So that whilst this imaginary security is so fondly maintained the most sacred appointment of Christianity is exposed to the contempt of buffoons and infidels; who there is too much reason to believe are now become the most considerable party in the kingdom."[2] The writer, who hotly denies that he is a Dissenter, goes on to implore Sharp, as being of no one political party and so universally esteemed and honoured, to take the matter up.

The archbishop carried into his personal relationships with Queen Anne the same strongly individualistic, non-party front towards politics which had alarmed his friends and dumbfounded his enemies. Anne had long admired his honesty of purpose, and delighted in his casuistical, practical, good-sense sermons. When still only Princess of Denmark she used frequently to single him out to be her special preacher, even, greatly daring, during the year 1687: "March 25th, 1687, Dr. Sharp, Dean of Norwich, preached at the chappel at Whitehall before the Princesse of Denmark."[3] On her accession to the throne Nottingham wrote to acquaint the archbishop with the new queen's favourable opinion of him. "I am now going", he informed Sharp, "to Burley having been here about 10 days to pay my duty to the Queen, and whether your Grace will not think it necessary for you to come and do so too I humbly submit it to you, but I ought to tell you I have good reason to believe that your Grace is more in her Majesty's

---

[1] "Tuesday, 4 Febr.—Yesterday the House of Lords (her Majesty present) in a committee, went thro the bill for the security of the Church of England; a clause was offered by the Archbishop of York, and seconded by the Earl of Nottingham, but rejected, 60 against 33": N. Luttrell, *A Brief Relation*, vol. vi, p. 134.

[2] L.-B.-S. MSS., Box 3, Bundle E. 1, Aug. 19, 1708.

[3] N. Luttrell, *A Brief Relation*, vol. i, p. 398.

favour and esteem, than any of your order. And judge whether
something more than the ordinary respect of a subject is not due
to Her from you; I presume your Grace will think your attendance
at the Coronation is indispensable, and I should not stay away till
you can no longer avoid coming."[1] Anne, indeed, insisted upon
his preaching her coronation sermon, despite the plea that he was
then suffering from an attack of the stone. "I hope by this time",
wrote Tenison on March 28, 1702, "your fit of the stone is safely
over. . . . This day I had a good deal of discourse with the Queen
in reference to the Coronation, which is ordered for April 23rd.
St. George's Day. I perceive it will be well taken if you be at it,
And I further believe you must preach the Coronation sermon if
God gives you health . . . it is to be short and suitable to the great
occasion. . . . Pray fail not of an answer to me as soon as you can.
. . . The Queen will expect that I bring it her sometime next week.
And your Grace's readiness to come and to preach is what she
will like best."[2] Sharp replied at once, declaring his intention of
attending the coronation at all hazards, and expressing his willingness to preach provided the queen really desired it and he himself
was not incapacitated by ill-health: "I do mean to set myself to
make a sermon upon the occasion. And I do likewise design to set
out from hence to London, on Monday, the 13th. But if anything
happens in the meantime that renders me incapable of prosecuting
either the one design or the other, I will give your Grace timely
noitce."[3] Canterbury promptly rejoined: "I received your Grace's
last night about seven of the clock. This morning I waited on the
Queen. She depends upon your Grace for the Sermon. You speak
of April 13 as the day you intend to set out. She observed that
allowing a week for the journey you would then have but three
days to shake off the fatigue. Perhaps 'twere better to have more
rest in Town before you preach; but you must be judge of that
yourself."[4]

After the coronation Sharp had the first of his many conferences with the queen on ecclesiastical affairs, when, as always, he
did not mince his words or hesitate to recommend men for their
characters and abilities rather than party bias. "I thank God", he
remarked in his diary, "I honestly spoke my thoughts about things
and persons. She promised me she would not alter her list of

[1] L-B-S. MSS., Box 4, Bundle K. 35, March 24, 1701/2.
[2] L-B-S. MSS., Box 4, Bundle K. 3.
[3] L-B-S. MSS., Box 4, Bundle K. 1, April 1, 1702.
[4] L-B-S. MSS., Box 4, Bundle K. 2, April 4, 1702.

chaplains. I did what good offices I could to my Lord Canterbury, Lord Norwich, etc."[1] Anne was anxious for him to hold a place in her household and offered the Almonry, together with a seat in the Privy Council. These he was induced to accept by the combined pressure of the queen, Nottingham and Godolphin: "The Queen will not let go her hopes", the last wrote, "that your Grace will be her Lord Almoner. She thinks it entirely necessary for her service, and she says it need not give you any trouble. For that you may depute any other Bishop, whom you please, to take her Majestie's orders in your absence."[2] He also became a commissioner for the Scottish Union, although he never attended any of the meetings.[3] Hereafter, throughout the entire reign, the archbishop was the close confidant of the queen in three capacities: as her spiritual counsellor, ecclesiastical adviser, and counsellor in state matters.

Considering the real power and influence of the crown at this time, shorn though it might be of its Stuart despotism, Sharp's privileged position made him a serious force to be reckoned with both in Church and State. And had he been a more ambitious, or even a party man, he might well have helped to change the course of history. But he was neither; and it was probably because he was neither that Anne trusted and confided in him so much. It is of interest to remember that she never dismissed him. The nearest he got to his discharge was when a strong whig Government came into power in 1708, pledged to carry the war to a successful conclusion, and demanding the axing of all tory officials. On this occasion, April 15, 1708, Sharp wrote in his diary: "I had some talk [with the queen] about Mrs. Masham, whom I found she hath a true kindness for. She seemed to be pleased that I would not at this time offer to resign my office till I was turned out. At least at present she said she would not turn me out."[4] She never turned him out.

Sharp's advice to the queen about politics was simple and vigorous. It was not to allow herself to fall either into the hands of whig or tory; but by utilising the services of the best men from all parties to direct her own policy, as far and as boldly as the Revolution Settlement allowed. For this purpose he encouraged her to attend the debates in the House of Lords; and, on one occasion at

[1] *Life of Archbishop Sharp*, vol. i, p. 315.
[2] L-B-S. MSS., Box 3, Bundle H. 27.
[3] See the article "John Sharp" in the *General Biographical Dictionary*, 1816.
[4] *Life of Archbishop Sharp*, vol. i, p. 331.

least, urged her to get an unpopular measure through Parliament
on the shoulders of the "Queen's Friends". George III, at a date
when the strength of the crown had been much further reduced,
made skilful use of these same "King's friends" in order to control
policy. And Anne, with her Stuart prestige and larger personal
power, would, it might have been thought, have made an even
better job of it. At one period of her reign, indeed, the "Triumvirate"—Marlborough, Godolphin and Harley—endeavoured with
the queen's support to put these ideas into practice; but the
pressure of parties, the high tories on the one side and the whigs
on the other, eventually rendered such a course impossible. Sharp,
who was a great admirer of Harley, backed this non-party Government, although his support remained limited by the fact that he
was not really interested in politics, apart from a few major issues,
and most of these were of an ecclesiastical nature.

Above all, he followed the dictates of his own conscience, and
not even Anne herself could always use the archbishop's vote and
influence as she wished. For again and again, when she pressed
him to follow her counsel, he refused to commit himself, and put
her off with such pleas as "I hoped she would give me leave
always to vote in Parliament according to my sentiments"[1] or "I
must vote according to my judgement."[2] However, in the majority
of such cases it is to be noted that he was usually found on the
side of the prerogative. An interesting example of this was to be
seen in the debates on the Place bill, which the tory Commons
were constantly seeking to force through the Lords in order to
limit the power of the executive over the legislature. Their object
was, as far as possible, to exclude all those who held office under
the crown from sitting in the Lower House and casting their votes
on the side of the administration. At an interview with the queen
on December 13, 1705, the archbishop was asked "to vote against
the bill for excluding officers".[3] Sharp then returned a non-
committal answer; but some four years later, when the subject
again came up between them, he was much more definitely opposed to her wishes: "I endeavoured to convince her it was a
good bill. But though I could not do that, yet I have stuck to my
point"[4]—the point, obviously, of meaning to vote for it, even if he
was "the only bishop of the bench that voted for that bill". Yet,
as a matter of fact, he must have changed his mind and joined his

[1] *Life of Archbishop Sharp*, vol. i, p. 302.   [2] Ibid., vol. i, p. 303.
[3] Ibid., vol. i, p. 300.   [4] Ibid., vol. i, p. 304.

brethren, since it is recorded that the Lords *unanimously* rejected the Place bill (February 4, 1709/10).[1]

During the non-party Government of the Triumvirate he certainly sided with the crown on all important issues, as, for example, against the "tack" in 1704 and the motion to call over the Electress Sophia in 1705. But with the whig-Marlborough-Godolphin ministry in office he was not always so accommodating. When Dawes and the high tory minority in the Lords attacked the Naturalisation bill of 1708/9, which was defended by Burnet,[2] Sharp came to their aid: "He voted against the commitment of it, March 15, and spoke . . . for the alteration of that clause where it was enacted, 'that it should be sufficient to qualify a man for naturalisation, that he received the sacrament in any Protestant congregation'. They would have had it inserted 'in any parish church', but it was carried against them. There were seven other bishops with them, and six against them."[3]

Later, indeed (February 10, 1710/11), when the Lords rejected a bill to repeal the Naturalisation Act, it received no support from the primate, perhaps because it was avowedly introduced to prevent the inflow of the Palatines.[4]

It would be interesting to know Sharp's exact relations with the most powerful political personalities of the day—Marlborough and his Duchess, Godolphin, Harley and Bolingbroke—and how far there was a tussle between them for the queen's attention, especially over episcopal appointments, which at that date were of the highest political significance. The available evidence goes to show that the archbishop sided, if he could ever be said to side with anyone at all, with Harley and Abigail Masham against the Duchess. Marlborough himself hardly comes into the picture. Harley was always Sharp's very good friend, and Godolphin also appears to have been friendly. On his appointment as Lord High Treasurer in 1702, Sharp wrote: "I sincerely rejoice as all do that have the favour to know you, at your Lordship's advancement to this new post. And I heartily pray that the management of it may be as easy and happy to yourself as without doubt it will be advantageous to the Queen and the whole kingdom";[5] to which sincere congratulations Godolphin cordially replied: "I know

[1] *Parl. Hist.*, vol. vi, p. 888. [2] Ibid., vol. vi, p. 780.
[3] *Life of Archbishop Sharp*, vol. i, p. 369. "Them" referred to: York, Carlisle, Chester.
[4] *Parl. Hist.*, vol. vi, p. 1000. For Sharp's views about the Palatines see Chapter X. pp. 274-276.
[5] L-B-S. MSS., Box 4, Bundle T. 31.

nothing in the world that could more encourage me to continue my constant inclination to deserve them from you."[1] He helped to secure the Almoner's seal for the archbishop, and was prominent in promoting the Bounty, which was one of Sharp's dearest projects. But later a coolness arose between the two men over the appointment of Bishops Dawes and Blackhall, which resulted in an open breach when the archbishop defended Dr. Sacheverell.[2] Bolingbroke was always too much of a Jacobite to win his confidence. For, despite non-juring and high-flying friends and sympathies, there was no more devoted partisan of the House of Hanover than the archbishop of York. His fears of popery, quite apart from his firm belief in the Revolution Settlement, would have made him oppose any attempt at a Jacobite restoration. He even endeavoured to sound the queen on this subject: "1708-9 Saturday February 5th. I had a great deal of talk", he noted in his diary, "about public affairs. I told her that the great jealousy of the nation was, that some people were too much inclined to the Prince of Wales. That all our fears were about Popery, and the eluding the Protestant succession, as established by law. She declared, that she verily believed all sorts of people in the nation, whether Whigs or Tories, were inclined to the Hanover family, as is settled by law. And that she knew *none of her ministers, but were in the same interest.* I am sure I interpreted her words to this sense. She seemed to adhere to the Protestant settlement, and seemed to have no manner of doubt about it, though I insinuated that all our jealousies did proceed from some of her ministers; and from the little care that was taken at the last invasion for the suppression of it. But she answered all this, and urged the address of Parliament, of thanks for that care that had been taken."[3]

Sharp's reference to "the last invasion" was to a scare in 1708 that the French would land in the north and be supported by a Jacobite rising. Mordecai Moxon, vicar of Lancaster, had written to the archbishop on March 1, 1700, to inform him of an embryo conspiracy of Roman Catholics and Jacobites in Lancashire; and

[1] L-B-S. MSS., Box 3, Bundle N. 20. On another occasion he wrote: "I have the honour of your Grace's letter and am always very pleased when I can have the good fortune of doing anything to your satisfaction, tho the occasions of it do not happen, as would be agreeable to me": L-B-S. MSS., Box 4, Bundle B. 12, June 30, 1705. Or again: "I should think myself very happy upon all occasions when I could help to pleasure any gentleman recommended by you": L-B-S. MSS., Box 4, Bundle L. 121.
[2] According to the *Life of Archbishop Sharp*, vol. i, p. 365, Godolphin was also much put out by Sharp's defence of the motion that the Church was in danger during the year 1705.
[3] *Life of Archbishop Sharp*, vol. i, p. 324.

of their "great hopes and expectations . . . of a wonderful and speedy Revolution by the landing of the late King James and a French Invasion". He suggested that "nothing can be more requisite, than to secure and imprison the persons, as well as to seize the Arms and Horses of the King's enemies and the betrayers of their native country to a foreign and implacable enemy". William ought to be informed immediately, for the danger was very great, "this last Act of disinheriting the Papists having driven them into desperation."[1] Sharp replied cautiously: "I have received your letter. And (as it was my duty) I shewed it to a Privy Councillor. He is of opinion, and so am I that this general intimation of dangers from Lancashire which you have given in it, will be of no great service to the public unless you will descend to particulars, and give some account of the persons that are engaged in these designs against the Government, and what measures have been taken by them, for bringing their ill designs to pass, what meetings they have had, what arms are provided, and where their arms are lodged. In a word whatever particulars of this nature (from which a proof may be drawn that there is such a conspiracy on foot as you suggest). If you shall think fit to transmit them to me, I do promise they shall be faithfully communicated to the Government."[2] As a result of this and other intelligence several suspected persons were rounded up; but the threat of invasion and rebellion did not actually come to a head until the April of 1706, when the House of Lords petitioned the queen that "for the safety of Her Majesty's Royal Person and Government, a more watchful eye should be had over them [i.e. the papists] for the future, and for that purpose, that a distinct and particular account should be taken of all Papists and reputed Papists in this kingdom with their respective Qualities, Estates and Places of Abode".[3]

Subsequently the Privy Council requested Sharp to order the bishops of his province to instruct their clergy "to take an exact and particular account of the number of papists" in their parishes and make a return. Furthermore, bishops "should proceed against such of the clergy as shall refuse or neglect to do their duty in respect of the said service, according to the utmost severity of the law".[4] The clergy were also expected to find out "what advowsons or rights of Presentation or Donation of Churches, Benefices or

[1] L-B-S. MSS., Box 3, Bundle O. 1.
[2] L-B-S. MSS., Box 4, Bundle P. 8, March 11, 1700.
[3] L-B-S. MSS., Box 3, Bundle No. I, Document 3.
[4] L-B-S. MSS., Box 3, Bundle No. I, Document. 4.

Schools are in the disposition of any papists". The archbishop found his suffragans only too eager to obey the Government in the matter. "Last night I received a letter from your Grace," wrote Nathaniel Crewe of Durham, on April 18, 1706, "together with a copy of a letter from the Privy Council to your Grace . . , I shall be very careful in observing and executing the several orders therein given."[1] "Your commands", declared Nicolson of Carlisle, "in observance of the new order of Council, shall be obeyed with all possible diligence."[2] Finally, Stratford of Chester, a bitter anti-papist, was exceptionally zealous in carrying out these orders.[3] The clergy, on the other hand, were not so forward. Canon S. L. Ollard, speaking of the recusant returns in the northern province for 1733, 1735 and 1743, as well as those for 1706, remarked: "One fact these Returns make crystal clear: the English clergy were not anxious to call attention to their Roman Catholic brethren. In answer to Archbishop Herring's searching questions, the parochial clergy for the most part preserved a discreet silence."[4] Nicolson, indeed, frankly admitted as much to Sharp. "Several clergy here", he wrote wrathfully, "have omitted the giving in the value of the estates of the papists and reputed papists in their several parishes. This shall be rectified."[5]

The official duties of the Almoner were to dispense the royal alms on Maundy Thursday: "April 13, 1704. This day the Arch-bishop of York, Lord Almoner to the Queen, delivered cloth and fish to as many poor women as her majestie is years old, according to custome, being Maundy Thursday."[6] But Sharp had also many other tasks to perform in connection with this office. "My Lord", he informed William Lloyd, bishop of Worcester, who had been William III's Almoner and still took an active interest in the royal charity, "There was not one of those things which you left in charge with me, to be recommended to Her Majesty, that was forgotten by me. What success my solicitations had, you shall now have account of. Those persons that you desired might be entered

---

[1] L-B-S. MSS., Box 4, Bundle B. 11.
[2] L-B-S. MSS., Box 4, Bundle V. 21, July 31, 1706. Later in September he wrote again: "In obedience to your Grace's late commands, I make this return of all the papists and reputed papists in my diocese; with such estimates of their respective estates as the several incumbents of the parishes where they reside were able to give": L-B-S. MSS., Box 4, Bundle V. 22.
[3] L-B-S. MSS., Box 4, Bundle B. 20.
[4] *Archbishop Herring's Visitation Returns*, Appendix A, vol. iv, p. 190. The figures in 1706 probably represented the householders only.
[5] L-B-S. MSS., Box 4, Bundle V. 21.
[6] N. Luttrell, *A Brief Relation*, vol. v, p. 413.

into the list of the Queen's Pensioners in Mr. Nicholas (an officer
in the place of such as were dead), (the Lord Canaris's daughter,
Madam la Chesne and her sister, and Monsieur la Pierre) were all
rejected. As indeed all pensions of this nature, as far as I can find,
are discouraged by my Lord Treasurer, till the Queen have more
money. And it is thought hard that any French Refugees should
put in for new allowances here, the Queen continuing the £15,000
per annum that was granted them by King William. As for those
that had pensions before, and which your Lordship desired might
be continued, their case stands thus: Mr. Yeates' Pension is settled,
and so is the £100 for the education of 2 students in Arabic learning. It is now put in Mr. Nicholas his list, and made payable to
me as Almoner, but I shall leave such a deputation to the Master
of St. Paul's School, as the Bishop of Oxford formerly gave.
Bernard Yates and his niece Pelgins are likewise continued, but
how much taken off I know not. Gaffarelli's pension likewise and
Madame Bastiquenarr's are continued. The Marquess de Neufille's
pension which was paid out of Lord Ranelagh's Office, is struck
off, the fund being ceased. Mrs. Croban's pension is also cancelled.
Mr. Hartman's son's pension, which you desired but for one year
more, is ordered to be paid out of the Almoner's quarterly allowance. These I think are all the particulars of which your Lordship
left memorandums with me, to be laid before the Queen. I had
put them all into writing and by the Queen's order lodged them
with my Lord Treasurer, before whom I read them first to the
Queen, and I have given you the answer that I had afterwards to
each of them.

"I have forgot Captain Baskervill whom the Queen remembered
and will be ready to put him into a Poor Knight of Windsor's
place, when any falls void, provided such application be then
made to her. I forgot likewise your Turk, to whom the Queen
according to your desire sent £10, and was paid by her to Boaz
the Jew. . . . As to Mrs. War, I will leave a memorandum with the
Sub-Almoner that he shall continue your allowance of £6 per
annum, to her out of the quarterly payment for occasional charity.
Tho' I beg leave to acquaint you that I am ordered to grant no
such sort of pensions till the number of the pensioners in the list by
death or otherwise be reduced to such a proportion, as that £800
per annum which is continued for that purpose, may be sufficient
to satisfy them all. As for your own concern to be discharged from
all demands from my Lord Montgomery, upon account of the

Welsh Rectories, I not only sent Dr. Dering, my Chaplain, to Mr.
A. Hornby to take care of that business, but I also spoke to him
myself last Sunday about it, and he has promised that he will take
care you shall be discharged. As for Peter Emy. I represented his
case to my Lord Treasurer some time ago. His answer was that I
should do it in writing by way of petition. Since Mr. Evans came
to town I have got the petition, which was formerly presented to
the Lords of the Treasury. . . . This Petition I mean to send tomorrow to Mr. Taylor with my recommendations of it to my Lord
Treasurer, his Lordship being now at Newmarket. As to speaking
to Charles Bernard for a ticket for Mr. Santley's sister to be
touched for the evil, if your Lordship was here you could certainly
be convinced that it is to no purpose. The Queen has hitherto
touched but 40 at a time, and there are now in London several
thousands of people, some of them ready to perish, come out of
the country waiting for her healing. Mr. Bernard will give no
tickets till most of these people be served. The Queen (for I spoke
to her today about it) will as she has strength (for she has lately
had the gout in both her hands) increase her number, and from
40 will I hope come to touch 2 or 300 at a time. And therefore I
hope in a little time there will be opportunity of getting Mr.
Bernard to serve your friend. . . . As for Mr. Makenzy, I remember
your Lordship told me the story of him as you now write it, but
you left no memorial of him in writing. And if you had, I believe
it would have been to no purpose as to getting him any pension.
But I will leave a note with the sub-Almoner to be as kind to him
as he can. . . . About the Arabic Charity, I have already told you
that the £100 per annum is settled by my Lord Treasurer, and
how that is to be disposed of I do not know. Why may not £10 per
annum be sufficient for the Professor at Oxford, and £40 go to
Mr. Marshall, and the other £50 go to the encouragement of a
student of the same learning in the University of Cambridge, £10
of which shall be allowed to his teacher? This is my Lord of Canterbury's proposal, which I would have your Lordship's sense of."[1]

Sharp had, apparently, the greatest difficulty in obtaining the
necessary money from the treasury for these multitudinous purposes, and was frequently compelled to dip into his own pocket or
borrow from that of the queen. "If my Lord Treasurer", he once

[1] See "John Sharp, Archbishop of York, to William Lloyd, Bishop of Worcester," in
English Historical Review, vol. v, p. 121, published by permission of the late G. Lloyd-
Baker, Esq.

told her, half in jest, half in earnest, "would not pay up his arrears, it would be necessary for them to shut up shop, for they should have no money for the Maundy."[1] The treasury, too, proved very slack in paying the archbishop's own legal fees. "Whereas it has been represented to My Lord Treasurer", wrote William Lowndes from the treasury chambers on March 3, 1705/6, "that the several sums contained in the inclosed account are in arrear to his Grace the Archbishop of York and to Dr. Pearson Archdeacon of Nottingham for pensions, synodalls and procurations. My Lord directs you to signify his Lordship's commands to the Receiver General forthwith to satisfy what is due thereupon, and for the future to make punctual payments thereof from time to time as they shall become due, so that there may be no cause of complaint."[2]

No man was more adept than the archbishop in helping lame dogs over stiles and the deserving into good jobs; and much of his surviving correspondence is taken up with this subject. Indeed, he was always pestering his more influential friends to find posts for his protégés. "He is a poor man in a miserable dejected condition," Sharp wrote to Godolphin about a certain Mr. Peters, "having to his other afflictions this new one added of the loss of his wife."[3] The Lord Treasurer replied promising to do what he could.[4] "I spoke", reports Nottingham about another of the archbishop's swans, "to Mr. Secretary Hedges in favour of Mr. Chamberlain, but afterwards upon his representation of Mr. Tucker's case . . . and that Mr. Chamberlain had obtained it and in a manner supplanted Mr. Tucker, her Majesty was pleased to allow it to Mr. Tucker, but has declared she will take care of Mr. Chamberlain some other way."[5] About a second the Earl said: "Capt. Gibson whom your Grace recommends was I think employed in the pacquet-boat to Calais, but that service is at present suspended: the person himself I do not know but it shall always be sufficient to induce me to serve any man that your Grace would have me do so."[6] Mr. Hill of the Admiralty was, too, always ready to oblige Sharp. "If he [Mr. Randall of the victualling office] is to be removed", he confided to the primate, "I will not fail to make the best use I can of your Grace's recommendation with all

[1] *Life of Archbishop Sharp*, vol. i, p. 326.
[2] L-B-S. MSS., Box 4, Bundle L. 49.
[3] L-B-S. MSS., Box 4, Bundle T. 30.
[4] L-B-S. MSS., Box 3, Bundle N. 20. Oct. 4, 1701.
[5] L-B-S. MSS., Box 4, Bundle A. 40, July 2, 1702. *Cf.* Additional MS. 29584, pp. 87-94.
[6] L-B-S. MSS., Box 4, Bundle A. 37, July 22, 1702.

possible attention in favour of Mr. Watkinson."[1] Even political
opponents like Lord Wharton were inveigled into the archbishop's
net. "Your Lordship", Sharp wrote to him, "received my applications to you at London in the behalf of Mr. Fairfax with so much
goodness, that I have no reason to refuse him, what he came to
desire of me this morning, viz that I would be again his remem-
brancer to your Lordship for some office or employment that your
interest may procure for him. He is a very honest gentleman. . . .
And I doubt his circumstances are so encumbered, that without
some help his family is in danger of being ruined."[2]

Frequently, however, the archbishop's kindness of heart outran
his discretion and he found himself politely snubbed for his pains,
as when Godolphin, replying to a request to find employment for
a certain gentleman in one of the country mints, commented
sarcastically: "But I doubt this matter is a little misapprehended
by the gentleman in the country. The officers employed to look
after the country mints must be persons deputed by the officers of
the mint here, and of the best knowledge and experience they can
find. . . . Several gentlemen from other parts of the kingdom and
from Yorkshire too, have made applications of the same kind with
what your Grace has been pleased to send me, and received the
same answer."[3] And even to such a good friend as Nottingham all
the archbishop's swans were not as white as he loved to paint
them. "I understand", the Earl wrote, "your Grace has prevailed
with the Queen to continue Mr. Palmer in the Teller's place, but
since you permit me to speak with great freedom I will write so
too and am confident this will be a great disservice to the Queen
and some reflection on yourself, how charitably soever you meant
it, and in conclusion no great advantage to Mr. Palmer, for certainly a man of his character can't long be kept in that station
which he once forfeited and never deserved."[4] Nottingham, however, went on to suggest that "because your Grace is concerned
for him" the queen might give him a pension of £1,000 a year
instead. Sharp in reply admitted that he had recommended
Palmer because "I could not in humanity refuse it, having had a
friendship with him this 25 years, and received a great many
obligations from him, and withall knowing his circumstances to
be very compassionable." Nevertheless he readily agreed to

[1] L-B-S. MSS., Box 4, Bundle F. 16, May 22, 1703.
[2] L-B-S. MSS., Box 4, Bundle T. 26.
[3] L-B-S. MSS., Box 4, Bundle L. 121.
[4] L-B-S. MSS., Box 4, Bundle A. 22, 1702.

Nottingham's suggestion, declaring that Mr. Palmer had "reason to take it for a very great favour".[1]

The archbishop, of course, was snowed under with applications for this kind of help, often from persons of quality;[2] and among the many others who benefited were members of his own family, including his cousin, John Weddell.[3] But, in spite of all the extra work the Almonry entailed, Sharp showed himself to be exceedingly jealous of its rights and would suffer no invasion of his privileges, so much so that in March 1706/7 he firmly and successfully opposed an attempt by the Lord Chamberlain to present two Maundy women.[4] He was not, on the other hand, averse to making use of his lordship in a different capacity. For one of the duties of the Almoner's office was to provide clergymen to preach before the queen. At the best of times this would have been an invidious task, but with party passions running so dangerously high it was quite impossible to escape criticism. Anne had, indeed, promised to excuse Sharp from this duty when he was out of town, which fact enabled him to write the following letter to the then Lord Chamberlain, the Earl of Kent, on April 30, 1705: "My Lord— Your Lordship being at Newmarket when I came out of Town, so that I had not an opportunity of waiting on you as I intended, I am forced to give you the trouble of this letter, which is to acquaint you, that when I took my leave of her Majesty the other day, she was pleased to grant me this favour, that while I was in the country I should be excused from providing preachers before her, on those days which shall fall to the Lord Almoner's turn, that is to say: Ascension Day, the 29th of May and Whitsunday. But that you should take care of those turns. And accordingly she ordered me to signify the same to you. This in truth is no more than what she graciously promised me, when she conferred on me the office of her Almoner, tho' it was my misfortune to forget the acquainting you with it, when your Lordship came to be Lord Chamberlain and through that neglect some difficulties happened the last year in getting preachers for those days. I therefore humbly beseech you to take care of those three days, which are now a

[1] L-B-S. MSS., Box 4, Bundle T. 2, May 16, 1702. It is possible that this Mr. Palmer was a relation of Mrs. Sharp. His father wrote to the archbishop thanking him for his intervention (L-B-S. MSS., Box 4, Bundle M. 3, June 27, 1702): "Her Majesty . . . has given my son £2,000 a year in consideration of his former services."
[2] E.g., Lady Catherine Jones: L-B-S. MSS., Box 4, Bundle E. 38.
[3] "Mr. Weddel I put into a way proper for him immediately and will take all the care of him I can." (Signed) J. Pelham, Oct. 4, 1698: L-B-S. MSS., Box 4 Bundle M. 23.
[4] Life of Archbishop Sharp, vol. i, p. 330.

coming, which your Lordship may do either by ordering the Chaplains-in-waiting to perform those courses as they fall, or by sending your letter to such persons, as her Majesty or your Lordship shall think fit."[1] Kent politely replied, promising to "supply the days which belong to your Lordship";[2] but was evidently unprepared to put himself out, since his secretary was merely instructed to get into touch immediately with "Her Majesty's Chaplains in Waiting . . . to give you notice that you officiate before her Majesty on those days".[3] The following year he was much relieved to hear that the archbishop intended to do this work himself. "I", he hastened to inform Sharp, "am very glad that your Grace has appointed the preachers for the usual days this year because none can do it so well as yourself. The Queen is very well satisfied with the persons you have named."[4] Others were not so easily pleased, for the archbishop chose his men for thier preaching abilities regardless of their political sympathies. Amongst others he twice invited Thomas Brett, then vicar of Betteshanger and later to become a celebrated non-juring bishop. On the first occasion Sharp wrote to him: "I had the favour of your letter for which I thank you. I am glad you mentioned the 5th November, for in truth I quite forgot the Dean of Rochester ever spoke to me about your preaching before the Queen either on that day or any other: so bad is my memory. But since I find you are willing to undertake that service I will depend on you for a sermon before Her Majesty on the 5th November and I am sure I shall never forget it."[5] Dr. Pratt, dean of Rochester, was Brett's old tutor, who had recommended him to the archbishop. The sermon seems to have been a success, for on November 29, 1712, Sharp again got into touch with Brett, asking him if he would supply his own place on May 29, 1713.[6] This address was also well liked by the queen, and on May 30 Brett received her command to print the sermon "delivered in St. James's Chapel yesterday".[7] It is an interesting commentary on the state of the Queen Anne episcopate that Brett's second invitation to preach came at a moment when he was lying under the censure of the archbishop of Canterbury, because of his famous sermon on the

[1] L-B-S. MSS., Box 4, Bundle T. 7.
[2] L-B-S. MSS., Box 4, Bundle B. 13, May 8, 1705.
[3] L-B-S. MSS., Box 4, Bundle B. 14, May 14, 1705.
[4] L-B-S. MSS., Box 4, Bundle B. 15, April 18, 1706.
[5] H. Broxap, *The Later Non-Jurors*, p. 20. *Cf. Brett MSS.*, vol. i, f. 401.
[6] *Brett MSS.*, vol. i, f. 530.
[7] H. Broxap, *The Later Non-Jurors*, p. 21. *Cf. Brett MSS.*, vol. i, f. 566.

Absolution and Remission, which Tenison considered popish. Two years later Brett resigned his livings and became a convert to the non-jurors (July 1, 1715).

Naturally the extension of invitations to such men to preach before the queen, even though personally acceptable to Anne herself, evoked a great deal of criticism from clergy and laity alike; with the result that Sharp used ruefully to remark that "if anything happened to be taken amiss in a sermon, he was pretty sure to hear of it, and obliged to apologise either for his clerk or for his choice".[1] Again and again the archbishop asked the queen to relieve him of the Almonry, pleading ill-health and a general unfitness for the task; and even suggesting a successor, his friend Bishop Moore of Norwich. Once at least "he did it upon his knees".[2] But, protesting her own love for him and confidence in his abilities, she stubbornly refused to grant him his discharge. Yet, strangely enough, when everyone, including the queen herself, expected him to resign, he tenaciously clung to office, surviving the strong whig Government of 1708/10.

During the trial of Dr. Henry Sacheverell in 1709/10, Anne, although never actively intervening on his behalf, showed unmistakably which way her sympathies lay. She constantly attended the proceedings in Westminster Hall; and when finally the doctor was found guilty by 69 votes to 52, the knowledge that the queen desired a light sentence got him off with a three-year suspension from all preaching activity and the public burning of his sermons. As everyone now knows, this trial dug the grave of the whig cabinet and enabled the tories under Harley and Bolingbroke to effect a *coup d'état*, which gave them the reins of government for the next four years, brought about the Peace of Utrecht, an intensified persecution of the Dissenters, and raised the hopes, albeit prematurely, of the Jacobites. What part (if any) Sharp played in this tory revolution is not known. Certainly he favoured Dr. Sacheverell, equally certainly he disliked the whigs, especially the Duchess and Wharton. His own position under the 1708 Government was highly insecure, entirely dependent indeed upon the personal favour of the queen. Robert Harley had proved a staunch friend on more than one occasion, notably during the

---

[1] *Life of Archbishop Sharp*, vol. i, p. 327.
[2] Ibid., vol. i, p. 329. "April 26, 1705. 'Tis said the Archbishop of York has resigned his place of Lord Almoner to her Majestie and will be succeeded by the Bishop of Norwich": N. Luttrell, *A Brief Relation*, vol. v, p. 544.

"Carlisle Affair", and Abigail had been friendly.[1] Furthermore, all his best friends and most of his interests lay in the tory party and in tory plans. He, too, like Anne, ardently desired peace,[2] and both were convinced that the whigs would never give it them. Latterly he had become much more hostile to the Dissenters (who were patronised by the whig lords), in particular fearing the influence of their schools. The tories he knew had promised to pass an occasional uniformity bill and possibly other restraining measures, while still preserving intact the principles of the Act of Toleration. As regards the Jacobites, Sharp had long ago convinced himself that so long as Harley was in control the Hanoverian succession would be perfectly safe. Finally, the triumph of the tories meant the virtual eclipse of Canterbury, with whom he was now on very strained terms. The whigs, for their part, were well aware of the preponderant and growing influence of York on Church matters: "Somers wrote to Tenison as early as June 1707 urging him to write to the Queen about Church appointments, 'if the way of talking is difficult' since 'the Archbishop of York never suffers her to rest'."[3] All these factors point to the conclusion, for which there is little direct evidence, that at this crisis in his country's fortunes he used his great influence with the queen in support of Harley and against the Junto.

It was maliciously reported that Sharp had written a letter to Dr. Radcliffe, his physician, who was also a personal friend of Sacheverell, wholeheartedly applauding the latter's stand and endorsing the extreme sentiments expressed in his sermons. The existence of such a letter was, of course, immediately denied by its supposed author, who declared "that he refused to peruse his answer to the articles of impeachment which the Doctor [Sacheverell] himself brought him, and would have shown him. But he told him, that upon his trial he could do him no favour, but he would do him all the right and justice that he could."[4]

Dr. Radcliffe, who figures in this incident, was one of the ablest, but most eccentric, medical practitioners of the age. He had attended William III and Anne, and mortally offended them both

---

[1] Cf. L-B-S. MSS., Box 4, Bundle E. 38, over Lady Catherine Jones' allowance.
[2] Harley (then Lord Oxford) wrote to Sharp in February 1712/13: "Her Majesty has commanded me to tell your Grace that the great affairs of Peace, and of settlement after it for the preservation of the constitution in Church and State being to come before the Parliament; the Queen desires your Grace's assistance and that you will hasten your coming to Town": L-B-S. MSS., Box 4, Bundle L. 105.
[3] G. M. Trevelyan, Ramillies, p. 319.
[4] Life of Archbishop Sharp, vol. i, p. 383.

by his caustic tongue. He said of the former: "I would not have the king's two legs for his three kingdoms"; and told the queen that her distemper was nothing but the vapours.[1] Sharp, on the other hand, did not resent such freedom of speech, while he appreciated the doctor's undoubted devotion and liberality to the Church, especially the help he gave to the Scottish episcopalians. Radcliffe died in 1714, and two years later a *Life* of him appeared, wherein the close friendship subsisting between the two men was illustrated by the following anecdote: Radcliffe seriously considered retiring in 1710 owing to ill-health, but Sharp persuaded him to continue his practice; which he did with such good effect that shortly afterwards he was the means of saving the archbishop's life. Certainly he had a wide following among the nobility, gentry and clergy. Henry Finch wrote to the archbishop on one occasion about his sister in London, "who hath been under Dr. Radcliffe's care about her eyes which are still bad, however we shall go home now and follow the Doctor's prescriptions there since he says her recovery is like to be a work of time".[2] Robert Nelson reported on November 11, 1711, that he had been healed by the doctor, who "has by the blessing of God not only overcome my fever, but has abated the swelling, so that I am now in a fair way of recovery".[3]

The archbishop more than kept his word to Sacheverell that he would help him if he could, as his subsequent conduct at the doctor's trial fully bears out.

Sacheverell had incurred the hostility of the whigs owing to two sermons, one of which he had preached at the Derby assizes in the August of 1709 on the subject of the "Communication of Sin", and the other and more violent address on November 5, 1709, before the lord mayor at St. Paul's, from the text 2 Cor. xi. 26: "In perils among false brethren." The mayor, Sir Samuel Garrard, although he subsequently denied the charge,[4] allowed the sermon to be printed and 40,000 copies were sold. The House of Commons, prompted by the ministry, and especially by Godolphin, who was irritated by a scarcely veiled reference to himself as Volpone, the wily fox, decided that both sermons were "malicious, scandalous, and seditious libells, highly reflecting upon her Majestie and the Government, the late happy Revolution, the Protestant Succession by law established, and both

---

[1] *D.N.B.*: "John Radcliffe." [2] L-B-S. MSS., Box 3, Bundle B. 6.
[3] L-B-S. MSS., Box 3, Bundle N. 23.
[4] N. Luttrell, *A Brief Relation*, vol. vi, p. 523.

Houses of Parliament, tending to alienate the affections of her Majestie's good subjects, and create jealousies and divisions among them",[1] and immediately proceeded to Sacheverell's impeachment. Accordingly, on January 10, 1709/10, four articles against Sacheverell, drawn up by the Commons' committee, were laid before the Lords. These showed that in his sermon at St. Paul's the doctor had attacked "the necessary means used to bring about the happy Revolution", pronounced that the Toleration Act was "unreasonable", the Church of England to be in danger "under her Majestie's administration", and that the same ministry was undermining the whole constitution.[2] These were grave charges. But as Sacheverell proved in a long-winded reply they were very far from the truth. He denied, in fact, that he had attacked either the Act of Settlement or the Act of Toleration, and in reaffirming that the Church was in danger he cast no slur on the administration: "He humbly conceives that he has no where reflected on the ministry, he having in his sermon so clearly made out who those persons were that designed the ruin of the church viz. the dissenters."[3] Here, as later during his trial in Westminster Hall, he successfully made the point that it was the High-Church party that was being condemned in his person: "I am the person impeached," he said, "yet my condemnation is not the thing principally aimed at," and cleverly appealed to the High-Church bishops for support. "I could", he declared, "also appeal for the same (my character and behaviour) to a Right Reverend Lord, that now sits upon the Bench of Bishops,"[4] and caused his counsel, Mr. Phipps, to quote a passage from one of Sharp's sermons, preached before the Lords on January 30, 1700, on the subject of non-resistance and passive obedience, which, he had then pronounced, "must be of obligation to all christians".[5] The appeal was answered; yet not so much for the sake of Sacheverell as in the interest of high-churchmanship, which the archbishop believed to be seriously threatened by the combined power of the whigs, the Dissenters, and the Marlborough-Godolphin group of political opportunists. Along with

[1] N. Luttrell, *A Brief Relation*, vol. vi, p. 522.
[2] Ibid., vol. vi, pp. 532-535. *Cf. The Tryall of Dr. Henry Sacheverell,* published by order of the House of Peers, 1710, pp. 3-5.
[3] Pamphlets *re* the Trial of Sacheverell, in possession of London Library—No. II: "Dr. Sacheverell's Answer to the Articles of Impeachment exhibited against him in Parliament, Jan. 25, 1709/10." Reply to Article IV.
[4] Ibid., No. III: "The speech of Henry Sacheverell D.D. upon his impeachment at the Bar of the House of Lords, in Westminster Hall. March 7th, 1709/10."
[5] *The Tryall of Dr. Henry Sacheverell*, published by order of the House of Peers 1710, p. 154.

Nottingham, Rochester, Buckingham and others he frankly acknowledged that the sermons were poor stuff, but alleged that they
were being used as levers to attack the freedom of the pulpit.

Nottingham actually struck the first blow for Sacheverell "when
he demanded to know whether it was not necessary in impeachment trials to indicate the precise words alleged to be criminal".[1]
In this he was supported by the unanimous opinion of the judges.
Nevertheless by sixty-five votes to forty-seven, the Lords decided
"that by the law and usage of Parliament in prosecutions by
impeachments for high crimes and misdemeanours by writing or
speaking, the particular words supposed to be criminal are not
necessary to be expressly specified in such impeachments".[2] This
cynical flouting of the law, despite the precedent of Dr. Main-
waring's case quoted in its defence, led to a vigorous protest by
thirty-two Lords headed by Sharp. Henceforth the archbishop
came out openly on the side of Sacheverell, and, in the course of
the debate on the articles, made a vigorous speech in his defence.
"There is a matter", he said, "of great consequence before us,
which relates to things both spiritual and temporal, divine and
human. A member of the Church of England stands impeached
at the Bar of the House of very high crimes and misdemeanours,
the particulars of his Charge hath been read before us with his
Answer thereto, the latter of which in my judgement seems very
pertinent to the matter, tho' how far satisfactory to the learned
judges in the sense of the law, I am not able to determine; tho' I
humbly conceive the laws of this land do not, or at least ought not
to contradict the laws of God. A true minister of Christ should
according to the Doctrine of the Cross neither be afraid nor
ashamed to instruct and admonish the people committed to his
charge in the true principles and grounds of religion faithfully and
honestly, without favour or affection, hope of reward or fear of
displeasure, according to their conscience, not only to tell them
from the pulpit what they ought to do but what they ought to
avoid, and those truths I think are visible enough to be read in the
Old and New Testament. But if the person here meant has been
too warm in his zeal for the Church against hypocrites (who are
the worst enemies to the Christian Religion) and thereby has
given offence to those it may concern, yet they are to consider
whether they are too good to amend, or too great to be reproved.

[1] A. S. Turberville, *The House of Lords in the Eighteenth Century*, p. 98.
[2] *Proceedings of the House of Lords*, edit. E. Timberland, vol. ii, p. 269.

The skilful surgeon always searches the bottom of the wound before he applies an healing plaster, lest when it is skinned over it should break out with more fury and contagion than before, so a true pastor of the Church must tell his hearers of their faults and the danger thereof, and not cry peace, peace, to a people just ready for destruction. My Lords, the Church was never yet without enemies, and I fear hardly ever will, so long as the Grand Enemy of our salvation is let loose among us. And if there be no bold shepherds in the time of danger to watch the motion of the wolves in sheep's clothing, how can the flock be safe?"[1]

By a majority of nineteen the Lords secured Sacheverell's condemnation; but this was to prove a pyrrhic victory leading almost immediately to the defeat of the whig administration. The tories were to enjoy their own again, Harley to take Godolphin's place, and York to eclipse Canterbury.

[1] *The Bodleian MSS.*, MS. Rawl. D. 383, fol. 65.

CHAPTER IX

THE CHURCH MILITANT

QUEEN ANNE was reluctant to regard Church appointments as mere counters in the game of political expediency, although Sarah Churchill, a strong anti-clerical, was always at her elbow urging her to do so. To Sarah livings and bishoprics were simply political bribes to be used in the interests of the crown and, incidentally, of the whigs. But Anne had other ideas. The Church of England was very dear to her heart, and she was determined so far as lay in her power to appoint men who, for piety and learning, irrespective of party, would do her credit. She clearly expounded these views to the Duchess on July 17, 1706: "I . . . must answer that part of your last letter that concerns my Lord Keeper [Cowper] and his livings. I have a very good opinion of him and would depend upon his recommendations on any occasion sooner than on most peoples'. But as to this particular, I think the crown can never have too many livings at its disposal, and therefore though there may be some trouble in it, it is a power I can never think reasonable to part with: and I hope that those that come after me will be of the same mind. I own I have been very much to blame in disposing of those livings, but when these are filled up, there shall be no more complaints of me on that account. You wrong me very much in thinking I am influenced by some you mention in disposing of Church preferments. Ask those whom I am sure you will believe, though you wont me, and they can tell you I never disposed of any without advising with them, and that I have preferred more people upon others' recommendations than I have upon his, that you fancy to have so much power with me."[1]

"His" probably referred to Robert Harley, who had by now, with Abigail's aid, commenced his back-stair intrigues. "Those whom I am sure you will believe" may include among others the archbishop of York, who was almost invariably consulted by the queen when there were livings to fill or bishops to nominate. Actually at this stage Harley's influence over Church appointments was very slight, although the Churchills and Godolphin,

[1] B. Curtis Brown, *Letters of Queen Anne*, p. 211.

terrified of his intrigues, grossly exaggerated it. The real tussle lay between Sarah, the whig Junto and their clerical allies, including Tenison, on the one side, and Sharp on the other.

During William III's reign, when Tenison's influence was in the ascendant, the two archbishops had worked together amicably enough. William, busy with his wars and political intrigues, showed no very great interest in Church matters, and set up several clerical commissions, notably in April 1695[1] and again on May 9, 1700,[2] in order to take as much of this kind of work as possible off his shoulders by recommending suitable men for preferment. On these commissions the two archbishops acted together in company with their brethren of Salisbury, Worcester, Ely, Lichfield and Coventry, and Norwich. Their task was to recommend names to the king for any vacant bishopric, or living above £20 per annum. If William should be out of England they had power to dispose of the less important ones on their own initiative. As a rule the king accepted their decisions without question, but on occasion he would override them in the interests of his friends. For instance, in May 1700 Lord Jersey informed the commission that it was the king's pleasure that a prebend should be conferred upon his chaplain. This apparently high-handed action, which flatly contradicted the terms of the commission, so infuriated Burnet that he advised Tenison to resign. Sharp, however, and Simon Patrick, bishop of Ely, were of the opinion that William had the right to override his own instructions.[3] Tenison wisely took the latter's advice, informing his fellow-metropolitan on May 23, 1700, that William had appointed Mr. Stapylton to a prebend at Worcester. "Mr. Stapylton", he added, "is my Lord's [Jersey's] Chaplain and a very good man."[4] On another occasion the king insisted upon a reluctant commission nominating one of his chaplains to the living of Greens-Norton in place of their own recommendation. "When I told the king", Tenison ruefully remarked, "he might over-rule our representation, if he did not agree to it, he answered: I do not care to break in upon the Commission, but I would have this done by the Commissioners upon my direction."[5]

[1] H. C. Foxcroft, *Supplement to Burnet's History of My Own Time*, p. 406. *Cf.* N. Luttrell, *A Brief Relation*, vol. iii, p. 466.
[2] Le Neve, *Lives of the Archbishops*, pp. 247-254.
[3] See Foxcroft and Clarke, *Life of Gilbert Burnet*, pp. 374 and 375.
[4] L-B-S. MSS., Box 4, Bundle L. 63.
[5] L-B-S. MSS., Box 4, Bundle L. 62, May 14, 1700.

As there were never enough livings of any value to go round, the commissioners quickly found themselves overwhelmed with applications when one fell vacant. "There is a living in Cornwall called Stoke Climsland (value about £220 per annum) now void," reported Tenison to Sharp on October 2, 1701. "The King is Patron . . . the persons who at present apply are: Mr. Lowrey . . . he has no living. Dr. King . . . an Army chaplain of some standing. Mr. Noyes of King's College, Cambridge, an Army chaplain of long standing. Mr. Saul, an Army chaplain, who has a living of £100 per annum in county Bucks, but would quit it for this. Mr. Burrington once chaplain to the Duke of Ormonde, who finds he had formerly a promise of it. Mr. Ellis, brother to Secretary Ellis, and chaplain to the Duke of Ormonde. Dr. Atterbury, well known to your Grace. Mr. Charles Harwood not known to me . . . Mr. Hern, the Speaker's chaplain . . . it seems he has not distinguished himself much."[1] At this period Canterbury certainly seems to have valued York's opinion and frequently accepted the latter's suggestions. "The Dean of Coventry is dead," Tenison wrote on September 2, 1697. "By this reason a Prebend of Windsor is void. The King allows he said Mr. Hill should have the next. Sir William Trumball came to me as from the King telling me that the King had given the next vacant Prebend of Windsor to his brother Trumball. From the King himself I have heard nothing. The Princess (believing Mr. Hill will not accept it) has mentioned Dr. Pratt, the chaplain of the Duke of Gloucester, commanding me to let her earnest desire be made known both to the King and to the Commissioners . . . by her speaking and writing two several letters to this effect, your Grace will perceive that 'tis not probable she will be well pleased with a disappointment. I acquainted Her Highness with what Sir W. Trumball had said, but, notwithstanding that, she pressed the matter; so that I offer it to your Grace's serious consideration. She is a very good friend to the Church, and Dr. Pratt has served her 8 years; and I think he's a very honest man, tho' not, perhaps, of the highest form in learning. I shall expect your Grace's opinion as soon as you can conveniently send it."[2] Sharp naturally supported the Princess Anne, all the more readily as Pratt happened to be a personal friend of his.

[1] L-B-S. MSS., Box 4, Bundle L. 69. *Cf.* L-B-S. MSS., Box 4, Bundle L. 68, Aug. 2, 1701, where Tenison tells Sharp of the large number of applicants for the living of Great Hallingbury in Essex.
[2] L-B-S. MSS., Box 4, Bundle L. 55.

Consequently "brother Trumball" withdrew his candidature and the doctor was appointed.

Nearly two years later Tenison consulted him again, this time about a new dean for Chichester. His own nominee was Dr. Willis; but there were several other possibilities, including Dr. Thomas Hayley, the bishop of Worcester's choice, who eventually proved successful. "I desire", wrote Canterbury, "that this may not be determined till I hear your Grace's opinion."[1] Sharp, who had favoured Dr. Gee, now suggested that he should be consoled with a prebend in Westminster and the rectorship of St. Margaret's. This was agreed to; and when the commissioners actually made the appointment in the November of 1701 they naturally took the archbishop of York's approval for granted, "presuming", Tenison told him, "upon your Grace's consent, having heard you favourably speaking of his fervour."[2]

Sharp's approval was, moreover, taken for granted by his brother of Canterbury on other and less obvious occasions, as in the case of the deaneries of Exeter and Lincoln, which fell vacant the same year: "We are thinking of Dr. Wake for Exeter, who had the Queen's promise, and Dr. Willis for Lincoln. There is such pressing that we have not time to deliberate long. We (viz. the Bishops of Worcester, Ely and Norwich with myself) hope we have hit your Grace's mind." That was not quite true, since both the new deans were opposed to the high-flying school of churchmanship towards which, to the disquiet of his many Low-Church friends, Sharp now tended to lean more and more closely. However, up to the time that Anne succeeded to the throne there had been little friction between the two archbishops, who were in the habit of consulting each other fairly frequently. On February 2, 1694/5, Tenison expressed the hope that he would see Sharp "a little before the session begins next year; for it seems to have been our great failure that we have not by consultations, digested our matters relating to the good of Church and State before we are to use them."[3] When Lord Jenyns asked Tenison to present "one Mr. Idle" to the living of Wakefield in Yorkshire, the archbishop referred the whole matter to Sharp. "I shall be directed by you," he wrote, "your Grace can best judge and therefore (as I said formerly) I will be for the man you think will do best service in that church."[1] Again, on Sharp's advice he prevented the University of Cambridge from giving an unsatisfactory clergyman named Trenwick a living in their gift;[2] and whole-heartedly collaborated with him in suppressing such scandals as pluralities or simoniacal contracts and in upholding the decisions of the Church courts against writs from Chancery.[3] On July 4, 1695, Tenison apologised for failing to secure for Sharp's nominee, Dean Davies, the bishopric of Down and Connor. "For my Lord Capel", complained Canterbury, "insists so much upon the presenting of Dr. Walkinton . . . the King will be unwilling to deny his request."[4]

Five years later, when it was believed that Dean Fairfax could not recover from an attack of apoplexy, and remembering York's peculiar interest in the Norwich diocese, he suggested: "Your Grace will let me know who you would desire for a succeeding Dean (Dr. Prideaux or Trimnell)."[5] Sharp replied in favour of Prideaux, because of "his long services to that Church, and the circumstances he is in, which are unlikely to be ever mended, if he be disappointed of this place".[6] But as Fairfax made a totally unexpected recovery, nothing could then de done in the matter. Eventually Sharp did, through the agency of Lord Nottingham, procure Prideaux this appointment, for which the new dean gave him scant thanks.[7] Humphrey Prideaux, a learned but disagreeable person, seemed always ready to bite the hand that fed him. Barely had he taken up his duties as dean before he accused the archbishop of stealing the chapter minute book;[8] and finally penned the following, quite untrue, account of their relations: "But this hard fate hath always attended me ever since my first acquaintance with you that although I never had any intentions towards you but of affection and service to the best of my power, yet all my endeavours hereto have been taken by the contrary handle and I have lost your friendship by such means whereby others would have got it. But since there is such an adverse genius against me I will struggle no longer with it I having not now health enough left to enable me to bear a London journey, do not now expect to see your Grace any more, and I will take care that for the re-

[1] L-B-S. MSS., Box 4, Bundle L. 65 and 66, Sept. 24 and Oct. 8, 1700.
[2] L-B-S. MSS., Box 4, Bundle B. 8, April 29, 1697.
[3] L-B-S. MSS., Box 4, Bundle A. 13; B. 1; R. 2; L. 58.
[4] L-B-S. MSS., Box 4, Bundle L. 53.
[5] L-B-S. MSS., Box 4, Bundle L. 64.
[6] Life of Archbishop Sharp, vol. ii, p. 49.
[7] Ibid., vol. ii, p. 50, 1702.
[8] L-B-S. MSS., Box 3, Bundle N. 29, June 13, 1702.

maining part of my life nothing now from me shall ever come in your way to disturb you. However, I hope we shall meet in Heaven and there will be no misunderstanding or mistakes there."[1]

York and Canterbury were again in consultation in September 1698, "as to the Prebend of Worcester void by the death of Dr. Blagrave", which apparently the bishop of that see had demanded for his youngest son. Indeed, he made himself so unpleasant on the subject that Tenison feared it might "cause the breaking the Commission, which some are very desirous to do".[2]

In the autumn of 1701 a new bishop of Bangor was required. "Your Grace," wrote Canterbury, "is desired with all speed to send your thoughts about a new bishop to succeed in Bangor." Sharp proposed Dr. Bull, who was turned down on the grounds of nationality and age. "If Dr. Bull had been a Welshman", Tenison told him, "I would have been for him, tho' indeed he seemed to me last session exhausted and broken."[3]

At the beginning of Anne's reign Thomas Smith, bishop of Carlisle, died, whereupon Canterbury left the new appointment entirely in York's hands: "I hear that the Bishop of Carlisle is dying or dead; your Grace will have heard the truth before this comes at you. The King thought of Dr. Robinson . . . I meddle the less because 'tis in your Grace's province."[4] Sharp recommended the fire-eating archdeacon of Carlisle to the queen, not perhaps a very wise choice so far as the ecclesiastical peace of the North was concerned; but Nicolson was duly grateful.[5]

Another bishop who largely owed his translation to the archbishop's friendship was Lloyd of Lichfield and Coventry, who went to Worcester in 1700.[6]

The Low-Church school of bishops, which greatly predominated during the reign of William and Mary, had come to regard Sharp almost as one of themselves. He was bound to them by many ties, particularly because of his strong friendship for Tillotson and other old companions of his London days, like Tenison, Wake and Stillingfleet. He had, too, personal links with Nonconformity, and was noted for his violent antipathy to Rome and all forms of Jacobitism. Certainly most of his actions up to the beginning of

[1] L-B-S. MSS., Box 3, Bundle N. 30, May 10, 1704.
[2] L-B-S. MSS., Box 4, Bundle L. 57, Sept. 28, 1698.
[3] L-B-S. MSS., Box 4, Bundle Q. 42, Sept. 9, 1701.
[4] L-B-S. MSS., Box 4, Bundle K. 2, April 4, 1702.
[5] L-B-S. MSS., Box 4, Bundle L. 90 and 91.
[6] L-B-S. MSS., Box 4, Bundle L. 58, April 7, 1699.

1702 seemed to confirm this impression and proclaim him at any rate a moderate member of that section of the Church. Now, however, he began to break away from these leading strings and to pay more attention to the advice of Nottingham and his other friends among the high-fliers.

His favoured position in relation to Queen Anne, commencing with the preaching of the coronation sermon, aroused the jealousy first of Burnet and later of Tenison, who found themselves and their Low-Church allies being pushed more and more into the background.

William's system of controlling appointments through a commission over which Canterbury had presided amicably enough, even if at times a trifle autocratically—"I perceive", wrote the bishop of Norwich to Sharp on June 28, 1695, "it continues still a secret who shall succeed the late Dean of Lincoln . . . the closeness used in this matter has given offence to some of your Grace's brethren in the Commission"[1]—now came to an abrupt end. Anne was fully determined to manage her own patronage, guided by the archbishop of York alone, and Sharp himself was not sorry to assert his independence. Tillotson was dead and times had changed, especially with reference to the Dissenters, who appeared a far greater menace to the Church than either the Roman Catholics or Jacobites.

His first success in this independent rôle came with the nomination of George Hooper to the bishopric of St. Asaph, and was stage-managed in alliance with Nottingham. "My Lord", the latter wrote on June 2, 1703, "'Tis fit I should acquaint your Grace how the Queen has disposed of the Bishopric of St. Asaph, the Dean of Canterbury has accepted it and I am preparing the warrant, but her Majesty is pleased to allow him to hold his deanery with it; and also the canonry of Exeter for 2 years that he may the easier pay his first fruits. Probably he will be advanced to a better Bishopric before the two years are expired."[2] The latter prophecy was fulfilled in 1704 with Hooper's translation to Bath and Wells after Kidder's death in the "Great Storm".

Then came Atterbury's presentation to the Carlisle deanery and his triumphant institution in the teeth of bitter whig opposition. Again, in 1704 and 1705 the high-churchmen William Beveridge[3]

---

[1] L-B-S. MSS., Box 4, Bundle L. 117.   [2] L-B-S. MSS., Box 4, Bundle B. 30.
[3] See *Life of Archbishop Sharp*, vol. ii, p. 43. Here Beveridge informed the archbishop: "You was an instrument, I believe, in God's hand, to call me to his high office in the Church."

and George Bull were nominated respectively to the sees of St. Asaph and St. David's. Both were Sharp's personal choices, and were certainly very learned and deserving candidates for episcopal honours; although it might have been argued that their great age would prevent them from ever becoming very active bishops. But the archbishop was determined on their enthronement. He long strove unsuccessfully to secure Bull a bishopric; but, as he informed Bishop Lloyd, he had so sung his praises to Queen Anne in March 1703/4 that she could not decently pass him over any more. "I told her", he said, "a great many things . . . as particularly the thanks that were given him by the Bishop of Meaux in the name of the General Assembly of the Clergy of France, for his Books in defence of the Catholic Faith against the Socinians. I likewise told her Majesty of the ill usage he had met with from some party men in Gloucestershire in being turned out of the Commission of the Peace for no other reason than I could hear of but that of his zeal in prosecuting immoral men according to the statutes. I hope I have left such impressions upon her Majesty concerning him that she will be very ready to shew him any mark of her favour that she can."[1] These representations had their effect, for when two years later Anne appointed Bull to St. David's she told Sharp "she would not have done it, but for the great character he had given her before of this Dr. Bull".[2]

Nevertheless Sharp was not uniformly successful. Tenison, backed by Godolphin and the whigs, secured the nomination of Wake to the bishopric of Lincoln, in spite of his opposition. Sharp had hoped to land this prize for his friend and protégé Sir William Dawes, whom he looked upon as his natural successor in the northern archbishopric, and wished to train up in the way that he should go. But for once the queen was against him, and to his amazement "refused persons . . . for being Tories".[3] For a while, however, the issue hung in the balance, enabling that staunch tory champion Francis Atterbury to write hopefully from Chelsea on May 1, 1705: "We are still in suspense here as to the Bishop of Lincoln." But he was compelled regretfully to add: "Sir W. Dawes, I find now by an intimate acquaintance of his, begins to despair of it."[4]

Tenison, who was rendered intensely uneasy about this budding rivalry between Canterbury and York, wrote to Sharp on July 24,

---

[1] E.H.R., vol. v, p. 122.
[2] Life of Archbishop Sharp, vol. i, p. 337.
[3] Ibid., vol. i, p. 336.
[4] L-B-S. MSS., Box 4, Bundle V. 12.

1705, in connection with the recent appointment of John Potter as his domestic chaplain, a choice acceptable to both archbishops: "I hope we shall one day agree in others. If not I am sure on my part charity shall prevail; and I think it will on your Grace's also."[1]

In 1707 Bishop Moore of Norwich, a particular friend of Sharp, was translated to Ely on his recommendation; but the archbishop's biggest triumph that year lay in the appointment of the tories Dawes and Blackhall to the bishoprics of Chester and Exeter respectively. This caused a considerable flutter in the dovecots. Marlborough was furious, but for the wrong reason. He suspected Harley of endeavouring to obtain two more tory votes in the House of Lords. Anne quickly disabused his mind of that supposed grievance: "As to what you say, that I must put my business in Mr. Harley's hands or follow the Lord Treasurer's measures, I should be glad you would explain yourself a little more on that. For I know no measures the Lord Treasurer has, but what were laid down when you were here, and I do not know I have broken any of them; for I cannot think my having nominated Sir William Dawes or Dr. Blackhall to be bishops is any breach, they being worthy men; and all the clamour that is raised against them proceeds only from the malice of the Whigs, which you would see very plainly, if you were here. I know this is otherwise represented to you, and I believe you have been told, as I have, that these two persons were recommended to me by Mr. Harley, which is so far from being true, that he knew nothing of it till it was the talk of the town; and I do assure you these men were my own choice. They are certainly very fit for the station I designed them; and indeed, I think myself, obliged to fill the bishops' bench with those that will be a credit to it, and to the church, and not always take the recommendations of 29, who, as all the world knows, is governed by 26."[2] 29, the archbishop of Canterbury, on the advice of 26, the whig Junto, had already sought to intervene, only to be snubbed for his pains. The real victor was Sharp, who had at length secured a bishopric for Dawes. Two other letters are worth quoting in this connection. The first is from a disinterested spectator, Nathaniel Crewe, bishop of Durham, who wrote to the archbishop of York on May 31, 1707, before the nominations had been made: "I am yet of opinion that the Bishop of Exeter[3] will

[1] L-B-S. MSS., Box 4, Bundle B. 9a.
[2] B. Curtis Brown, *Letters of Queen Anne*, p. 230, Sept. 1707.
[3] This was Sir Jonathan Trelawny of "And shall Trelawny die?" fame.

be Bishop of Winchester. For I know for certain (but this is to yourself) that before I came out of Town Dr. Blackhall (a worthy city minister) was sent for by the Queen, and that she offered him his choice of the Bishoprics of Exeter and Chester. I advised him to pitch upon the former. The very next day I came out of Town and so have heard no more of this matter from any certain hand. But by a letter I had this last week I find that the common report of the Town is that Dr. Blackhall will be declared Bishop of Exeter and Sir William Dawes Bishop of Chester, I could be well pleased if this news was true. Tho' I am afraid Sir William Dawes will not be fond of Chester since the living is gone from it. Today I hear that our Dean of Ripon[1] is talked of for the Bishopric of Chester. Well: I pray God direct the Queen in her choice, and if so, it is indifferent to me whom she pitches upon, to fill the vacant places."[2] The other is from Sharp himself, addressed to Sir William Dawes: "Hon. Sir—Is there any hope of your coming among us? May we believe what has been told us over and over again that you are designed for the Bishop of Chester? If so God and the Queen be thanked. We are all here very much pleased with it, but I must confess I shall still be doubtful till we hear of it in the prints that you have kissed her Majesty's hand for the Bishopric. But however doubtful as I am at this time, take the thing for granted because my business now is at the earnest desire of Dr. Stratford the last bishop's son to recommend a secretary to you if you be not yet provided of one. . . . Will you give me leave to ask you in good earnest whether the Bishopric of Chester has been offered you or no? If it has why you have not accepted it. It is not so mean a bishopric as perhaps you may have represented to you. I am told from those that know it very well that it may be valued at £900 per annum without the living of Wigan. And if so I take it to be as good as Lincoln. If you have any enquiries to make either as to the particulars of the revenue or the state of the Diocese I shall be glad to receive your commands and will get you the best information I can."[3] Dawes replied thanking the archbishop for his "kind packet", and continued: "I hope matters will fall out so, that I may have the honour of your Grace's own hands, in my Consecration. I do not hear that any nomination is like to be made suddenly; on the contrary, I have reason to believe, that none will be made, till the Queen's coming to Town in Winter; and abou:

[1] Christopher Wyvil.   [2] L-B-S. MSS., Box 3, Bundle H. 18.
[3] L-B-S. MSS., Box 4, Bundle T. 29, July 2, 1707.

that time, I hope your Grace will be in Town likewise. . . . I shall apply myself, with all diligence, to follow your Grace's directions, in order to prepare myself as well as I can, for that great work, to which I am like to be called."[1]

Victory, however, was tempered by defeat, for Anne could not always ignore the claims of Tenison and the whigs. Dr. John Tyler, dean of Hereford, was nominated to the see of Llandaff in 1706 on their recommendation; while in the next year Dr. Henry Godolphin, brother of the Lord Treasurer, went to the deanery of St. Paul's, and Dr. Francis Hare, chaplain to the Duke of Marlborough, accepted the prebend there, which the former vacated. This was a direct rebuff to the archbishop of York, who had written to the queen on September 19, 1705: "We had it in several letters by the last post that Dr. Sherlock the Dean of St. Paul's was dangerously ill and not like to recover. Now, Madam, taking it for granted that if he die your Majesty will pitch upon Dr. Godolphin to succeed in the Deanery, I humbly beg if this happen, that your Majesty would be pleased to remember Mr. Finch (our Dean of York's elder Brother) for the Residentiary's place at St. Paul's that the Dr. must quit, upon his taking the Deanery."[2] At the same time Potter succeeded to the regius professorship of divinity at Oxford, now vacant by the death of Dr. William Jane. York had proposed George Smalridge for this post, who had gratefully acknowledged his good offices. "I most humbly thank your Grace", he wrote on May 15, 1707, "for your kind concern for me. I do not know what information your Grace has received about the disposal of the Professorship; but I hear no more of it. . . . My Lord of London did the last week press Her Majesty very earnestly in my behalf. Her Majesty was pleased to say that she would take time to consider of it. . . . I am not at all anxious . . . and am fully satisfied with the honour that has been done me by the good wishes and offices of so many worthy persons; among whom I am especially obliged to your Grace."[3]

All these were whig successes, and others were to follow before Anne could shake herself free of their toils, which during the middle period of her reign so firmly hemmed her in. Sharp himself at this time barely escaped being dismissed from his post as Lord Almoner, and had to stand by inactive while the low-churchmen carried all before them. Dr. Trimnell, a staunch whig and Sunder-

land's chaplain, was made bishop of Norwich in 1708, while Dr.
William Fleetwood, another low-churchman, stepped into
Beveridge's vacant place at St. Asaph. It is interesting to note in
passing that Sharp, who was certainly no partisan, had previously
helped Trimnell up the clerical ladder by securing him the living
of St. James', Westminster, three years earlier. "Your Grace was
so kind in relation to Dr. Trimnell", wrote Sunderland to the
archbishop on that occasion, "before you went out of Town, that
makes me now take the liberty of troubling you again. . . . My
Lady Marlborough has promised to speak to the Queen for the
first vacancy in the Church of Westminster, but withall said, that
if your Grace would join in the request it would be much more
effectual; as I should never my Lord have troubled you about
this, but that I know you think of Dr. Trimnell's merit, as I do,
so I am sure the good opinion you have of him, will obtain my
pardon from you for this trouble."[1]

Encouraged by these successes, the Junto now tried to force
either Dr. Hayley, dean of Chichester, or Dr. Willis, dean of Lincoln, upon Anne as the new bishop of Chichester. But by this
time the obstinate queen had dug in her heels and she flatly refused
to consider them, although careful to assure both Tenison and the
Duke of Somerset, who waited upon her with their advice, that
the new bishop "should be a person acceptable".[2] Eventually
Manningham, dean of Windsor, a moderate and acceptable to all
parties, was appointed. This pyrrhic victory of 1709 constituted
the Junto's last; for in the general election of 1710 the tories were
returned to power with an overwhelming majority.

The alliance between the whigs and the Low-Church bishops
and clergy had, on the whole, worked badly. Tenison possessed
little influence with the queen and had never received the firm
backing of his lay friends to which he felt himself entitled. Anne
was no easy heifer to drive; and Sharp, her spiritual counsellor,
lurked in the background, not to speak of Harley and his back-
stair allies. On the other hand, the understanding between Harley
and Sharp functioned fairly smoothly during the next three years.
They were both resolved to promote only the moderates and keep
all extremists at bay; and so they usually agreed without difficulty
on most appointments. But on the few occasions when their paths
crossed, the archbishop generally emerged as victor. In a letter

[1] L-B-S. MSS., Box 4, Bundle Q. 70, June 10, 1705.
[2] See N. Sykes, "Queen Anne and the Episcopate", in E.H.R., vol. l, pp. 433-464.

written to the Earl of Oxford on November 5, 1712, Anne remarked: "The living that is vacant in Yorkshire is what I promised
the Archbishop of York last spring to give to Mr. Drake, whenever
it should fall."[1] Evidently Harley had desired this living for one of
his tory friends, but Sharp secured the prize. Nevertheless co-
operation rather than rivalry was the hallmark of their relationship. So early as October 21, 1704, Harley had written to the
archbishop: "And as to that of Greenwich the Queen will take
care of it as you desire when it happens to be vacant; if there be
any need of a sollicitor in the case to put her Majesty in mind of
it your Grace may be sure of your humble servant."[2] Since neither
Swift nor Sacheverell fulfilled the essential condition of moderation, they failed—high-churchmen though they were and contrary to all expectation—to acquire the lawn sleeves they so much
desired. Instead, the sees of St. David's and Bristol, which were
again empty, fell to the Hanoverian tories Bisse and Robinson
(1710); and the former, a personal friend of Harley, was quickly
translated to Hereford, when Adam Ottley, archdeacon of Salop
and canon of Hereford, another tory moderate, took St. David's
(1713). At this point the increasing infirmities of Sharp, the de-
cline of Harley's influence, and the insistent clamour of Bolingbroke and Harcourt, the new Lord Keeper, let in the high-fliers,
beginning with Atterbury. It is interesting to note that during this
peak period of the archbishop's influence he was neither wedded
to the tories nor uniformly successful: "At another time, when he
recommended, the reason given for the refusal was, that the person
he proposed was a notorious Whig (1713)."[3]

Strangely enough, his greatest success came after his own death,
when his known wishes were respected by Anne, and Dawes was
raised to the northern archbishopric in place of the far better
qualified and influential Robinson, who had to rest content with
the powerful and lucrative see of London.[4] Canon Stratford of
Christ Church, Oxford, wrote to Harley on the subject: "The poor
Archbishop of York is dead. The chief competitors for that see, I
believe will be Hereford and Chester. I may tell your Lordship
whom I can trust, that our friend the Bishop of Hereford never at
first desired a bishopric so much as he now does a better. He gave
so many proofs when he was at Hereford of his designing to leave

[1] B. Curtis Brown, *Letters of Queen Anne*, p. 384.
[2] L-B-S. MSS., Box 4, Bundle Q. 59.
[3] *Life of Archbishop Sharp*, vol. i, p. 336.   [4] Ibid., vol. i, p. 332.

them the first moment he could, that he had lost himself in that diocese before he was well in possession of it. Chester (Dawes) will certainly vote against you if he has not York, and I am afraid will not be firm to you, if he has it."[1]

Anne, as is well known, took her Church duties very seriously, and had a sensitive conscience both concerning sins of omission and commission. Whenever possible she made a careful preparation before receiving the sacrament, and was scrupulous in observing her private devotions. Once, when relations between Anne and the Duchess Sarah were very strained, the latter wrote a long letter to the queen recounting her many services, and flavoured it with extracts from *The Whole Duty of Man*, directions from the Prayer Book, and the remarks of Jeremy Taylor on the obligation of reconciliation before receiving communion. A little later at the service itself Anne bestowed a pleasant smile upon her old friend; but as Sarah shrewdly surmised, "the smile and pleasant look, I had reason afterwards to think were given to Bishop Taylor and the Common Prayer Book and not to me."[2] In such matters she more usually consulted the archbishop of York, who came to act, as he himself recorded on several occasions in his diary, in the capacity of the queen's spiritual counsellor. In such a rôle he was able to influence and direct her mind and conscience in many ways. Among other things he drew her attention to what he termed the indecency of Saturday night play-acting, Good Friday shopping, and various sabbatarian offences; with the result that Anne wrote to Tenison on December 10, 1710, concerning the summoning of Convocation and the business it should pursue: "It is with great grief of heart that we observe the scandalous attempts which of late years have been made to infect the minds of our good subjects by loose and profane principles openly scattered and propagated among them. We think the consultations of the clergy particularly requisite to repress these daring attempts and to prevent the like for the future."[3] Here was the authentic voice of Sharp advocating reforms directly sponsored by the Church and not by the mixed Societies for the Reformation of Manners.

One of the most criticised of Lord Keeper Wright's decisions was that for dissolving the Savoy Hospital on July 13, 1702, and annexing the revenues to the Crown.[4] Admittedly the state of the

[1] *The Portland MSS.*, vol. vii, p. 178, Feb. 5, 1713/14.
[2] Neville Connell, *Anne*, p. 211.
[3] B. Curtis Brown, *Letters of Queen Anne*, p. 311.
[4] Campbell, *Lord Chancellors*, p. 244.

hospital had long been unsatisfactory and was a matter of deep concern to the bishops;[1] but this high-handed action in destroying it aroused the archbishop of York's violent indignation, and he informed the queen "that she ought to restore it again; nay, and to refund all the money she had received from it, for it was sacrilege to touch those revenues."[2] Nothing if not thorough, he went further and caused a memorial to be drawn up on the subject[3] and presented to Anne. This contained a short account of the hospital's history and constitution from the reign of Henry VIII, its founder, until the present time. The establishment originally consisted of a Master and four chaplains, with ample endowments. Most of the revenues, however, had been appropriated by Edward VI and settled upon a new hospital at Bridewell, although Mary I had partially restored them from other sources. During the seventeenth century the statutes were neglected and both the Mastership and chaplaincies became sinecures to be bestowed by the crown on its favourites. Charles II, for example, gave the Mastership to Sheldon, bishop of London and afterwards archbishop of Canterbury, "for his great services to the Crown". Later Dr. Killigrew enjoyed it for the same reason. It was worth about £300 a year. There is an interesting letter from Edward Fowler, bishop of Gloucester, on the subject, who informed Sharp during the summer of 1700: "I . . . went on Tuesday fortnight to Hampton Court, got my fill of discourse with the King. I told him that the late Archbishop of Canterbury informed me quickly after my nomination to Gloucester, that he having made his request to both their Majesties, that the Mastership of the Savoy might be annexed at its next avoidance to Gloucester Bishopric. They both graciously granted his request." But this promise had not been fulfilled, and now William fobbed him off by saying that "he would not dispose of this Mastership till he had had the state of the hospital laid before him."[4]

Upon complaints of neglect and misuse the hospital had been visited several times during the reigns of Charles II, James II, and William and Mary; but nothing was done about it, except that the commissioners reported to William after their last visit

[1] March 22, 1700/1: "Yesterday, the archbishops of Canterbury and York, with several civilians, met at the Savoy, and open'd a commission under the great seal of England for visiting the master thereof, in order to reform what is amiss there": N. Luttrell, *A Brief Relation*, vol. v, p. 30.
[2] *Life of Archbishop Sharp*, vol. i, p. 318.
[3] L-B-S. MSS., Box 3, Bundle C. 3.
[4] L-B-S. MSS., Box 4. Bundle L. 89, June 16, 1700.

"that in as much as the present Chaplains did not begin the abuses and violations of the statutes, but only followed the erroneous practices of their predecessors, they and all other belonging to the Hospital should be continued in their respective places with the usual salaries and incomes". Sharp's memorandum continued: "Notwithstanding which report July 31st 1702 at another 4th visitation made by the Lord Keeper, Sir Nathan Wright, he was pleased to deprive the four Chaplains, though whatever corruptions there had been they prevailed long before their time, and they never received any manner of profit by them. This is as to the dishonour and loss of all the four Chaplains, so more especially to the almost utter undoing of one of them who has nothing left, but a small vicarage for himself and family to subsist on."[1] Yet, despite all his efforts, the archbishop was unable to obtain for them any redress.

In the launching of what came to be known as "Queen Anne's Bounty" Sharp played a more important and successful part. Burnet originally suggested the idea to William III, and actually drew up "two memorials upon it, which he presented to the King, one in 1696, and the other in the year following".[2]

Anne, then Princess of Denmark, read these reports and supported them by her own arguments. But William, no great lover of the Church of England and conscious of the tremendous difficulties in the way of its successful prosecution, besides having other and more urgent matters on his mind, quietly shelved the whole project. It was nothing less than to take the first-fruits and tenths— i.e., the first year's revenue of a benefice and a tenth part of the annual income, which had been originally paid to the Pope, but annexed by Henry VIII to the crown—and form a fund for the augmentation of poor livings. The chief obstacle to the scheme lay in the fact that much of this money had already been settled by Charles II upon his mistresses and natural children, and so was no longer crown property. Still, Burnet persevered, enlisting the

[1] L-B-S. MSS., Box 3, Bundle C. 3.
[2] *Life of Archbishop Sharp*, vol. i, p. 339. Watson, bishop of St. David's, suggested a different origin in a letter to Sharp dated April 19, 1701. "When last I waited upon my Lord of Canterbury", he wrote, "I gave him an extract of an opinion that was drawn up by a great civilian [Sir Henry Spelman] and presented to our late King, to show the way to augment vicarages and pensions and to provide better maintenance for the poor clergy . . . and thinking what may be useful in one province may be so in the other, and knowing your Grace's zeal for the . . . interest of the Church and Religion", he hoped the archbishop would accept a copy of Spelman's treatise and "join with the other Archbishop and his Bishops" in forwarding the design: L-B-S. MSS., Box 4, Bundle L. 76.

active co-operation of Somers and Godolphin, who, as Lord Treasurer in Anne's first ministry, was the man to find the money, since from the time of Queen Elizabeth the Exchequer had collected these dues.

After the second rejection of the Occasional Conformity bill by the Lords with Anne's tacit approval (1703), many of the High-Church party began to doubt of her zeal for Anglicanism; and there was much talk of the Church being in danger. Here, then, seemed an admirable opportunity for restoring her prestige with the tories and smoothing any ruffled clerical feathers by laying before Parliament and the country such a princely proposal as the "Bounty" would appear to be. Accordingly Godolphin approached Sharp, "to whom he gave the first intimation of her Majesty's disposition to give back the first-fruits and tenths to the Church"[1] (January 6, 1704), secured his ready help and sent him to the queen to settle the whole matter forthwith. Godolphin, Sharp and Anne thereupon drafted the following message, which was sent to the House of Commons: "Her Majesty having taken into her serious consideration the mean and insufficient maintenance belonging to the clergy in divers parts of this kingdom, to give them some ease, has been pleased to remit the arrears of the tenths to the poor clergy. And for an augmentation of their maintenance her Majesty is pleased to declare, that she will make a grant of her whole revenues arising out of first-fruits and tenths, so far as it now is, or shall become, free from incumbrances, to be applied to this purpose. And if the House of Commons can find any proper method by which her Majesty's good intentions to the poor clergy may be made more effectual, it will be a great advantage to the public, and very acceptable to her Majesty. St. James, February 7th 1703/4."[2] The Commons replied: "We are justly sensible of Your Majesty's pious concern for the church of England, and of the great advantage it will receive from your Majesty's unparalleled goodness, in giving up such a part of Your Majesty's revenue towards the better provision for the poorer clergy."[3] And the resulting Act of Parliament, 2 & 3 Anne, c. 2, had a smooth passage through the Lower House, but encountered some opposition in the Lords, where the whig majority were largely hostile, since they were strongly opposed to the clause repealing the statute of mortmain, and so enabling people to leave money for the

[1] *Life of Archbishop Sharp*, vol. i, p. 339.
[2] Ibid., vol. i, p. 340; *Parl. Hist.*, vol. vi, p. 328.   [3] *Parl. Hist.*, vol. vi, p. 330.

augmentation of benefices. But the archbishop threw all his weight into the scale and for once secured the united support of the bishops,[1] who, together with the queen's friends and high-fliers, carried the day, although only by a majority of seven. This Act empowered the queen to form the corporation of the Bounty, on which all the revenue of the first-fruits and tenths was settled; while providing that any charitable person who so desired "might by deed or will give to the Corporation lands, tenements, and hereditaments, goods and chattels, towards the augmentation of the clergy".[2] The corporation could also make purchases without licence in mortmain. Later, on November 3, 1704, the governors were nominated by letters patent. They consisted of two distinct classes: First, a number of peers and officers of State appointed for life; and secondly, episcopal and other governors sitting by virtue of their offices. The total number was not more than two hundred.

Both Houses of the Canterbury Convocation felt constrained to present to the queen a united address of thanks for so magnificent a gift; and the archbishop of York with his northern brethren decided to join with them. Naturally the bishops expected that Tenison would act as spokesman; but he was, at the time, confined to his bed, and Sharp would have taken his place but for an unfortunate incident which further exasperated relations between the two archbishops. This began with a letter which Tenison's whig friends, working upon his jealousy of the tory archbishop of York, persuaded him to write to the latter.[3] "Since your Grace sent to me . . . for the copy of the Address as being the person to read it to the Queen", declared Canterbury, "I have heard some hints about it, together with this argument which I cannot well answer. The Bishop of Worcester, being my substitute for this time in Convocation, is, according to the words of the instrument of substitution, to do all that I should do if present; and consequently he is to read the Address, otherwise he gives up the power entrusted with him. This is an occasion on which all possible unanimity is to be endeavoured after; and, therefore, I hope your Grace will consider of this point with my Brethren in such calm and private manner that all things may be done decently and in order."[4]

---

[1] "The bishops were so Zealous and unanimous for the bill that it was carried": *Parl. Hist.*, vol. vi, p. 330.
[2] Le Fanu, *Queen Anne's Bounty*, p. 9. See also Burnet's account of the Bounty in the *History of My Own Time*, vol. v, pp. 118-123.
[3] *Life of Archbishop Sharp*, vol. i, p. 342.
[4] L-B-S. MSS., Box 4, Bundle K. 4a, Feb. 14, 1703/4.

Tenison's argument, in fact, was that as Lloyd represented the archbishop of Canterbury in Convocation, he must also do so in delivering an address from Convocation. This happened to be strictly correct and according to precedent, but unhappily and only too obviously reflected Tenison's political bias. The matter was now further complicated by Lloyd's refusal to undertake the task, since he had the greatest esteem and friendship for Sharp, whom he once advised his son to take for his pattern,[1] and had no desire to supersede him. Whereupon, as time pressed, Canterbury found himself compelled to inform York: "My Lord of Worcester is persistent in the refusal of reading the Address, so that I must desire your Grace to do it, lest a greater evil follow: For I would not for all the world that there should be any miscarriage upon this occasion."[2] Sharp, however, was not impressed, and in his reply clearly expressed his reluctance to intrude where previously he had not been wanted. "I beg of you, therefore", he suggested, "if the Bishop of Worcester persists in his refusal, that your Grace would be pleased some time tomorrow, to send your deputation to the Bishop of London (who will be in the House tomorrow, and who in your Grace's absence may expect such a substitution) or to any other of the Bishops whom you shall think fit to attend the Queen with the address of your Convocation."[3]

Such an answer disturbed Canterbury not a little, who wrote hurriedly and urgently from his sick bed: "I received your Grace's this morning about 7 in bed and still full of pain. The proposition in your Grace's letter added to it. For, unless your Grace goes, this matter will not now do well; for the form cannot be altered without consent of both Houses as I think. If you consult my letter you will see it to be written upon some sudden hints from others, and that your Grace was desired only to speak of it privately to some of my Brethren. I must repeat my desire that your Grace will carry it, otherwise mischief may insue, which I would by all means prevent."[4] Faced by this appeal, Sharp eventually decided to undertake the office in order to preserve at least an appearance of unity in the Church. A little later he presented a further address from his own Convocation of York, drawn up by himself. To both these addresses the queen returned a gracious answer in which she referred to her desire to help those of the clergy "who faith-

[1] L-B-S. MSS., Box 4, Bundle L. 98.
[2] L-B-S. MSS., Box 4, Bundle K. 4b, Feb. 14, 1703/4.
[3] *Life of Archbishop Sharp*, vol. i, p. 343.
[4] L-B-S. MSS., Box 4, Bundle K. 5, Feb. 15, 1703/4.

fully do their duties to God and the Church".[1] A two-edged compliment, as Lord Halifax duly noted, dryly remarking to Sharp: "We know what the Queen means in her answer to your York address; but we cannot so well understand her answer to that of the Convocation here."[2] During the first ten years the governors of the Bounty were mainly employed in trying to get rid of existing charges on the revenue, consisting of annuities worth £10,950.

Already by an Act of Queen Elizabeth, vicarages under £10 per annum and rectories under £7 per annum had been excused the first-fruits; now, Act 5 & 6 Anne, c. 27, all livings under £50 were exempted from the first-fruits and tenths, numbering nearly four thousand parishes out of a total of ten thousand.

Sharp took an active part in these early labours. For example, it is recorded by Mr. Ecton, "Receiver of the Tenths", that "In March 1711, the Lord Archbishop of York was desired to represent to the Queen, the inconveniences resulting from the present quorum of the Governors, to wit, a Bishop, a Judge, and a Privy Counsellor, who must be always part of every Court, and the want of a new Charter on other accounts, etc. Which matters the Queen referr'd to the Attorney-General."[3] The new charter was granted in 1713. The archbishop also made himself responsible for pressing the claims of the Irish clergy; but nothing seems to have been done in this direction. The greatest immediate blessing the poorer clergy derived from the Bounty was the remission of all arrears to those in debt for their tenths and first-fruits. These were often considerable, as James Gardiner, the bishop of Lincoln, reminded the archbishop when the latter recommended a certain clerk for the vacant living of Owston. "There is no haste of presenting him," he suggested. "It may not be amiss, if your Grace think fit, to clear the arrears of tenths first, which neither Dr. Knighton, nor Mr. Horbury [recent incumbents] have yet done."[4] At a later date he finally reported: "I have by further searching found that Mr. Horbury was instituted to Oweston May 9, 1690, so that there is 9 years of arrears of tenths for which he is accountable in his own time, besides 4 more before."[5] Nevertheless Godolphin, as Lord Treasurer, strove to deny them this blessing

[1] *Life of Archbishop Sharp*, vol. i, p. 346.   [2] Ibid., vol. i, p. 346.
[3] Mr. Ecton, *A State of the Proceedings of the Corporation of the Governors of the Bounty of Queen Anne*, p. 6, 1720.
[4] L-B-S. MSS., Box 4, Bundle L. 94, Oct. 14, 1699.
[5] L-B-S. MSS., Box 4, Bundle L. 95.

by maintaining that it was unfair to the Exchequer "to remit the arrears of tenths, which from some persons were considerable".[1] Against this cynical attempt to undermine the queen's gift Sharp flung his whole weight with such effect that the claims were dropped.

The Convocation controversy during the late seventeenth and early eighteenth centuries is, of course, well known.

It began when, soon after the Restoration, in 1664, Lord Clarendon and Archbishop Sheldon arranged for the clergy to surrender their right of taxing themselves in Convocation.[2] The immediate result of this step was the complete disappearance of a sitting and acting Convocation during the reigns of Charles II and James II. William III revived it only in order to pass Tillotson's Comprehension Scheme of 1689. But Convocation reassembled in an ugly mood. The proctors were firmly convinced that it was shortly going to be abolished, and aggression could only be successfully met by a swift counter-attack; while their antagonism towards the State also involved them in a fierce internecine struggle between the two Houses themselves, *i.e.* the tory High-Church clergy and the whig Low-Church bishops. The Comprehension Scheme was rejected; and a clamour led by Atterbury, who had not then entered the Lower House, was raised for sitting Convocations, *i.e.* "that the King had no more authority to prevent their meeting than he had to refuse to summon the Parliament".[3] Wake replied for the crown and a heated pamphlet war broke out. When Convocation met again in 1700 the tactics were changed and an attack was made not on the king but on Archbishop Tenison and the House of bishops. Again Atterbury, now archdeacon of Totnes with a seat in the Lower House, headed the tories. The immediate question at issue was whether or no the archbishop had the right to adjourn or prorogue the House of clergy. This battle continued in and out of Convocation until Anne found herself compelled to intervene and demand "the due subordination of Presbyters to Bishops"[4] in 1706.

Nothing daunted, the high-fliers, who considered that the Church had become endangered by the Act of Union with Scotland, proposed to address the House of Commons against it (1707). Whereupon the queen retorted by ordering Tenison to prorogue Convocation for three weeks until the Union had safely passed

---

[1] *Life of Archbishop Sharp*, vol. 1, p. 347.   [2] N. Sykes, *Edmund Gibson*, p. 25.
[3] Ibid., p. 27.   [4] B. Curtis Brown, *Letters of Queen Anne*, p. 182

through Parliament. The clergy were furious and roundly declared
that "since Henry VIII's time no prorogation had taken place
during the sitting of Parliament."[1] Anne's patience was at an end,
and she wrote sternly to Tenison complaining of the Lower
House's "plain invasion of her supremacy", and threatening that
if "anything of a like nature be attempted for the future will make
it necessary for Us . . . to use such means for the punishing offences
of this nature as are warranted by laws".[2] However, the tory
reaction of 1710 restored the Lower House to favour, and Atterbury, now its prolocutor, recommenced his attacks on the bishops.

The obvious protagonist in all these squabbles was Francis
Atterbury, but strangely enough behind him there sometimes
loomed the figure of the archbishop of York. Actually Sharp was
only officially concerned with his own York Convocation, which
during the years of his primacy met very occasionally for the most
formal of business. The records contain nothing except the names
(and there are very few of these) of those who attended.[3] The one
sign of life it displayed was to address the queen on the matter of
the Bounty. But to make up for the inertia of the north, the south
had more than its fair share of troubles, and Sharp seemed not unwilling to try his hand at stilling the waters. Godolphin, during
Anne's first tory ministry of 1702, had suggested to the queen that
Sharp might be persuaded to keep his friend Atterbury in check.
At this stage Marlborough and Godolphin were still working with
the high-fliers and had no desire to offend them, while anxious to
prevent friction with the moderates and whigs for the sake of getting on with the war. Accordingly Godolphin brought Sharp and
Atterbury together, optimistically remarking: "I hope it may be
a good foundation for the peace of the Church and a great advantage to her Majesty's service from it."[4] Sharp, working through
Atterbury in the Lower, and through Hooper, bishop of St. Asaph,
in the Upper House, succeeded in persuading Tenison to agree to a
meeting of the representatives of both to thrash out the differences
at issue. Nothing, however, could permanently heal the divisions
between them, which the known rivalry of the two archbishops
only aggravated, since the Lower House claimed and to a certain
extent received the sympathy, if not the active support, of York.
The latter certainly did it good service in 1710 when, taking ad-

[1] N. Connell, *Anne*, p. 170.
[2] B. Curtis Brown, *Letters of Queen Anne*, p. 219.
[3] *The Records of the Northern Convocation*, pp. 329-331. (The Surtees Society, vol. 113.)
[4] L-B-S. MSS., Box 4, Bundle K. 29.

vantage of the tory reaction, he persuaded Anne to forgive and forget, and allow Convocation once more to sit and act. Having obtained her consent, and entirely ignoring the claims of Canterbury, he called a meeting "at the Bishop of Rochester's, where the Earl of Rochester, Mr. Harley, and the Bishop of Bath and Wells were present".[1] Sharp, apparently, presided and suggested three topics for Convocation's consideration: the state of the Church, the affair of the King of Prussia, and the turning of the writ *de excommunicato capiendo* into a writ *de contumaci*. Further conferences were arranged, when Atterbury, the new prolocutor, and some of his friends, together with the bishops of Bristol, St. David's and Exeter, strong supporters of York, were called in for consultation. The archbishop's proposals were considered and amended; and finally the revised minutes were laid before the queen and accepted by her. A royal licence was then issued specifying the subjects to be discussed by Convocation, but, as a studied slight to Tenison, omitting to nominate him as president.[2]

The two archbishops disagreed on another issue, that of lay baptism. The eccentric Henry Dodwell had raised the whole question in an acute form by proclaiming that only those who were baptised by episcopally ordained clergy possessed immortal souls. Furthermore, pamphlets were printed and circulated declaring that for this reason the Dissenters were not Christian at all, and existed in a state of damnation. Whereupon, as Burnet puts it, "the Bishops thought it necessary to put a stop to this new and extravagant doctrine."[3] Accordingly Tenison brought the matter up in 1712 at the annual dinner he regularly gave to the bishops at Lambeth on Easter Tuesday. This occasion, indeed, was frequently used to discuss Church policy or problems. In 1699, for example, the subject was the Societies for the Reformation of Manners, with special reference to a circular letter that Tenison intended to send into every diocese, cautiously commending their activities. "I heard", wrote Fowler angrily to Sharp, "most of the Bishops were invited to dinner at Lambeth, on Easter Tuesday. I was not; nor my Lord of London. . . . And 'tis like, then the letter was read to them; and their approbation desired."[4] Fowler, a too zealous advocate of the Societies, had been purposely omitted

[1] *Life of Archbishop Sharp*, vol. i, p. 351.
[2] N. Sykes, *Church and State in the Eighteenth Century*, p. 297. *Cf.* B. Curtis Brown, *Letters of Queen Anne*, p. 311.
[3] Burnet, *History of My Own Time*, vol. iv, p. 371, edn. 1753.
[4] L-B-S. MSS., Box 4, Bundle L. 88, April 18, 1699.

from the invitation, as Tenison himself carefully explained to his brother archbishop. For Fowler had been busily canvassing among the bishops for signatures to his "Book", and Canterbury felt that this should be stopped. "We then met," he explained, referring to the Lambeth dinner party, "and I proposed the stopping of hands and doing something ourselves, it being, I suggest, most absurd for the College of Bishops to be led in such a manner."[1]

Again, on April 3, 1706, Dr. Sherlock, dean of St. Paul's, wrote to the archbishop: "On Saturday last I heard a great piece of news that the Bishops at Lambeth on Easter Tuesday had some debate about the controversy between the Bishop of Gloucester and me, and did conclude to silence the dispute, and oblige us to put an end to it at our peril."[2]

So in the year 1712 the principal topic discussed round the dinner table by thirteen bishops was lay baptism. Sharp, who was one of those present, afterwards noted in his diary: "We all agreed, that baptism by any other person, except the lawful ministers, ought as much as may be to be discouraged; nevertheless, whoever was baptised by any other person, and in that baptism the essentials of baptism were preserved, that is, being dipped or sprinkled in the name of the Father etc. such baptism was valid and ought not to be repeated."[3] It was one thing to agree to such a principle during an informal conversation, but quite another to sign his name to a public declaration on the subject, which Tenison, seizing on the opportunity as a chance of pleasing the Dissenters and whigs, and scoring off the High-Church party, now expected him to do.[4] Consequently, in the brief correspondence which passed between them on this matter, Sharp, supported by his stout allies the bishops of Chester, Exeter and St. David's, flatly declined to have anything to do with a project which, so he shrewdly surmised, was principally aimed at his many friends among the nonjurors. "I can", he wrote, "by no means come into the proposal your Grace has now made in your letter; in that we should all *declare*, under our hands, the validity of lay-baptism. For I am afraid this would be too great an encouragement to the dissenters to go on their way of irregular uncanonical baptisms."[5] The learned but eccentric Henry Dodwell had recently written in his

---

[1] L-B-S. MSS., Box 4, Bundle L. 58, April 7, 1699.
[2] L-B-S. MSS., Box 4, Bundle Q. 72.
[3] *Life of Archbishop Sharp*, vol. i, p. 370.
[4] L-B-S. MSS., Box 4, Bundle K. 29.
[5] *Life of Archbishop Sharp*, vol. i, p. 373. *Cf.* L-B-S. MSS., Box 3, Bundle H. 30.

book on baptism: "Immortality was a special gift of God to those only who had been baptized into the Communion of the Church and that no baptism was valid except such as was administered through the hands of the lawfully, that is to say episcopally ordained clergy." In this contention he was supported by Hickes, Wagstaffe, Brett and Laurence. Laurence, also a non-juror, was a close friend of Sharp and received the archbishop's support in his wordy warfare with the whig Fleetwood, who in *The Judgement of the Church of England on Lay Baptism* had come out strongly on Tenison's side. In a letter to Brett dated May 14, 1712, Laurence wrote: "The enclosed answer to Bishop Fleetwood's Judgement of the Church of England (as he calls it) I hope will prevail with you to pardon my thus long silence, especially when I tell you that not only my writing that book was the occasion thereof, but also my making some additions and alterations in my Book on Lay Baptism for a third edition, which God willing must speedily come forth if an order from the Queen and Council does not first put a stop to it. For my Lord Archbishop of York has told me that the Lord Treasurer assured him last week there would speedily come out such an order to stop all our and your pens from meddling any more in this matter of Lay Baptism."[1] Sharp proved right, for the crown was anxious to let sleeping dogs lie. Nevertheless, after the Bishops' Declaration, which he had refused to sign, had been rejected by the Lower House of Convocation the principle continued to be debated outside for some time. But as nothing further was done, it eventually died a natural death. Sharp's attitude had aroused the wrath of Burnet, who accused him of turning his coat. This was not true. The fault lay rather with Tenison, who had seized upon a privately expressed opinion and tried to exalt it into a public declaration in the interests of his own Church and political party. Sharp was right to refuse to be stampeded into a false position. But Burnet's disappointment is understandable, if what he believed was true, namely that the Lower House led by Atterbury might have listened to Sharp if he had supported the Declaration, but would have nothing to do with Tenison.

It would be correct to say that the older Sharp became the more hostile he grew towards dissent, and probably as a necessary corollary more definitely High Church. As a boy he had been influenced by a puritanical father; but his years at Cambridge and later in Kensington House had nipped these leanings in the bud. How-

[1] Broxap, *The Later Non-Jurors*, p. 16.

ever, his great friendship with Tillotson and marriage connection with Baxter, besides his long struggle against popery at St. Giles', made him very tolerant of dissent. He hoped much from Tillotson's Comprehension Scheme, and his own two controversial works on conscience were written with the express desire of attaining this end. Its failure saddened him; and his attitude gradually changed from friendly neutrality to dislike, from dislike to active hostility, as the recovery of Nonconformity, based on an understanding with the great whig lords and the Low-Church bishops, became clearer. At St. Giles' his chief enemies had been the Irish papists, but in Yorkshire the Roman Catholics were insignificant. The recusant returns of 1706, when a Jacobite rising was feared, record monotonously in parish after parish "no papist".[1] Dissent, on the other hand, was strong. Its schools were better organised and more numerous than the Anglican, its chapels were well attended, its ministers aggressive, especially in such populous places as Leeds, Bradford and Hull. As has already been seen, the Nonconformist ministers had tried hard to capture the Societies for the Reformation of Manners, and were endeavouring to interpret the Toleration Act in the widest possible sense to their own advantage.[2] Sharp himself bitterly complained of "dissenting ministers taking upon themselves to perform parochial offices, to the grievance and detriment of the clergy of the Church Established".[3]

"There have been several couples since I came to this parish", wrote the Reverend R. Banks, vicar of Hull, to the archbishop on March 6, 1692, "who have had the matrimonial banns thrice published, and because they are not asked out before the Prohibited times, in which the Ecclesiastical Court will not allow us to marry them without licence; they have upon our refusal, gone to be married by the Non-conformist Minister, whereby we not only lose our dues, but usually our parishioners too, who are too often by this means seduced to a conventicle."[4]

Eventually, in 1704, Sharp consulted Lord Justice Holt as to how to remedy this unsatisfactory state of affairs. "I have, my Lord", he told him, "complaints from some of my clergy, that the non-conformist ministers do them a great deal of prejudice, by

---

[1] *Archbishop Sharp's Book*, vol. iii, marginal notes, Bishopthorpe MSS. See also *Archbishop Herring's Visitation Returns*, Appendix A, vol. iv, p. 190.
[2] Richard Frankland's case: L-B-S. MSS., Box 3, Bundle B. 15; Box 4, Bundle P. 11; Box 4, Bundle L. 115.
[3] *Life of Archbishop Sharp*, vol. i, p. 360.   [4] L-B-S. MSS., Box 4, Bundle Q. 8.

taking upon them to marry, bury, christen children, and church women within their families. And when they have expostulated this matter with them, they affirm that the Act of Indulgence doth allow them to do all this."[1] Holt's reply was not very helpful: "As to the non-conformists' marrying, they may be proceeded against in the ecclesiastical court for marrying without licence, or publication of the banns, or for clandestine marriages, which the Act of Toleration doth not indulge them in. But as for christenings, churching of women, and burials, I know not how to deal with them."[2] Finally, in 1705, the archbishop raised the whole question in the debate on the tory motion that the Church was in danger, only to be shouted down by Wharton and the whigs.

After Tillotson's death Sharp's links with low-churchmanship were largely broken; and when old friends like Burnet, Tenison, Wake and Nicolson became antagonistic he was forced back on the High-Church party, where his defence of Atterbury and Sacheverell, his attacks on dissent, his friendship for Harley, Nottingham and Rochester were widely welcomed. Towards the end of his life all his chief supporters among the bishops were strong tories. He spoke and voted consistently for the Occasional Conformity bill when freed from the "tack." The Reverend Richard Stretton, writing to Thoresby in the spring of 1703 about this bill, remarked: "All King William's bishops that were in town, and some others, were all right and tight [i.e. opposed the bill], only your Archbishop of York turned head upon them. He is much blamed for causing her Majesty to have the misfortune to appear so zealous for it. It is commonly said, and I never heard it denied, that when this bill was first framed, her Majesty sent for him, and asked him if he thought in his conscience, that this bill did interfere with, or did undermine the Act for Toleration, and he should say in his conscience he did believe not. Some think (that love him well) he was strangely surprised, or his conscience was not duly informed and consulted, that could give such an answer. But the influence of his old patron the Earl of Nottingham (from whose vassalage he broke in King William's time) hath brought him over to be the head of the high church party."[3]

For the first time in his life the archbishop was accused, not unjustly, of adopting an intolerant attitude towards the Dissenters when he and the bishop of Lincoln attacked their schools in 1705. They also expressed great horror at the "prevailing irreligion" and

[1] Life of Archbishop Sharp, vol. i, p. 360.   [2] L-B-S. MSS., Box 4, Bundle Q.8
[3] R. Thoresby, Letters of Eminent Men, vol. i, p. 436.

"licentiousness of the press".[1] Yet no man was ever less of a persecutor than Sharp. Again and again he reiterated perfectly
genuinely his determination to observe and defend the Act of
Toleration; and no individual Nonconformist ever suffered at his
hands. Indeed, as in the case of Thomas Wainman, minister at
Bingley,[2] many lived to bless his name. Furthermore, he would
never allow his clergy to attack them in their sermons, being
"shocked to hear them vilified and maltreated in the pulpit,
which he abhorred should be prostituted to such purposes".[3] At
the same time he was absolutely convinced that the sects were
once again becoming a real danger to the Church. Whig lords and
Nonconformist tradesmen represented the richest interests in the
country; and the Hanoverian heirs to the throne were inclined to
favour them both. Consequently the archbishop saw many dangers ahead. These he strove to counteract not merely by destructive opposition, but by endeavouring to convert the Hanoverians
in advance through the introduction of Anglicanism into their
country, by improving and increasing the Anglican schools in his
diocese, and above all by pressing for the appointment of good
churchmen as bishops. Events proved his fear groundless; but few
men have the gift of reading the future correctly.

In conclusion it will not be out of place to quote the archbishop's
own considered opinion of the Church which he loved and fought
for: "If we take our measures concerning the truths of religion,
from the rules of the Holy Scripture, and the platform of the primitive churches; the Church of England is undoubtedly, both as to
doctrine and worship, the purest church that is at this day in the
world; the most orthodox in faith, and the freest on the one hand
from idolatry and superstition; and, on the other hand, from the
freakishness and enthusiasm, of any now extant. Nay, I do further
say, with great seriousness, and as one that expects to be called to
account at the dreadful tribunal of God, for what I now say, if I
do not speak in sincerity, that I do in my conscience believe that,
if the religion of Jesus Christ, as it is believed in the New Testament, be the true religion (as I am certain it is) then the communion of the Church of England is a safe way to salvation, and
the safest of any I know in the world."[4]

[1] Additional MS. 28242, f. 84.
[2] *Archbishop Herring's Visitation Returns*, vol. ii, pp. 109 and 224.
[3] *Life of Archbishop Sharp*, vol. i, p. 357.   [4] Ibid., vol. i, p. 355.

CHAPTER X

FOREIGN AFFAIRS

LIKE Wake, Bull and other leading divines of the day, Sharp took a keen interest in religious matters outside the English boundaries; and was "very desirous of seeing the English Church strengthened and the Protestant interest consolidated by a closer union with sympathisers on the Continent".[1]

The Grand Alliance against Louis XIV, although professedly a political union containing the Roman Catholic Emperor, was also in another sense a Protestant league against the greatest Roman Catholic protagonist of the age. England, Prussia and Holland represented, with the possible exception of Sweden, the strongest and best elements in the Reformation. Holland, suspicious of England and content with its own strong brand of Calvinism, seemed sterile ground for the Anglican missionary. Nevertheless it is interesting to note that an Anglican church had been set up in Amsterdam and served by Dr. John Cockburn from 1698 until 1709. Cockburn, who had been appointed by Compton, was also friendly with Sharp. It was, indeed, through Cockburn that the archbishop became acquainted with M. Le Clerc,[2] of whom more will be heard in the next chapter; and on several occasions he was able to do the chaplain a kindness. Writing to the archbishop towards the end of 1703, Cockburn spoke of his help "in settling that affair concerning this church by obtaining her Majesty's positive order for paying her Royal allowance"; and went on to complain that Burnet had been trying to injure him with the governors of the Society for the Propagation of the Gospel, but that his accusations were unfounded. "I have lived", he declared, "fairly and peaceably with all English, Dutch and French clergy and laity, private persons and others in the Government and have been honoured among them above what modesty would on another occasion allow me to say."[3] Early in 1703/4 he wrote again to thank Sharp for his efforts on his behalf: "I do acknowledge", he declared, "the same divine providence in introducing me to the acquaintance of your Grace whom by the report

[1] C. J. Abbey, *The English Church and its Bishops*, vol. i, p. 105.
[2] *Life of Archbishop Sharp*, vol. ii, p. 35.
[3] L-B-S. MSS., Box 4, Bundle Q. 65, Dec. 14, 1703.

of fame I honoured and revered it before; and now feel to have a spirit answerable to your sacred character, for nothing else could be the motive of such generous concernment to a poor stranger." It was his pension that Cockburn was worrying about. "I did not press so much the payment of the Queen's pension from an impatient desire of fingering money," he continued, "but because that was indeed all my subsistence; for the congregation here as yet cannot maintain the minister, and the small gratuities which some who are able gave formerly are not forthcoming since the news of that pension."[1] Burnet and "others of his gang", as he called them, on the other hand, were endeavouring to get his pension stopped and himself recalled. Sharp appears to have done what he could for Cockburn, judging from the following letter he sent him on April 2, 1704, but without a great deal of success: "Rev. Sir, I received yours that very night I came to Town. And the next Friday after, happening to be the day of the monthly meeting of the Governors of the Corporation for Propagating etc. I resolved to take that opportunity of getting the matter you writ to me about propos'd to the Assembly. Accordingly I was there, and your letter to me was read by the Secretary. But whether you will have any good effect of it, I am very doubtful. A vote did indeed pass that a sum of fifty pounds should be allowed to you for one year longer, and likewise that it should be referred to the committee to inform themselves of the state of your Church at Amsterdam, and to make their report of it at the next meeting. But presently after we parted; I was told that the former part of this vote was irregular, for that no grants of money can be made without a previous summons of all the members who are to be acquainted with it, which in this case of yours was not done: so that I have reason to be afraid, that at the next meeting this vote of the continuance of your pension will be rescinded. However I have done for you what I can, and I had a mind to let you know it.

"Pray say nothing of what I have writ to you, about your own affairs, for fear it be taken ill of me by some here. But you may make the best interest you can with your friends for yourself."[2]

Hanover and Prussia seemed to offer more promising fields for conquest.

The Princess Sophia of Hanover, heiress to the English throne, was especially anxious to consolidate her position in influential

[1] L-B-S. MSS., Box 4, Bundle K. 36; Feb. 1, 1703/4.
[2] L-B-S. MSS., Box 4, Bundle T. 13.

Anglican circles, and particularly with the Church. This happened to be all the more difficult because, while privately of the Reformed faith, her own official religious beliefs and those of her son were Lutheran. Neither of these Churches would appeal very strongly to the Anglican high-flier, although they were likely to find more favour in the eyes of low-churchmen such as Tenison or Burnet. Sharp himself, anxious as he was to promote good relations with the Hanoverian heirs, yet had to walk warily lest either his words or actions be misconstrued. Atterbury, writing on May 27, 1704, to inform him of a design of M. de la Mothe, an exiled Huguenot minister, to promote goodwill between English and continental Protestantism, remarked: "He hath heard it seems that your Grace did in the House of Lords say, that, if you were abroad, you would willingly communicate with the Protestant Churches, where you should happen to be; and he thinks it will be of moment to give an account of the words which your Grace used on that occasion."[1] Sharp, somewhat tartly, refused his permission "for reasons you very well know . . . and therefore I shall take it kindly of M. de la Mothe if he mentions not my name at all upon this occasion."[2] The archbishop feared, in fact, lest his words, which were concerned exclusively with continental Protestants, might be used by the Dissenters at home to encourage the practice of occasional conformity. M. de la Mothe scrupulously respected the primate's wishes; but others were not so conscientious. "There is another writer", Atterbury indignantly declared, "who hath mentioned something as said by your Grace in the House of Lords, for which I am sure he had no leave, and which I dare say your Grace never said in the manner he represents it."[3] This was the Jacobite author of a book entitled *Les interests de l'Angleterre malentendus dans la guerre présente*, which was printed at Brussels in 1703 and later smuggled into Holland and England, where it was represented as the work of an Englishman. Cockburn had already warned Sharp about this work: "I crave leave", he wrote, "to acquaint your Grace with a book which I have obtained a sight of with great difficulty. I have given some account of it to my Lord Nottingham, but there is a passage or two concerning your Grace which I only write to yourself. The author it seems carries some prejudice against your Grace. For in the Preface he says that he has published it to shew what the English are, for whose generosity he

---

[1] L-B-S. MSS., Box 3, Bundle N. 3.   [2] *Life of Archbishop Sharp*, vol. i, p. 378.
[3] L-B-S. MSS., Box 4, Bundle K. 67.

had an esteem but now has lost it, because they have none. And instances your Grace sending 18 guineas for the dedication of the Harmony.[1] This vexed Mr. Le Clerk to the heart when I told him. In the back of the book also he praises you for favouring the papists and opposing all severe acts against them for this reason because they kept the old Religion of the Nation. It is in French but pretended to be translated from an English MS. It is most malicious and dangerous at this time. A further account of it you may have from my Lord Nottingham."[2]

So far as the archbishop was concerned this represented a deliberate attempt to twist certain of his words in order to imply that he favoured the English Catholics against the Government, a gross calumny on so strong an anti-papist. Strangely enough it was not the only attempt. His sermon of 1674 urging Dissenters to rejoin the Church of England had been used in 1704 to bolster up the arguments of an anonymous writer seeking to reconcile the Anglicans to Rome.[3]

In 1702 Sharp had presented Sophia with his coronation sermon, which he entrusted somewhat curiously to the hands of Toland, the free-thinker. Toland, who was apparently *persona grata* with the electress, faithfully fulfilled his task, but not in person as Sharp's biographer implies:[4] "When, in 1702, Toland found it convenient again to quit England for Germany, he left the court of Hanover unvisited; nor does he seem to have reappeared there till 1707."[5] The electress returned a letter of thanks that delighted the archbishop. "It was a great presumption in one", he replied, "to offer so mean a thing as my sermon to so great a princess; and your pardon for it was all I could expect. But that your Electral Highness should vouchsafe me a letter of thanks for it, and that so extremely gracious a one, this was a favour as much beyond my hopes, as it was above my merits. But thus you charm all the world with your condescending goodness."[6]

Two years later Bagnall, chaplain to Edmund Coley, the English envoy extraordinary at Hanover, came home on leave bearing another gracious message from Sophia to Sharp. "She

---

[1] This accusation was unfounded, as Sharp, who apologised for the smallness of the sum—"I would have made a better, if I had been richer"—also presented Le Clerk with a number of "the most valuable books printed in England, which he knew were to M. Le Clerk as money". See *Life of Archbishop Sharp*, vol. ii, pp. 38-42.
[2] L-B-S. MSS., Box 4, Bundle K. 36.
[3] *Life of Archbishop Sharp*, vol. i, p. 61.   [4] Ibid., vol. i, p. 273.
[5] A. W. Ward, *The Electress Sophia*, p. 368.
[6] *Life of Archbishop Sharp*, vol. i, p. 276, Sept. 4, 1702.

spoke of your Grace", Bagnall assured him, "with particular esteem and respect"; and also, incidentally, expressed her willingness to do something for the archbishop's kinsman, Cholmondley, who was travelling on the continent at the time.[1] But when Lord Haversham introduced his famous motion into the House of Lords, inviting Sophia over to England, the archbishop was caught between two stools. Sophia, his gracious correspondent, seemed anxious to come; but Anne, his present mistress, was bitterly hostile to such a step. Sharp recorded in his diary: "Wednesday, Oct. 24, 1705. When I came home to dinner, I found that a messenger had been sent by the Queen to order me to wait on her at five o'clock in the evening. Her business was to tell me what she had heard. That a motion would be made in our House to send for the Princess of Hanover, in pursuance of what my Lord Rochester had threatened in a speech the last Parliament, and to persuade me to use my interest with my friends not to come over into that notion; which I readily promised her, and told her, that I would always oppose it, as looking upon that project to proceed from nothing but a pique to her Majesty."[2] He tried at first to prevent its introduction by a personal appeal to Rochester; but when that failed he could do nothing more except to vote against the motion. Yet before doing so and supporting the whig Regency bill, he was careful to reinsure himself with Sophia through the good offices of his Hanoverian agent, Dr. Hutton, who was also a friend of Harley, and repeated "to her Highness the Electress assurances of his integrity with respect to her interests in this kingdom."[3] In this mission he succeeded so completely that he could inform the archbishop: "She knows you very well her fast friend, and is satisfied of the proof your Grace hath given her."[4] Nevertheless Sophia also conveyed a pretty broad hint that, provided she was first created Princess of Wales, she would be only too pleased to come over to England, should she ever be asked to do so. In face of Anne's stubborn opposition such an invitation was quite impossible; and so, after the tories had been returned to power in 1710, she began to agitate instead for a little English court at Hanover together with a substantial civil list, both, of course, to be paid for by the English Exchequer. Sophia always professed herself a tory, just as her son, the elector, proclaimed himself a whig, and for this as well as other reasons Sharp was

---

[1] L-B-S. MSS., Box 4, Bundle K. 52. [2] *Life of Archbishop Sharp*, vol. i, p. 308.
[3] Ibid., vol. i, p. 270. [4] L-B-S. MSS., Box 4, Bundle K. 18, Oct. 1705.

persuaded to support her demands. In return she promised to favour his design "of introducing the Liturgy of the Church of England at Hanover, and procuring a chaplain of the Church of England at the Queen's expense to attend on the Princess Sophia".[1] Dr. Ayerst, chaplain to the Earl of Strafford, the English ambassador at The Hague, was suggested for the post by George Smalridge, who took a keen interest in these negotiations. "It would certainly be of great service to the Church", he wrote to the archbishop on July 18, 1711, "that our Liturgy should be used at the Court of Hanover; and since there is so good a disposition there towards it, I hope by your Grace's influence it may be compassed. If that design should succeed, Mr. Ayerst seems to have a very good right to officiate as chaplain. He has given sufficient proofs of his prudence and good affection to our Church, and being well known there would I doubt not be very acceptable to Madam the Electress. . . . If your Grace shall be pleased to honour Mr. Ayerst with a letter, one directed to him, chaplain to the British Ambassador at the Hague, will find him by the post."[2] Strafford, formerly Lord Raby and ambassador in Berlin, and Ayerst were certainly well suited to this type of work, for they had already helped to start the Prussian negotiations, of which more will be heard later on. Leibnitz, Sophia's confidential adviser, and Sharp now entered upon a protracted correspondence, with Ayerst acting as intermediary, in order thoroughly to explore the possibilities of such an important move. But it soon became obvious to the archbishop and his advisers that Sophia was simply utilising the idea of an English chaplain at Hanover as a means, first of securing the little English court she so much hankered after, and secondly of strengthening her ultimate claim to the succession. Leibnitz, of course, denied all this. "That Princess", he said, "having too elevated a mind, and being too content with her present condition . . . to form any pretensions or make any demand."[3] So the scheme hung fire; and although a serious attempt was made to link it up with similar negotiations with Prussia, it never got beyond the stage of a paper project, to be eventually swallowed up in the Peace Conference, to which Strafford was transferred.

Frederick I of Prussia, who had married the electress' daughter, Sophia Charlotte, was more disinterested in his desire to create an

[1] *Life of Archbishop Sharp*, vol. i, p. 279.
[2] L-B-S. MSS., Box 4, Bundle K. 26.   [3] *Life of Archbishop Sharp*, vol. i, p. 282.

episcopate and introduce a liturgy, approximating to the Anglican, into his kingdom. Thereby he no doubt hoped to unite those two great German Protestant Churches the Lutheran and Reformed. Accordingly, on the advice of a Reformed divine, Dr. Ursinus, to whom he had given the title of bishop, and Dr. Daniel Ernestus Jablonski, his principal chaplain, Frederick had the English liturgy, in preference to all others, translated into High Dutch, and seriously considered making use of it in his own royal chapel and possibly in the cathedral church. First of all, however, he ordered Ursinus to send copies of this translation to Queen Anne and the archbishop of Canterbury in order to obtain the approval of the Mother Church, both for the design as a whole and concerning the correctness of the German translation. "A gracious and satisfactory reply was received from Queen Anne,"[1] but Tenison remained curiously silent. Whereupon Frederick, offended by his indifference, dropped the scheme entirely for several years. It has been suggested that the archbishop's silence was due to the fact that he never received his copy of the liturgy;[2] a more likely explanation is that he would ultimately have answered Ursinus, but took longer over it "than suited the impatience of his Prussian Majesty",[3] whose sharp demand for an immediate reply in turn incensed the archbishop. Certainly, whatever the truth may have been, Tenison refused then and afterwards to take any part or interest in these negotiations.

It was entirely owing to the zeal and energy of Jablonski that the project survived this unexpected rebuff. Jablonski, indeed, was a remarkable man, much esteemed in the Moravian Church. Both his father, Peter Jablonski, and grandfather, Comenius, had been bishops of the Bohemian Church, and he not only followed in their footsteps but obtained "at the same time the superintendency of the Bohemian Brethren out of Poland". He was consecrated on March 20, 1699, at the synod of Lissa with the consent of the Elector Frederick III, afterwards Frederick I of Prussia, whose principal chaplain he then became, and henceforward called himself "the Bishop of the Unity in Poland".[4] This famous divine had already twice visited England, had met and conversed with many prominent English churchmen, although apparently not with Sharp, and had become as a result a fervent admirer of the Angli-

---

[1] See W. S. Gilly, *Waldensian Researches*, pp. 386-390.
[2] *Life of Archbishop Sharp*, vol. i, p. 409.
[3] W. S. Gilly, *Waldensian Researches*, p. 386.
[4] D. Cranz, *Unitas Fratrum*, pp. 70 and 141.

can liturgy. Ursinus, too, despite Tenison's rebuff, seemed well
disposed towards it; but he was now an old man and afraid of
offending the king by reopening negotiations without the royal
sanction. The British envoy at Berlin, Lord Raby, and his chaplain,
Dr. Ayerst, were deeply interested in these events from the first
and encouraged the Prussian ministers to persevere, assuring them
of Queen Anne's sympathies.

Meanwhile Frederick, although he had abandoned his Anglican
model, still desired to secure union, or at least law and order, in
Church worship; and proposed that his clerical advisers should
each draw up a plan for worship and discipline and submit it to
Baron Printz, President of the Council of Ecclesiastical Affairs in
Berlin. Among the rest Jablonski sent in his contribution, which
was based on that of the English liturgy; and found it favourably
received. Whereupon, acting solely on the advice of Raby and
Ayerst and without consulting either the king or Printz, he decided to write directly to the archbishop of York as a person who
carried weight with the Queen and was likely to pursue the scheme
with energy. He entrusted the letter to Dr. Hobart, a friend of
Sharp then residing in Berlin, who also enclosed a short, clear-cut
résumé of the history of the negotiations to date, together with a
copy of Jablonski's plan for a form of public worship suitable to a
united Prussian Church. This packet found its way via George
Smalridge to Sharp on October 10, 1710; and a direct correspondence was immediately opened between the two principals
concerned. The archbishop appeared enthusiastic. "You may", he
told Jablonski, "whenever you please, freely communicate your
mind to me, as I shall make no scruple of doing the like to you.
And you may likewise assure yourself of all the assistance that I
can give you towards the furthering that noble pious work, which
I understand you are now pursuing. I thank you heartily for the
papers you sent me containing your thoughts concerning the
public worship of God, directed to Baron Printz. I agree with you
in every particular, and hope his Prussian Majesty will be so
affected with it as to establish things according to your plan. And
I know no public worship in Christendom that comes up so well
to your measures as that used among us in the Church of England."[1] He promptly sought to engage the active support of the
queen, Harley and St. John, who were now at the head of the
Government, in this enterprise. He even stirred up Tenison to get

[1] *Life of Archbishop Sharp*, vol. i, p. 415.

the matter discussed in Convocation. Two men he found especially useful for his purposes: Dr. Ernest Grabe, an extremely learned man and a fervent admirer of the Anglican Church, was a Prussian divine who had been resident in England since 1697 and "was perfectly acquainted with the state of the matter, with Jablonski's character, and with the disposition of the King of Prussia and his courtiers and his divines".[1] Grabe had been ordained a deacon in 1700 by Bishop Lloyd of Worcester, and, apparently, priested by one of the non-juring bishops. Oxford gave him a chaplaincy at Christ Church, while Anne, besides continuing William's pension of £100 per annum, employed him in the royal library at St. James'. Despite his long residence in England, he remained on excellent terms with the King of Prussia; so much so that Nelson, wrongly, ascribed to his zeal alone the plan for introducing the English liturgy both into Prussia and Hanover, "by which means he would have united the two main bodies of Protestants, in a more perfect and Apostolical Reformation, than that upon which either of them did yet stand, and would thereby have fortified the common cause of their Protestation against the Errors of Popery."[2] Again, in a long letter to Sharp on the occasion of Grabe's last illness and death, Nelson spoke of him in the very highest terms.[3]

Robert Hales, the archbishop's other chief helper, represented a very different type. For if Grabe was a student and a bit of a recluse, Hales appeared as the man of action. Some years previously he had been employed by Anne to enquire into the conditions of Protestants abroad, especially of the distressed churches in France, the Palatinate and Silesia, and had drawn up a memorial on the subject, which through the good offices of Sharp was subsequently laid before Harley. Hales was also a servant of the Society for the Promotion of Christian Knowledge and travelled widely in their service. Many of his letters to the Society are still extant, advocating, for example, the conveying of books and other assistance to the French Protestants in the galleys, and reporting on the condition of the Helvetic churches.[4] One sentence from a letter of 1701 is particularly significant in view of future events. "Many Divines in Germany and Switzerland", he wrote on April 11, "are for attempting an Union of Protestants and that the impending War is likely to promote it."[5]

[1] *Life of Archbishop Sharp*, vol. i, p. 418.   [2] R. Nelson, *Life of Bull*, p. 403.
[3] L-B-S. MSS., Box 3, Bundle N. 23, Nov. 11, 1711.
[4] Allen and McClure, *History of the Society for Promoting Christian Knowledge*, pp. 112-117.
[5] Ibid., p. 116.

Yet another valuable ally was Robinson, the new bishop of
Bristol, who through his contacts with the court of Sweden kept
in close touch with continental Protestantism, and actually took
the responsibility for reopening direct negotiations with the King
of Prussia. Frederick was friendly, but cautious. He had not forgotten or forgiven his former rebuff, and when apprised of the
new advances remarked that "he was yet of the same mind he had
formerly been and recommended the scheme to be adjusted by
them and Dr. Jablonski, but in a secret way, that a good and solid
foundation might be laid for it before it was made public."[1] Baron
Printz expressed his feelings in even more direct terms: "We continue, on our parts, in the same favourable dispositions, and are
ready to enter into whatever measures may contribute to the good
success of this affair. But as hitherto it has been treated in England
with so great an indifference, that they have not vouchsafed to
give any answer to the overtures that have been made by us, nor
to the version of the English Liturgy, translated into our German
language, so we would not expose ourselves to the like hazard, by
making any further advances without being assured of an answer
from the part of England."[2] Hence the negotiations started under
considerable handicaps that ultimately wrecked them altogether.
Jablonski, recognising the difficulties, urged the early establishment of direct personal contacts as the best method of dispelling
suspicion. Lord Raby, he suggested, should be authorised by the
queen to open discussions on the spot, and Hales should be sent
to Berlin on a special mission. Neither suggestion was ever seriously
considered in England. St. John, indeed, wrote to Lord Raby informing him that "her Majesty desires that you would take some
proper opportunity of speaking to Monsieur Prinz, to the bishops,
and to any others who may concern themselves in so laudable a
design . . . to assure them that her Majesty is ready to give all
possible encouragement to that excellent work";[3] but this was
scarcely the beginning of any definite negotiations. Lord Raby,
too, despite his keen interest in the scheme, was suddenly for
political reasons created Earl of Strafford and transferred to The
Hague, where in partnership with Bishop Robinson he became a
plenipotentiary at the Peace Conference. Sharp earnestly pressed
for the despatch of Hales, but with little or no result. St. John,
deeply concerned with the coming peace terms, was only half-

hearted in the matter; while even Anne herself professed to be too busy to attend to it. The archbishop records grimly in his diary: "Thursday, March 1st 1710/11. I would have read Dr. Jablonski's two letters to her; but she was in haste. . . . Tuesday, April 3rd. Before twelve oclock I went to the Queen; but she was so busy, I did no business with her, but only put her in mind of Dr. Jablonski's letters."[1]

The Government, however, was anxious, in the interests of the Grand Alliance, to keep on friendly terms with Frederick, and so was fully prepared to promise anything in general terms in order to prolong the negotiations. Anne expressed herself ready to give a thousand pounds towards buying a site for a Prussian church in London; and St. John assured Herr Bonet, the Prussian envoy, that both the queen and the clergy had a warm regard for Prussia and desired "entering into a negotiation to create an union between the Protestant Churches here and beyond the sea; but", as Bonet shrewdly added in his letter to the king, "without entering into any particulars".[2] These last words typify the attitude of all the parties concerned in the negotiations, with the exception of Sharp, Jablonski, Ayerst and possibly Robinson, who hoped for definite results. Herr Bonet's statement to St. John had matched his own in caution: "I told him I was not yet honoured with your Majesty's [Frederick's] commands upon this affair, nor was I yet instructed in the scheme to be proposed, no more than I was acquainted with the dispositions of the people, who are often jealous and prepossessed against novelties, and that their inclinations ought to be consulted before we made any step of this nature, who must be instructed and prepared by degrees, before they will enter into any new measures, be they ever so good. But I added, that I would not fail to lay the Queen's inclinations in this affair before your Majesty."[3] He then gave it as his opinion that whereas conformity between the Prussian and the English Church would be welcomed in England by the mass of the clergy and people, the whigs were bitterly hostile to the design, and so were their friends the Hanoverian heirs. St. John, too, would not commit himself to anything more definite than promises; and until he did so the once-rebuffed Frederick would make no sign.

Jablonski in a long letter to Sharp dated April 28, 1711, unerringly put his finger on the weak spots: the withdrawal of Lord

[1] *Life of Archbishop Sharp*, vol. i, p. 425.   [2] Ibid., vol. i, p. 428.
[3] Ibid., vol. i, p. 427.

Raby and the non-appearance of Hales. Meanwhile Printz had
suggested to Jablonski that he might profitably utilise the delay by
setting down on paper his considered opinion on the whole subject; which, nothing loth, the latter proceeded to do, producing
a treatise entitled *His Project for introducing Episcopacy into the
King of Prussia's Dominions*, and sent it to the baron on May 7,
1711. This treatise, together with his earlier reflections on Herr
Bonet's letter to Frederick, were translated into English and
copies were despatched to Sharp by Ayerst, who himself bitterly
complained of the non-arrival of Hales just at the time when everything seemed set for definite action.   He recognised, however, the
many difficulties facing the negotiators and suggested to the archbishop as a way out of them that "perhaps they [the negotiations]
might still go on better, if the House of Hanover were applied to
in the same affair."[1] This was a shrewd and statesmanlike move,
since it had become obvious that the English Government was
reluctant to proceed in the face of the combined opposition of
the whig-dissent-Hanoverian interests; but could the Elector be
bought off, then the whig opposition might be overborne. Sharp
continued to press Harley and St. John for the despatch of the
Hales mission to Berlin. "I would beg leave to put your Lordship
in mind of Mr. Hales," he wrote to Harley on July 21, 1711. "He
is capable of doing great service towards the promoting that noble
design that is now on foot of having episcopacy and our Liturgy
established in Prussia; he being very well known there and in all
parts of Germany. I have had several letters from Dr. Jablonski,
wherein he earnestly presses that he (Mr. Hales) may be sent
abroad for that purpose, under some public character. I could
heartily wish that your Lordship would concert and settle this
affair with Mr. Secretary, St. John, who is very well apprized of
this whole business, and is no stranger to Mr. Hales."[2] Still nothing
was done. Nevertheless Ayerst, who had now arrived in Holland,
was very hopeful about a settlement. He succeeded in bringing
Jablonski and Leibnitz together and trusted that the new marriage
alliance between the courts of Prussia and Hanover would help to
heal the old enmity. For ever since Queen Sophia Charlotte's
death in 1705 Frederick and the Elector had been at daggers
drawn: "In 1711 the Electress Sophia, speaking of a melancholy
journey of her son-in-law, observes that it was a Divine punishment on him that he should hate the Elector without any reason

[1] *Life of Archbishop Sharp*, vol. i, p. 437.   [2] Ibid., pp. 437-438.

whatever."[1] Now the marriage of Frederick's son, Frederick William, to the elector's daughter, Sophia Dorothea, seemed about to open a fresh and happier chapter in the relations between the two countries.

It was therefore decided by Sharp, Leibnitz and Jablonski to proceed along the lines of first introducing the English liturgy into Hanover, where Ayerst should be appointed the first Church of England chaplain with his salary paid by Anne. But when it came to a practical application of this agreement, somehow, somewhere, things began to go wrong. Unfortunately most of the correspondence between the three principals concerned has been lost, and hence it is difficult to assess accurately the cause for the complete failure of the negotiations. It seems probable that the zeal of the churchmen had outrun that of the laity. Sharp, Robinson, Leibnitz, Jablonski and Ayerst were undoubtedly sincere; but it is extremely doubtful whether the same could be said of the Elector, Frederick or St. John. It may also be presumed that St. John's "betrayal" of the Allies by secretly negotiating his own terms of peace with France, his disclosure of their military secrets, and final open desertion of them in the field, was largely responsible for the failure of this proposed Church union. Actually Prussia did very well for herself at the Peace of Utrecht and was perfectly satisfied with her treatment; but the Elector of Hanover never forgave Bolingbroke and the tories for their conduct in the last campaign of the war. Furthermore, it must be owned that Bolingbroke himself strongly favoured a post-war alliance with France at the expense of the Dutch and other old allies.[2]

Be this as it may, it is certain that a great opportunity, never to be revived, had been lost for making Anglicanism the unifying force among continental Protestants; and for this failure the tory bishops are not to be blamed.

A desultory correspondence was still carried on between the archbishop and Dr. Jablonski, as also between the doctor, the Earl of Strafford and the bishop of Bristol, during the years 1712 and 1713, but it had been robbed of all real value, and the net result was merely the establishment of a fund by Frederick for the education of Prussian divinity students at the English Universities. Frederick's death on February 25, 1712/13, followed in the next

---

[1] A. W. Ward, *The Electress Sophia*, p. 358.
[2] See G. M. Trevelyan, *The Peace*, vol. iii, "England under Queen Anne," chapters xi, xii and xiii.

year by Sharp's, put a final end to this grand design: "Frederick William was one of the last men in the world to trouble himself about the ideas of Church union."[1]

Protestants suffering from want or persecution always aroused Sharp's practical sympathy, particularly in the case of the victims of Roman Catholic persecutions. The strange story of Elizabeth Vasconcellos is an interesting example of this. Elizabeth Chester was a Devonshire girl and a member of the Church of England. She emigrated with her uncle, who was killed during the voyage, to Madeira, where she met and married a Spanish physician named Vasconcellos. Repeated attempts were made to persuade her to become a Roman Catholic, but they all failed. Whereupon during her husband's absence in Brazil she was kidnapped, sent to the Inquisition in Lisbon, and foully tortured until she recanted and signed the various documents put before her. On her release, however, she hastened to recount her story to John Milner, British Consul-General in Lisbon, and to Joseph Wilcocks, afterwards bishop of Rochester, who then ministered to the English Factory in Lisbon. Wilcocks referred the case to Sharp, who endorsed its accuracy and befriended the unfortunate girl.[2]

William III had soon after his accession granted a pension of some £425 to be distributed among certain distressed Vaudois ministers and schoolmasters. This was supplemented by collections among the clergy themselves, in the organisation of which the archbishop took an active part. Thomas Smith, bishop of Carlisle, wrote to Sharp on July 3, 1699, enclosing some £63 for the fund "from the parishes of this Diocese", besides £10 out of his own pocket and £5 from the dean and chapter. His letter makes it perfectly clear that the archbishop had been authorised to collect contributions from the northern province and send them to London.[3] Later, as Almoner, he demanded and obtained from Anne the continuation of William's pension. "The expelled Vaudois" were not, however, the only people included in this brief; for French refugees are also specifically mentioned as benefiting from the collections.[4]

In July 1698 Sharp was approached in a letter by the Senators of the hard-pressed Protestant Churches of the Palatinate, who also enclosed a lengthy memorandum[5] wherein they set out in

[1] C. J. Abbey, *The English Church and its Bishops*, vol. i, p. 106.
[2] L-B-S. MSS., Box 3, Bundle O. 22.   [3] L-B-S. MSS., Box 3, Bundle O, 37.
[4] L-B-S. MSS., Box 4, Bundle L. 68, March 14, 1698/9.
[5] L-B-S. MSS., Box 4, Bundle N. 12 (a Latin document).

great detail the sufferings of their pastors and schoolmasters from the French invaders on the one hand and from the Roman Catholics on the other, and concluded with the following piteous appeal: "Most humbly and earnestly asking that the Holy Bond which unites us may please your Grace to help towards the salvation of this Church either by graciously giving orders for some collections to be taken or by means of other gifts. And to commend this cause with all your Grace's authority, and to promote it together with the Right Reverend Bishops and the very venerable clergy."[1] In January 1698/9 they ventured "to repeat those facts which in our letter . . . of last year we took the liberty of submitting to Your Grace about the distressed and miserable state of the Church of the Palatinate"; pointing out that things had got very much worse during the interval, and throwing themselves on the generosity of the Anglican Church. "We trust", they implored, "that the Church of the Palatinate will not be left without solace and a charitable subsidy, but be comforted by the Anglican Church, the well-known patron of indigent ministers and other distressed members of the Church."[2]

The archbishop was much affected by these appeals and suggested first to Tenison and then to Compton that they should "petition the King for a brief or order for a private collection among the clergy".[3] "As to the Palatinate", Tenison replied on May 29, 1699, "nothing is yet done. My Brethren have gone as far as they have been able."[4] Compton was more explicit: "I . . . am not yet able to tell you what course will be taken for the relief of those poor Protestants in the Palatinate. I wish that treaty at Ryswick could have prevented this misfortune, which is likely to fall upon many more of the Protestants in Germany. The King does not think it proper at this time to have a brief for them because he reasonably judges it may be a prejudice to that for the Vaudois; but he will prescribe some other way, which when determined, you will be sure to hear of."[5]

It was, indeed, scarcely surprising that William refused to sanction the issuing of another brief. For already in 1691 the king and queen had ordered a further general collection from "well disposed people throughout England and Wales" to redeem their subjects sold into slavery at Algiers. The result had been disap-

---

[1] L-B-S. MSS., Box 4, Bundle N. 18 (translation from the Latin).
[2] L-B-S. MSS., Box 4, Bundle N. 19 (translation from the Latin).
[3] *Life of Archbishop Sharp*, vol. i, p. 400.
[4] L-B-S. MSS., Box 4, Bundle L. 60.   [5] L-B-S. MSS., Box 3, Bundle O. 36.

pointing; and consequently Sharp received a letter from the privy council dated October 10, 1695, "earnestly recommending" him "to write effectively to the respective Bishops within your Province" in order to secure better returns from the parishes. He was also to report "the names of the Parishes (if any) that neglect to make any contribution towards so pious a work".[1] The wretchedly paid parson had therefore to contribute towards the needs of the Vaudois, the French refugees and the Algerian slaves; it seemed hardly fair to burden him with those of the Palatinate Churches as well.

Nevertheless Sharp did not forget their sufferings, and in May 1709, when it appeared possible that peace might be made, he advised Anne "to order her plenipotentiaries to concern themselves about the Protestant religion, both in France, the Palatinate, the Vaudois, Silesia, etc.";[2] to send a special paid expert abroad, who would go into the matter on the spot and co-ordinate all the necessary relief work; and finally to read and digest a memorial already prepared by Robert Hales on this very subject, which would shortly be presented to her by the bishop of Ely.

Hales was certainly doing much good work. Among the archbishop's MSS. is a long letter from a certain M. Calandrin, minister and professor of divinity at Geneva, which is addressed to Hales and discusses the sufferings and religious constancy under affliction of the French Huguenots condemned to "the Gallies of France". Hales is most gratefully thanked for helping them "to everything that might tend to their relief, establishment and comfort", and for interesting the Helvetic churches in their case. Throughout he is described as representing "that . . . most illustrious and Religious Society which applies itself in so holy and laudable a manner to the advancement of true Piety"[3] (*i.e.* S.P.C.K.).

Two years later Baron Printz in a letter to Lord Raby reinforced Sharp's arguments by suggesting that the Prussian negotiations would go very much faster if Anne "gave proof of her royal bounty and gracious zeal, as to procure by her powerful solicitations, that liberty of conscience and free exercise of religion to the

---

[1] L-B-S. MSS., Box 3, Letters from the Privy Council, No. 1.
[2] *Life of Archbishop Sharp*, vol. i, p. 402.
[3] L-B-S. MSS., Box 4, Bundle N. 9, 1699. Calandrin went on to say that certain slaves "were delivered by the favourable intercession of his British Majesty, as well of his subjects of the Principality of Orange, as of the English and Scotch nations". So the collections in England for the redemption of slaves were not wasted.

poor reformed in Silesia, as the Imperial Court had granted to the other Lutheran Protestants by the mediation of the King of Sweden".[1]

But curiously enough, strong churchwoman as she was, the queen remained throughout her entire reign largely indifferent to the sufferings of Protestants abroad. The Hales memorial went unread, and nothing of moment was done either in Silesia or the Palatinate. However, when in 1710, owing to the ravages of war and persecution, more than 10,000 of the Protestant inhabitants of the Palatinate emigrated to England "in a state of destitution",[2] they met with much sympathy and charity from Anne and her bishops. Eventually many of them were transplanted to Ireland or America; but not before they had aroused the wrath of the English labouring classes by sharing their food and competing for their employment during a period of lean harvests.

The archbishop, because of his efforts in these and other directions, soon came to be regarded as a legitimate target for the appeals of all oppressed Christians from near and far.

The dean and clergy of Jersey approached him in September 1703 concerning their grievances over the tithes. They were, or so they claimed, the victims of unscrupulous tax gatherers; and suggested as a remedy that the clergy should themselves "rent the said impropriated tithes in their respective Parishes at the same yearly value, as prized in the last Extent Book . . . the said Dean and Clergy giving securities for the payment of the same". By this means they would escape "the iniquity of the farmers of the impropriated tithes", while her Majesty's revenues would not suffer. They quite frankly admitted that they had come to the archbishop because of his widely famed kindness of heart and great influence with the queen.[3]

Wilson, the new bishop of Sodor and Man, submitted for his approval "some constitutions which I got lately passed into laws, and now I send an apology for not laying them before your Grace before they were confirmed. I saw the necessity for some such acts to be passed, and I took an occasion of proposing these at a time when several matters relating to the civil settlement, were offered to me for my assent and I got these confirmed with less opposition. I hope your Grace will approve of what has been done,

[1] Life of Archbishop Sharp, vol. i, p. 421.
[2] G. M. Trevelyan, The Peace, vol. iii, " England under Queen Anne," p. 37.
[3] L-B-S. MSS., Box 3, Bundle O. 8 and 9, Sept. 4, 1703.

and particularly in the matter of the commutations, which were become so very scandalous, and so impossible to be kept any other way, that I was forced to hinder the future practice by a law. The people of a faction being generally related to each other, and the Vicars General necessarily being natives of the country, and having the ecclesiastical authority lodged with them in the Bishop's absence; and sometimes exercising their power unknown to him when upon the place, they managed it with partiality, making the poor offenders to do penance, and taking from the others monies, but so small a fine, as a crown for an adulterer, that if it had been applied to pious uses, would have signified little. Whereas now all do penance, who shall have deserved it, and I hope the instances will not be so many as to render the punishment cheap and contemptible, especially since, by another act, they that relapse are treated with severity to make others fear."[1] Sharp certainly approved of these constitutions,[2] which were sound and statesmanlike and gave to the Isle of Man a religious settlement that stood the test of time.[3]

The archbishop was an ardent supporter of the Society for the Propagation of the Gospel in Foreign Parts, as Robert Nelson handsomely acknowledged in a letter written to Sharp on August 31, 1700. Here he thanks the archbishop for his generous contribution to the Society's funds, but especially for his frank support and patronage of its members, "and that your Grace approves of their zeal in endeavouring to disperse those clouds of ignorance which overwhelm a great part of mankind, as well as of the methods they make use of to that purpose."[4]

Most of the Society's work was done in the American colonies, and with that part of the world Sharp kept in close touch. "I have an account from North Carolina (where my eldest son Charles is settled)", wrote Miles Gale of Keighley on October 28, 1705, "that the Quakers grow numerous and Christianity is at a low ebb; that they had but one Minister after the Church of England, and even he of an ill life, and was fled from thence, which case I beg of your Grace to consider."[5] Two other letters are especially worth quoting from in this connection. "May it please your

---

[1] L-B-S. MSS., Box 4, Bundle L. 78, March 5, 1704.
[2] For a copy of these *Constitutions for the Bishoprick of Man agreed upon in Convocation 1704 and passed into laws*" see L-B-S. MSS., Box 3, Bundle B. 2.
[3] A. G. Bradley, *Our Centenarian Grandfather*, pp. 163-167.
[4] L-B-S. MSS., Box 3, Bundle N. 22.
[5] L-B-S. MSS., Box 3, Bundle D. 6.

Grace", wrote E. Jennings, Esq., Secretary for the Colony of Virginia, from Ripon Hall, York River, on June 15, 1702, "Being made sensible of your Lordship's great goodness and kindness to my brothers and relations, and that your Grace hath been pleased to extend it to me tho' so remote and a stranger and in so particular a manner to be the chief instrument of his late Majesty's honouring me with the place of Secretary of this colony, I take the first opportunity to return my exceeding thanks, and should be very proud that fortune would give occasion for your Grace's command on me that I might demonstrate my earnest desire of obeying, and my grateful sense of your Lordship's favour. I take leave to give your Grace the assurance that I will study and labour to advance and maintain your interest of the Church and clergy, to discharge the trust reposed in me with loyalty and integrity, and so demean myself that your Lordship may not be censured for your generous and candid recommendation, but that I may deserve the continuance of your Grace's good opinion and favour."[1]

The other was from Lord Cornbury, Governor of New York: "My Lord, I had the honour of your Grace's letter of the 9th of April by the hands of the Reverend Mr. Brook, on the 22nd of July, in a very few days he was very desirous to be at the place for which the Honourable Society designed him, and in order thereto he desired me to direct him what place would be fittest for him to reside at. I told him that the places designed by the Society to be under his care were some of them very remote from the others. That Amboy which was intended to be the chief town was but very small and very few inhabitants, that Elizabeth Towne and Woodbridge were populous places, but full of dissenters, that I looked upon Elizabeth Towne to be the place where he was the most wanted. He very readily resolved to go thither. I recommended him to Colonel Townley, at whose house he now lies. He has by his behaviour here, fully answered the excellent character your Grace is pleased to give of him. I think we are very happy in having so good a man among us, and I intreat your Grace to believe that I shall always think myself very happy when I have it in my power to serve any person who is honoured with your Grace's Recommendation, to which I shall always pay the utmost regard. This being the first time that I have ventured to trouble you with my scribble, I was not willing to be too tedious, but beg

[1] L-B-S. MSS., Box 4, Bundle H. 4.

leave to trouble your Grace by the next conveyance with an account of the Church in these parts."[1]

Above all, the Scottish Episcopalians were especially successful in securing the archbishop's support and sympathy, and for two reasons: First, because the archbishopric of York had originally covered the lowlands of Scotland as well as the north of England, and this connection had never been wholly severed. Consequently Sharp felt bound to interest himself in the sufferings and privations of his co-religionists in Scotland after the Revolution. Secondly, because as an Anglo-Catholic he most heartily detested the principles of the more rigid Presbyterians, who were now in control of the Scotch Church.

In 1688, when it became known that William had landed in England, rioting broke out in the south-west of Scotland, the Cameronian country, where the Episcopalians were especially hated. "Companies of armed men", so it was later complained, "to whatsoever parish they came, if the Minister was at home, and not so securely protected by his parishioners, as that they were afraid to attack him, they carried him out to the market-place of the town or village where he resided, or to the most public place of the parish, if it had no town in it; and there giving him names in abundance, pulled his gown over his ears, and tore it in many places, dislodging his family, and throwing the furniture out of his house, and threatening him with death if ever he should return to the place to preach any more."[2] Others were ducked and beaten, and in all more than 260 Episcopalians were expelled in the west of Scotland alone. In fact, south of the Tay few churchmen were left in possession, their places being taken by the Presbyterian clergy, who had escaped Claverhouse's dragonnades. North of the Tay, however, where the majority of the people were Episcopalian and Jacobite, the ministers kept their livings by bowing to the storm, conforming to Presbyterianism, and taking the oaths of allegiance and assurance. This was largely due to William III's personal and energetic intervention, since he desired to conciliate Presbyterian and Episcopalian alike. But once the Act of 1690 had proclaimed Presbyterianism to be the National Church of Scotland, its Assembly resolved to exterminate Episcopacy root and branch. Consequently, despite the king's declaration that all Protestants were to enjoy their own religious worship without dis-

---

[1] L-B-S. MSS., Box 4, Bundle B. 16, Sept. 12, 1705.
[2] *Somers Tracts*, vol. xii, p. 359.

turbance, he could not prevent the persecutions from going on. These were very bitter and prolonged;[1] although Daniel Defoe was always very scornful of Episcopalian complaints in view of the way the Presbyterians had been treated by Claverhouse. "Yet we do not find", he wrote, "that the utmost violence complained of amounts to any more than an over-hasty turning the said episcopal ministers out of the parsonage houses . . . and this but a few; but as to any personal injury, such as wounding or killing of any, I do not find that any such thing is charged upon them."[2]

Nevertheless Sharp received many piteous appeals for succour from his distressed brethren over the border. "We, the suffering clergy of this National Church of Scotland", declared Mr. St. George of Glasgow on February 15, 1695, "were . . . violently and illegally dispossessed of our churches and livelihoods."[3]

"The Reverend James Chalmers bearer of this", another correspondent informed the archbishop some six years later, "has Commission particularly to inform your Grace that the Episcopal clergy in Scotland (however qualified according to law) are in a deplorable condition through the violent and illegal proceedings of presbyterian judicators."[4] In view of the fact, however, that the Scottish Episcopalians were almost certainly Jacobites to a man, Sharp quickly found it was not easy to help them. But since the poverty of the dispossessed was one of their main trials, he concentrated his efforts in striving to "procure collections for their relief".[5] For there were, he was told, "some hundreds of poor episcopal ministers deprived of bread, and all means of earning it, except what proceeds from a free, generous and Christian charity".[6] But William, who had already authorised collections for the Vaudois, French Protestant refugees and Algerian slaves, did not see his way clear for issuing another brief; and so Sharp had to rest content with persuading some of his fellow-bishops and noble lay friends to give handsomely out of their own pockets towards helping their distressed Scottish brethren.[7]

With the accession of a High-Church queen and the mooting of an Act of Union the Scottish Episcopalians hoped for better

[1] *Somers Tracts*, vol. xii, p. 363.
[2] Daniel Defoe, *Memoirs of the Church of Scotland*, pp. 313 and 314.
[3] L-B-S. MSS., Box 3, Bundle M. 15.
[4] L-B-S. MSS., Box 3, Bundle M. 6, Nov. 18, 1701.
[5] *Life of Archbishop Sharp*, vol. i, p. 387.
[6] *Somers Tracts*, vol. xii, p. 360.
[7] *E.g.*, Burnet and the Earl of Thanet. See L-B-S. MSS., Box 4, Bundle K. 54.

treatment, and promptly appealed to Anne "to take them into her royal protection".[1] At the same time Alexander Rose, bishop of Edinburgh, wrote to Sharp to tell him that "the deplorable circumstances of our suffering clergy, scarce otherwise to be relieved save by supplies from abroad, have obliged me to offer their case both to my Lords of Canterbury and London"; and trusted that Tenison and Sharp would put their heads together and devise some sort of assistance.[2] But this was easier said than done. Anne had no desire to antagonise the powerful Presbyterian Church of Scotland, which could make or mar the proposed Act of Union. Hence her aid to the Episcopalians was conditional upon the need to keep Scotland as a whole friendly to England. The archbishop of York adopted a much more partisan attitude. He had himself appointed, indeed, as one of the commissioners for the Union; but as he frankly admitted, he was interested in its success only in so far as it benefited the Scottish Episcopalians: "At the private meetings of the English Commissioners, the Archbishop of York argued that Episcopacy ought to be restored in Scotland under the Union, though Nottingham hesitated and Rochester said it was impossible to suggest it in the negotiations."[3] The Presbyterians were not unnaturally deeply suspicious of the English high-churchmen; and when in 1703 the Earl of Strathmore demanded an Act of Toleration and Fletcher of Saltoun put in a plea for another of Comprehension their anger was aroused, while Anne's own mild attempts to intervene merely added fuel to the flames, provoking riots against the Episcopalians in Edinburgh, Glasgow and elsewhere. Henceforth, until the Union was safely passed, the queen turned a deaf ear to all the archbishop's entreaties, both verbal and written. In March 1706 she actually gave her consent to an "Act Anent Intruders into Churches", which aimed at convicting deprived Episcopalian clergy, who with the support of their bishops were trying, in districts where the people were friendly towards them, to creep back into the churches from which they had been evicted.[4] This measure, of course, opened wide the door to the persecutors, and the Episcopalians were soon complaining that even those who had previously conformed were now being imprisoned: "The ministers of the meeting-houses of Perth and Elgin were both put in jail, by the magistrates of these respective

---

[1] *Life of Archbishop Sharp*, vol. i, p. 389.
[2] L.-B-S. MSS., Box 3, Bundle M. 5, June 21, 1702.
[3] G. M. Trevelyan, *Ramillies*, vol. ii, "England under Queen Anne," p. 231.
[4] *Somers Tracts*, vol. xii, p. 366.

burghs, though they daily pray for the Queen, and were ready to qualify themselves to the Government."[1]

After the Union was an accomplished fact things were quieter for a while; but in 1709 appeals and complaints began again to pour into the archbishop's letter-bag, telling of yet another persecution of the Episcopalians, whose old enemies the Presbyterians now accused them, perhaps not unjustly, of being ready to support the abortive Jacobite invasion of the previous year. The bishop of Edinburgh pointed out to Sharp "how Acts of Parliament are wrestled, especially that establishing the Union as if they meant to debarr people from any other form of worship but what's in use among the Presbyterians".[2] The old Countess of Lauderdale expressed herself even more plainly: "We thought the storm was over till now that it has broke out afresh and the design seems only to be levelled against them who kept the English service of which sort we had two very flourishing houses, where the service was very regularly performed and the same was attended by many good people of good quality and good sense, and this is a very sad affliction to all of them and to myself more especially, who am old and infirm, being lodged conveniently in the neighbourhood of one of them. It was shut up by order of the Magistrates on Friday the fifth instant." She begged Sharp to make "your representation of it to the Queen".[3] Matters came to a head with the imprisonment of an Episcopalian clergyman named James Greenshields.

Greenshields, who had been in Ireland, returned to Scotland in 1709 and established a meeting-house in Edinburgh opposite to St. Giles', the citadel of Scottish Presbyterianism, where he used the Church of England liturgy and was largely patronised by the English colony. Greenshields had taken the oaths, but even so the Edinburgh Presbytery ordered him to desist, and on his refusal had him arrested by the civil authority and thrown into the Tolbooth. From here he appealed first to the Lords of Session, who rejected his plea,[4] and finally to the House of Lords, where more than a year later, after the tory reaction in England, his case was tried and the decree of the Lords of Session and the sentence of the Edinburgh magistrates were reversed with costs against that

---

[1] *Somers Tracts*, vol. xii, p. 361.
[2] L-B-S. MSS., Box 3, Bundle M. 9. *Cf*. L-B-S. MSS., Box 3, Bundle M. 7.
[3] L-B-S. MSS., Box 3, Bundle M. 4.
[4] The Presbytery argued that Greenshields' offence was that, by using the English liturgy, he had introduced innovations in worship contrary to the Act of 1707. Greenshields, on the other hand, declared that as a fully qualified Episcopalian minister he had every right to use the Episcopalian form of worship in his own meeting-house.

city.[1] Among Greenshields' strong supporters was the archbishop of York, who had already received a long letter and memorial[2] from him, setting out his case in great detail.

In his letter, after describing what had happened, Greenshields reminded Sharp, and through him the high tories, that "There is a very great zeal here for the English Liturgy, and if I should fail upon whom they have made the first attack, it would discourage us all."[3] The bishop of Edinburgh, who transmitted the memorial to the archbishop, added in a covering letter: "This harsh treatment of our brother plainly shows that whatever pretences our enemies make for their prosecutions, yet Episcopacy and the English service are the main ground of the quarrell. They rage exceedingly to find the service of the Church take so mightily with such multitudes among us. . . . Wherefore they are now plainly above board, by all means whether legal or otherwise to have it entirely suppressed."[4]

In yet another direction Sharp was instrumental in compelling the National Assembly to hold its hand; for in October 1709 the clergy of Aberdeen had informed him that "the names of such of them as were enrolled to be prosecuted before the Justiciary Court, were scored out, and none of them met with any trouble from the late circuit."[5]

The tide of reaction had set in; and during 1712 two measures were passed through Parliament that must have delighted the archbishop's heart. The first was an Act of Toleration, which stated it "to be free and lawful for all those of the Episcopal communion in that part of Great Britain called Scotland, to meet for the exercise of Divine worship, to be performed after their own manner by pastors, ordained by a Protestant bishop, and to use in their congregations the liturgy of the Church of England, if they think fit, without any let, hindrance, or disturbance from any person whatsoever";[6] and the second, the restoration of lay patronage in the Church of Scotland. Both the Episcopalian and the Presbyterian clergy were also compelled to take the oath of

---

[1] *Lockhart Papers*, vol. i, p. 347.
[2] "A true representation of the case of James Greenshields, a minister of the Church of England, given in a memorial to his Grace My Lord Archbishop of York, to be by his Grace humbly represented to Her most sacred Majesty, and to Her Majesty's most Honourable Privy Council": L-B-S. MSS., Box 3, Bundle M. 10.
[3] L-B-S. MSS., Box 3, Bundle M. 13, Sept. 9, 1709.
[4] L-B-S. MSS., Box 4, Bundle K. 65.
[5] *Life of Archbishop Sharp*, vol. i, p. 397.
[6] Mackinnon, *The Union of England and Scotland*, p. 414.

abjuration and to pray for the queen and electress, thus robbing
these measures of any possible suggestion of Jacobitism.

The archbishop continued his efforts to raise funds in England
for the relief of the dispossessed, and in this matter found Anne
much more sympathetic than William had ever been. Various
Scottish bishops, including Edinburgh, Aberdeen and the aged
Dr. John Paterson, archbishop of Glasgow, "burdened with age
and infirmities, eleven children and great poverty",[1] received
pensions, as did also several of the inferior clergy. Paterson had
been the friend and colleague of the tragic Archbishop Sharp of
St. Andrews; and among the archbishop of York's correspondence
there is an interesting epistle linking the two Sharps together.
Alexander Sharp of Scotland, an old Episcopal clergyman who had
been chaplain to the archbishop of St. Andrews, wrote on May 15,
1695: "Be pleased to know that I am one of the dispirited clergy
yet remaining in the kingdom of Scotland"; and went on to appeal
for help because "I find a magnetical power, a charming and
stable strength in the name of Sharp . . . and my relation to my
dear martyred Lord and patron the Archbishop of St. Andrews."[2]

Paterson, a very old and sick man, expressed in several letters
his deep sense of gratitude for the archbishop's kindness and "Her
Majesty's royall bounty".[3]

Ireland represented another field of Sharp's activities. About
this period there seems to have been a considerable ebb and flow
of clergy across the Irish Channel. Greenshields, as stated above,
returned to Scotland from a cure in Ireland; and his was only one
of many comings and goings. Consequently Sharp found himself
engaged in a correspondence with several of the Irish archbishops
and bishops. On October 19, 1703, the archbishop of Armagh
wrote to say that he had at last succeeded in fitting one of Sharp's
candidates, Mr. Brook, into a curacy in the Dublin diocese.[4] Some
four years later York suggested his further promotion: "It may
now be in your Grace's power to do him a kindness by putting him
into some post that will be vacant through the removals that will
be made upon the death of the late Archdeacon of Dublin."[5]
Another of Sharp's choices, however, proved less satisfactory.
"Mr. Charles McNeal an Augustinian Fryer being recommended

[1] *Life of Archbishop Sharp*, vol. i, p. 399. [2] L-B-S. MSS., Box 3, Bundle M. 2.
[3] L-B-S. MSS., Box 3, Bundle M. 16, 17, 18, 19, 20, 21, 22, 24, dated from March 1704 to February 1705.
[4] L-B-S. MSS., Box 4, Bundle L. 73.
[5] L-B-S. MSS., Box 4, Bundle T. 55, Sept. 5, 1707.

to me by his Grace the Lord Archbishop of York", wrote the archbishop of Tuam to the bishop of Limerick, "as one that might do more good in his native country than in England, I permitted him to preach sometimes occasionally in my diocese, but having run away with the daughter of one of my clergy, and lived with her as his wife, before he was married to her by any of my clergy, alledging he was married by some Romish Priest, he was enjoined penance in the consistory of Tuam, and having performed part of it in the Church at Castle-bar, the rest was remitted to him on some appearance of his being penitent, which I pray God grant may be real, and that he may bring forth fruits worthy of Repentance".[1] A month later the bishop of Limerick informed Sharp that McNeal was returning to England and would wait upon him: "He seems to be very sensible of his crime and penitent for it and a clergyman in whose parish he has sojourned for some time of late, gives a good account of his carriage and life whilst under his care".[2]

The archbishop in his turn was frequently petitioned for favours by his Irish colleagues. The bishop of Kilmore, for instance, tried to persuade him in April 1703 to procure a pension from the queen for the widow of an Irish major who had been serving in the "Colonial Indies Regiment . . . he has left little but 8 small children."[3]

It has already been seen how Sharp failed to secure for Dean Davies the bishopric of Down and Connor, but in the disposal of that of Cork and Ross he was more successful. Lord Wharton, then Lord-Lieutenant of Ireland, desired this for the unsatisfactory Dr. Lloyd, fellow of Trinity College, Dublin; but Anne on the archbishop's recommendation rejected his advice and appointed Dr. Brown, Provost of the same College, instead.[4]

A clergyman beneficed in England who accepted a cure of souls in Ireland was obliged as a rule to resign his former living. This applied, apparently, even to bishops; for, as Tenison told Sharp, "Dr. Huntingdon is now confirmed Bishop of Raphoe so that his living of Hallingbury Mag: in Essex nigh Bishop-Stortford in Hertfordshire is void and in the gift of the King."[5]

There were, however, ways and means of evading such a resig-

[1] L-B-S. MSS., Box 4, Bundle B. 17, Jan. 5, 1705.
[2] L-B-S. MSS., Box 4, Bundle B. 18, Feb. 19, 1705.
[3] L-B-S. MSS., Box 4, Bundle L. 74, April 16, 1703.
[4] Swift, *Prose Works*, vol. iii, pp. 314-315.
[5] L-B-S. MSS., Box 4, Bundle L. 68, April 2, 1701.

nation, at least for a time, as can be seen from the following case which the archbishop submitted to his legal advisers: "John Clayton Clerk", Sharp explained, "about Midsummer 1697 left his cure of Crofton (of which he is rector) to go over into Ireland with the M of Winchester one of the Lords Justices as his Lordship's Chaplain. This he did with the leave of the Ordinary but withall promising to come back again to his cure if he was not in a little time (half a year or thereabouts) better provided for in the Kingdom of Ireland.

"A year is now elapsed since his going, and he himself has owned that he is presented to a very good living in that kingdom, but he defers taking Institution and Induction to that living out of design to hold Crofton till he has received the tithes of this next harvest that will be due there about Michaelmas next. At least it does not appear by any certificate that he has taken institution to the Irish living. And it is certain he said he would not till after Michaelmas. The Query is whether the matter thus standing the Rectory of Crofton be now actually void this Midsummer yet. So as that the Ordinary may lawfully admit thereto a clerk presented by the patron, there being no notice given or proof made of Clayton's being legally possessed of his Irish benefice nor, any resignation made by him of Crofton, nor any sentence of deprivation yet passed upon him I beg of you to consider the Act made for the relief of the Irish Protestant Clergy in the first year of King William and Queen Mary, or any other Acts or Canons, which you know of that may seem to relate to this matter."[1]

The archbishop was the more concerned because the patron of Crofton, Lord Stamford, threatened legal proceedings unless his chaplain should be instituted there immediately.[2] "I am of opinion", replied Sharp's lawyer, "that if Mr. Clayton have not taken institution to a living in Ireland nor made a resignation of his living of Crofton; his bare non-residence (tho' for a year's time and tho' it be without the consent of his ordinary) will not make the living of Crofton void; but there must in such a case be a monition against the incumbent to reside and then in case of failure a sentence of deprivation and till such sentence of deprivation be passed the patron has no title in my opinion to present (since the living remains full) and in case he do present the Ordinary ought not (as I conceive) nor can legally grant institu-

[1] L-B-S. MSS., Box 4, Bundle N. 7.
[2] L-B-S. MSS., Box 4, Bundle A. 55, June 28, 1698.

tion thereupon, nor does any *Quare impedit* lie against him for his refusal, in such a case, and I know of no law, statute, canon, or ecclesiastical constitution that contradicts this. And as to the statute I. William and Mary concerning the Protestant Irish clergy I conceive it no way relates to this case Mr. Clayton never having been beneficed in Ireland heretofore."[1]

A little later Lord Stamford wrote to Sharp again to say that he had at last procured a certificate of Clayton's having been installed into the prebend which went with his Irish living, and added: "I take that the one cannot be without the other . . . so now I hope you will institute him [the chaplain] into Crofton without any further delay."[2] But Lord Stamford was mistaken. It was perfectly lawful for an English benefice *cum cura animarum* to be held conjointly with an Irish benefice *sine cura animarum, i.e.* a cathedral prebend.

During Queen Anne's reign a certain Irish clergyman, the Reverend John Richardson,[3] with the support of Archbishop King of Dublin, commenced a propaganda campaign for the wholesale conversion of the Irish papists by preaching to them in the Irish tongue, and by distributing the Bible, Prayer Book and Church Catechism printed in the Irish characters. The matter was warmly taken up by the Lower House of Convocation, which in 1709 passed a resolution commending these suggestions, and further suggesting "that fit persons be provided and encouraged to preach catechise and perform Divine service in the Irish tongue . . . and that application be made to her Majesty for granting letters patent to erect a corporation capable of receiving and disposing charitable contributions for promoting the conversion of papists in this kingdom."[4] This resolution was coldly received by the Upper House, and no doubt would have been quietly pigeon-holed but for the popular support it received in the country at large, where a memorial on the subject was drawn up by several prominent Irishmen, headed by the bishop of Kilmore, and presented to the Duke of Ormonde, then Lord-Lieutenant. Ormonde, who was in England at the time, consulted the archbishop of York. The latter, who had already been approached by Richardson and King, was enthusiastic and promised to use his influence with the queen to forward the proposals. These were as follows: First, that

[1] L-B-S. MSS., Box 4, Bundle N. 7, July 14, 1698.
[2] L-B-S. MSS., Box 4, Bundle A. 56, Aug. 15, 1698.
[3] Author of *History of Attempts to Convert the Popish Natives of Ireland*, published 1712.
[4] R. Mant, *History of the Church of Ireland*, vol. ii, p. 218.

the Bible, Prayer Book and various standard commentaries and devotional works, including *The Whole Duty of Man*, should be translated into Irish, distributed to the people and reinforced by a preaching campaign in Irish; secondly, that charity schools should be erected in every parish in Ireland for the instruction of the children in the English tongue, the Catechism and Church doctrine; finally, that the queen should be asked to grant a charter for the setting up of an incorporated society of bishops and laymen especially qualified for putting such a programme into action.[1] Accordingly Ormonde laid the memorial before the primate, Archbishop Marsh of Armagh, and a gathering of his fellow-archbishops and bishops. Here it was received with a marked lack of enthusiasm, except by King, who, as the bishop of Killaloe afterwards informed Sharp, "left us in some anger, saying that what was proposed should be done whether we would or no". Killaloe, representing the majority view, opposed the memorial, which he declared, "when thoroughly examined into, will be found to be nothing else, but an unprofitable amusement and some unformed offspring of some undigested thoughts". He went on to point out that proposals one and two contradicted each other. "The whole tenour of this proposal [the first]", argued the bishop, "runs counter to the design of the second: This tending to encourage and propagate the Irish language, whereas the second is for setting up Charity schools to teach the Irish children the English tongue in every parish in order to destroy and abolish that of the Irish and promote the English interest thereby."[2] Even the archbishop of Dublin was doubtful about the wisdom of the charity schools, which were admirable institutions where all the people were Protestant, but dangerous when it became a matter of teaching papist children to read and write. They might perhaps be converted while at school, but so long as their parents remained Roman Catholics would certainly eventually relapse. On the other hand, he strongly favoured the proposal to preach to the Irish in their own tongue.[3] In passing, he related to Sharp an amusing anecdote about a similar scheme which was unsuccessfully pressed on James I by Dr. Daniel, then archbishop of Tuam: "The King asked him what was the Irish for a raw egg (the Irish is very harsh) and the Archbishop pronouncing the words to him, he

[1] L-B-S. MSS., Box 3, Bundle B. 35a.
[2] L-B-S. MSS., Box 3, Bundle B. 35b.
[3] L-B-S. MSS., Box 3, Bundle B. 34 and 35c.

19

replied: is that a language to put the work of God in? My dog
Jowler can speak as good language as that."

In view, however, of the weighty support behind the memorial,
the bishops concealed their dislike of it, adopting the face-saving
formula that, while generally approving of its principles, before
they could proceed any further they would require "the advice
and assistance of Parliament and Convocation".[1]

Meanwhile a similar petition, sponsored by Sharp and Ormonde, was presented to Anne, who licensed Convocation to
legislate on this subject at its next session. Richardson, with the
help of Swift and the Governors of the S.P.C.K., also procured
6,000 copies of the Prayer Book, Church Catechism and Lewis'
Exposition of the Church Catechism, printed with the English and Irish
in parallel columns, and had them distributed partly in Ireland
and partly in the Highlands of Scotland. Yet when Convocation
finally met again in 1711 the memorial was talked out of court,
owing to the stubborn opposition of Marsh and the majority of his
fellow-prelates—a fact that King in his letters to Swift and Sharp
never ceased to lament.[2]

The archbishop was also interested in the Churches of the Near
East, several of which seemed to be in poor shape about this
period. In 1706 he had helped certain Armenian bishops, who had
arrived in England to solicit funds, by recommending their case
to the queen.[3] Towards the end of his life, in the summer of 1713,
he received another and heart-rending appeal from no less a
personage than Samuel, the Patriarch of Alexandria. At that time
the Egyptian Church was suffering from what Samuel described
as "intolerable calamities", both material and spiritual. Consequently he despatched a mission to England headed by Arsenius,
the archbishop of the Thebais, and the abbot Gennadius to try
to obtain some help. They arrived in the spring of 1713; but,
according to a letter sent to Sharp by Arsenius the following
August, were not at first very successful in their endeavours. "For
three months have passed", complained Arsenius, "since we came
to this place, yet we have not accomplished any of our tasks, to be
exact we have hardly started with them; for up till now we have
not found any patron or protector here for the distressed Patriarchal See."[4]

---

[1] R. Mant, *History of the Church of Ireland*, vol. ii, p. 222.
[2] Ibid., vol. ii, pp. 224-229.
[3] *Life of Archbishop Sharp*, vol. i, p. 402.
[4] L-B-S. MSS., Box 4, Bundle Q. 79 (translation from the original Latin).

Sharp himself gave £10, for which the Egyptians were patheti-
cally grateful; but otherwise practically no donations were forthcoming, and although armed with three patriarchal letters,
addressed respectively to the queen and the two archbishops, they
had not yet succeeded in reaching Anne's presence. The archbishop of York was their main hope both of approaching the queen
and also of securing the generous support of the English Church.
"We furthermore beseech your Grace", wrote the Patriarch, "to
recommend those whom we have sent, and to acquaint others
with our unhappy case and misfortunes; and that you would not
only speak, but write letters in our favour; that you would entreat
the Queen, Her Majesty, and exhort the nobility, magistrates, and
all pious and well disposed Christians that are put under your care,
and live within your diocese, to espouse our cause. . . . We beg your
Grace to pity us, and lend us your helping hand; and that we, who
are unable of ourselves, may by your assistance get clear of our
great misfortunes."[1] No doubt Sharp would have gladly responded
to this appeal; but the following autumn he was disabled by
sickness and never saw the Queen again.[2]

[1] L-B-S. MSS., Box 3, Bundle K. 25 (translation from the original Greek).
[2] *Life of Archbishop Sharp*, vol. i, p. 325.

CHAPTER XI

CONCLUSION

WE have traced as accurately as possible the story of John Sharp the public servant of Church and State; finally, then, let us consider him in his purely private capacity as a man, and above all a man of God. In this way he will appear before us under various guises—as husband, father, friend, benefactor, a student of literature and of the mind, an earnest seeker after truth, all of them illustrative of his true character and personality.

In Mrs. Sharp the archbishop found as loving and faithful a consort as could be desired. Her principal task lay in the bearing and rearing of his fourteen children, to whom there are frequent references in the archbishop's correspondence. On June 28, 1695, the bishop of Norwich congratulated Sharp on the birth of a daughter and promised that both he and his wife would act as godparents at the christening. He added by way of postscript: "I apprehend 5 guineas to be but a proper and agreeable sum to the occasion."[1] Lady Nottingham sent similar felicitations on another happy advent. "I must wish your Grace and Mrs. Sharp", she wrote, "joy of the daughter, which I rejoice in being to have the relation of Godmother to her."[2] It is sad to have to record that only two children of each sex survived their father.

Mrs. Sharp, of course, like other virtuous ladies of her generation, remained very much in the background of her lord's public life; but there is much evidence to show that in private she pulled many of the wires that determined his actions, particularly his charities.[3] On more than one occasion she herself directly intervened to help a deserving case. A certain Mrs. Jegon was in trouble in March 1700, and was told by the archbishop's wife to go to "Mr. Nicholas Suger of York, who is ordered to pay you the sum of twenty guineas whenever you call for it at his house . . . and if you have need of a further supply write to me at the Archbishop of York's house in Duke Street, Westminster."[4] The provision of

---

[1] L-B-S. MSS., Box 4, Bundle L. 117.   [2] L-B-S. MSS., Box 4, Bundle A. 43.
[3] *Life of Archbishop Sharp*, vol. ii, p. 56.
[4] L-B-S. MSS., Box 4, Bundle T. 47, March 15, 1700.

hospitality for all those countless guests who flocked to the open house kept by the Sharps at Bishopthorpe was yet another of her multitudinous duties; in whose performance, judging from the many profuse letters of thanks still extant from rich and poor alike who had partaken of the archiepiscopal board and lodging, she proved herself to be an admirable caterer and *châtelaine*. Lordly bishops like Crewe of Durham,[1] noble laymen such as Nottingham and his brothers,[2] the saintly Simon Patrick of Ely,[3] the heretic Whiston,[4] the antiquary Ralph Thoresby,[5] and the more usual Yorkshire incumbent or curate,[6] were equally loud in their praises. The archbishop's official position also entailed at various times the bestowal of presents upon and the exchange of courtesies with not only his near neighbours but leading officials throughout his province. Mrs. Sharp, too, took much of this kind of work off his shoulders. "Do pray", wrote John Sharp junior to Heneage Finch on August 3, 17ℵ0, "put my mother in mind of a buck for the Mayor of Ripon on or about the 15th day of this month."[7]

Only one action of hers may have caused Sharp a slight uneasiness, when she brought her mother, the dissenting Mrs. Moseley, to spend her declining years at Bishopthorpe Palace.[8]

The two surviving sons, John and Thomas, were both to be a credit to their parents and upbringing.

John, who as a young man was inclined to spend more money than he ought and to sow some wild oats, became in time a noted tory member of the House of Commons under Queen Anne, earning the nickname of "Spitfire" for his zeal in the interest of the Church of England. His father, however, could always rely upon him to vote as the former deemed expedient, as when he helped to defeat the "tack" in 1704. A monument to his memory in Wicken Church, Northamptonshire, records with true eighteenth-century unction that he was "Eldest son of Dr. John Sharp, Archbishop of York. He served his country and her late Majesty Queen Anne, in several Parliaments, and at the Board of Trade. He was a polite Scholar, an accomplished gentleman, a most affectionate Husband and Father, a true friend and a desirable Companion.

---

[1] L-B-S. MSS., Box 4, Bundle L. 103.   [2] L-B-S. MSS., Box 3, Bundle B. 4.
[3] L-B-S. MSS., Box 4, Bundle L. 104.
[4] William Whiston, *Memoirs*, vol. i, p. 245.
[5] R. Thoresby, *Diary*, vol. i, pp. 245, 307, 309, 348, 438, 452.
[6] L-B-S. MSS., Box 4, Bundle D. 13.   [7] L-B-S. MSS., Box 3, Bundle K. 7.
[8] See Surtees Society, vol. 65, p. 340: "This summer Mrs. Moseley, Mother to Mrs. Sharp, died at Bishopthorpe where she had lived some years and was buried in York Minster"—*i.e.*, May 22, 1698. *Cf.* L-B-S. MSS., Box 3, Bundle K. 4.

Beloved and esteemed by all who knew him, he died much lamented at Grafton Park, March 9th, 1726. Aged 49."

Thomas, a younger brother, took holy orders and bade fair to rival his father's attainments. For although he never actually became a bishop, he was renowned for his learning, especially in Hebrew, and rose rapidly from being a fellow of Trinity College, Cambridge, and chaplain to Archbishop Dawes, to the arch-deaconry of Northumberland in 1723, in conjunction with which he also held prebends at Southwell, York and Durham. He was the author of his father's biography.

The archbishop gave all his sons a thoroughly good education. During the debate in the Lords in 1705, on the motion that "the Church was in Danger," Sharp said "his two sons were taught by Mr. Ellis, a sober virtuous man, and a man of letters, and who had qualified himself according to law when they were sent to him; but when the Abjuration-Oath was enjoined, that, it seems, he refused it, which, as soon as he was apprised of, he took his sons from him."[1] The names of these sons are not mentioned and their identity remains obscure, since John certainly attended Leeds Grammar School under Thomas Dwyer, B.D.,[2] before proceeding to Christ's, Cambridge. Thomas also began his education at Leeds, which pleased Dwyer very much. "I return my most humble thanks", he wrote to the archbishop on May 24, 1703, "for your Grace's generous present to our library and to myself. And as I am under the greatest obligations in the world to serve your Grace to the utmost of my power, so I assure you I will faithfully endeavour it in my love and care of Mr. Sharp. And I heartily pray to God that the effects of it may be seen in that child's improvement both in piety and learning, to your Grace's satisfaction."[3] He completed his schooling, however, at St. Paul's, London, and was admitted to Trinity,[4] where eventually he won a fellowship.

The two surviving daughters were Anne and Dorothy. Dorothy remained unmarried, but Anne became the wife of Dr. Heneage Dering, the archbishop's chaplain, in 1712. Heneage was the son of Christopher Dering, who had been the private secretary of Heneage Finch at the same time that Sharp was his chaplain. The two men had become friends, with the result that in later years

---

[1] *History and Proceedings of the House of Lords*, edit. E. Timberland, vol. ii, p. 158.
[2] R. Thoresby, *Ducatus Leodiensis*, p. 84.
[3] L-B-S. MSS., Box 4, Bundle C. 16.
[4] See J. Venn and J. A. Venn, *Alumni Cantabrigienses*, vol. iv, p. 49.

Heneage (called after his father's old patron) secured the post first as private secretary and then as chaplain to the archbishop. The marriage took place in Bishopthorpe chapel, with Sharp himself officiating at the ceremony.

Sharp's affection for the members of his family is well illustrated in a letter that he wrote to Dering on hearing of the death of another daughter, Elizabeth.

St. James Street
May 4th, 1713.

"Dear Son,

  I had yours the last night which brought us the sad news of my daughter's death at which we are all here very much concerned and heavily troubled. But God's will must be submitted to in all things. My poor wife is extremely afflicted at it. And so no doubt is yours. I pray God to comfort them both. I thank you for your care of her funeral, and that she is buried at York Minster. I will take care that all the expenses of it shall be paid you by Mr. Suger. I heartily send my blessing to your wife, my daughter, and earnestly beseech God not only to support her under these afflictions, but to bless her with health and give her a happy delivery from her burden in due time. My wife and I hope to see you both a good while before that time comes. Wishing all health and happiness to you and her with my wife's blessing to you both, and all good wishes of your friends here

I am, Dear Son, your most

Affectionate Father

Jo. Ebor."[1]

The archbishop had an equally deep concern for more distant relations. When a certain Thomas Hutton proposed to marry his cousin, Miss Moxon-Verney, he took infinite trouble enquiring into the young man's character and financial stability, and commissioned another cousin, John Weddell, the lawyer, to investigate the whole matter thoroughly. Hutton and his father made far-reaching promises, but in Weddell's opinion they could and would never be fulfilled. Consequently he informed Sharp, that "in my weak judgement renders this match not a very suitable one".[2] A little later he wrote again triumphantly to announce that the match had been broken off, and Cousin Moxon "begs the favour

---

[1] L-B-S. MSS., Box 3, Bundle L. 1.
[2] L-B-S. MSS., Box 3, Bundle E. 13, Sept. 8, 1698. See also L-B-S. MSS., Box 4, Bundle F. 7, 8, 9a, 9b, 10.

of presenting her duty to your Grace and returning her humble thanks for the great trouble your Lordship hath received in this affair . . . I presume she will never engage herself in any other amour without the advice and approbation of your Lordship."[1]

No man was ever a better friend than John Sharp, and his friendships stood fast in adversity as well as in fair weather. He did not hesitate, for example, after the Revolution of 1688, to visit Jeffreys in the Tower, an act which so amazed the late Lord Chancellor that he cried out: "What! dare you own me now?"[2]

When Lord Nottingham lay under a cloud in 1694, or, as he quaintly put it in a letter to the archbishop, "Tho' the King and people too have given me my quietus," he expressed his deep appreciation of Sharp's endeavours to secure his brother Henry, also suspect by William, the deanery of York.[3] Robert Nelson, the non-juror, was likewise much indebted to his help and support: "Sharp, Archbishop of York, must by no means be omitted from the list of Robert Nelson's friends, the more so as he was mainly instrumental in over-coming the scruples which for many years had deterred Nelson from the communion of the National Church."[4] That learned but eccentric divine William Whiston, who had been banished from Cambridge and deprived of his degree because of his strange Arian heresy, put it on record: "I sent a copy of my MS Fourth volume, or an account of the primitive faith concerning the Trinity and Incarnation, to Dr. Sharp, the Archbishop of York, that very good, that very honest man, that excellent preacher and great friend to Mr. Clark and myself."[5] The Jacobite bishop Crewe of Durham, who narrowly escaped being deprived of his bishopric at the Revolution, and had been compelled to retire from public life, was loud in the praise of the archbishop's continual kindness and hospitality. "Your Grace's extraordinary favours to me", he wrote, "in time of difficulty can never be sufficiently acknowledged, I am sure they shall never be forgotten by me. I can truly say my respects to your son, a very ingenious hopeful person, are seconded with my affec-

---

[1] L-B-S. MSS., Box 3, Bundle E. 14, Jan. 19, 1698/9.
[2] *Life of Archbishop Sharp*, vol. i, p. 97.
[3] L-B-S. MSS., Box 4, Bundle L. 109, Oct. 13, 1694.
[4] Overton and Abbey, *English Church in the Eighteenth Century*, p. 44.
[5] *Life of Archbishop Sharp*, vol. ii, p. 7. Whiston claimed that the archbishop agreed with him on the question of the length of Christ's Ministry. See *Memoirs*, vol. i, p. 115.
Such men were certainly the archbishop's friends; but it would be totally untrue to say that he in any sense accepted their teaching. This applied (equally) to Nonconformists like Baxter and Firmin or deists like Toland, who was told: "I would, as I had occasion do him right": *Life of Archbishop Sharp*, vol. i, p. 274.

tions, and my wishes for your Grace's health and happiness, are
as hearty as they are for the public good of the Church; a great
share of which (God be thanked) is under such a protection, as
can never (during your Grace's primacy) want the true Apostolic
endeavours for its preservation."[1] The archbishop's MSS. are,
indeed, full of letters from contemporary bishops and noble laymen expressing their unqualified admiration for his character
and actions. "I desire not to be forgot", begged the Marquis
of Northampton, "in those prayers you offer up to the throne of
Grace, that I may rejoice in the happiness of being forever your
Grace's most humble and obedient servant."[2]

"I have received the honour of your Grace's letter," acknowledged the Duke of Somerset, "and shall in this affair . . . as I desire
likewise in all other affairs whenever I can be so happy, to concert
with so great and so good a man, as my Lord Archbishop of York."[3]

"My Lord", declared John Williams, bishop of Chichester, "you
always study how to gratify and oblige your friends, and are the
most successful in it in the world."[4]

Bishops Moore of Norwich and Lloyd of Worcester appear to
have been his particular friends in the episcopate; and with Lloyd
he carried on a long and intimate correspondence both as regards
the affairs of the Almonry and the former's apocalyptic studies in
the Book of Daniel.

Sharp, begging Lloyd to forgive his bluntness, such as he dared
not have used with any other bishop except Norwich, demanded
that the fruits of these studies should be published as soon as
possible. For in his opinion a most important work was proceeding
far too slowly. "At this rate of a sheet a year", he declared, "our
children perhaps may live to see it, if God so long continue your
life and health. . . . In truth if you go on in this way, I cannot help
thinking, that all the pains you take in your studies, is more for
your own pleasure and amusement, than for the good of the
public, considering how uncertain human life is."[5] Lloyd defended
himself by pleading attacks by Whiston, which had to be answered,[6] ill-health,[7] and the enmity of one John Laughton, a

[1] L-B-S. MSS., Box 4, Bundle A. 60, Aug. 26, 1704.
[2] L-B-S. MSS., Box 4, Bundle A. 63, May 18, 1703.
[3] L-B-S. MSS., Box 4, Bundle A. 45, Oct. 24, 1702.
[4] L-B-S. MSS., Box 4, Bundle L. 106. Sept. 25, 1700.
[5] L-B-S. MSS., Box 3, Bundle II: Correspondence between Archbishop Sharp and
Bishop Lloyd, Letter I, Oct. 18, 1704.
[6] Ibid., Letter II, May 4, 1709.
[7] L-B-S. MSS., Box 3, Bundle O. 21, March 6, 1708/9.

prebendary of Worcester, who had preached against him in the cathedral, obliging the bishop to vindicate himself.[1] All these causes had contributed towards delaying publication. "For . . . which faults", Lloyd pleaded, "I ask your Grace's pardon, and promise to make any satisfaction that I am able."

But perhaps Sharp's kindly, friendly spirit was seen at its best in his dealings with his inferiors. In *Archbishop Herring's Visitation Returns* of 1743, some of the older clergy quite gratuitously paid tribute to a prelate thirty years in his grave. W. Steer, curate of Swinton Chapel, Doncaster, wrote: "I do not pretend to advise you, who are so much my superior; and so well versed in ecclesiastical matters; you cannot tread after a better man than Archbishop Sharp."[2]

The following anecdote has been told about the archbishop as a practical example of his kindness to the "down and out":[3] Sharp was, apparently, in the habit of taking a saddled horse along with his carriage on a tedious journey, lest, growing tired of sitting, he might prefer to ride. One day, a few years before his death, he was riding in this manner, a mile or so in advance of his carriage, while returning from London to Bishopthorpe, when a young, masked horseman suddenly appeared, presented a pistol, and demanded, in a "faultering tone of voice", his money or his life. Sharp with great composure advised the youth to remove the dangerous weapon and tell him his trouble. The highwayman, however, persisted in his demand for money; whereupon the archbishop said bluntly but kindly: "Hear me, young man, come on with me. I, you see, am a very old man and my life is of very little consequence; yours seems far otherwise. I am named Sharp, the Archbishop of York; my carriage and servants are behind. But conceal your perturbations and tell me what money you want and who you are: And on the word of my character, I'll not injure you, but prove a friend. Here, take this"—giving him money—"and tell me how much you want to make you independent of so dangerous and destructive a business as you are now engaged in." The young man promptly broke down and confessed that he detested his present occupation, but was heavily in debt and this had seemed the only way out of his troubles. Sharp arranged an appointment with him in the near future, when he advanced him some fifty

---

[1] L-B-S. MSS., Box 3, Bundle O. 23, Feb. 27, 1710.
[2] *Archbishop Herring's Visitation Returns*, vol. iii, p. 88.
[3] L-B-S. MSS., Box 3, Bundle B. 59: "Anecdote of Archbishop Sharp taken out of the *Craftsman or Says Weekly Journal*, Feb. 1st, 1777."

pounds, the extent of his liabilities. Naturally the archbishop never expected to see his masked friend again; but a year and a half later he reappeared to refund the money and express his deep gratitude. "My Lord", he said, "you cannot have forgotten the circumstance at such a time and place; God and gratitude will never suffer them to be obliterated from my mind. In me, my Lord, you now behold that once most wretched of mankind. And now by your inexpressive humanity rendered equal, perhaps superior, in happiness to millions of mankind. Oh, my Lord (tears for a while prevented his utterance), 'tis you, 'tis you that have saved me, body and soul. 'Tis you that have saved a dear and much-loved wife, and a little brood of children whom I tendered dearer than my life. Here is that fifty pounds. But nowhere, never, shall I find a language to testify what I feel. Your God is your witness, your deed itself is your glory, and may Heaven . . . be your . . . everlasting reward! I was the youngest son of a wealthy man. Your Lordship knew him I am sure. —— is my name. Marriage alienated his affections, and my brother withdrew his love and left me to sorrow and penury. . . . A month since my brother died a bachelor and intestate. What was his becomes mine, and now by your astonishing goodness I am at once the most penitent, the most grateful and happiest of my species."

From the day of his consecration the archbishop rapidly acquired a reputation for willingness to expend unlimited time, energy, money, tact and patience in helping the deserving in all walks and conditions of life. With the result, of course, that the requests for aid found among his MSS. are so many and diverse that it is impossible to do more than mention a few of the more outstanding and little known. The following letter from a Mrs. Greaves to her brother, Leonard Wilberfoss, at York, is a typical example of the kind of family dispute which was only too frequently brought to Sharp's notice:

BEVERLEY,
June 2, 1704.

"DEAR BROTHER,

I am sorry that I have occasion to let you know the troubles I have undergone, which I have concealed so long as patience would permit me. I am daily abused by my husband, who beats me till I am oft black and blue. The marks of his anger I carry about me at this present. He calls me all the ill names that can be, as whore, drunkard, thief, etc. He hath turned me out of doors several times, one of which I was forced to lie in the yard all night, and in the morning abused me and told me I had been with my gallant. He hath turned me out of bed and locked me out of his chamber, nay, even he encourages his servants to abuse me. He hath taken all the keys from me and hath given them to the upper maid to keep. I am a perfect stranger in the house. Anything that he sees me have a hand in, whether meat or drink he will not touch it, for he says that I put poison in it. He hath discharged me of coming in his shop, and says I sit there to cheat him. He not only abuses me, but all my relations. He hath struck me both before brother and sister Trippett. He calls me and sister Lambert and sister Chapelow the three furies of hell. He calls my sister Chapelow by the same names he calls me. He is to go to his Grace the Lord Archbishop of York about some town's business, and he designs to let his Grace know what a bad wife he hath. Therefore would desire you if you can anyways speak to his Grace, to acquaint him with his good qualities and ill-usage of me, and if you think it convenient to shew his Lordship my letter. They have put him into the spiritual court about his getting his servant, Easter, with child. He was at Hull yesterday, and as soon as he came home he kicked me out of the house. I went very submissively to desire entrance last night, but he refused me. So was forced to lie at brother Lambert's last night. He will give me no more than the law will allow me. Nay, I did but desire my night clothes, which he denied me, Dear Brother, if you have any affection for me, pray send me your assistance in this my misfortune, knowing not what to do without your kind help. We have not laid together for a month. I have several witnesses of his denying me entrance. Pray Brother come over to this town that we may make some end in this matter. I should have writ ere this, but for fear it should have troubled you and mother, but the matter is gone so high that I could forbear no longer. Pray excuse this trouble from your disconsolate sister.

JANE GREAVES.[1]

On another occasion he was asked to deal with an even more delicate problem—a Roman Catholic husband and Anglican wife who could not agree about the education of their children. Nicholas Stratford, bishop of Chester, who also interested himself in this affair, was violently prejudiced against the papist; but

[1] L-B-S. MSS., Box 4, Bundle E. 14.

Sharp, apparently, treated him with the greatest courtesy and impartiality. The agreement finally arrived at was that the husband would be responsible for the education of his five sons, the lady for their two daughters.[1] Several other cases of a similar nature include one of a proposed marriage of an uncle to his niece; when, remembering the archbishop's classical education, the defendant rashly quoted the precedent of the Emperor Claudius who married his niece Agrippina.[2]

On a slightly different plane Sharp often acted as a mediator or peacemaker in family disputes over money or land. Lady Lampson sought his assistance in helping her to recover some money belonging to her late husband, Sir Wilfred Lampson. She pointed out that he had left his family in such straitened circumstances "that 'twill be extremely difficult to get the poor children even a tolerable education. I am, as I ought to be, ashamed of being so troublesome to your Grace; but I am sure when you consider it is the cause of the fatherless and widow that will plead a better excuse than I can."[3]

Another good example of this kind of thing is to be found in a protracted correspondence between members of the Lowther family from 1700 to 1704. Here the main protagonists were Sir William Lowther and his son, with Lord Maynard of Easton Lodge, near Dunmow, Lady Lowther, "Parson Lowther", and Mr. Stanhope all interested parties. The archbishop was appealed to from every side. "My son [-in-law] Lowther", wrote Lord Maynard, "telling me that your Grace has been so very obliging as to undertake the deciding of a troublesome as well as chargeable dispute that has been for some time between Sir William and him, I thought myself obliged to acknowledge your Grace's great favour in it, and do hope you will find his cause so just that there will be no difficulty in giving of it of my son's side, he being a man of so much honesty and honour, that I cannot think he would do an ill thing to any gentleman, much less to his father."[4] And eventually Sharp succeeded in restoring harmony and facilitating a settlement.[5]

He also loved to act as a peacemaker among men of his own cloth; as when, for example, he sought in 1699 to compose the

[1] L-B-S. MSS., Box 4, Bundle L. 79, Oct. 4, 1697.
[2] L-B-S. MSS., Box 3, Bundle O. 45.
[3] L-B-S. MSS., Box 4, Bundle J. 1.
[4] L-B-S. MSS., Box 4, Bundle U. 27, Oct. 30, 1701.
[5] See L-B-S. MSS., Box 4, Bundle U. 1-33.

differences between the dean of York and Dr. James, one of the
prebendaries, over the question of the latter's residence. "I heartily
wish", he concluded, "that while you are together you may live
like friends and brethren, and that you may part so."[1]

Lack of space alone forbids the quotation of many other cases;
but in conclusion let us record the following interesting story, told
by Susannah Wesley, the mother of the famous John, of how the
archbishop helped her when Samuel, her husband, was imprisoned
in Lincoln Castle for debt. " 'Tell me', says he, 'Mrs. Wesley,
whether you ever really wanted bread?' 'My Lord', said I, 'I will
freely own to your Grace that, strictly speaking, I never did want
bread. But then I have had so much care to get it before it was eat,
and to pay for it after, as has often made it very unpleasant to me.
And I think to have bread on such terms is the next degree of
wretchedness to having none at all.' 'You are certainly in the right,'
replied my Lord, and seemed for a while very thoughtful. Next
morning he made me a handsome present, nor did he ever repent
of having done so."[2]

When in residence at Bishopthorpe Sharp felt compelled to keep
an open house; although, since he was not of a particularly con-
vivial disposition, this tried his patience as well as drained his
purse. However, he did not fail to entertain all his guests with
agreeable and if possible serious conversation, but always carefully
choosing his subjects to suit his audience, even should it mean
conversing with a Yorkshire fox-hunter about horse racing. The
fare, too, provided on these occasions was certainly not
Spartan, judging from the trouble the archbishop took in im-
porting the very best wines from London via Hull, and choice
venison from the estates of Lord Burlington and other noble
friends.[3]

There is an amusing story—not so amusing from the archbishop's point of view—of how at a most inconvenient moment in
1701 his wines miscarried and eventually turned up under very
mysterious, not to say highly suspicious, circumstances in the
cellars of Sir Godfrey Copley of Sprotborough.[4] Sharp was most
indignant, especially as Sir Godfrey appeared reluctant to part
with them. "Word sent me from Hull", noted the archbishop on
October 29, "that my wine was in Sir Godfrey's cellar and that

[1] L-B-S. MSS., Box 4, Bundle T. 21 and 22.
[2] M. Watt, The History of the Parson's Wife, p. 52.
[3] L-B-S. MSS., Box 4, Bundle L. 116.
[4] See L-B-S. MSS., Box 4, Bundle Q. 9, and Box 3, Bundle G. 19, Sept. 1, 1701.

care would be taken that it should be sent me. From that time I have waited patiently, but nothing I see comes of it . . . my wine should have been sent down in the middle of June."[1] Ultimately a threat of legal proceedings secured their restoration.

The Yorkshire clergy were Sharp's most frequent visitors. "The meanest man in his diocese who wore a gown . . . was welcome at his table as often as he pleased."[2]

But if Sharp could be a good and generous friend he was also a bad enemy, as Swift found to his cost when the archbishop advised Anne "that her Majesty should be sure that the man whom she was going to make a bishop was at least a christian".[3]

Another *bête noire* was the bishop of Salisbury. At one period during Tillotson's lifetime Burnet and Sharp had been very good friends, for the latter was then attacking the Roman Catholics and championing the cause of comprehension. But as the archbishop's high-churchmanship became more pronounced, and his attitude towards the Dissenters more hostile, their friendship waned. Burnet had received the news of Sharp's nomination to York with joy. "So the king named him (Tillotson)", he wrote, "and the Archbishop of York dying soon after, Sharp (now Dean of Canterbury) was promoted to that see; so that these two sees were in a month's time filled with two of the greatest prelates, the best preachers, and worthiest men that perhaps ever sat in them."[4]

Later, after Sharp had voted against the attainder of Sir John Fenwick, and when on Queen Anne's accession it became obvious that he was to take the place of Burnet and Tenison as the royal adviser in ecclesiastical matters, the former changed his attitude: "Sharp by a great error of Tillotson's was made Archbishop of York. He has proved an ill instrument and has set himself at the head of the party; but has suffered much by it in the opinion of many, who looked on him before as a man of integrity and simplicity. But few do now retain that opinion, as with regret I confess I do not. I have observed too much art and design in him to be able to think of him as I wish I could do."[5]

The reign of Queen Anne was one of the high-water marks in

---

[1] L.-B.-S. MSS., Box 4, Bundle T. 89.
[2] *Life of Archbishop Sharp*, vol. ii, p. 51.
[3] "John Sharp" in the *General Biographical Dictionary*, 1816. *Cf. Life of Archbishop Sharp*, vol. ii, p. 262.
[4] H. C. Foxcroft, *Supplement to Burnet's History of My Own Time*, p. 359.
[5] Ibid., p. 504.

the production of English literature, and since the Church still
represented one of the nerve centres of the nation and the clergy
its best educated section, it is small wonder that "religion" figured
very largely in this output; and the bishops, especially the archbishops, were some of the chief literary critics. Sharp was a sound
but by no means brilliant classical scholar, his sermons were never
more than mediocre,[1] his literary achievements were extremely
meagre; and yet no sooner had he been elevated to the throne of
York than authors, orthodox and heretical, well established and
obscure, High Church, Low Church, no Church, besought his
public approval of their works as the sure key to successful sales.
"I herewith return you the manuscript which you sent me from
Mr. Stephens," wrote the archbishop to his brother Joshua on
August 15, 1707, "he would have me to recommend it to some
bookseller. I have read it over and I do truly believe that the lady,
who was the author of these meditations, was a very pious devout
good woman, that the meditations themselves are very savoury
and I should think cannot but promote virtue and piety in all well
disposed persons that read them, especially those of the devout
sex, as Bishop Taylor styles womankind. Nor have I any objection
either as to the matter, which is very useful, or the style, which is
very natural and unaffected. If this recommendation will be any
encouragement to a bookseller to print this work you may with
Mr. Stephens his leave offer it to Mr. Rogers or Mr. Ailmer or
whom you think fit. But tho' you may shew them this letter yet I
would not have any notice taken of this my recommendation in
print."[2]

The more eccentric and unorthodox the publication the more
anxiously and tirelessly he was pursued. "May it please your
Grace", wrote William Whiston on February 26, 1701/2, "to
accept of the tender of a small present of my *Short View of the
Chronology of the Old Testament*, and of the *Harmony of the Four*

---

[1] They were, nevertheless, extraordinarily popular:
   Kidder, Bishop of Bath and Wells: "I must humbly thank you for your sermons you intended me": L-B-S. MSS., Box 4, Bundle L. 102, April 20, 1700.
   Crewe of Durham thanked him for "two excellent sermons": L-B-S. MSS., Box 4, Bundle L. 103.
   Lloyd of Lichfield: "Pray let me see your farewell sermon, and the pamphlet that is written against it": L-B-S. MSS., Box 4, Bundle L. 96, Jan. 10, 1692.
   Stratford of Chester: "I had the favour of receiving your excellent sermon, which I read over with as much satisfaction as, I think, I ever did any. If atheists and devils would seriously consider it, they would certainly be convinced by it, were they not fatally blinded by their own lusts": L-B-S. MSS., Box 4, Bundle L. 84, Aug. 13, 1700.
[2] L-B-S. MSS., Box 4, Bundle T. 28.

Evangelists; which I have at last completed. I hope the endeavours
I have used to afford new light to those difficult points will be
acceptable; and in some measure advantageous to all those, who
earnestly study the sacred scriptures. The favourable acceptance
both myself, and my former attempt met with from your Grace
makes me not at all doubt of the like kind reception of this more
general important, and useful design."[1] Whiston, who at this time
was deputy to Newton in the Lucasian professorship at Cambridge,
succeeded the latter in 1703 with the approval of many of the
bishops, including Sharp. He even expressed the hope that the
archbishop would find him "a sinecure or prebend or donative to
make up my salary a competency to me". In 1710, however, he
wrote to the archbishop in a very different strain, replying to
Sharp's appeal of August 6, 1708, "that it will be a great sin in
you to disturb the peace and unity of the Catholic Church by
endeavouring to impose new articles of faith upon us about the
Blessed Trinity, different from, or contrary to, the definitions of
the Council of Nice",[2] together with a spirited defence of his
heresies: "Since I have now completed my designs, and am going
to print my dissertation on Ignatius' Epistles with the Epistles
themselves; my essay on the Constitutions, with the Constitutions
themselves; and my *Account of the Primitive Faith of Christians*,
severally in the order wherein they are here mentioned. I thought
it would become me to acquaint your Grace with it; that still, if
your Grace, and the rest of the Bishops please, all or any of these
may come to a solemn and public examination before they are
printed. I plainly find that hitherto the learned are no ways able
to oppose the evidence that I have in these matters; as indeed I
have all along known that it was too strong to be opposed." But
he went on passionately to declare that no such full and impartial
examination would be allowed, for the simple reason that Sharp
and his brother bishops were biassed by "worldly interest, fears
for the reputation of parties, and dread of the greatness of the
alterations to be made in faith, worship, practice and discipline".
Hence he must and would proceed to the publication of his dis-
coveries on his own account and leave the truth to vindicate itself.
"I could add", he concluded tartly, "many more things here, not
unworthy of your Grace's notice. But since your Grace was not
pleased to return any answer to my second letter, I cannot with
any assurance promise myself one to this. So I shall satisfy myself

[1] L-B-S. MSS., Box 3, Bundle N. 39.   [2] *Life of Archbishop Sharp*, vol. ii, p. 135.

in giving your Grace this information before I proceed further, that no blame may any way lie upon me in this matter."[1]

Another heretic, the deist Toland, had already submitted to the archbishop's scrutiny his own highly debatable book, *Mr. Toland's Defence of Himself*. Sharp dealt very frankly and bluntly with his theories: "We fell a talking about his books and principles. I dealt very freely with him as to both."[2]

On the other hand, Sharp always endeavoured to be as charitable as possible in the case of innocuous eccentrics, whom he criticised cautiously and gave praise wherever he could. Dr. Comber, dean of Durham, sought to maintain that tithes were due to the clergy by divine right. Sharp replied: "I do confess to you, that all your arguments, direct or consequential, singly taken, or taken altogether, do not in my opinion come up to the point that you would prove."[3] The dean was persuaded not to publish; and Dr. Grew likewise suppressed the chapter on "Church Government" in his *Cosmologia Sacra* owing to the archbishop's friendly criticisms.[4] Sharp was equally tactful with the high-flying effusions of the non-juring Dodwell and Hickes; but, despite political differences, could honestly approve and applaud Burnet's great work on the Thirty-Nine Articles, although with certain mental reservations, particularly as regards non-episcopal ordinations.[5] "I kept that work seven years by me before I put it in the press," Burnet himself noted; "many Bishops read it, Tenison, Sharp, Stillingfleet, Patrick, Hall and Williams. It lay some considerable time in both Universities and was read by many, all approving of it and desiring me to print it."[6]

The archbishop's interest in books and authors was not, however, by any means confined to those of his own country. In particular he carried on a correspondence and exchanged books with M. Le Clerc, a learned professor at Amsterdam.[7] The following letter from Sharp, which has never before been published, is typical of many that passed between them:

"SIR—I had the favour of your obliging letter a quarter of a year ago, but did not receive your *Ars Critica* till yesterday. I do hereby return you my hearty thanks for that kind present, which

[1] L-B-S. MSS., Box 3, Bundle N. 40, Sept. 5, 1710.
[2] *Life of Archbishop Sharp*, vol. i, p. 274.   [3] Ibid., vol. ii, p. 14.
[4] L-B-S. MSS., Box 4, Bundle R. 34.   [5] *Life of Archbishop Sharp*, vol. ii, p. 25.
[6] H. C. Foxcroft, *Supplement to Burnet's History of My Own Time*, p. 507.
[7] *Life of Archbishop Sharp*, vol. ii, pp. 34-42.

comes very seasonably for an excellent entertainment for me in
my journey into the North whither I am hastening. I am much
troubled at the account you give me of the treatment you met with
from Mr. M——. It was unfortunate that I sent my letter by him,
but in truth that was the first opportunity I had of writing to you.
I would wish a better understanding between you and Dr. Cave
who is really a very good man as well as a learned. It happens that
my Bookseller has just now published a new edition of my sermons
in one volume; I have ordered Mr. Smith to send them to you as
a testimony of my sincere respects, tho' I am at the same time out
of countenance to present such trifles to you. We hope shortly for
a good edition of Irenæus from Oxford; and when it comes out I
will take care to send it you, I am with hearty wishes of your good
health, etc.
Jo. EBOR."[1]

Neither was the archbishop too proud to discuss literary topics
with his parochial clergy, nor even to read and criticise their MSS.
The Reverend Clement Elis conducted a voluminous correspondence with him on this subject, and submitted many of his
own sermons and devotional treatises for his metropolitan's perusal
and, if necessary, correction.[2] Benjamin Brown, rector of Sundridge, and N. Drake, vicar of Sheffield, acted on several occasions as Sharp's unofficial agents for procuring books both at
auctions in England and from publishers overseas.[3]

In the course of a busy life the archbishop himself found time
for a pleasant recreation, that of the numismatist. He collected
coins industriously from all quarters, and kept in close touch with
some of the best authorities of the day, notably Evelyn, Archdeacon Nicolson and Ralph Thoresby.[4] On August 31, 1696,
Sharp visited Thoresby's museum and came away amazed at the
splendour of his collection. "He said", Dering afterwards informed
the antiquary, "it was the richness of your collection of coins that
showed him the poverty of his own."[5]

The archbishop's is the first signature in the museum's album,
and after it he added the motto: "Omnia vobis cum charitate
fiant."[6]

[1] L-B-S. MSS., Box 3, Bundle N. 7, March 23, 1699.
[2] Cf. L-B-S. MSS., Box 4, Bundle D. 4, 6, 8; Bundle T. 19.
[3] L-B-S. MSS., Box 4, Bundle C. 8, 11; Bundle Q. 31.
[4] See R. Thoresby, Letters of Eminent Men, vol. i, pp. 319 and 343; vol. ii, p. 286;
Diary, vol. i, p. 328; Thoresby Society, vol. xxi, pp. 74, 95, 163; L-B-S. MSS., Box 3,
Bundle N. 35 and 36.
[5] Thoresby Society, vol. xxi, p. 49.   [6] Ibid., vol. xxi, p. 54.

Thoresby advised Sharp to write an authoritative book on coins, but the latter was not to be drawn. "I found it", he remarked, "a good divertisement in the evenings. But I find I am too apt to make a business of that which should only be a recreation."[1] At his death he left his coins to Thoresby, together with some unpublished treatises entitled *Observations on the Coinage of England, Observations on the Scots Money,* and *Of the Irish Coins.*[2]

Sharp was also an able antiquary in other directions. When the "Old White Chapel of the North" near Bradford, which had long been in ruins, was rebuilt in 1706, he refused to consecrate it on the ground that an ancient yew tree grew in the churchyard. This, he declared, proved it to be already holy ground, since it was the custom in Saxon times to erect a cross and plant a yew tree in the centre of a newly consecrated burial-ground.[3]

Apart from these researches his only other secular amusement appears to have been an appreciative study of Shakespeare's plays and poetry; and he was wont to say, half in jest, half earnest, that the Bible and Shakespeare had made him archbishop of York.

Sharp corresponded with Thoresby on another and, in his eyes, a much more important subject, namely the latter's conversion to the Church of England. "I have often wondered", he wrote to him on March 16, 1696/7, "how a person of such curious learning and good knowledge and, withal, of such goodness of temper and undesigning honesty, as I always took you to be, could possibly have entertained such prejudices against our way of worship, as to be of a different communion from us."[4] Thoresby conformed in 1699; and undoubtedly he was largely persuaded to do so by the archbishop's eloquent letters, his treatises on conscience, and his sermons, all of which Sharp had gladly and tirelessly pressed upon the famous antiquary.[5] The chief reason for his long hesitation, as he confessed to the archbishop, was the fear of the wrath of his relations, who would certainly and immediately disown him and his family. "I must be", he lamented, "the unhappy occasion of debates, censures, etc. And as to relations, I disoblige them all to a man."[6] But in the end Sharp, with the aid of a famous casuist,

[1] "Archbishop Sharp's Observations on the Coinage of England," in *Bibliotheca Topographica Britannia,* 1764.
[2] *Harley MSS.* 4119.
[3] W. Cudworth, *Round about Bradford,* p. 97.
[4] R. Thoresby, *Letters of Eminent Men,* vol. i, p. 273.
[5] *Cf.* Ibid., vol. i, pp. 319, 324, 366, 370, 391; and L-B-S. MSS., Box 3, Bundle N. 33 and 34.
[6] L-B-S. MSS., Box 3, Bundle F. 5, May 20, 1699.

John Humfrey,[1] prevailed and Thoresby became a member of the Church of England, which he soon saw to be the strongest bulwark against popery in the country.

His admiration for the archbishop's character and preaching abilities had always been unbounded. In 1697 he recorded in his diary: "It may not be amiss to insert here a passage relating to the excellent Archbishop of York, who coming to confirm, preached incomparably; we were forced to go a full hour before the bells ceased, to secure places in our own pews, the church being so crowded as was never known in the memory of any person living. . . . At the conclusion he spoke most affectingly as to the office of confirmation."[2] Some two years later he made the following entry: "I received a most comfortable letter from my Lord Archbishop of York, answering many objections against my conformity, and gave me great satisfaction."[3]

Sharp kept in close touch with his old College of Christ's, and was frequently consulted by the then Master, Dr. John Covell. The two had been friends in their student days, and were now able to help one another in various ways. On August 12, 1700, Covell wrote to the archbishop: "I shall always be ready to comply with your desires, especially when they are coincident with my own. Sir Thompson is an ingenious and deserving lad, and I have long set my heart upon him to do him good; and in this affair, he shall not fail of my favour as far as justice will permit. Here are likely to be four competitors, all his seniors. How our public examinations may distinguish them, I cannot tell. I have long since advised and encouraged this youth to study hard, and perhaps he may have the mastery. He hath several friends amongst the fellows, but we must be eight to make a majority. The senior of all the competitors is Master of Arts of the second year, kinsman to Mr. Waterhouse (now leaving us) and formerly sizar to Mr. Standish, who I presume will lean to his interest. If your Grace thought fitting, to give him a line or two, it might at least make him indifferent. Mr. Smithson is kinsman to my Lord of Lincoln, and a letter from my Lord to him in Sir Thompson's behalf may do him some kindness, though I perceive Mr. Smithson is addicted likewise to Mr. Waterhouse's interest. The competition will lie chiefly there. Your son

[1] R. Thoresby, *Diary*, vol. i, p. 362: "Archbishop Sharp had recommended my case to a very eminent divine, Mr. John Humfrey, noted as well for his moderation as piety, who to use his own expression, was though a Nonconformist minister, a conformist parishioner."
[2] R. Thoresby, *Diary*, vol. i, p. 313.   [3] Ibid., vol. i, p. 329.

(if you approve of it) may write to some of these (if they were of his intimate acquaintance), Mr. Every, Mr. Bevin, Mr. Broughton especially (who I believe would love to be courted by such a hand), Mr. Burton, Mr. Sherwell, Mr. Palmer. I should be very glad if Sir Thompson could find seven for him. I would then without fail consummate the matter. You may perceive how ready I am to gratify your desire and to approve myself.

Your Grace's, etc.
JOHN COVELL."[1]

In a postscript he made the suggestion that the Earl of Nottingham might be induced to influence his two fellows, Dr. Hobart and Mr. Palmer. Two months later he wrote again triumphantly to say: "Your favourite, little Thompson is chosen and admitted Fellow of Christ College" after "a very severe canvass."[2] In his turn the archbishop was appealed to to promote a certain Martin Sharp, whom Covell recommended "to your Grace . . . upon a new emergency wherein your assistance would highly oblige both him and me". He went on to add that Mr. Sharp was "as deserving a person as any of his standing in our University".[3]

Sharp did not find himself on such easy and familiar ground in his dealings with another College in another University, Queen's, Oxford, of which he was the official visitor.[4] In the autumn of 1704 the fellows had to elect a new Provost in the room of the late Dr. Halton. Dr. William Lancaster was chosen, and his name sent in to the archbishop with a request for confirmation. This he would willingly have given, but unfortunately Lancaster's rivals, Dr. Crosthwait, Francis Thompson and others, now informed him that the election was invalid, since the fellows had violated the statutes and perjured themselves by nominating a man who was not himself an actual fellow of the College.[5] Whereupon Sharp wrote to Dr. Lancaster proposing a postponement of the confirmation until these technical flaws had been investigated and cleared up. "If this delay be no inconvenience to you", he suggested, "I shall be glad, because . . . there will be time given for the removing some difficulties or scruples which I must confess at the present, I do

[1] L-B-S. MSS., Box 3, Bundle G. 4.
[2] L-B-S. MSS., Box 3, Bundle G. 5, Oct. 12, 1700.
[3] L-B-S. MSS., Box 3, Bundle G. 30, March 26, 1709.
[4] L-B-S. MSS., Box 3: "Commission to the Vice-Chancellor of Oxford and others for visiting Queen's College. With the return thereof, made Sept. 25th, 1704."
[5] L-B-S. MSS., Box 4, Bundle O. 51, 54, 57.

labour under as to this matter of your confirmation."[1] Lancaster, of course, defended himself and the validity of his election at great length,[2] and received the support of many friends both within and without the College, including William Pearson, the archdeacon of Nottingham, who acted as his representative with the archbishop.[3] The whole question turned on the interpretation of the word "fellow". Lancaster argued that once a fellow always a fellow, even if, as in his case, he had accepted a College living worth more than ten marks. "For a Fellow preferred", he wrote to Pearson, "has a . . . relation to the College always, and this evidently shows it, that he is bound by oath to the College when sworn at his admission to be a Fellow and that as long as he lives."[4] Crosthwait, on the other hand, strongly denied all this: "One of the rights of a Fellow of Queen's College I take to be this, that he has a right to appear as a candidate for the Provostship when there is a vacancy, which right he forgoes, when he has got a living inconsistent with a Fellowship. . . . It must of necessity signify an actual Fellow; and cannot signify a Fellow promoted."[5] Crosthwait, however, had acquired an unsavoury reputation at Oxford as a perpetual fault-finder. "He has been always looked on", wrote Dr. Charlett of University College to Sharp, "as a common blunderer, to be treated only in ridicule, not in earnest or anger."[6]

Another friend of Sharp also pressed for Lancaster's confirmation. This was Dr. John Mill. "After a great deal of trouble", he wrote, "your Grace has had by appeals and letters from Queen's College before and since their late election, I am pressed by some of that Society to do them what good offices I can with your Grace in the order to the confirmation of the person they have elected."[7]

Eventually Lancaster proved and won his case, and was confirmed. Later he became Vice-Chancellor of Oxford.

No man loved his home more ardently than Sharp; and certainly the palace of Bishopthorpe, standing with its back to the broad Ouse, set amid lovely gardens, with a fine façade, was worthy of his love. He carefully studied its architecture and history, the fruits of which research are still to be found in one of his MS. volumes:[8] "And to this day we owe much of our knowledge of the

[1] L-B-S. MSS., Box 4, Bundle T. 84.   [2] L-B-S. MSS., Box 4, Bundle O. 45, 50.
[3] L-B-S. MSS., Box 4, Bundle O. 56.   [4] L-B-S. MSS., Box 4, Bundle O. 50.
[5] L-B-S. MSS., Box 4, Bundle O. 54, 57.
[6] L-B-S. MSS., Box 4, Bundle O. 46.   [7] L-B-S. MSS., Box 4, Bundle K. 24.
[8] *Archbishop Sharp's MSS.*, vol. ii, section ii.

residence to his descriptions."[1] The archbishop was very fond of trees and shrubs,[2] especially the yew and lime. The avenue of lime trees which he planted is still the finest in the gardens.

Something yet remains to be said of the archbishop's private devotional life.

It was from his loyalist Anglican mother that he inherited his Catholicism, his love of authority, his sense of decorum in worship, and his ritualistic observances. "On many points of doctrine he was a high churchman; he entirely agreed with Nelson . . . in regretting the omission in King Edward's second Prayer Book of the prayer of oblation . . . but, with a curious intermixture of Puritan feeling, he told one of his Non-conformist correspondents that he did not much approve of musical services, and would be glad if the law would permit an alteration."[3] But it was his father's influence that shaped his private devotions, which from first to last were Protestant in tone and content. Here was the individualist seeking to make his own peace with his Maker. Like Cromwell and other great Protestants he wrestled in prayer, sometimes scaling the heights of heaven, sometimes wallowing in the depths of despair, but always struggling onward confident of God's ultimate mercy and forgiveness. He, too, after the fashion of the Puritan saints, had had his day of conversion, although naturally of a less catastrophic nature than theirs: "On Sunday, June 24, 1688, I began to apply myself more diligently to the work of religion, and spent that summer well. And I thank God most heartily since that I have never relapsed. So that at the present writing hereof, I have above three years lived with a constant sense of religion. Blessed be the name of God for ever and ever. And, O blessed God, continue thy mercy to me, and be pleased every day more and more to perfect that good work, which I hope hast begun in me."[4] June 24 became henceforth his spiritual birthday, to be observed more and more solemnly and intensely as the years went by. In 1711, for example, he recorded in his diary: "1711. June 24th. Fourth Sunday after Trinity. This being my anniversary day for my returning of thanks to God for his wonderful mercies to me, now twenty-three years ago, I resolved to spend this day as devoutly as I could. Accordingly I said my prayers most heartily alone, and with my wife, and with my

---

[1] Canon Solloway, *York Minster Historical Tracts*, No. 25.
[2] See L-B-S. MSS., Box 3, Bundle H. 39, and Bundle T. 33.
[3] Overton and Abbey, *English Church in the Eighteenth Century*, pp. 44-46.
[4] *Life of Archbishop Sharp*, vol. ii, p. 65.

family in the chapel. Afterwards, before I went to Church, I said the prayers which I use on my birthday as devoutly as I could, and devoted myself to God's service for the next years; begging humbly, that if I live another year, I may at the end of it present myself improved in every grace and virtue. I then went to the minster, where I thank God I said my prayers and received the sacrament with as devout desires as ever I did. But I was not so bright as I am sometimes. I came home in the coach alone. So that I had a conveniency of conversing with God all the way, which I did as heartily as I could. In the evening I walked in my gardens, and repeated my thanksgivings, and renewed my vows. So also I did just before I went to bed; prostrating myself upon the ground, and earnestly begging God's grace and presence the following year."[1] 1713 was the last year he observed this private festival, when his devotions were even more elaborate.

Sharp's cultivation of the spiritual life went back well beyond 1688. He had always, from his Cambridge days onwards, endeavoured to practise such exercises; but his busy early years at St. Giles' severely handicapped their performance. However, on becoming prebendary and later dean of Norwich, he took advantage of his position to spend long periods away from London, finding the peace of Norfolk more congenial for these devotional purposes.

His own troubles in 1686, together with a strong foreboding, so nearly realised, that the Anglican Church was about to endure another intensive period of persecution, deepened his desire for purely religious strength and comfort. And, as has been seen, it was amid the dangers and stresses of the fateful year 1688, when the destiny of England and of the Church hung in the balance, that his conversion occurred.

Sharp, being naturally more Catholic than Protestant, never allowed these private devotions to run away with him. They remained strictly private and personal, and were not permitted to intrude either into his public work or worship except in so far as this progress in the life of the spirit influenced his whole character for good.

Apart from his spiritual birthday, the archbishop made a point of strictly observing his natural birthday on February 16: "He kept this anniversary . . . twenty-two times after he was Archbishop." Other occasions of especially religious importance in his

[1] *Life of Archbishop Sharp*, vol. ii, p. 69.

eyes were the first and last days of the year, and July 5, the day of his consecration.

He regularly performed the daily offices of the Church; but he also set aside Sundays and Thursdays for particular acts of praise and thanksgiving, and Wednesdays and Fridays as fasts or days of humiliation. Saturday was kept as a time of preparation for the celebration of the holy communion. Sharp set great store by such preparations, which were not confined to Saturdays, but observed before any of the great festivals of the Church's year: "Dec. 24, 1707. I was most devout at home to prepare for Christmas day."[1] Like all Catholics, the archbishop attached tremendous import- ance to the celebration of the Eucharist, and rarely failed to receive it every Sunday, even if on a journey or actively engaged in other business. On the few occasions when he found it impos- sible to do so, "he endeavoured to obtain the effects and blessings of it by an eucharistical oblation of his own prayers in private."[2]

During Thursday, the other weekly period of thanksgiving, he used, if possible, when in residence at Bishopthorpe, to make his acts of praise out of doors. At one time he would walk as far as the little church of Acaster,[3] set in the midst of the fields and about a mile from the palace, repeating his prayers as he went. These were concluded in the porch of the church itself, which he termed "his oratory". Later he abandoned the practice in favour of his own garden, where he constructed a "Temple of Praise". This consisted of "a close grass-plot walk, lying north and south, and hedged on each side with yew, so thick and high, as to be com- pletely shaded at all times of the day, except noon. On the east it hath a little maze or wilderness, that grows considerably higher. The entrance into it at each end is through arches, immediately bounded by a hedge of horn-beam at one end, and a fruit wall at the other. So that from within the walk, scarce anything is to be seen but verdure and the open sky above."[4] Here Sharp spent a great many happy hours pouring "out my soul to God in an unusual ardent manner".[5]

As he grew older his Protestant fervour increased, soaring above Catholic decorum: "I never was in such transports of devotion

---

[1] *Life of Archbishop Sharp*, vol. ii, p. 76.   [2] Ibid., vol. ii, p. 77.
[3] Acaster Malbis was originally the home of the Fairfax family, who became possessed of the manor there in the early fifteenth century. This is of interest when it is remembered what a good friend Sir Thomas Fairfax proved to the Sharps at Brad- ford during and after the Civil Wars.
[4] *Life of Archbishop Sharp*, vol. ii, p. 78.   [5] Ibid., vol. ii, p. 79.

hardly as I was when I came home from the Minster, being alone in the coach. I never prayed more heartily and devoutly in my life. And I hope God will hear my prayers, which I put up for grace and mercy with tears."[1] He certainly fasted more than was good for him, and his health became affected. This was already far from robust. But the result of illness upon his deeply devotional mind was only to make him lean all the more heavily upon Divine help and guidance. And he undertook many an arduous task while in indifferent health confident that God would not suffer him to fail in its fulfilment. Bodily fitness normally plays a big part in a man's life for good or ill; and Sharp seems to have had but a poor constitution. He suffered from fever at Cambridge, and more than once during his sojourn in Kensington House he had had to return home to recover his health in his native Yorkshire air. However, when he finally settled down at St. Giles' he was fit enough. He was then thirty-one years old. At forty he had definitely thrown off his youthful maladies and possessed a clear head and a sound body. He could work exceedingly hard seven days a week at parochial tasks, and far into the night in order to prepare his sermons. Indeed, his story at this period abounded in mental and physical energy. But at fifty in the seventeenth century a man was old; and even if he had lived abstemiously and sprang from sound stock he was liable to be crippled by such common complaints as the stone or gout. Fowler, bishop of Gloucester, wrote to Sharp on April 6, 1695, bitterly lamenting his lack of good health: "The truth is that I am good for nothing, most cloudy headed and dispirited and preyed upon by that which you call the spleen and I by a worse name. I have a little wondered to find some so zealous for the resurrection of the self-same body; for I owe not so much kindness to mine, as to find myself much concerned to have that honour done it; but it may be that many souls are more beholden to their bodies, than ever mine was to my body."[2] Patrick of Ely was another bishop whose health was poor; and, of course, the lower clergy did not escape any easier. The Reverend Stephen Penton of Ripon described his ailments to his archbishop in much detail: "colick in my stomach, a torment so exquisite as to make death more desirable than Christianity will justify. Vomiting, purging gave no relief . . . my urine was more full of jaundice than saffron itself."[3]

---

[1] *Life of Archbishop Sharp*, vol. ii, p. 80.   [2] L-B-S. MSS., Box 4, Bundle O. 44.
[3] L-B-S. MSS., Box 4, Bundle M. 18, June 26, 1699.

In his later years Sharp suffered chiefly from the stone. He begged to be excused from attending Queen Anne's coronation for this reason, and it remained with him on and off for the rest of his life. The principal remedies prescribed by Dr. Radcliffe were rest and the drinking of the water at Bath. The archbishop received many letters sympathising with his condition and suggesting all sorts of amusing remedies. "I . . . take the liberty", wrote Lady Masham on July 23, 1701, "to recommend to you Bohee tea . . . I experimentally know it to be a most excellent remedy." She suggested that it should be drunk "twice a day . . . before the drinking of the tea eat 8 or 10 walnuts; which may be kept all or the greatest part of the year good; and which it is believed did contribute to the effect which followed upon drinking the tea. Mr. Locke has a great opinion of this prescription."[1]

The smallpox was a frequent visitor at Bishopthorpe. Sharp informed Crewe on February 23, 1694/5, that "the small pox has been much about us";[2] and in 1700 the archbishop himself was reported to have been one of its victims: "Sept. 12, 1700. 'Tis said the Archbishop of York is fallen ill, and his physicians fear 'twill be the small pox."[3] Twelve days later gossip declared that his life was despaired of: " Here is a report as if the Archbishop of York was dead of the small pox, but not certain."[4] Tenison wrote directly to Bishopthorpe to say that he had received news "that your Grace was dangerously ill and this day it is in one of the prints", but having just heard from Sharp he said he would now kill the rumour.[5]

Bad health was taken for granted, especially by the middle-aged. Burnet made it a matter of great self-congratulation that he got off so lightly himself.

Sharp, on the other hand, was thankful for small mercies: "I had a most prosperous journey, and God carried me through my work in every place more prosperously than I could have expected, considering in how low state of health I was when I set out."[6] Again, he asked God to forgive him because "I was this noon so peevish and disordered in my mind, that in truth I could not say my prayers in the chapel; nor could I help it, being incapable of thinking. I impute it to my dispiritedness upon taking the vomit."[7]

[1] L-B-S. MSS., Box 3, Bundle O. 10.   [2] L-B-S. MSS., Box 3, Bundle H. 16.
[3] N. Luttrell, *A Brief Relation*, vol. iv, p. 686.   [4] Ibid., vol. iv, p. 690.
[5] L-B-S. MSS., Box 4, Bundle L. 65.
[6] *Life of Archbishop Sharp*, vol. ii, p. 63.   [7] Ibid., vol. ii, p. 86.

The archbishop's other main bodily affliction was the gout, which was not improved by his taste for a glass of good wine. "I had so tired myself with walking", he recorded in his diary under the date March 31, 1711, "that I drank wine to refresh myself before my usual time, and then I sat prating with Mr. —— a good while, and I told him a great many stories of myself, for which I was afterwards grieved."[1]

Sharp had a weakness for another of the indulgences of the flesh: a pipe of tobacco. The famous Admiral George Rooke helped to supply his needs in this way:

> JERMAN ST.
> *April 20,* 1699.

"MY LORD
      Having lately had a small parcel of Parmas tobacco from Spain; I do humbly presume to send your Grace part of it, which I beg your acceptance of, and that you will please to give me leave to own myself with real respect and duty etc.

> G. ROOKE."[2]

His last illness commenced at the beginning of December 1713. He was once more advised to drink the waters at Bath; but the journey proved too much for him and he died shortly after his arrival there. It is recorded that up to the very end he insisted on having the daily family service performed in his presence, when he could murmur the responses. The words of the communion office were also frequently on his lips. He had no fear of death, for as he whispered to Mrs. Sharp "he should be happy."[3] So passed a great churchman and a saintly character on February 2, 1714, aged 69; and may we not add that all the trumpets sounded for him on the other side? He was archbishop of York for twenty-two years, longer than any of his predecessors since the Reformation. He died with Herbert's lines on his lips:

> "Ah my deare angry Lord
>   Since thou dost love, yet strike;
>   Cast down, yet help afford;
> Sure I will do the like.
> I will complain, yet praise;
> I will bewail, approve:
> And all my soure-sweet dayes
>   I will lament and love."

---

[1] *Life of Archbishop Sharp*, vol. ii, p. 88.
[2] L-B-S. MSS., Box 4, Bundle E. 39.   [3] *Life of Archbishop Sharp*, vol. ii, p. 92.

Shortly after his death a pamphlet was printed entitled "The Late Archbishop of York",[1] which contained a short account of his life, work and characteristics, couched, of course, in the most laudatory style. Nevertheless the author, a clergyman, was not far from the mark when he paid his late metropolitan this glowing tribute: "In the Government of his Diocese we of the Clergy had all the Demonstrations we could wish for, not only of Paternal Affection, but even of Brotherly Condescension. As our Superior, upon all proper occasions, he laid before us, without any unbecoming Reserve, the obligations of our sacred Function; which he might do with the greater Authority and Earnestness, because he was himself what he admonished us to be. As our Fellow-labourer in the Work of the Ministry, he behaved himself with such Meekness, Humanity, and Good-Nature, as if he had been our Equal; never looking supercilious or disdainful upon the meanest of our Order, but kindly admitted them to disclose their Grievances, and solicit his Assistance, when he was capable of doing them any Justice, or procuring them any reasonable Favour which their Circumstances required. Neither did he confine his Benevolence to those of his own Profession: but to all sorts of People, who resorted to him, either upon Business or as respectful Visitants, he was easy of Access, affable and courteous, never assuming or morose, but ever pleased and cheerful, allowing and encouraging all innocent Communications in Discourse which might render Conversation agreeable and useful."

[1] L-B-S. MSS., Box 3, Bundle H. 21.

APPENDICES TO THE CHAPTERS

APPENDIX TO CHAPTER II

SEVENTEENTH-CENTURY SHORTHAND

IT has been suggested[1] that the remarkable development of the art of shorthand in the seventeenth century was the direct result of the Reformation. The sermons of the early reformers were rarely published, and if their hearers desired to remember the chief arguments of these discourses and later use them in defence of their Protestantism against the Roman Catholics, the voluminous taking of notes became a necessity at sermon-time. This widespread practice of note-taking led inevitably to the creation of various shorthand systems and the publication of a number of textbooks by shorthand experts. The art quickly permeated the schools, where it was strongly encouraged and became very popular, and we find, for example, John Brinsley, master at Ashby-de-la-Zouch early in the seventeenth century, the author of *Ludus Literarius*, recommending his scholars to take down the entire sermon in shorthand on Sunday, and then "after sermon-time the whole was to be revised and each scholar to set 'downe the sum of every chief head, faire and distinctly in the margent over against the place'. . . . By this help, (he concluded), they will be able to understand and make a repetition of the sermon, with very little meditation, yea to do it with admiration for children."[2]

Thomas Shelton, on the other hand, wrote in 1659 that the practice of shorthand enabled preachers "to outlive themselves", and "should the revolution of times bring forth such as the Marian day (which God avert) when one small epistle of the New Testament was at the rate of five pounds . . . how precious then notes of wholesome divinity (taken in this art)."[3]

[1] Hon. Ion Keith-Falconer in his article on shorthand in the *Encyclopædia Britannica*, 9th edition.
[2] W. F. Mitchell, *English Pulpit Oratory*, p. 74.
[3] See Foster Watson, *The English Grammar Schools to 1660*, pp. 67 and 68.

APPENDIX TO CHAPTER VI

NO FEE FOR BAPTISM

"IT has always been a maxim of ecclesiastical law that no sacrament of the church shall be denied to anyone upon the account of
any sum of money, though it has been said that immemorial
custom may in certain special cases warrant the demand for a fee
after the sacrament has been performed. In England, however,
the exception to the general law with respect to baptism appears
never to have been admitted."[1] Mr. Leech's "profits of the
christenings" were therefore in all probability purely voluntary
offerings made to the officiating minister by the grateful parents
and other members or friends of the family.

APPENDIX TO CHAPTER VII

SECRETARIES OF STATE

"THERE were two Secretaries, known from their respective connection with the management of foreign affairs as the Secretaries
for the Northern and Southern Departments. The Secretary for
the Northern Department was in charge of relations with the
Empire, the United Provinces, Russia, Poland, and the Scandi-
navian countries; the Secretary for the Southern Department was
in charge of relations with the other European countries and also
of Irish and Colonial business in so far as it was a matter of
Secretarial concern. . . . Both Secretaries dealt with English
domestic business indifferently. Prior to 1706 the rule, to which,
however, there were occasional exceptions, was that the senior
Secretary held the Southern Department, which was regarded as
the more important, and the junior Secretary the Northern Department."[2] Harley was the Southern Secretary, Hedges the
Northern, in 1704.

[1] Sir Robert Phillimore, *The Ecclesiastical Law of the Church of England*, vol. i, p. 664,
1873.
[2] M. A. Thomson, *A Constitutional History of England*, vol. iv, pp. 438-439.

APPENDIX TO CHAPTER VIII

ARCHBISHOP SHARP AND THE OCCASIONAL CONFORMITY BILLS

THE Occasional Conformity bills, which caused such heartburn-ings among both whigs and tories in Queen Anne's reign and were so dear to the soul of Lord Nottingham, seemed equally important to the archbishop. Every time the bill appeared in the House of Lords he voted and spoke on its behalf to the chagrin of many of the whig bishops, notably Burnet. For Sharp strongly approved[1] of this attempt to prevent Dissenters obtaining office under the crown or in the corporations by means of occasionally receiving the sacrament at their parish church and so evading the Test Act.[2]

On the other hand, when the high tory Commons, in their exasperation at its repeated rejection by the Lords, attempted to "tack" this bill to the land tax, the main financial prop of the war effort, convinced that the whigs and moderate tories dared not throw out the latter, Sharp, in the interests of queen and country, which he put above party and even his own personal convic-tions, helped, as has already been seen, to secure the defeat of the "tack" in the House of Commons. By so doing he remained true to his principles. Neither can it be said that he had previously behaved inconsistently in allowing Baxter to come to Holy Com-munion at St. Giles' or by encouraging the dissenting Ralph Thoresby "to receive the Sacrament monthly, at his parish Church".[3] For, as his sermons and other writings go to prove, the archbishop was at any rate for the greater part of his life an ardent believer in the theory that the mass of the Dissenters could yet be persuaded to rejoin the National Church either by argu-

---

[1] *Life of Archbishop Sharp*, vol. i, p. 367.
[2] The preamble to the Occasional Conformity bill of 1702/3 reads as follows: "Whereas the laws do provide that every person to be admitted into any office or em-ployment should be conformable to the Church, as it is by law established, by enact-ing, that every such person, so to be admitted, should receive the Sacrament of the Lord's Supper, according to the rites and usage of the Church of England; Yet several persons dissenting from the Church . . . do joyn with the Members thereof in receiving the Sacrament of the Lord's Supper, to qualify themselves to have and enjoy such offices and employments, and do afterwards resort to Conventicles or Meetings for the exercise of religion in other manner than according to the Liturgy and Practice of the Church of England:" G. M. Trevelyan, *Select Documents of Queen Anne's Reign*, pp. 27 and 28.
[3] R. Thoresby, *Letters o ¹Eminent Men*, vol. i, p. 324.

ment or example. And what finer example could be found than that some of the very best of their number attended, if only occasionally, Anglican services? Sharp had no objection to occasional conformists as such; what caused him acute anxiety was the fact that in so many cases the sacrament had been used by an unrepentant schismatic for the purpose of worldly advancement, while the conscientious Anglican parson was debarred from repelling him "from the communion, as by the rubric they were empowered to do".[1] In other words, by advising Thoresby to communicate he thereby eventually won a convert to Anglicanism; but if he had opposed the Occasional Conformity bills he would merely have supported the Dissenters' demand for office.

APPENDIX TO CHAPTER X

BRIEFS

In the seventeenth century it was unusual to take collections during the church services. Instead, when money was needed for charitable or other purposes, a letter known as a "brief" would be issued from the crown or bishop and ordered to be read by the clergy at service time to their assembled flocks, urging them to subscribe. This practice, of course, was copied from the Roman Church, but with the difference that the crown took the place of the Pope. The clergy had also to act as collectors, handing over the total contributions from their parishes to the diocesan, who in the case of a crown-brief despatched the full amount raised by his diocese to the Privy Council. The crown, however, only issued briefs for charitable appeals on a nation-wide scale in such instances as those of the Vaudois, French refugees and the Algerian slaves. The bishops were concerned with the smaller but much more numerous local needs. An example of the latter is to be found in the brief which was published in York for procuring subscriptions towards the rebuilding of St. Mary Southwell in 1711.

[1] *Life of Archbishop Sharp*, vol. i, p. 368.

APPENDIX TO CHAPTER XI
ARCHBISHOP SHARP'S DOMESTIC CHAPLAINS

WHEN Sharp succeeded to the archbishopric of York in 1691 he took over Lamplugh's two chaplains, Dr. Palmer and Mr. Pearson, while Heneage Dering became his private secretary. "1691. This summer Dr. Sharp, dean of Canterbury, was promoted to the see of York," wrote Dering in his autobiography. "He made me his secretary."[1]

Charles Palmer, D.D., a son of Sir William Palmer of the Hill, Bedfordshire, was also canon residentiary and prebendary of Grindal. A few years after Sharp's enthronement, however, he married a widow named Wickham and resigned his chaplaincy; for it seems to have been a recognised custom at Bishopthorpe that the post of domestic chaplain was vacated by marriage. His place was filled by Edmund Wickens, the tutor of John Sharp the younger and a kinsman of the bishop of Worcester.[2] William Pearson, Nicolson's cousin, likewise married in 1696,[3] when Samuel Terrick was nominated in his stead. Two more years elapsed; and then, as Dering recorded, "Mr. Wickens married Mrs. Dorothy Richardson, niece to the Archbishop . . . the Archbishop had got for him the rectory of Kirbythore, in Westmoreland, from the Earl of Thanet. Her brother, Mr. Richardson, succeeded as chaplain."[4] Terrick went next, after he had been married to Mrs. Ann Arlish of Nedlington "by his Grace in the chapel, on Sunday the 12th day of November 1699".[5] Dering himself took the post, being ordained deacon in Bishopthorpe chapel on February 9, 1701, and priest the following July. He had a long innings; for despite his rapid promotions, culminating in the deanery of Ripon in 1711, he retained his chaplaincy until his own marriage to the archbishop's daughter Anne in Bishopthorpe chapel during January 1712. Then, finally, he retired. "At Michaelmas", he remarked, "I quitted the secretary's place to Mr. Richardson; and Mr. Lamplugh came down chaplain in my room, when the Archbishop returned in the summer to Bishopthorpe."[6] The next

---

[1] H. Dering, *Autobiographical Memoranda* (Surtees Society, vol. 65), p. 338.
[2] L-B-S. MSS., Box 4, Bundle L. 96.
[3] Miss Watkinson, daughter of the chancellor of York.
[4] H. Dering, *Autobiographical Memoranda*, p. 340.
[5] *Bishopthorpe Register*.
[6] H. Dering, *Autobiographical Memoranda*, p. 344.

year John Richardson became precentor of York and a residentiary, and "Mr. Marsden succeeded him as chaplain". Marsden and Lamplugh, a grandson of Sharp's predecessor, appear to have been in office at the time of the archbishop's death. Robert Marsden, it is interesting to note, made his returns to Archbishop Herring in 1743 as rector of Rempstone, Bingham, to which living he had been instituted in 1702.[1]

[1] *Archbishop Herring's Visitation Returns*, vol. iv, p. 119.

GENERAL APPENDICES

APPENDIX A

THE TORRE MSS.

[On page 137, vol. ii, of the *Life of Archbishop John Sharp*, edited by Thomas Newcome, is a somewhat lengthy footnote dealing with the Torre MSS. This footnote has taken the place of a section of the original MS. *Life* now in possession of Lt.-Col. A. B. Lloyd-Baker, which for some obscure reason was omitted from the published text. The omission and subsequent insertion of the footnote were apparently the work of the author, Archdeacon Sharp, and not of the editor.

Here is the original text in full, sandwiched in between the sentences "These were left at his death by his executors to the use of his successors" (page 137) and "Then, as to the Archbishop's other enquiry" (page 138).]

"He was exceedingly assisted in all these collections, but more especially in the notitia last mentioned, by those large and curious MSS. volumes upon the same subjects which were wrote by that great and indefatigable antiquary Mr. James Torr, now in the possession of the Dean and Chapter of York by the gift likewise of the Archbishop's executors.

"Extraordinary use hath been since made of these Books of Mr. Torr's, and gratefully acknowledged, by the learned and ingenious author of the *History and Antiquities of York City, and Cathedral Church*. Fol. published An. 1736, who hath also in his Preface done that justice to Mr. Torr's memory which is very well deserved: And which otherwise would have been attempted here, tho' it could not have been so effectually done as it now is by his hand. But as there are two points in his said Preface (and both in the same paragraph) that may yet receive a little illustration from a circumstance or two that he could not come to the knowledge of, a few words upon each, will be seasonably spent in this place, especially as they will be found to relate as much to the Archbishop as to Mr. Torr.

"The first is his remark upon the prodigious industry and application of that laborious Gentleman, when he came to methodise his material for the West riding and to transcribe them did within the space of four months and half (tho' at different times and as it were at two heats) run thro' 1200 columns in Fol. in a small close hand: 'He began to transcribe for the former part of the volume Sept. 4, 1691 and finished it Oct. 27 the same year. And for the latter on March 1691 and completed it June 9, 1692. This volume contains no less than one thousand two hundred fifty five columns in folio mostly close writ and in a very small but legible hand.' Mr. Drake's Preface.

"This may not easily be paralleled: yet it is surprising what pains some persons will take in this particular kind of work. The Archbishop himself was an instance of this who in the space of two months went thro' his epitome or extracts of this great vol. of Mr. Torr's and likewise thro' another Archdeaconry; which make part of his notitia of the Diocese in 4 volumes above mentioned: Diary Feb. 6 1694. 'I brought home with me (viz. from York) Mr. Torr's book of the York and Westriding livings.' April 12, 1695 . . . 'My time has been altogether (except writing letters and doing necessary business) taken up in the making my notitia of the Parishes in my Diocese. And just in the space of two months viz. between Feb. 6 and April 6 I have gone through the Archdeaconries of Ebor and Cleveland, except the synopsis or preface to the three Deaneries of Cleveland which I did this week.'

"And in less than 2 more he went in the same manner thro' the other 2 Archdeaconries and the Peculiars. So that in less than 4 months time (tho' not computed altogether) he made an abstract of all Mr. Torr's 4 volumes as appears by memorandums of his own: Diary. Aug. 3 1695 'Most of my work hath been my going on with my Notitia of the livings of this diocese which I have now finished and bound up in four volumes. In less than four months time I finished my transcriptions out of Mr. Torr's four books viz. the 4 Archdeaconries and the Peculiars. But my completing my catalogues of the incumbents and the times of their institutions and such other finishing work took up some weeks besides etc.'

"This may serve not only to support the credit of what is related of Mr. Torr's almost incredible assiduity, but to stand for a proof or specimen of the Archbishop's; who could abide by and dispatch a work of this nature and extent amidst the interruptions of business and company and other daily and unavoidable intrenchments upon his time, to which persons of more private lives and characters are not subject. Indeed they only who have both seen his books and Mr. Torr's can make any just judgement of the pains taken by each of them in digesting and copying out what they did in so short a time.

"The other remark of the author of the Antiquities, which will admit of a little more light thrown upon it (for he owns himself there is a difficulty in it which is beyond his solution) is that which he makes upon the intrinsick value of Mr. Torr's Collections: 'This almost invaluable Treasure was given to the Dean and Chapters Library by the Executors to the last will of the late Archbishop Sharp. No doubt the worthy sons of that very eminent Prelate imagined they had an unquestionable right to make this present. I shall not enter further into this affair, which by the good Archbishop's death, and other persons concerned is now rendered inscrutable. Yet this I may venture to say that there never was a *quantum meruit* paid to the author's Relict or his heir for them.' Pref. to Ant. of York.

"He makes some doubt whether the Archbishop's executors (tho' they made no doubt of it themselves) had really a right to dispose of them as they did, on a supposition that there never was a *quantum meruit* paid for them either to Mr. Torr's widow or heir.

"What is a proper consideration for such valuable things, is not easy to say. If Antiquaries only were to be the judges (and they ought to be the best judges too) such simple collections would be deemed like jewells of extraordinary size unratable. Or supposing the *quantum meruit* in this case easily determinable, yet it is impossible to judge, as there are no *data* in this account to proceed upon, how far what was paid for them fell short of their just price upon estimation. And when neither of the extremes or terms of the question, necessary to the understanding it or stating it are given, no wonder, if the truth and reasonableness of this remark be rendered altogether as inscrutable as the Executors' right to Mr. Torr's Mss. Tho' no doubt the worthy Author of it imagined (like them) that he had an unquestionable right to make it.

"If the affair be so perplexed that nothing can now with any certainty be made out—All must depend upon conjectures. And every one is equally free to make them. The ingenious Author of the Preface has made his; to which is allowed its *quantum meruit*. But there is still room left for many more as that there might be more done by the Archbishop for the widow or her friends by way of compensation for these books than the bare payment of money. If not; yet that the sum given, whatever it was, might be more than the widow had any prospect or hopes of getting from any other hand. And it might also be more than the Archbishop himself, (tho' he judged it not a full equivalent) would have given at that time to any other Proprietor of them, except himself: He having already made all the use of them that he could propose.

"If it be said that he should not have set a less value upon them with regard to the widow's property in them on account of his having extracted their quintescence himself, let it also be remembered that he himself might claim the chief property in all the materials of them. They were the quintescence of his registers and all the most valuable records to be found in his archives and offices. To which without his and his predecessors special favour Mr. Torr could never have had access. And after they had freely permitted this most industrious bee to suck and drain their choicest flowers, he and his successors might claim some right to partake of the honey. Mr. Torr himself was so sensible of this, that as soon as his Books were finished—This was publicly in the Vestry of York Minster Nov. 21, 1694, on which day the Archbishop took the vol. relating to the Archbishops home with him. Feb. 6 following he took the Vol. relating to the York and West-Riding livings. And so the remaining volumes in their order. This appears from his Diary—he laid them before the Archbishop and allowed him the perusal and use of them *ad libitum*. An use he did make a very considerable one; in a little time, and with as little inconvenience to Mr. Torr as was possible. Taking but one vol. at a time, and returning the last of them within a few months. If he was not bound to pay for this loan then, neither was he bound to pay the widow for it, when the books were not in any respect of that consequence to himself as they would have been, had not Mr. Torr in gratitude paid this respect to him and his see.

"However that the satisfaction made to the widow whether by purchase, or otherwise, was sufficient, accepted as an equivalent, and thankfully acknowledged, one may not only conjecture but venture to say, from hence, that it is neither to be conceived that the Archbishop should be tempted to strain a point, in which either his honour or generosity were concerned for the sake of what was of so little consequence to himself, or that Mrs. Torr and her son should never complain to him in his life-time of a hard bargain if such had been made, or upon any such complaint made, or even dissatisfaction shewn by them, he should not make them proper amends some way or other before his death.

"It is true Mr. Torr, the son, soon after the Archbishop's decease, put in his claim to these books, yet very modestly and civilly, as one that rather presumed a right than asserted it. All the opportunities that he could have desired in making out his claim would have been given him by the Executors, if they had not divested themselves of a property in the books by presenting them or promising them to the Church of York before he signified his pretensions, however they might be grounded. So that they could give him no other satisfaction or answer than that they found them in the Archbishop's possession, in which they had remained several years (above 13) without any demand upon them, and had been purchased, as they were informed of his mother. That therefore they had made no question of their right to dispose of them as they pleased, which having already done they were no longer interested in them; and if he could make out a better right to them than the Church of York had thro' their gift, he had the remedy in his own hands. Thus the matter stood, and here it ended. Nor did the executors at that time either know any more of this affair, or make any further enquiry into it; till lately, and after it appeared that their right to dispose of the books was a little questioned, and yet the truth of the matter represented as inscrutable, extraordinary pains were taken to gather up what could be learned from the Archbishop's own Diary and papers about it. And from this examination it now appears, that the very worthy Mr. Francis Drake Vicar of Pontefract in whose neighbourhood at Syndal Mr. James Torr died in July 1699 came within less than three months after that gentleman's decease to the Archbishop with a generous offer from the widow of her husband's Mss as a present. But the Archbishop after proper acknowledgements made of her kind intentions and obliging proffer, told Mr. Drake it would not be right in him to accept them *gratis*. But if she would likewise accept of a present from him, which he named, and could not dispose of them to more advantage, (For he would not be an hindrance to her making the best of them) he would on this condition accept them from her.

"Receiving no answer to this overture in the time he expected it, he wrote the following letter to Mr. Drake as taken from the copy of it that was made by his secretary and endorsed with his own hand 'My letter to Mr. Drake about Mr. Torr's MSS.'[1]

---

[1] This letter is published in the *Life of Archbishop Sharp*, vol. ii, Appendix I, p. 109, ed. by T. Newcome.

BISHOPTHORPE
Oct. 28, 1699.

"SIR—Having heard no more from you about Mr. Torr's manuscripts and being in a little time for a journey to London I give you the trouble of this to desire you to let me know how that affair stands viz. whether Mrs. Torr continues the same kind intentions towards me that you acquainted me she had when you was last at Bishopthorpe, and if so whether I may send for the books before I go to London. I told you then and I beg of you to tell her that I take myself extremely obliged to her for the kind offer she made by you; and as I do return my hearty thanks so I shall be glad of all opportunities whereby I may express these thanks in real services. But how generous soever her offer was I told you I thought it did not become me to accept it without some sort of acknowledgement; such a one at least as might be equivalent to what she might have made of the books in my judgement if she had sold them. And therefore I desired and do desire that she would accept of a present of 20 guineas from me, which I will send when you order me to send for the books. I do by no means propose this sum as a just price for them, for I do not intend to purchase them; but that Mrs. Torr may be no loser by her kindness to me. And if she can make greater advantage of them, I think I ought not to suffer her respects for me to be her hindrance.

"I must ever own my obligations to good Mr. Torr, whose death I was extremely sorry for, and whose memory shall be always dear to me, which I shall endeavour to shew by a careful preserving of his collections if they come into my hands. I beg my humble service to Mrs. Torr, to whom I wish all comfort and happiness. Accept of the same service and good wishes to yourself and Mrs. Drake, and be pleased to give me an answer to this as soon as you can.

I am Sir
Your affectionate friend and brother
JO. EBOR.

"That Mrs. Torr did upon this make use of the liberty the Archbishop gave her of trying whether she would make more of the books by sale, or in any other way of disposing of them, is highly probable: because it was very near a twelve month before she sent them to him, and when they came he was something better than his word; for instead of 20 he gave her 25 guineas for them: Diary Oct. 6, 1700. 'This day likewise came Mr. Torr's books for which I gave 25 guineas. And a guinea to the minister that came along with Mr. Lister to bring them, and 5s to the servant.' At the foot of the copy of the letter above mentioned he likewise made this entry: 'Memorandum. I gave 25 guineas.'

"Now if this sum was really deficient, or the widow was not well used in this matter, Mr. Drake himself will seem as much, if not more, concerned in it than the Archbishop, as acting for her, and being instrumental in their disposal after this manner. He might not indeed have those high notions of their value, which his worthy son has since entertained from the experience of their usefulness to him in his antiquities. But he might perhaps have a stronger sense upon his mind of the fitness and reasonableness that they should be rather in the custody and possession of the Archbishop, than in any other hand. And he did not think it wrong that they should be disposed of, even without any consideration, in so proper a way. This was probably his sentiment, and a just one too. It is the same that afterwards moved the Archbishop's Executors to deposit these books (as a donation) in the Church of York, after they had lodged their father's abstract or epitome of them in the hands of his successor.

"If the mention of these several circumstances of which the Author of the Antiquities plainly appears not to have been apprised, hath set the whole affair on a more plausible footing than he left it, none perhaps will be more ready than himself to acknowledge it. For he hath expressed so much respect both for the Archbishop and his executors in his short remonstrance of an insufficient compensation to Mr. Torr's family, that it cannot be doubted he would be pleased to see them stand clear of all blame in this matter; and willing to express his veneration for Mr. Torr's labours in a way something less exceptionable, viz. by only congratulating the Dean and Chapter of York upon their coming so easily and fortunately into the possession of what he justly styles an almost invaluable treasure."

APPENDIX B

SELECTED DOCUMENTS FROM THE ARCHBISHOP'S MSS.

[THE Abjuration Oath caused much heart-searching among high-churchmen. The Earl of Nottingham, as the two following letters show, felt such conscientious scruples, scruples which none the less he was able with Sharp's help to satisfy.]

Jan. 10, 1701/2.

"MY LORD,

Your Grace's letter of the 7th is so extremely obliging that I should be most unworthy of your favour if I should press anything that is in the least inconvenient to your own affairs. I must own, that how dreadful soever the prospect of our affairs is to me, that particular reason which made me wish for your Grace's company was the Oath of Abjuration with which we were threatened and is now before us and will be read a second time on Monday before this can reach you; how this is consistent with the belief of God's Providence or how they, who formerly trembled at it can now be advocates for it I can't imagine nor can I reconcile so very different sentiments; I know Toland has lately published a book wherein this is recommended, but I am sure I am not of his Church in my faith and I think I ought not to be so neither in my practice. In so great a matter I do not wish too indulgent a confessor, and I am sure you are a faithful one; But since I can't have your advice, the safest side in conscience is to refuse it and if your Grace should not approve my judgment by your own practice at least your charity would not impute my error to an ill cause, and either way I should be screened from censure.

I must tell you that this Oath is to be voluntary but however it must be tendered to all members of both houses who will be summoned to attend for that purpose, perhaps your Grace will think it more decent to prevent that summons, and I can assure you there are many who daily inquire after you and very impatiently expect you, but I must forbear all importunity on my part, that you may not repent your promise of gratifying me in this request. Your pardon and Blessing are humbly begged by your Grace's most obedient and most faithful

and humble servant
NOTTINGHAM."

BURLEY,
April 7th, 1702.

"MY LORD,

If the Postmaster of Stamford had not kept your Grace's letter of March 31st two or three days longer than he ought, I should sooner have returned my humble thanks to your Grace for it, however I hope this will reach Bishopthorpe before you leave it, that my wife may have the honour of seeing your Grace here, tho' I shall be gone to London, towards which place I set out tomorrow: where I must determine my scruples before I can have the happiness of discoursing with your Grace about them, which I extremely desired: for tho' your Grace has truly stated both, of which the first is much the easiest Resolved, and tho' your Grace Reasons very justly upon the Second, yet I apprehend the argument is founded upon a principle, which I can't entirely come up to, and therefore, since it is the duty of a subject actively to obey, as far as is consistent with his own conscience, I have been endeavouring to draw the conclusion from my own premises, such principles I mean as I have been bred up in tho' of late they have been much out of fashion, that I might Reconcile my practice to my faith, tho' there are some men will never believe that any thing I do is a good evidence of it. What I have said upon this subject, I think is just and true but it would have been a great satisfaction to me to have had such an assurance of it as your Grace's approbation; however when I wait on your Grace in London, I will beg your leave to lay my thoughts before you, that if I have argued aright I may be confirmed by you in my opinion. Or, if amiss I may correct my error which, as it shall be short, so I hope, it will not be a very great fault, since I have examined the matter as well as I could, and consulted such others too as I could meet with and speak to with confidence.

I am extremely grieved to hear your Grace has been so long indisposed. I believe that gentle exercise and motion of a coach may be rather an advantage than prejudice to your health, which I heartily wish may be so reestablished as that your life may be as easy to yourself as it will be useful to our Church. I humbly beg your Blessing upon

Your Grace's most obedient humble servant
NOTTINGHAM."

[In the following letter Whiston seeks to secure the support of the two archbishops for his heretical views on the Trinity. Sharp's reply is to be found in the *Life of Archbishop Sharp*, vol. ii, Appendix I, p. 135, where he says: "I do by no means approve of the design which you tell me in your letter you are upon."

CAMBRIDGE,
July 17, 1708.

"MAY IT PLEASE YOUR GRACE,

Having been lately examining, with all the care, Application and Impartiality I could, the *original doctrines* of Christianity, concerning the Everblessed *Trinity*, and the *Incarnation* of our Lord and Saviour, both in the New Testament, and in the most primitive antiquity; and having in that Enquiry observed, as tis very easy to do, that the opinions of the *two*, and almost *three first Centuries* were very different from those of the *fourth* and following ones, I think it my duty to propose the Consideration and Examination of these matters to the *Christian World*; but more especially to the *Protestant Churches*: Because they have never yet been examined in any public manner, either at, or since the *Reformation*: and because the common doctrines appear all along to have been settled and established by the *See of Rome*, and thence to have been propagated to the rest of the Christian World. It seems to me plain that the *Scripture*, the *Apostolical Fathers*, and, in the main, the *second Century* do agree in the explication of these sacred doctrines: Nay, even the body of the Christian Church appears to have been of the same Opinions so low as the *Council of Antioch* itself, in the latter part of the *third Century*: abating only one or two particular persons, contradicting themselves, and such parts of the Church as were under the influence of the *Bishops of Rome*; who ever since the days of *Pope Victor* have taken upon them to be the Arbitrators of these and other controversies among Christians. I hope your Grace will believe that I am *honest* and *sincere* in my *Intentions*; and that if I were not fully convinced of the great *importance* of what I have to propose I would not trouble your Grace or the world in the matter. I am sure I have no difficulty upon me in believing *mysteries*, whenever I find them revealed by God: Nor have I the least design to detract from the great Dignity of, or from the Divine Worship due to the *Son of God* and the *Blessed Spirit*: On whose *Redemption* and *Sanctification* all my own hopes of salvation are entirely grounded. But I cannot easily believe that the doctrine of the *fourth* and following Centuries, I mean that which at length prevailed in them, can be purer than that of the *two first*; that *Vigilius Tapsensis, Athanasius*, or Councils themselves can make *Articles of Faith*; or that their *late* authorities can excuse me or any honest Christian from examining and embracing the *original Faith which was once delivered to the Saints,* and received in the *first ages* of the Gospel. As to the most proper *method* of proposing these matters to the public, I shall have the greatest deference for your Grace's judgement and directions, and those of my Lord Archbishop of Canterbury; who, as the principal guides of this Church, have a just right to be consulted in matters of this nature and moment. For my own part I not only *believe* but *know* that, for the main, what I affirm to be the ancient doctrine is so, having examined all the certainly genuine and most ancient books and fragments hitherto published. I have also a pretty complete *Collection of the Testimonies* by me, and a Short *Chronological Account* by what steps the Primitive Faith was gradually either altered or improved, till it came to the model of the Creed of *Vigilius Tapsensis,* the *Standard of modern Orthodoxy* in these matters. So that I think myself in some measure prepared to give an authentic account of the Faith of the *two first Centuries.* Nor do I find any plain Testimonies to be alledged on the other side. But then, because in some particular I may easily have made mistakes or omissions; because, as a peaceable member of this church, I ought to consult its unity and quiet as much as possible; and because, if it may be, I would have this matter calmly and fairly debated and settled by the learned, before it comes into the hands of the Ignorant; upon all these accounts I humbly propose it to your Grace's consideration what way I should take in the particular management of this matter. My own thoughts are that it might be convenient to have some copies transcribed, or rather a few printed for the use of the Learned. But if any other method shall be proposed, which may better attain the same ends, I shall very readily comply with it. I am aware that several political or prudential considerations may be alledged against either the doing this *at all* or at least the doing it *now.* But then, if the sacred truths of God must be always suppressed, and dangerous corruptions never enquired into, till the *Politicians* of the world should say it were a *proper time* to examine and correct them, I doubt it would be long enough ere such examination and correction could be expected in any case. I think myself plainly obliged in point of *duty* to communicate my collections to the Public Consideration; and therefore from this *Resolution* in general no worldly motives whatever, by the blessing of God, shall dissuade me. But as to the particular Propositions themselves when they are sent your Grace will please to look upon them as a somewhat hasty Account I do not say of *mine own* Opinions, for they are of small consideration but of the Opinions of the *two first Centuries of the Church of Christ*, ready for all well grounded alterations, corrections, and improvements; if my own further enquiries, or the suggestions of the Learned shall make any of them necessary hereafter.

I most humbly crave your Grace's pardon for the great freedom and boldness of this address; with the continuance of the candid and favourable opinion of me, my intentions, and labours which hitherto your Grace has been pleased to afford to

Your obliged and most obedient Servant
WILL: WHISTON.

(I have sent the same letter to the Archbishop of Canterbury.)"

THE FUNERAL EXPENSES OF ARCHBISHOP SHARP

	£	s.	d.
Sending to York	0	12	0
To the blue coat men at York	0	5	0
To the poor at Bishopthorpe	2	0	0
To Dr. Chambers	2	3	0
Mourning	1	1	6
Mrs. Smal's mourning	7	14	10
Mrs. Musgrave's bill for Coach and Horses	9	10	0
Scutcheons at York	12	16	0
Fees at the Minster	6	11	0
To Mrs. Townley's Coachman	0	10	0
Rosemary	0	5	0
Brook's bill for a Coach	4	0	0
Mr. Jackson at Ripon for cloth	1	8	3½
Scutcheons at Ripon	3	12	0
Making clothes	0	7	0
	52	15	7½
Dr. Chambers' bill	1	9	6
Smithson for the Coffin	3	0	0
	57	5	1½

[The following letter from Bishop Crewe of Durham conveys the sense of uneasiness in the North, an uneasiness due both to fears of Scotland and France, in the summer of 1707. There is also

an interesting reference to Trelawny's expectation of the bishopric of Winchester.]

DURHAM CASTLE
May 23rd, 1707.

"MY LORD,

The great trouble I gave your Grace last year in my
Journey southward, made me forbear a repetition of it in my
return this summer; and therefore this waits upon your Grace
with an earnest enquiry after your health, as well as with hearty
wishes for its long continuance. The unexpected turn of affairs
abroad, together with the surprising insults upon our coasts at
home, makes a great drawback from rejoicings here: Thus the
Lord gives, and the Lord takes away, and we must all patiently
submit to his holy will and pleasure. However we are very quiet
in this place; and free from the wonted noisiness of Scottish com-
minations; only some trading persons I doubt, have adventured
too far upon prohibited goods, and are so deeply immersed in the
applauded French wines, that they are puzzled how to import
their advantageous bargains into these southern parts of Great
Britain for want of a safe land convoy. The Reverend and cautious
Judges have skilfully avoided giving their opinions in this matter,
but when this point comes into Westminster Hall, I believe a very
indifferent lawyer may easily conjecture which way the determination will go. But it is not so easy to guess who shall succeed
in Winchester notwithstanding the most ensured expectations a
certain brother had. If there should be a retraction of this, the
storm, where-ever it falls, will be very violent and furious. The less
dependence any man has upon persons and things in this world,
and the more he puts his trust and confidence in Almighty God,
the happier will his condition be here as well as here after, which
is the highest of all preferments.

Your Grace will pardon this interruption, and believe me, etc.

N. DURESME, CREWE."

[The archbishop of York frequently found himself a court of
appeal from the decisions, omissions or demands of his suffragans.
It has already been seen how Atterbury and Todd had invoked
his aid against the bishop of Carlisle. Durham and Chester, as
well as Carlisle, found members of their flock writing to York
about their reputed iniquities. Stratford wrote to Sharp, who had

22

sent him back one such complaint: "I shall make the best use I can of the letter your Grace sent enclosed; the author of it (I doubt not) means well, but is a man of a very unhappy restless temper, ever complaining; so that if your Grace should give him encouragement, you will be frequently troubled with his letters": L-B-S. MSS., Box 4, Bundle L. 81, Jan. 22, 1700.

The following memorial against Crewe was sent to the archbishop anonymously in the summer of 1703. Again he immediately communicated its contents to the bishop, who promised to investigate the alleged grievances: L-B-S. MSS., Box 4, Bundle L. 103.]

"The following memorial is humbly offered to your Grace's consideration by your dutiful unknown humble servant, A. H. an inhabitant of the County Palatine of Durham.

1. No minister of Hunstenworth, tho' the Bishop of Durham has a considerable estate in that parish in right of his lady.
2. The south wall of Darlington Churchyard is down to the ground, which ought to be repaired by the Bishop of Durham.
3. A Quaker licensed by the Bishop to teach school in Whitbourne Church.
4. The chancells of Aukland, Barnard Castle, Gainford, Whorlton and Meddomley are all in a ruinous condition."

APPENDIX C

A BRIEF INVENTORY OF THE LETTERS AND PAPERS IN THE MUNIMENT ROOM AT HARDWICKE COURT, GLOUCESTER, THE PROPERTY OF LT.-COL. A. B. LLOYD-BAKER

BESIDES the MSS. relating specifically to Archbishop Sharp there is much other material at Hardwicke Court; in particular the papers of Bishop Lloyd of Worcester, a contemporary of the archbishop, and those of his son and grandson, Thomas and Granville Sharp.

The boxes of MSS. may roughly be classified as follows:

Larger Boxes

Boxes Nos. 1 and 2	...	...	Granville Sharp.
Boxes Nos. 3 and 4	...	...	Archbishop Sharp.
Box No. 3	...	...	Thomas Sharp.
Box No. 21	...	...	Granville Sharp.
Box No. 22	...	...	Lloyd Papers (family papers).
Box No. 23	...	...	Ditto.
Box No. 27	...	...	Bishop Lloyd.
Box No. 28	...	...	Miscellaneous.
Box No. 30	...	...	Pedigrees and papers of the Lloyd and Baker families and Bishop Lloyd MSS.

Smaller Boxes (Lower Muniment)

Box No. I	...	...	Miscellaneous.
Box No. II	...	...	Manuscripts of Granville Sharp.

It will be noted that the archbishop and his son share a box. Nor is this the only source of confusion, since some of the former's MSS. are also to be found in Box No. 2, notably the MS. *Life*; while Bundle W in Box No. 4 consists almost entirely of petitions addressed to Bishop Lloyd as Lord Almoner.

A full catalogue of all these muniments would require a complete book in itself; so here, in the limited space at my disposal, I propose simply to outline, briefly and generally, the contents of Boxes Nos. 3 and 4.

My method is as follows:

In the case of the smaller bundles, where the papers are mostly homogeneous, a general heading must suffice; in that of the larger, which usually contain letters, the number of items will be given, the initial letter of the majority of the correspondents (surnames beginning with a similar letter often appear to be grouped together), and the names of the more important of them. As a general rule it can be assumed, where it is not otherwise stated, that the vast mass of this correspondence is the product of the parochial clergy of the archdiocese of York, and it is addressed to the archbishop.

Box No. 3

1. Bundle of letters relating to the Societies for the Reformation of Manners.
2. Papers relating to the revenue of the Archbishopric of York.
3. Sermon of Mr. Cockburn, January 25, 1712.
4. Commission for the Visitation of Queen's College, Oxford, with the Return, September 25, 1704.
5. Articles relating to Ireland, Scotland, foreign trade, and papers of the Privy Council.
6. Correspondence between Archbishop Sharp and Bishop Lloyd.

Bundle A: Papers of Thomas Sharp.

Bundle B: 59 items; initial F; papers of Thomas Sharp; Finch family; constitutions for the bishopric of Man; case of Frankland, archbishop of Dublin and bishop of Killaloe; memorial to Duke of Ormonde; anecdote of Archbishop Sharp.

Bundle C: 7 items; state of the Savoy Hospital, letters of congratulation from Christ's College and University (Cambridge) on the nomination of Sharp to the archbishopric.

Bundle D: 44 items; initial W; Christopher Wyvil (dean of Ripon), Wake.

Bundle E: 27 items; initial W; Cousin Weddell, Wyvil.

Bundle F: 31 items; initial T; Ralph Thoresby, Hugh Todd.

Bundle G: 55 items; initial C; John Covell, Master of Christ's College, John Chamberlayne, Dr. Cockburn, Knightley Chetwood.

Bundle H: 65 items; initial K; Sir John Kay, Tillotson, Sharp to bishop of Durham, paper *re* Lord Almoner, memorial on the Episcopal clergy of Scotland, letter and declaration on the subject of lay baptism, Address of Thanks to the Queen for the Bounty.

Bundle K: 35 items; papers of Thomas Sharp; John Sharp junior to Heneage Dering.

Bundle L: 4 items; Archbishop Sharp to Heneage Dering *re* death of Elizabeth Sharp, will and funeral expenses of the archbishop.

Bundle M: 24 items; concerned entirely with the deprived bishops and clergy of the Episcopal Church of Scotland.

Bundle N: 44 items; Dr. Atterbury, Bishop Beveridge, correspondence between Archbishop Sharp and M. Le Clerk, Dr. Gale, Lord Treasurer Godolphin, Chief Justice Holt, Robert

Nelson, John Potter, Humphrey Prideaux, Tillotson, Thoresby, William Whiston.

Bundle O: 46 items; Mordecai Moxon *re* possible invasion of Lancashire, clergy of Jersey, Bishop Lloyd of Worcester, case of Elizabeth Vasconcellos, Bishops of Norwich and Carlisle, Archbishop Sharp to Dr. Grew, list of papist bishops and priests indicted. October 1700.

(*N.B.*—Bundles M, N, and O were selected as proper for presentation to the British Museum, but were never handed over.)

Box No. 4

Bundle A: 81 items; initials A and N; Lord and Lady Nottingham and many other members of the nobility; archbishop of Canterbury (Tenison); bishops of Norwich, Durham, Carlisle, Chichester, Gloucester; Sir W. Dawes, Lord Keeper Wright, Mr. Noyes.

Bundle B: 69 items; archbishop of Canterbury (Tenison); bishops of Durham, Chester, Carlisle; archbishop of Tuam, bishop of Limerick, Lord Treasurer Godolphin, Lord Chamberlain Kent, Lord Nottingham, others of the nobility, *e.g.* Lord Cornbury, Governor of New York, Lord Chief Justice Holt, Lord Chancellor Somers, Lord Keeper Wright.

Bundle C: 24 items; initial D; Drake of Sheffield, Drake of Pontefract, Lady Dixie, Lady Dalton, Heneage Dering.

Bundle D: 24 items; initial E; Prebendary Clement Elis of Southwell.

Bundle E: 48 items; initials G and R; Dr. Grahme, Dr. Grew, Cousin D. Oughton of Whitby, Lady Catherine Jones, Admiral Rooke.

Bundle F: 47 items; initial H; Sir Willoughby Hickman, Mr. Hill of the Admiralty.

Bundle G: 76 items; papers relating to Sharp as dean of Canterbury, *e.g.* correspondence of Mr. James Proast.

Bundle H: 28 items; initial J; Mr. E. Jennings, Secretary of Virginia, Dr. James, Jefferson of Beverley.

Bundle J: 20 items; initial L; Lady Lowther, Lee of Wakefield, William Lowndes.

Bundle K: 69 items; initial S; archbishop of Canterbury (Tenison); bishops of Carlisle, Salisbury and Edinburgh; Archdeacon Nicolson, Dr. Mill, Dr. Smalridge, Lord President Leeds, Lord Treasurer Godolphin, Lord Nottingham, Dr. Cockburn, Mr. J. Bagnall *re* Electress Sophia, Chief Justice Holt, Dr. Stainforth, Mr. Alexander Stanhope, Dr. Atterbury.

Bundle L: 122 items; archbishop of Canterbury (Tenison); primate of Ireland; bishops of London, Kilmore, St. David's, Man, Chester, Gloucester, Carlisle, Lincoln, St. Asaph, Coventry and Lichfield, Bath and Wells, Dur` am, Ely, Chichester, Norwich; Lord Oxford, Earl of Thanet, Lord Nottingham, Lord Wharton, Lord Treasurer Godolphin, Sir W. Dawes, Earl of Rochester, others of the nobility.

Bundle M: 34 items; initial P; Palmer family, Stephen Penton of Ripon, W. Popely of Southwell, Archdeacon Pearson.

Bundle N: 19 items; Dr. Pratt *re* Savoy Chapel, M. Calandrin of Geneva to Robert Hales, Bland's public confession, Latin documents *re* the Palatinate.

Bundle O: 76 items; material relating to the ecclesiastical courts at York; Dr. Lancaster, Dr. Charlett, Dr. Crosthwait, W. Pearson, Dr. Bouchier, Mr. Thompson, all concerned with the election of Provost for Queen's College, Oxford, Sir James Bradshaw.

Bundle P: 30 items; Sharp's sermon (1688) before the Convention, Sharp to Mr. Drake *re* Torre MSS., London address to sovereign, Sharp's answer to Moxon *re* Lancashire dangers, Sharp to Justices of Wakefield *re* Frankland, Edward Finch, Sharp's answer to Whiston, verses by Bishop of Gloucester, Dr. Grew, Irish State Papers.

Bundle Q: 79 items; initial B; Archdeacon Booth, Dr. Breary, archbishop of Canterbury (Tenison); bishops of Gloucester, Bristol, Worcester, Salisbury, Ely; Lord Nottingham, Lord Treasurer Godolphin, Secretary Harley, Knightley Chetwood, Dr. Cockburn, Lord Sunderland, Dr. Sherlock, Dr. Newton, M. Le Clerk, W. Whiston, Dr. Mill, archbishop of Thebais.

Bundle R: 38 items; consisting entirely of "copies" of the replies Archbishop Sharp sent to his correspondents (long-hand).

Bundle S: 81 items; ditto (short-hand).

Bundle T: 89 items; ditto (long-hand).

Bundle U: 33 items; concerned with a dispute over property between Sir William Lowther and his son. The archbishop acted as a mediator. Others involved included Lady Lowther, Parson Lowther, Lord Maynard and Mr. John Stanhope.

Bundle V: 50 items; disputation between Nicolson, Atterbury and Todd in the Carlisle diocese; Mr. Mompesson, Mrs. Cholmley, Lord Keeper Wright.

Bundle W: 59 items; petitions addressed to the bishop of Worcester as Lord Almoner.

BIBLIOGRAPHY

(CONTAINING A LIST OF THE CHIEF AUTHORITIES USED)

UNPUBLISHED SOURCES

The Lloyd-Baker-Sharp MSS.:

    Box 3. Bundles A to O
    Box 4. Bundles A to Z

British Museum MSS.:

    Additional MSS. 4292, 5841, 11396, 11397, 15551, 21506, 22910, 29584,
      29588
    Sloane MS. 3943
    Lansdowne MSS. 785, 987
    Egerton MS. 2543
    Harley MS. 4119

Bodleian Library MSS.: Rawlinson MS. D. 383, f. 65

Public Record Office: Calendar of State Papers Domestic, 1660-1714

Lambeth Act Book, vol. ii

York Diocesan Registry: Act Books and Register of Archbishop Sharp

Church Registers:

    St. Peter, Bradford
    St. Giles-in-the-Fields, London

The Norwich Cathedral Chapter Minute Book, 1681-1689

Southwell MSS.:

    Archbishop Lamplugh's Visitation Enquiries and their Answers, 1690
    Archbishop Sharp, ditto, 1693
    MS. relating to the Great Fire at Southwell, 1711

Bishopthorpe MSS.:

    Archbishop Sharp's three MS. volumes
    Letters of Joseph Wood, vicar of Sandall
    Letters and petitions relating to the curacy at Haworth
    Documents relating to Southwell affairs

Historical MSS. Commission:

    Reports 1, 2, 5, 7
    Report 8, part i
    Report 10, part iv
    Report 13, part vi
    Dartmouth MSS., vol. i
    Le Fleming MSS.
    Portland MSS., vols. ii-vii
    Stuart MSS., vol. i
    Verulam MSS.
    Ancaster MSS.

PUBLISHED SOURCES

Life of Archbishop Sharp, 2 vols., ed. T. Newcome, 1825
Archbishop Sharp's Sermons, 7 vols., 1734-1738
Archbishop Sharp's Works, 7 vols., 1754
Archbishop Herring's Visitation Returns, 5 vols., ed. S. L. Ollard and P. C. Walker, 1929
Burnet's History of My Own Time, 2 vols., ed. O. Airy, 1897-1900
Burnet's History of My Own Time, 4 vols., 1753
Burnet's History of My Own Time, 4 vols., 1818
Supplement to Burnet's History, ed. H. C. Foxcroft, 1902
Letters of Queen Anne, ed. B. Curtis Brown, 1935
Queen Anne's Bounty, Le Fanu, 1920
A State of the Proceedings of the Governors of the Bounty, J. Ecton, 1721
Liber Regis Vel Thesaurus Rerum Ecclesiasticarum, J. Ecton, 1721
Collectanea Bradfordiana, A. Holroyd, 1873
Round about Bradford, W. Cudworth, 1876
Life and Correspondence of Abraham Sharp, W. Cudworth, 1889
Ducatus Leodiensis, R. Thoresby, ed. T. Whitaker, 1816
Diary of Ralph Thoresby, 2 vols., ed. O. Hunter, 1830
Letters of Eminent Men addressed to R. Thoresby, 2 vols., 1832
Letters addressed to R. Thoresby (Thoresby Society, vol. 21), 1912
Diary and Correspondence of J. Evelyn, 4 vols., ed. H. B. Wheatley, 1879
Alliance in Church and State: The Problem of the Non-Jurors, L. M. Hawkins, 1928
History of the Non-Jurors, T. Lathbury, 1845
The Later Non-Jurors, H. Broxap, 1924
The Non-Jurors, their Lives, Principles and Writings, J. H. Overton, 1902
Life in the English Church, 1660-1714, J. H. Overton, 1885
The English Church in the 18th Century, J. H. Overton and C. J. Abbey, 1887
A History of the English Church, 1675-1714, W. H. Hutton, 1903
English Preachers and Preaching, 1640-1670, C. F. Richardson, 1928
English Pulpit Oratory from Andrews to Tillotson, W. F. Mitshell, 1932
Religion in England under Queen Anne and the Georges, 2 vols., J. Stoughton, 1878
Lives of the Lord Chancellors, vol. iv, J. Campbell, 1846
Memoirs of the Life and Writings of Mr. William Whiston, 2 vols., 1753
Later Stuart Tracts, ed. G. A. Aitkin, 1902
Somers Tracts, vols. ix-xiii, 1809-1815
The Tryall of Dr. Henry Sacheverell, 1710
Pamphlets relating to the Sacheverell Trial (in the London Library)
History of St. Giles-in-the-Fields, R. Dobie, 1829
Some Account of the Hospital and Parish of St. Giles, J. Parton, 1819
Nell Gwynne, Arthur Dasent, 1924
The Growth of Stuart London, N. G. Brett-James, 1934
A Collection of Cases and Other Discourses lately written to recover Dissenters to the Communion of the Church, by Divines of the City of London, 1698
A Rebuke to the Informers against Non-Conformists, Owen Stockton, 1675
Studies in English Puritanism, 1660-1688, C. E. Whiting, 1931
Nathaniel Lord Crewe, C. E. Whiting, 1940
The Later Stuarts, G. N. Clark, 1934
Edmund Gibson, N. Sykes, 1926
Church and State in the 18th Century, N. Sykes, 1934
A Brief Historical Relation of State Affairs, 6 vols., N. Luttrell, 1857
The History and Proceedings of the House of Lords, vols. i and ii, ed. E. Timberland, 1743
The House of Lords in the 18th Century, A. S. Turberville, 1927

PUBLISHED SOURCES (continued)

Life of Tillotson, T. Birch, 1753
Memorials of Ripon (Surtees Society, vol. 78), 4 vols., 1835
The Records of the Northern Convocation (Surtees Society, vol. 113), 1835
Yorkshire Diaries (Surtees Society, vols. 65 and 77), 1835
Valor Ecclesiasticus, vol. v, 1834
Life of Bull, R. Nelson, 1846
State Trials, vol. xii, ed. T. Howell, 1812
The English Church and its Bishops, vol. i, C. J. Abbey, 1887
Life of Gilbert Burnet, H. C. Foxcroft and T. E. S. Clarke, 1907
Anglicanism, ed. E. More and F. L. Cross, 1935
Prose Works of Jonathan Swift, 12 vols., ed. Temple Scott, 1907
Life of Mr. Richard Baxter, Silvester, 1696
Life of Thomas Ken, E. H. Plumptre, 1888
Bishop William Nicolson's Episcopal Correspondence, 2 vols., ed. J. Nichols, 1809
History of England, vol. ii, T. B. Macaulay, 1849
The English Revolution, G. M. Trevelyan, 1938
England under Queen Anne, 3 vols., G. M. Trevelyan, 1930-1934
History of Christ's College, Cambridge, J. Peile, 1900
The Importance of the Reign of Queen Anne in English Church History, F. W. Wilson, 1911
History of Southwell, W. D. Rastall, 1787
The English Church in the 17th Century, C. S. Carter, 1909
English Constitutional Conflicts in the 17th Century, J. R. Tanner, 1928
A Constitutional History of England, 1642-1801, M. A. Thomson, 1938
Thomas, third Lord Fairfax, a short memorial of the Northern Actions; during the war there, from the year 1642 till the year 1644 (*An English Garner*, vol. ii), 1903
The Lord General, M. A. Gibb, 1938
Caritas Anglicana, G. V. Portus, 1912
The Electress Sophia and the Hanoverian Succession, A. W. Ward, 1919
The History of the Union of England and Scotland, J. Mackinnon, 1896
Unitas Fratrum, D. Cranz, 1780
History of the Society for Promoting Christian Knowledge, W. O. B. Allen and E. McClure, 1898
History of the Church of Ireland, vol. ii, R. Mant, 1840
Parliamentary History, vols. v and vi, ed. W. Cobbett, 1808
History of the Parson's Wife, M. Watt, 1943

ARTICLES

"Archbishop Sharp" (*York Minster Historical Tracts*), Canon Solloway, 1927
"John Sharp", *The General Biographical Dictionary*, 1816
"John Sharp", *Biographia Britannica*, 1763
"Archbishop Sharp's Observations on the Coinage of England, Scotland, and Ireland", *Bibliotheca Topographia Britannica*, 1764
"John Sharp", in *The Dictionary of National Biography*
The English Historical Review, "Letter: John, Archbishop of York, to William Lloyd, Bishop of Worcester, dated 31st of March, 1703": 1890, vol. v, p. 122
"Queen Anne and the Episcopate", by N. Sykes, 1935, vol. l, pp. 433-464
Review of English Studies, "Dean Swift and Ecclesiastical Preferment", by C. H. Firth, January 1926

INDEX

347

Printed in Great Britain by
Billing and Sons Ltd., Guildford and Esher
F6859